MULTIMEDIA – A MULTIDISCIPLINARY APPROACH TO COMPLEX ISSUES

Edited by **Ioannis Karydis**

Multimedia – A Multidisciplinary Approach to Complex Issues
Edited by Ioannis Karydis

Published by InTech
Janeza Trdine 9, 51000 Rijeka, Croatia

Technical Editor Sonja Mujacic

Cover Designer InTech Design Team

Additional hard copies can be obtained from orders@intechopen.com

Multimedia – A Multidisciplinary Approach to Complex Issues,
Edited by Ioannis Karydis
p. cm.
ISBN 978-953-51-0216-8

For EU product safety concerns:
IN TECH d.o.o., Prolaz Marije Krucifikse Kozulić 3, 51000 Rijeka, Croatia,
info@intechopen.com or visit our website at intechopen.com.

Meet the editor

Ioannis Karydis was born in Athens, Greece in 1979. He received a BEng (2000) in Engineering Science & Technology from Brunel University, UK, an MSc (2001) in Advanced Methods in Computer Science from Queen Mary University, UK and a PhD (2006) in Mining and Retrieval Methods for Acoustic and Symbolic Music Data from the Aristotle University of Thessaloniki, Greece. He has contributed to more than 25 academic publications and currently is a contract lecturer at the Ionian University, Greece. His research interests include music databases, music information retrieval (indexing & searching), music genre classification, musical similarity using contextual information, continuous querying in musical streams, cultural information systems and privacy issues in databases. A full and up-to-date CV can be found in http://www.ionio.gr/~karydis/

Contents

Preface

Multimedia is interdisciplinary a field by nature. One can identify principles, concepts and theories from communication and computer science, physics, psychology, music, graphic arts and many other disciplines in such data [Tannenbaum, 1999]. In addition, multimedia are renowned for their rich character, stemming from their formation based on combination of different content forms.

The widespread penetration of digital capturing and processing devices and the high bandwidth interconnections between web-users, coupled with the aforementioned multidisciplinary and rich character of multimedia, led their use to be a *sine qua non* in many forms of digitised expression.

Setting aside the enormous expansion of use of multimedia content in web pages under the auspices of Web 2.0, the most prominent example of the ever-increasing use of multimedia comes from socially aware and contextually rich video streaming services. In both terms of creating and consuming such content, YouTube service [YouTube, 2012] states that "48 hours of video are uploaded every minute, resulting in nearly 8 years of content uploaded every day, while over 3 billion videos are viewed a day".

Although research in the discipline of multimedia is far from young, such growth of multimedia content creation and consumption is unprecedented and calls for new methods in order to ensure efficiency and effectiveness of the methods utilised. In addition, latest developments in terms of hardware, networking issues, security and semantic information extraction require re-evaluation of the currently used techniques to suit new requirements.

This book is organised into 5 major sections addressing multimedia topics in peer-to-peer & wireless networks, security characteristics in multimedia, semantic gap bridging for multimedia content and novel applications for managing multimedia content & metadata.

Ioannis Karydis
Dept. of Informatics, Ionian University
Greece

References

Tannenbaum, R. S. (1999). Theoretical Foundations of Multimedia. W. H. Freeman.

YouTube. (2012). YouTube Statistics. Available: http://www.youtube.com/t/press_statistics. Last accessed 19th Jan 2012.

Part 1

Multimedia and Peer-to-Peer Networks

1

Peer-to-Peer Multimedia Distribution on Radio Channel and Asymmetric Channel

Danilo Merlanti[1] and Gianluca Mazzini[2]
[1]*Department of Engineering, University of Ferrara, Ferrara,*
[2]*Lepida S.p.a., Bologna,*
Italy

1. Introduction

In the Internet and Communication Technology (ICT) field, sharing and distribution of information is very important. Various mechanisms and techniques are used to manage information; one of these is based on peer-to-peer networks. In today's world and in the near future, the exchange and distribution of information will be a very important aspect in the workplace and in daily life. Consequently, mobile devices, devices for home entertainment, personal computers and office terminals must have the mechanisms to achieve the above functionality. Thus the peer-to-peer networks can be used to achieve (Tomoya & Shigeki, 2003) the following: Video conferences or phone calls (Bakos et al., 2006), in which more users can communicate together simultaneously. The distribution of multimedia contents provided by a single source node, for example: streaming distribution of TV contents or radio broadcasting contents (Ciullo et al., 2008; Leonardi et al., 2008; Mazzini & Rovatti, 2008). An example of a real-time algorithm used to create a simple distribution peer-to-peer network on asymmetric channels is given in article (Mazzini & Rovatti, 2008) and the issues of performance of peer-to-peer file sharing over asymmetric and wireless networks is addressed in article (Lien, 2005). Information sharing, for example in a company, the peer-to-peer network system can be used by employees to allow them to work in a shared manner. In daily life, the peer-to-peer network system can be used for sharing personal information such as audio and video contents, documents and others. The more significant peer-to-peer applications used for this purpose are: Gnutella ("The Gnutella Protocol Specification v0.4"; Matei et al, 2002; Wang et al., 2007), Kademlia (Maymounkov & Mazieres, 2002), KaZaA ("http://www.kazaa.com."), Bit-Torrent ("http://www.bittorrent.com."), massively multiplayer online game (MMOG) (Carter et al., 2010; Tay, 2005).

The scenario discussed in this chapter is the distribution of multimedia contents provided by a single source node with an appropriate peer-to-peer network on asymmetric channels and on wireless channels.

This chapter is organized as follows, the scenario and the main hypotheses of the chapter are explained in section 2. Section 3 describes the peer-to-peer algorithms used to build the peer-to-peer distribution networks. In section 4 we present how is estimated the maximum delay of a peer-to-peer distribution network. In this section we present the theoretical optimum in which it is maximized the average maximum number of peers and it is minimized the average maximum delay of the peer-to-peer distribution network. Moreover the simulation results for the asymmetric channel are reported in the last part of this section. In section 5 we analyse the behaviour of the peer-to-peer algorithms in a simple radio channel. In this section we present:

- the radio channel characterization.
- The model used to establish the bit error probability of each peer of a peer-to-peer distribution network.
- The peer-to-peer network simulator used to simulate the behaviour of the radio channel in the peer-to-peer distribution network.
- The validation of the model of the peer-to-peer network in an unreliable environment (radio channel) through the simulation results.
- The results used to establish which peer-to-peer algorithm builds the best peer-to-peer distribution network in an unreliable environment.

The conclusion are presented in the last section of the chapter.

2. Scenario and hypotheses

The scenarios discussed in this chapter refer to the distribution of multimedia contents transmitted by a single source node with an appropriate peer-to-peer network in an asymmetric channel and in a wireless environment.

In this chapter we present two different classes of algorithms. The first class is based on the Tier based algorithm presented in the article (Mazzini & Rovatti, 2008). In this class we have a central entity (server) that manages the insertion of the new peers and the construction of the network.

The second class of algorithms, is based on a peer list. In this class we have a distributed system in which a new node gets from a server, the list of the nodes of the peer-to-peer network and then the new node periodically performs a query flooding to keep the list updated (such as Kademlia (Maymounkov & Mazieres, 2002) is a distributed hash table for decentralized peer-to-peer computer networks).

In this study we are not interested in how the network is managed (centralized or distributed). Instead, by using new algorithms we aim to: maximize the average maximum number of peers that can access the multimedia content and minimize the average maximum delay of the network, in the case of the asymmetric channel, and minimize the bit error probability of each node of the network, in the case of the wireless channel .

In our aim, the source node can be a home-user that streams multimedia content (i.e. audio/video) with a limited output bandwidth ($B < 2$) or a server with a higher output bandwidth ($B \geq 2$) which can supply the content to more than two users, where B is the output bandwidth of the source node.

In the case of the asymmetric channel the building of the network is done in real-time thus the algorithm we use creates a peer-to-peer network for streaming applications in which a source continuously provides content that must be played by a large and unknown number of home-users (Mazzini & Rovatti, 2008). For hypothesis each home-user (peer) is characterized by an asymmetric channel such as ADSL and each peer has a uniform distributed output bandwidth.

An ADSL system with a cooperative bit-loading approach for each peer of the peer-to-peer network (Papandreou and Antonakopoulos, 2003) is used to ensure this hypothesis.

In case of the wireless system, we assume that each peer is an access point and that the network infrastructure is produced by the algorithm in non real-time and the algorithms we use in this chapter suppose that the peer-to-peer network is created before the initializing of the stream; moreover it is supposed that the placement of the various access points (peers) is done so that all wireless links have the same signal to noise ratio.

In both cases, the source node transmits the content while the receiving nodes are able to accept partial streams, from more than one node, through their inbound link and to redistribute it to one or more further peers through their outbound links. In this way the source node supplies the multimedia content to a limited number of requesting peers. The peers, that directly receive the streaming from the source node, provide the multimedia content to the other requesting nodes through a peer-to-peer network. The structure of this network depends on the algorithm used for incremental construction of the peer-to-peer network itself.

The base algorithm considers the source bandwidth as a constraint and minimizes the maximum delay in terms of intermediate links (Mazzini & Rovatti, 2008) without considering the number of nodes that the network is able to accept in accordance with bandwidth constraints.

Below is a list of hypothesis used in the next algorithms:

- the nodes of a peer-to-peer network are characterized by asymmetric channels.
- All peers are always available during the streaming.
- The source node of the network has a finite output bandwidth B.
- The inbound bandwidth of each node is adequate to accept the content.
- All bandwidths are normalized with respect to the bandwidth required to acquire the multimedia content. In this way the bandwidth required to acquire the multimedia content is normalized to 1.
- With respect to the bandwidth referred to above, the output bandwidth of each i-th peer is $0 < \Omega_i < 2$ and Ω_i can be different from Ω_j for each i-th and j-th peer of the network with $i \neq j$.
- Instead in the Mazzini-Rovatti Algorithm (Mazzini & Rovatti, 2008) all the peers have the same output bandwidth value $\Omega \in (0,1)$.
- The delay of each link is normalized to 1.
- In the case of the wireless channel all the links between couple of peers feature an identical signal to noise ratio.

3. Algorithms

In this section we give a brief description of all the algorithms used in this chapter. There are two classes of algorithms that we are going to consider.

3.1 Tiers based algorithms

The first group of algorithms we will consider are classified under the Tier based algorithm (based on Mazzini-Rovatti Algorithm (Mazzini & Rovatti, 2008)). The first new algorithm we introduce is the Tier based algorithm (T). This algorithm is formulated by making a generalization of Mazzini-Rovatti Algorithm (Mazzini & Rovatti, 2008) with an output bandwidth of each peer distributed between 0 and 2. The second new algorithm we introduce is the Tier based algorithm with network Reconstruction (TR). The TR algorithm is formulated from the T algorithm we introduce above and its aim is to maximize the number of the peers accepted in the network. In this algorithm the output bandwidths of the peers of each tier are greater than the output bandwidths of the peers found in the next tier. Moreover when the network produced by the T and TR Algorithms don't accept a new peer for the first time, they don't accept more peers. The third algorithm we introduce is the TR Algorithm without Input Blockage. In this algorithm, if a new peer is not accepted in the network, this peer is inserted into a waiting queue. When a new node able to increase the residual output bandwidth of the network is inserted, the algorithm takes the peers from the waiting list and tries to re-insert them.

A simple analytical formula for the maximum number of nodes accepted in a T network is:

$$n_T = \lfloor B \rfloor + \sum_{i=1}^{T} \lfloor B_i^* \rfloor, \; B_i^* = \sum_{k=1}^{\lfloor B_{i-1}^* \rfloor} \Omega_{k,i} \tag{1}$$

where B_i^* is the output bandwidth of the i-th tier of the network, i = 1…T and T is the maximum number of tiers. B_{i-1}^* is the output bandwidth of the previous tier (available output bandwidth of the previous tier), $B_0^* = B$ and $\lfloor B_i^* \rfloor$ is the maximum number of peers of (i+1)-th tier. $\Omega_{k,i}$ is the output bandwidth of the k-th peer contained in the i-th tier.

3.1.1 State of the art

The state of the art is based on Mazzini-Rovatti's algorithm (Mazzini & Rovatti, 2008). In this algorithm and in the first three new algorithms, the distribution network is organized in "tiers" numbered from 1 onwards. Peers in the first tier are fed by the source. Peers in the j-th tier receive the content only from peers in the (j−1)-th tier. The number of tiers in the distribution network is indicated by T, that also indicates the maximum delay in terms of intermediate links. In Mazzini-Rovatti's algorithm (Mazzini & Rovatti, 2008) a new peer is inserted into the tier closest to the source node. We indicate with p_j the number of peers in the j-th tier. The overall bandwidth required to distribute the content to the j-th tier is p_j, while the overall bandwidth made available by the j-th tier is $\Omega \cdot p_j$. We assume a finite total output bandwidth B offered to the first tier by the source node. The elementary step of Mazzini-Rovatti's algorithm is "add a peer to the j-th tier if possible". We indicate this step with A(j). A pseudo-code for A(j) is the following:

```
case j = 1
        if B > p_1 then p_1 ++ else failed
case j = 2, . . . , T
        if p_{j-1} ≥ p_j + 1 then p_j ++ else failed
case j = T + 1
        if p_T ≥ 1 then p_{T+1} = 1  T ++ else failed
```

where a peer is added to the j-th tier if and only if the bandwidth emitted by the previous tier (i.e. the source if j = 1) is enough to accommodate it, namely if this bandwidth is ≥ 1. The new peer insertion algorithm has the following pseudo-code:

```
for j = 1 to T + 1
    if A(j) not failed then stop
next
failed
```

This algorithm tries to add the new peer to the smallest-delay tier within bandwidth constraints and fails if no more peers can be fed by peers in the same tier.

The new algorithms aim to maximize the number of accepted nodes (to increase the number of users that can have access to the content), minimize the reconstruction delay and minimize the maximum delay of the network (to provide a better service).

The next subsections describe and introduce new algorithms, adopted for the distribution of multimedia contents.

3.1.2 Tiers based algorithm (T)

The generalization of Mazzini-Rovatti's algorithm (Mazzini & Rovatti, 2008), with the new hypothesis that is " $0 < \Omega_i < 2$ for each i-th peer", is provided by the Tiers based algorithm (T). A pseudo-code for this algorithm is the following:

case j = 1

  if $B \geq p_1 + 1$ then $p_1{+}{+}$ else failed

case j = 2, . . . , T

  if $\sum_{i=1}^{p_{j-1}} \Omega_{i,j-1} \geq p_j + 1$ then $p_j{+}{+}$ else failed

case j = T + 1

  if $\sum_{i=1}^{p_T} \Omega_{i,T} \geq 1$ then $p_{T+1} = 1$, $T{+}{+}$ else failed

where p_j is the number of peers contained in the j-th tier (with j = 1…T) and $\Omega_{i,j-1}$ is the output bandwidth of the i-th peer contained in the (j−1)-th tier of the network and a new peer is added to the j-th tier if and only if the bandwidth emitted by the previous tier (i.e. the source if j = 1) is able to accommodate it. The new peer insertion algorithm has the following pseudo-code:

```
for j = 1 to T + 1
    if A(j) not failed then stop
next
failed
```

This algorithm tries to add the new peer to the smallest delay tier within bandwidth constraints and fails if no more peers can be fed by peers in the same tier.

In the next section we describe an algorithm that increases the maximum number of peers accepted in the network, by adopting an insertion algorithm with the reconstruction of the network itself.

3.1.3 Tiers based algorithm with network Reconstruction (TR)

In this algorithm the tiers nearest to the source node must hold the nodes characterized by the greatest output bandwidth values. To guarantee this aim, the insertion of each new node can trigger a possible reconstruction of the distribution network. The elementary step of the TR algorithm is indicated with the recursive function $A(j,\Omega_N)$. A pseudo-code for $A(j,\Omega_N)$ is the following:

case j = 1
    if $B \geq p_j + 1$ then $p_j{++}$
    else $<remove\ N_{m_j}>$, $<add\ N>$, $A(j+1, B_{m_j})$
case j = 2, …, T
    if $\sum_{i=1}^{p_{j-1}} \Omega_{i,j-1} \geq p_j + 1$ then $p_j{++}$
    else $<remove\ N_{m_j}>$, $<add\ N>$, $A(j+1, B_{m_j})$
case j = T+1
    if $\sum_{i=1}^{p_T} \Omega_{i,T} \geq 1$ then $p_{T+1} = 1$ $T{++}$ else failed

where p_j is the number of peers contained in the j-th tier (with j = 1…T) and $\Omega_{i,j-1}$ is the output bandwidth of the i-th peer contained in the (j−1)-th tier of the network. Ω_N is the output bandwidth of the new node N. N_{m_j} is the peer with the minimum output bandwidth of the j-th tier because the hypothesis of this algorithm is that each j-th tier (with j = 1…T-1) holds all the peers characterized by output bandwidths greater than the output bandwidths of the peers held in the (j+1)-th tier. B_{m_j} is the output bandwidth of the peer N_{m_j}. In this way the algorithm tries to add the new peer in the j-th tier if $\Omega_N > B_{m_j}$.

The new peer insertion algorithm has the following pseudo-code:

for j = 1 to T + 1
    if $\left(\min\left(\text{NodesOutputBandwidth}\left(\text{tier}_j\right)\right) < \Omega_N\right)\text{and}\left(j < T+1\right)$ then break
next
if $A(j,\Omega_N)$ not failed then stop else failed

This insertion algorithm tries to insert the new peer (N) in the j-th tier where the output bandwidth of the peer, characterized by the minimum output bandwidth, is less than the output bandwidth (Ω_N) of the new peer (N).

3.1.4 TR algorithm without Input Blockage (TRwIB)

The TRwIB algorithm derives from the TR algorithm. The TRwIB is the TR algorithm without Input Blockage.

The engine of this algorithm is the following:

- if the new peer can be inserted into the network (with network reconstruction if it is necessary) then the algorithm performs the insertion operation as the TR algorithm.
- Otherwise the new peer is inserted in a waiting queue; this queue contains the peers that are waiting a new node able to increase the residual output bandwidth of the network. When this event happens the algorithm wakes up the waiting peers and it tries to insert them. The peers, that are not inserted, are maintained in the waiting queue and they are waked up (by the insertion algorithm) if and only if a new peer, is able to increase the residual bandwidth of the network with its insertion.

The disadvantage of this algorithm is represented by the network reconstruction that introduces an additional delay to the network.

3.2 Peer List based algorithms

The second group of algorithms we will consider are classified under the peer list algorithm. The first new algorithm we introduce is the Peer List based Algorithm (PL). In this algorithm, the peer-to-peer distribution network is represented by a peers list, in which each peer is characterized by an id, its available output bandwidth and an id list of children nodes. At the beginning of this algorithm, the peers list contains only the source node. When a new node N wants access to the network, this peer requests, to the peers of the network, an amount of bandwidth equal to the bandwidth required to acquire the multimedia content. If N obtains the required bandwidth, from the network, then the new node is added to the network; otherwise the network isn't able to accept more peers. The second algorithm we consider is the PL algorithm with Reconstruction (PLR). This algorithm is formulated from the PL algorithm. The PLR algorithm inserts the new node (N) in the network if and only if N is able to increase the residual bandwidth of the network. In this case the PLR algorithm extracts the peer (of the network) with minimum output bandwidth and replaces it with the new node. The PLR algorithm exploits the increase of the residual bandwidth (brought by N) by re-inserting the extracted node. If N isn't able to increase the network residual bandwidth then the PLR algorithm doesn't insert N into the network and the network accepts no more peers. The third algorithm we consider is the PLR Algorithm without input blockage. In this algorithm, if the new peer is not accepted in the network, this peer is inserted into a waiting queue. When a new node able to increase the residual output bandwidth of the network is inserted, this algorithm wakes up and tries to insert the waiting peers.

A simple analytical formula for the maximum number of nodes accepted in a Peer List based network is:

$$n_{PL} = \left\lfloor B + \sum_{i=1}^{n_{PL}} \Omega_i \right\rfloor \tag{2}$$

where Ω_i is the output bandwidth of the i-th peer of the network. In this way from the formulas (1) and (2) it is immediately proof that $n_{PL} \geq n_T$.

In a Tiers based network the maximum depth is T. If we collect the unused bandwidth B_u of the tiers and if $B_u \geq 1$ we can supply one or more new peers. In this way, in a Tiers based network , if we supply one or more new peers using the unused bandwidth B_u then the Tiers based network degenerates into a Peer List based network and in this case the maximum depth is ≥ T + 1. Thus $depth_{PL} \geq depth_T$. Therefore the Peer List based networks are optimal with respect to the maximum number of nodes accepted by the network but they don't have the minimum delay in terms of the maximum depth.

In the TR, TR without input blockage, PLR and PLR without input blockage algorithms the insertion of a new peer can trigger a reconstruction of the network required in order to maintain order in the structure of the network. The reconstruction makes a delay. Thus the maximum delay of the network, in terms of the maximum depth of the network, has to be increased by the reconstruction delays.

3.2.1 Peer List based algorithm (PL)

In the PL algorithm the peer-to-peer distribution network is represented by a peers list, where each peer is characterized by an id, its available output bandwidth and the id list of children nodes. At the beginning, the peers list contains only the source node. When a new node N wants access to the network, this peer requests, to the peers of the network, an amount of bandwidth equal to the bandwidth required to acquire the multimedia content. If N obtains the required bandwidth, from the network, then the new node is added to the network; otherwise the network isn't able to accept more peers. The next algorithm is an improvement of this algorithm and it allows to increase the maximum number of peers accepted in the network.

3.2.2 Peer List based algorithm with Reconstruction (PLR)

This algorithm has the same behaviour as the PL algorithm, when the network is able to accept a new peer otherwise it tries to insert this peer with a reconstruction of the network. The algorithm inserts the new node (N) in the network if and only if N is able to increase the residual bandwidth ($B + \left(\sum_{i=0}^{n} \Omega_i\right) - n$, where n is the number of peers of the network) of the network. In this case the algorithm extracts the peer (of the network) with minimum output bandwidth and replaces it with the new node. The algorithm exploits the increase of the residual bandwidth (brought by N) to re-insert the extracted node. If N isn't able to increase residual bandwidth of the network then the algorithm doesn't insert N into the network and the network accepts no more peers. The PLR as well as TR algorithm may have network reconstruction.

The PLR algorithm has the analytical formulation (2) where the output bandwidths of the peers are $\Omega_1 \geq \Omega_2 \geq \ldots \geq \Omega_n > 0$ and n is the number of peers accepted by the network.

3.2.3 PLR algorithm without Input Blockage (PLRwIB)

The PLRwIB algorithm derives the PLR algorithm. The PLRwIB is the PLR algorithm without input blockage.

The engine of this algorithm is the following:

- if the new peer can be inserted into the network (with network reconstruction if it is necessary) then the algorithm performs the insertion operation as the PLR algorithm.
- Otherwise the new peer is inserted in a waiting queue; this queue contains the peers that are waiting a new node able to increase the residual output bandwidth of the network. When this event happens the algorithm wakes up the waiting peers and it tries to insert them. The peers, that are not inserted, are maintained in the waiting queue and they are waked up (by the insertion algorithm) if and only if a new peer, is able to increase the residual bandwidth of the network with its insertion.

The disadvantage of this algorithm is represented by the network reconstruction that introduces an additional delay to the network.

4. Asymmetric channel

For the analysis of the peer-to-peer algorithms we introduced in section 3, we formulate a theoretical optimum in which the maximization of the average maximum number of the peers and the minimization of the average maximum delay of the network is achieved. We compare the results, in terms of the average maximum number of peers and the average maximum delay of the network, of the algorithms presented above, with respect to the theoretical optimum.

4.1 Maximum delay of a peer-to-peer distribution network

To estimate the maximum delay of a peer-to-peer distribution network, we suppose to have two different cases:

- in the first case, the network is generated by an algorithm (such as the T algorithm or the PL algorithm) that doesn't use a reconstruction of the network. In this case the maximum delay of the peer-to-peer distribution network is defined as the maximum depth of this network.
- In the second case, the network is generated by an algorithm (such as the TR, TRwIB, PLR and PLRwIB algorithms) that uses a reconstruction of the network. In this scenario the maximum delay of the peer-to-peer distribution network is defined as the maximum depth of this network plus the amount of the delays generated by each reconstruction of the network. For the insertion of a new peer N, we have a reconstruction of the network when it is necessary to extract a peer of the peer-to-peer network, replace it with the new peer N and the insertion algorithm exploits the increase of the residual bandwidth (brought by N) to re-insert the extracted node. The reconstruction delay for the insertion of a new node is the amount of replacement delays. The delay produced by each k-th substitution of two peers (p_1 and p_2) is: $d_{s_k} = \sum_{j=1}^{M} S_{cp} / B(p_1, j) + \sum_{h=1}^{W} S_{cp} / B(p_1, h)$, where: $B(p_1, j)$ is the bandwidth between the extracted peer p_1 and the j-th parent peer of p_1, M is the number of the parent peers of the peer p_1, $B(p_1, h)$ is the bandwidth between the extracted peer p_1 and the h-th child peer of p_1, W is the number of the child peers of the peer p_1 and the peer p_1 sends to its parent nodes and its child nodes a control packet (with size S_{cp}) used to perform the node replacement. Thus the reconstruction delay for the insertion of the i-th node is:

$d_i = \sum_k d_{s_k}$ and $d_i = 0$ if the are no node replacements for the insertion of the i-th peer.

Therefore the total reconstruction delay of a peer-to-peer network is: $d = \sum_{i=1}^{n} d_i$, where n is the maximum number of peers accepted by the network.

4.2 Theoretical optimum

The theoretical optimum is achieved when the ratio between the average maximum number of peers (n) and average minimum possible maximum delay (d) of the network is maximized. We indicate with, $\overline{n_1}$, the mean maximum number of peers accepted in the network with an output bandwidth between 1 and 2 ($1 \le \Omega_i < 2$). We indicate with, $\overline{n_2}$, the mean maximum number of peers with an output bandwidth between 0 and 1 ($0 < \Omega_i < 1$). We have the average maximum number of peers in the network with the minimum possible value of T if and only if the peers (that access the network) are ordered with respect to their output bandwidth namely $\Omega_1 \ge \Omega_2 \ge \Omega_3 \ge \ldots \ge \Omega_n$, where Ω_i (for $i = 1 \ldots n$) is the output bandwidth of the i-th peer that has access the network. In this way there are no reconstructions of the peer-to-peer network and there are no reconstruction delays. With this conditions we can partially apply the theoretical formulation of the article (Mazzini & Rovatti, 2008) to achieve the optimum value of the ratio between n and T.

In this way the network is divided in two parts. In the first part there are all the peers with output bandwidth $1 \le \Omega_i < 2$ (with average output bandwidth $\overline{\Omega^1}$) and they receive the multimedia content from the source ($\overline{n_1}$ number of peers and $\overline{T_1}$ the average minimum possible maximum delay of the first part of network). In the second part there are all the peers with output bandwidth $0 < \Omega_i < 1$ (with average output bandwidth $\overline{\Omega^2}$) and they receive the multimedia content from the leaf peers of the first part of the network ($\overline{n_2}$ number of peers and $\overline{T_2}$ the average minimum possible maximum delay of the first part of network).

The average maximum number of peers accepted in the network is $\overline{n} = \overline{n_1} + \overline{n^*}$. When $\left(\sum_{i=1}^{\overline{n}} \Omega_i\right) / \overline{n} < 1$ the system reaches its maximum number of peers.

We suppose to have n_T number of peers wants to access the peer-to-peer network. Thus the number of peers of the first part of the network is:

$$\overline{n_1} = \lfloor n_T \cdot (1 - p) \rfloor \quad (3)$$

Where p is the probability that each i-th node has output bandwidth $0 < \Omega_i < 1$ and $1 - p$ is the probability that each i-th node has output bandwidth $1 \le \Omega_i < 2$.

The average minimum possible maximum delay (formulation of the article (Mazzini & Rovatti, 2008) section III) in a $\overline{n_1}$ - nodes (non necessarily tiered) peer-to-peer network fed by a source with bandwidth B is:

$$\overline{T_1} = \left\lceil \log_{\overline{\Omega^1}} \left(\frac{\overline{n_1}}{B} \cdot (\overline{\Omega^1} - 1) + 1 \right) \right\rceil \quad (4)$$

The formula (4) give us the average minimum maximum delay of the first part of the network, because it is achieved through the average maximum number of peers $\overline{n_1}$.

The output bandwidth provided by the first part of the network to the second part of the network is:

$$\overline{B_{N_1}} = B + \overline{\Omega^1} \cdot \overline{n_1} - \overline{n_1} = B + \overline{n_1} \cdot (\overline{\Omega^1} - 1) \quad (5)$$

where B is the output bandwidth of the source.

The total residual bandwidth of the second part of the network is:

$$\overline{B_{N_2}} = \overline{B_{N_1}} + \overline{n^*} \cdot (\overline{\Omega^2} - 1) \quad (6)$$

where $\overline{n^*}$ is the mean maximum number of peers accepted in the second part of the peer-to-peer network.

When $\overline{B_{N_2}} = 1$ the second part of the network reaches the maximum number of peers - 1. Thus from the formula (6) the average maximum number of peers of the second part of the network is:

$$\overline{n^*} = \left\lfloor \frac{\overline{B_{N_1}} - 1}{1 - \overline{\Omega^2}} + 1 \right\rfloor \quad (7)$$

Therefore the average minimum possible maximum delay of the second part of the network (formula presented in section III of the article (Mazzini & Rovatti, 2008)) is:

$$\overline{T^*} = \left\lceil \log_{\overline{\Omega^2}} \left(\frac{\overline{n^*}}{\overline{B_{N_1}}} \cdot (\overline{\Omega^2} - 1) + 1 \right) \right\rceil \quad (8)$$

The formula (8) give us the average minimum maximum delay of the second part of the network, because it is achieved through the average maximum number of peers $\overline{n^*}$.

With the formula (7) the formula (8) becomes:

$$\overline{T^*} = \left\lceil \log_{\overline{\Omega^2}} \left(\frac{1}{\overline{B_{N_1}}} \right) + 1 \right\rceil \quad (9)$$

In this way if we define:

$$\overline{n_2} = \overline{n^*} - 1 = \left\lfloor \frac{\overline{B_{N_1}} - 1}{1 - \overline{\Omega^2}} \right\rfloor \quad (10)$$

then the average minimum possible maximum delay (formulation of the article (Mazzini & Rovatti, 2008) section III) in a $\overline{n_2}$ - nodes (non necessarily tiered) peer-to-peer network fed by an equivalent source with bandwidth $\overline{B_{N_1}}$ is:

$$\overline{T_2} = \begin{cases} 0 & if\ \overline{B_{N_1}} < 1 \\ 1 & if\ \overline{B_{N_1}} = 1 \\ \left\lceil \log_{\overline{\Omega^2}} \left(\frac{1}{\overline{B_{N_1}}} \right) \right\rceil & if\ \overline{B_{N_1}} > 1 \end{cases} \tag{11}$$

The formula (11) give us the average minimum maximum delay of the second part of the network, because it is achieved through the average number of peers $\overline{n_2}$.

Thus $\overline{T_2} = \overline{T^*} - 1$ and $\overline{n_2} = \overline{n^*} - 1$. Using the formulas (7), (9), (10) and (11), we can simply show that: $(\overline{n_1} + \overline{n_2}) / (\overline{T_1} + \overline{T_2}) \geq (\overline{n_1} + \overline{n^*}) / (\overline{T_1} + \overline{T^*})$. In conclusion, if $\overline{B_{N_1}} > 1$, the optimum for the ratio between the average maximum number of peers and the average minimum possible maximum delay of the network is:

$$\frac{\overline{n_1} + \overline{n_2}}{\overline{T_1} + \overline{T_2}} = \frac{\lfloor n_T \cdot (1-p) \rfloor + \left\lceil \frac{\overline{B_{N_1}} - 1}{1 - \overline{\Omega^2}} \right\rceil}{\left\lceil \log_{\overline{\Omega^1}} \left(\frac{\overline{n_1}}{B} \cdot (\overline{\Omega^1} - 1) + 1 \right) \right\rceil + \left\lceil \log_{\overline{\Omega^2}} \left(\frac{1}{\overline{B_{N_1}}} \right) \right\rceil} \tag{12}$$

4.3 Results

The comparison of the algorithms is performed by using the ratio between the average maximum number of peers (n) and the average maximum delay (d) of the network over 1000 samples of peers. The simulator uses 1000 different samples (random generated) and each sample contains 1000 peers. We now briefly describe the network parameters followed when making the comparison of the performance of the algorithms we discussed about in section 3. The value of the output bandwidth of the source node is $B \in [1,10]$. p is the probability that each i-th node has output bandwidth $0 < \Omega_i < 1$ and $1-p$ is the probability that each i-th node has output bandwidth $1 \leq \Omega_i < 2$. We are supposed to have an uniform distribution for p , where $p \in [0,1]$. For each value of p between 0 and 1; with step of 0.01 in the simulation environment; the simulator uses 1000 different samples and each sample contains 1000 peers. We suppose that the size of the control packet used to replace a peer with a new peer is equal to 642 bits (where 192 bits are for the TCP header (RFC 793, 1981), 192 bits are for the IPv4 header (RFC 791, 1981), 96 bits of data make up of 32 bits for the IP address of the extracted peer, 16 bits for the port of the extracted peer, 32 bits for the IP address of the new peer, 16 bits for the port of the new peer and 162 bits for the lower layers). The simulation results give a map of the best algorithms with respect to the ratio between the average maximum number of peers and the average maximum delay of the network as functions in term of p and B . The space B, p; with $1 \le B \le 10$ and $0 \le p \le 1$; is divided in three areas. The first area has $1 \le B \le 2$ and $0 \le p \le 1$. In this area the PLR algorithm without input blockage is closest to the optimum because it produces random trees (with $n/d > 1$) while all the Tier based algorithms produce networks that are chains of peers ($n/d = 1$). The second area has $2 \le B \le 10$ and $0.46 \le p \le 1$. In this area the best algorithm is the TR algorithm without Input Blockage. The third area has $2 \le B \le 10$ and $0 \le p < 0.46$. In this area the best algorithm is the PLR algorithm without Input Blockage. The confidence intervals of n/d (with respect to B and p) have been evaluated for each algorithm and they have a maximum size of $4.6 \cdot 10^{-3}$, thus they are negligible in this approach.

5. Radio channel

We now briefly analyse the behaviour of the algorithms described above in a simple radio channel characterization; moreover the algorithm with the maximum percentage of bits correctly received is established.

5.1 Radio channel characterization

This subsection describes a simple radio channel characterization. Each wireless link between nodes is represented as an ideal wireless link with the following characteristics: the error probabilities over received bits are not independent (in the previous article (Merlanti & Mazzini, 2009) the error probabilities over received bits were independent). The average bit error probability with respect to small scale fading effects and coherent four phase PSK modulation is given as (Pages 785-486 formulas 14-4-36 and 14-4-38 of (J. Proakis, 1995)):

$$P_b = \frac{1}{2}\left[1 - \frac{\mu}{\sqrt{2-\mu^2}} \sum_{k=0}^{L-1} \binom{2k}{k} \left(\frac{1-\mu^2}{4-2\mu^2}\right)^k\right] \tag{13}$$

Where L is the order of diversity (for our channel L=4) and μ is the cross-correlation coefficient with perfect estimation given as (page 786 formula 14-4-36 or table C-1 page 894 of (J. Proakis, 1995)):

$$\mu = \sqrt{\frac{\overline{\gamma_c}}{1+\overline{\gamma_c}}} \tag{14}$$

Where $\overline{\gamma_c}$ is the average Signal to Noise Ratio with respect to small scale fading effects.

5.2 Analytical formulation model

In this section we present an analytical formulation (Merlanti & Mazzini, 2009) used to establish the bit error probability of each node of the network, produced by the previous algorithms. The main hypothesis used for this analytical model (and used in the simulator presented in the next section) are as follows:

- stationary network: during the simulation the system doesn't insert new nodes in the network because the aim is to estimate the network behaviour with an unreliable radio channel.
- Each segment sent by a peer i to another peer j has a constant and fixed dimension $d_{i,j}$.
- Each peer has one or more parent nodes from which it obtains the content; the content (namely the packet) is distributed among the parent peers with a static allocation, for example each peer receives the first segment of each packet from the first parent node, ..., each peer receives the n-th segment of each packet from the n-th parent node and so on.
- Each peer is identified by a unique peer ID; the peer ID of the source node is 0 and the network peers have incremental peer ID value starting from 1.
- The source node has each packet and transmits it to the peers directly connected to source node.
- The analytical formulation and the simulator considers only the uncoded communication between peers and the probability P_b is the average (with respect to small scale fading effects) bit error probability on decoded word. In this way if there is an error on a bit in the considered decoded segment then the entire segment is lost.

Consider the j-th node of the network:

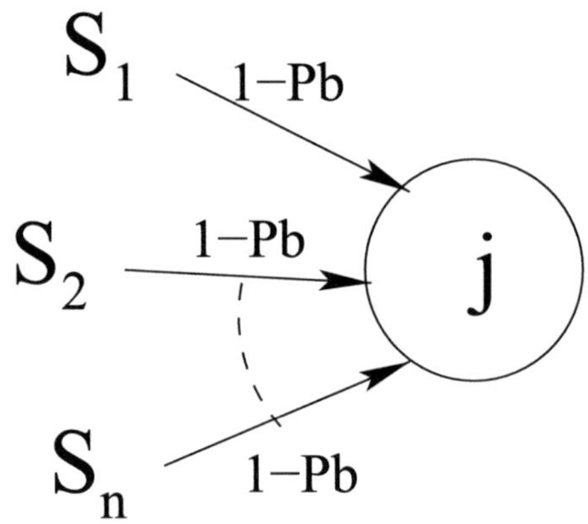

Fig. 1. j-th node of a p2p network

Suppose that the packet is divided in n segments and these are obtained from different parent nodes. So the j-th node receives the segments S_1… S_n of the packet from n different nodes. Each segment S_i (where i = 1…n) has g_i bits and suppose that these bits have different bit error probability namely, the first bit (b_1) of the segment S_i has a bit error probability equal P_{b1} ... the g_i-th bit (b_{gi}) of the segment S_i has a bit error probability equal P_{bgi}. In this way for each bit, the correct bit probability is: for the first bit is $P_1 = 1 - P_{b1}$ … for the g_i-th bit is $P_{gi} = 1 - P_{bgi}$. Now we have to establish the probability that the segment S_i is received correctly. A segment is correct if all the bits of this segment are received without errors. So the desired probability has the following expression:

$$P(S_i) = P_1 \cdot .... \cdot P_{g_i} \cdot (1 - P_b)^{g_i} \tag{15}$$

where P_b is the bit error probability of the radio channel and i=1…n. Therefore the average correct bit probability for the j-th node is:

$$\overline{P}(j) = \frac{\sum_{i=1}^{n} P(S_i) \cdot g_i}{\sum_{i=1}^{n} g_i} \tag{16}$$

This formula give us the wireless link model for each node of the network. Moreover, for the nodes directly connected to the source, the probabilities $P_1 \ldots P_{gi}$ for the segment S_i (where i = 1…n) have the following value:

$$P_1 = P_2 = \ldots = P_{g_i} = 1 \tag{17}$$

The bit error probability P_b of the radio channel, used in this section, is obtained through the formulas (13) and (14) with $\overline{\gamma_c}$ equal to the desired SNR.

5.3 Peer-to-peer network simulator

Each peer-to-peer network is simulated in the following way (Merlanti & Mazzini, 2009): for each packet transmitted by the source node S, the simulator analyses the peers in the order defined by their peer ID; for each i-th peer (where i = 1…n), the simulator performs the following operation: it searches the parent nodes of the i-th peer (we indicate this node with N). For each parent node N_f (N_f is the source node if N receives the packet from S), the simulator determines if N_f has the segment of the packet expected by N:

- if N_f has the segment then the simulator determines if N receives it without errors; this is done, whilst simulating the behaviour of the channel for each segment bit sent from N_f to N: the system generates a random number v uniformly distributed in [0,1); with this number the simulator establishes if the bit is lost or is correctly received. The bit is lost if $0 \leq v \leq P_b$. The bit is correctly received if $v > P_b$; where the parameter P_b is obtained through the formulas (13) and (14) with $\overline{\gamma_c}$ equal to the desired SNR. If the number of lost bits of the segment is greater than 0 then the entire segment is lost and therefore the simulator adds the number of bits of the segment to the number of bits lost by N. Otherwise the segment is correctly received and therefore the simulator adds the number of bits of the segment to the number of bits correctly received by N.
- If N_f doesn't have the segment, then the simulator adds the number of bits of the segment to the number of bits lost by N.

At the end of the simulation for each peer the system produces the number of the bits correctly received and the number of the bits lost.

5.4 Model validation through simulator

In order to validate the model of the network in an unreliable environment (radio channel) we use the autocorrelation test (pages 423-426 of the Book (Soderstrom & Stoica, 1989)).

We define the residuals $\varepsilon(t)$ as:

$$\varepsilon(t) = y(t) - \hat{y}(t) \tag{18}$$

where $y(t)$ are the simulated results about the average percentage of correctly received bits for each depth t of the network and $\hat{y}(t)$ are the results produced by the model.

If the model is accurately describing the observed data $y(t)$, then the residuals $\varepsilon(t)$ should be white. A way to validate the model is thus to test the hypotheses:

- H_0 : $\varepsilon(t)$ is a white sequence;
- H_1 : $\varepsilon(t)$ is not a white sequence.

The autocovariance of the residuals $\varepsilon(t)$ is estimated as:

$$\hat{r}_\varepsilon(\tau) = \frac{1}{N} \cdot \sum_{t=1}^{N-\tau} \varepsilon(t+\tau) \cdot \varepsilon(t) \tag{19}$$

where N is the maximum depth of the peer-to-peer distribution network.

If H_0 holds, then the square covariance estimates is asymptotically χ^2 distributed namely:

$$\frac{N}{\hat{r}_\varepsilon^2(0)} \cdot \sum_{i=1}^{m} \hat{r}_\varepsilon^2(i) \longrightarrow \chi^2(m) \tag{20}$$

where m is the number of degrees of freedom and it is equal to the maximum depth of the peer-to-peer distribution network.

Let x denote a random variable which is χ^2 distributed with m degrees of freedom. Furthermore, we define $\chi_\alpha^2(m)$ by:

$$\alpha = P(x > \chi_\alpha^2(m)) \tag{21}$$

For $\alpha = 0.01$ we have:

- if $\frac{N}{\hat{r}_\varepsilon^2(0)} \cdot \sum_{i=1}^{m} \hat{r}_\varepsilon^2(i) > \chi_\alpha^2(m)$ then we reject H_0.
- if $\frac{N}{\hat{r}_\varepsilon^2(0)} \cdot \sum_{i=1}^{m} \hat{r}_\varepsilon^2(i) \le \chi_\alpha^2(m)$ then we accept H_0.

We can see this property through the normalized covariance $\hat{r}_\varepsilon(\tau) / \hat{r}_\varepsilon(0)$. In this case $x_\tau = \hat{r}_\varepsilon(\tau) / \hat{r}_\varepsilon(0)$ and we plot (for each peer-to-peer algorithm, in the worst case, SNR = 4 dB) x_τ versus τ and a 99% confidence interval for x_τ.

Since $x_\tau \longrightarrow \mathbb{N}(0, 1/N)$ the lines in the diagram are drawn at $x = \pm 2.5758 / \sqrt{N}$. It can be seen from the figures 2 – 7 (for all the peer-to-peer algorithms) that x_τ lies in this interval. One can hence expect $\varepsilon(t)$ is a white process for all the peer-to-peer algorithms.

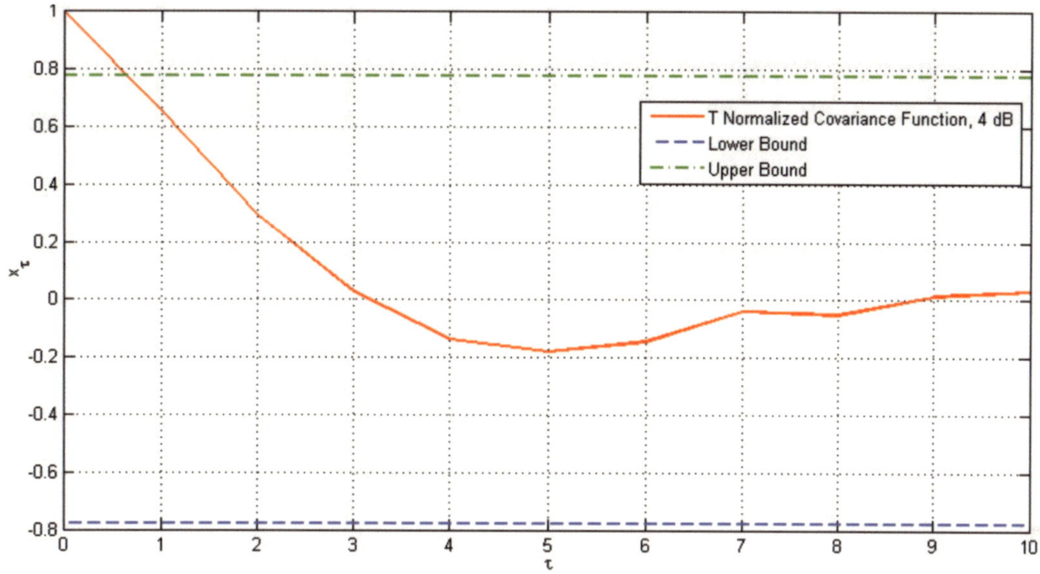

Fig. 2. Normalized covariance function of $\varepsilon(t)$ for the T algorithm in the worst condition (SNR = 4 dB)

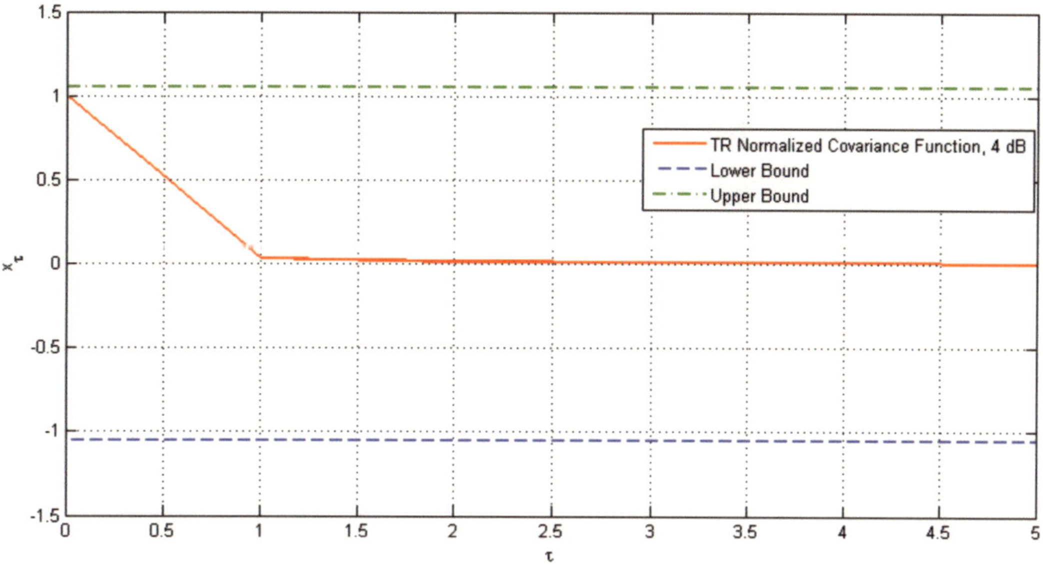

Fig. 3. Normalized covariance function of $\varepsilon(t)$ for the TR algorithm in the worst condition (SNR = 4 dB)

The result of the hypotheses test for each peer-to-peer algorithm is:

- T algorithm: the test quantity (20) is 17.5213 and $\chi^2_\alpha(m)$ is 24.7250 thus the variable $\varepsilon(t)$ is, under the null hypothesis H_0, approximately $\chi^2_\alpha(m)$.
- TR algorithm: the test quantity (20) is 14.0130 and $\chi^2_\alpha(m)$ is 16.8119 thus the variable $\varepsilon(t)$ is, under the null hypothesis H_0, approximately $\chi^2_\alpha(m)$.
- TRwIB algorithm: the test quantity (20) is 16.7519 and $\chi^2_\alpha(m)$ is 21.6660 thus the variable $\varepsilon(t)$ is, under the null hypothesis H_0, approximately $\chi^2_\alpha(m)$.
- PL algorithm: the test quantity (20) is 27.8567 and $\chi^2_\alpha(m)$ is 29.1412 thus the variable $\varepsilon(t)$ is, under the null hypothesis H_0, approximately $\chi^2_\alpha(m)$.
- PLR algorithm: the test quantity (20) is 57.1550 and $\chi^2_\alpha(m)$ is 63.6907 thus the variable $\varepsilon(t)$ is, under the null hypothesis H_0, approximately $\chi^2_\alpha(m)$.
- PLRwIB algorithm: the test quantity (20) is 154.0808 and $\chi^2_\alpha(m)$ is 180.7009 thus the variable $\varepsilon(t)$ is, under the null hypothesis H_0, approximately $\chi^2_\alpha(m)$.

In this case for all the peer-to-peer algorithms described above we observe that the prediction error $\varepsilon(t)$ is white with a level of significance $\alpha = 0.01$ thus the model is validated for all the algorithms.

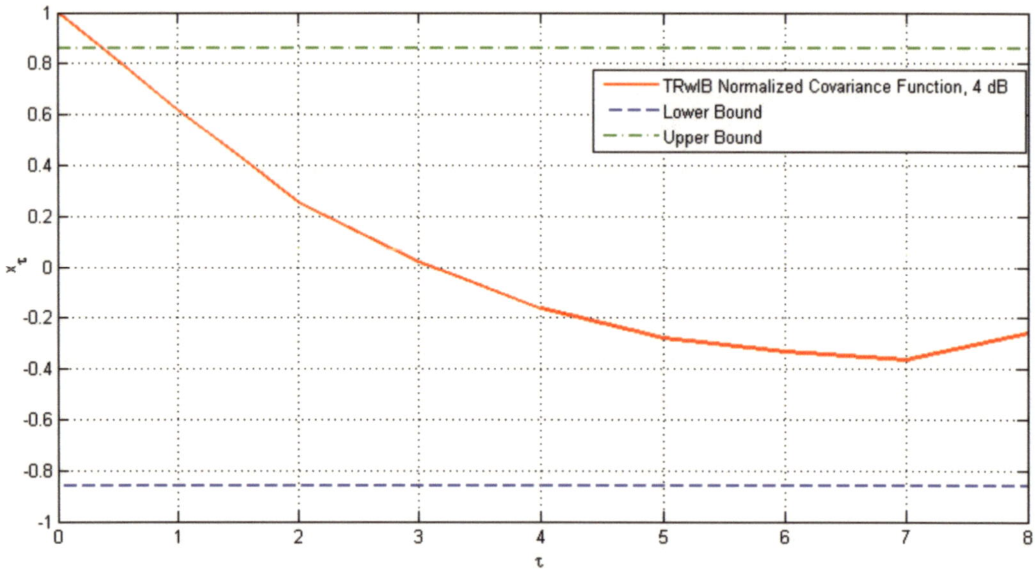

Fig. 4. Normalized covariance function of $\varepsilon(t)$ for the TRwIB algorithm in the worst condition (SNR = 4 dB)

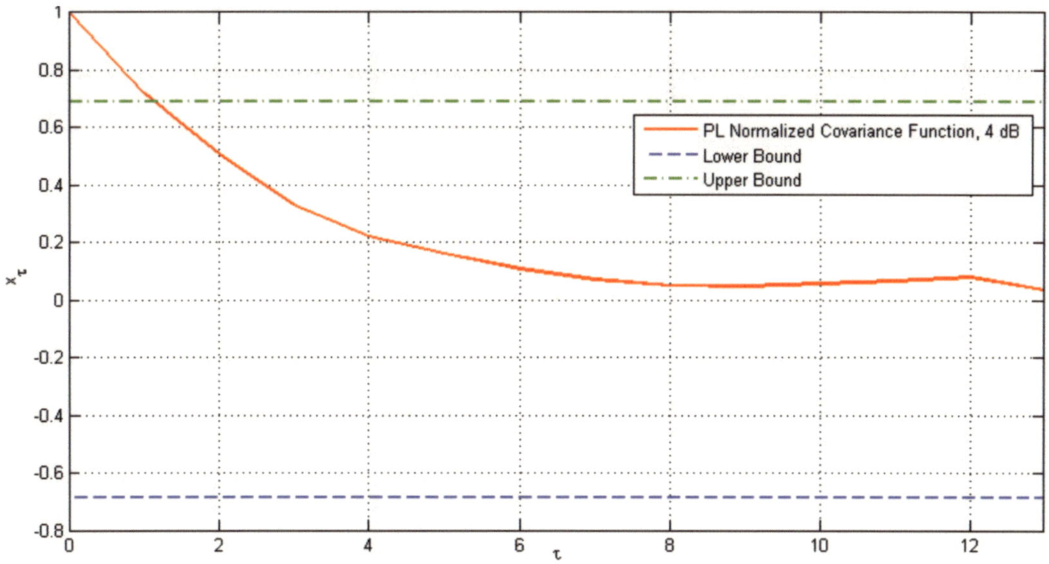

Fig. 5. Normalized covariance function of $\varepsilon(t)$ for the PL algorithm in the worst condition (SNR = 4 dB)

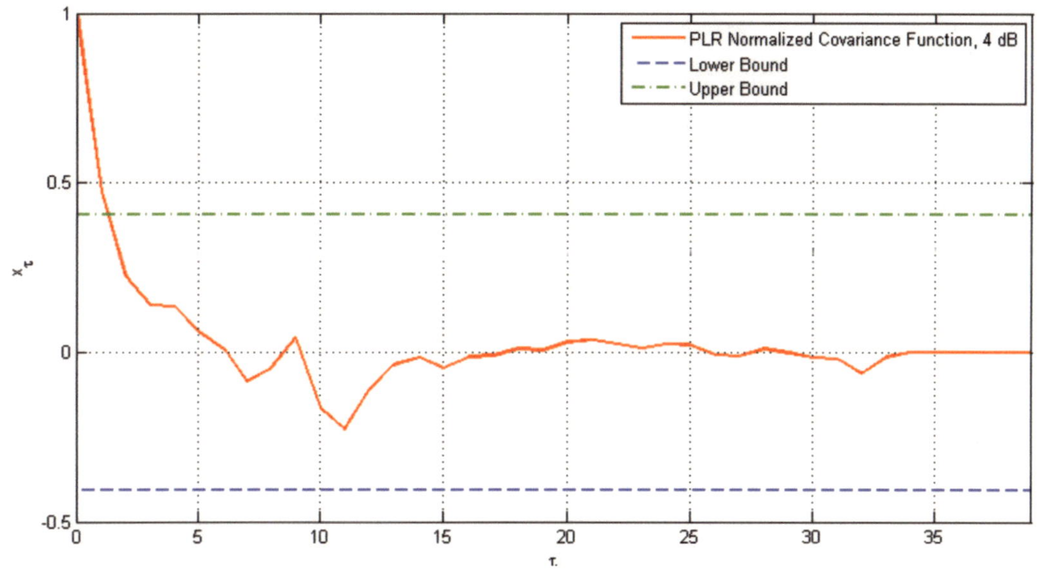

Fig. 6. Normalized covariance function of $\varepsilon(t)$ for the PLR algorithm in the worst condition (SNR = 4 dB)

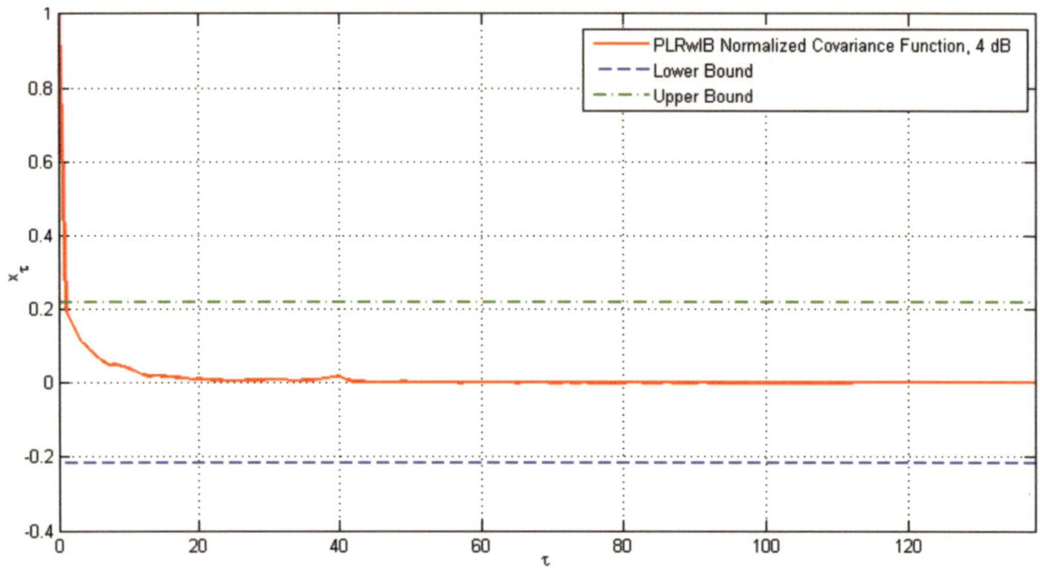

Fig. 7. Normalized covariance function of $\varepsilon(t)$ for the PLRwIB algorithm in the worst condition (SNR = 4 dB)

5.5 Results

The fundamental parameter used to analyze and compare the behaviour of the six types of peer-to-peer networks is represented by average percentage of correctly received bits as a function of depth level of the network. Through the simulation results we observe that by increasing the parameter of SNR (Signal to Noise Ratio) this produces an increase of the percentage of bits correctly received by each node of the network. Figures 8, 9 and 10 depict the comparisons of peer-to-peer networks under the six different types of algorithms we considered in section 3, with respect to the percentage of bits correctly received by each node with SNR = 4 dB, 7 dB and 10 dB. In this case the comparison parameter is the average percentage of correctly received bits as a function of depth level of the network. The best behaviour with respect to the average percentage of correctly received bits is obtained in the network generated by:

- the TR algorithm when the depth level is greater or equal to 4.
- The PLR algorithm and PLR algorithm without Input Blockage when the depth level is equal to 3.
- The PL algorithm when the depth level is less or equal to 2.

All the results, presented in this section, have been obtained by the following configuration parameters: number of bits supplied by the source node equal to 2048 Kbits divided in packets characterized by a length equal to 128 bits; we use the same sequences of peers, that require access to the network; dimension of each codeword is 16 bits and the number of bits that the receiver is able to detect and correct is 4 bits.

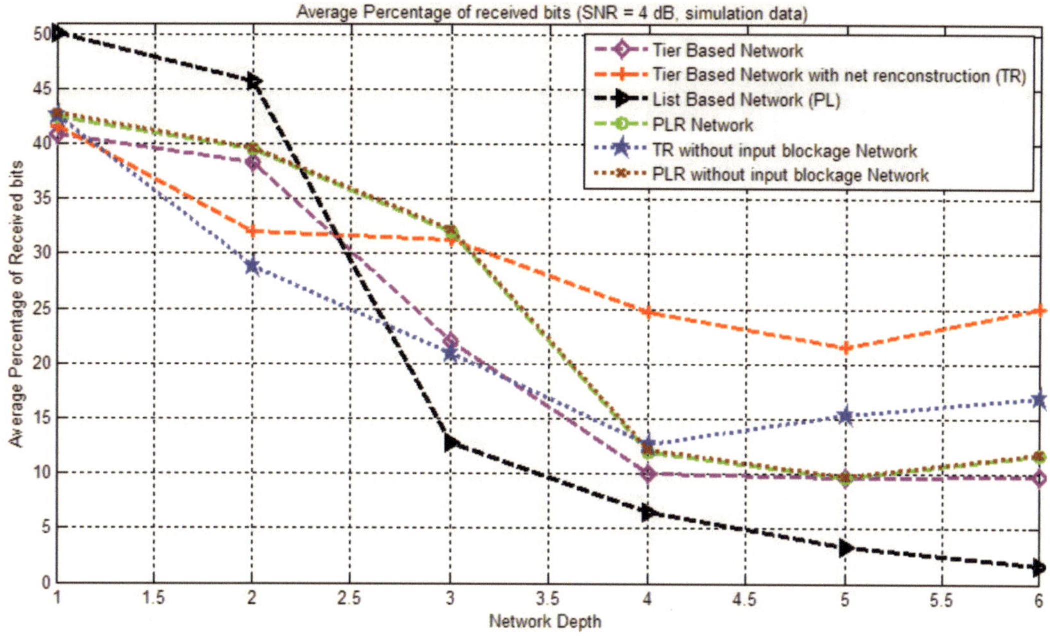

Fig. 8. Comparison, SNR = 4 dB

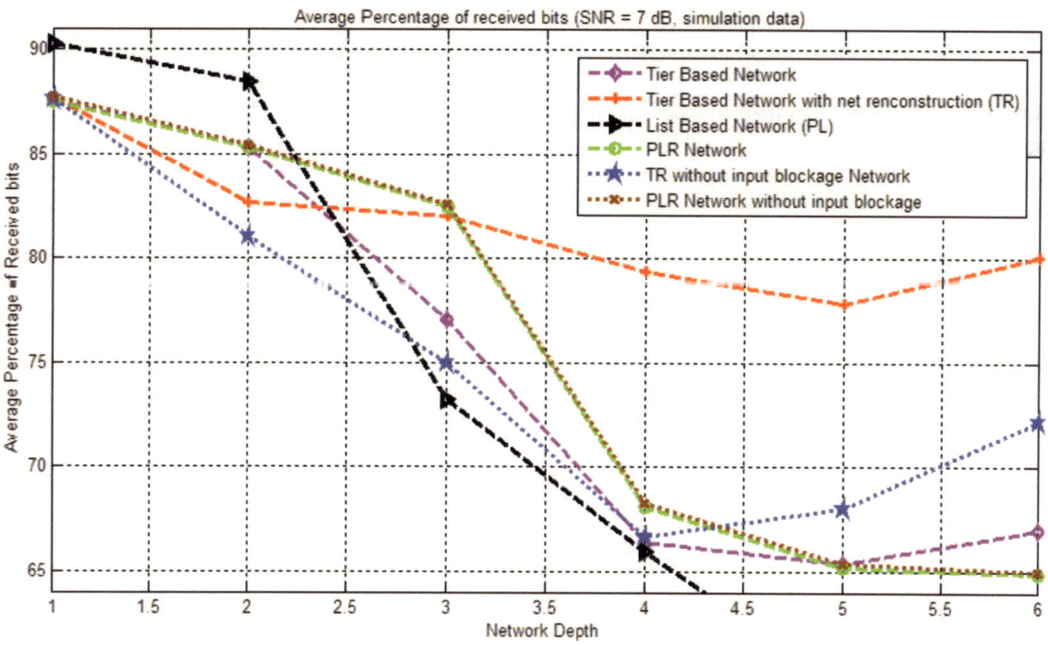

Fig. 9. Comparison, SNR = 7 dB

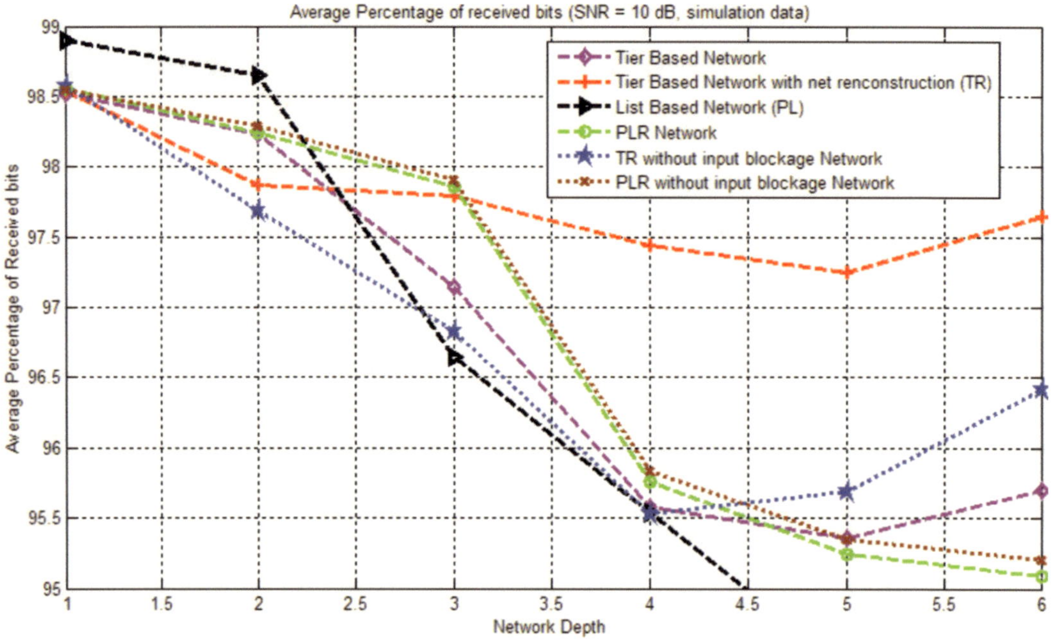

Fig. 10. Comparison, SNR = 10 dB

6. Conclusion

We can conclude that the maximization of the average maximum number of peers that can access the multimedia content and the minimization of the average maximum delay of the network is achieved, in the case of the asymmetric channel; when the source node is a home-user (where $1 \le B \le 2$) by using the PLR algorithm without Input Blockage, as in section 3 we showed that the PLR algorithm without Input Blockage is closest to optimum when $1 \le B \le 2$ and $0 \le p \le 1$. When the source node is a server (where $B \ge 2$) the best algorithm is:

- the TR algorithm without Input Blockage when $0.46 \le p \le 1$.
- The PLR algorithm without Input Blockage when $0 \le p < 0.46$.

We can also conclude that the TR and PLR algorithms without Input Blockage are a big improvement in comparison to Mazzini-Rovatti's algorithm (Mazzini & Rovatti, 2008) provided that new network conditions are followed, because they are suboptimal with respect to the theoretical optimum.

In the case of the radio channel, the best behaviour with respect to the percentage of correctly received bits is obtained in the network generated by:

- the TR algorithm when the depth level is greater or equal to 4.
- The PLR algorithm and PLR algorithm without Input Blockage when the depth level is equal to 3.
- The PL algorithm when the depth level is less or equal to 2.

7. References

Bakos, B., Farkas, L. & Nurminen, J. K. (2006). Peer-to-peer applications on smart phones using cellular communications, *WCNC 2006 proceedings*, ISBN 1-4244-0269-7, Las Vegas, Nevada, pp. 2222–2228, April 2006.

BitTorrent, http://www.bittorrent.com.

Boever, J. D. (2008). Value networks of peer-to-peer tv: An analysis of actors and their roles, *The Third International Conference on Internet and Web Applications and Services*, ISBN 978-0-7695-3163-2, Athens, Greece, pp. 686–695, June 2008.

Carter, C., Rhalibi, A.E., Merabti, M. & Bendiab, A.T. (2010). Hybrid Client-Server, Peer-to-Peer framework for MMOG, *Multimedia and Expo (ICME), 2010 IEEE International Conference on*, ISBN: 978-1-4244-7491-2, Suntec City, Singapore, pp. 1558 - 1563, July 2010.

Ciullo, D., Mellia, M., Meo, M., & Leonardi, E. (2008). Understanding peer-to-peer-tv systems through real measurements, *IEEE GLOBECOM 2008 proceedings*, ISBN: 978-1-4244-2324-8, New Orleans, Louisiana, pp. 1–6,November – December 2008.

KaZaA, http://www.kazaa.com.

Leonardi, E., Mellia, M., Horvath, A., Muscariello, L., Niccolini, S., & Rossi, D. (2008). Building a cooperative peer-to-peer-tv application over a wise network: The approach of the european fp-7 strep napa-wine, *IEEE Communications Magazine*, Vol. 46, No. 6, April 2008, pp. 20–22, ISSN: 0163-6804.

Lien, Y.-N. (2005). Performance issues of peer-to-peer file sharing over asymmetric and wireless networks, *ICDCSW '05: Proceedings of the First International Workshop on Mobility in Peer-to-Peer Systems*, ISBN : 0-7695-2328-5, Ohio, USA, pp. 850–855, June 2005.

Ma, M., Ma, Y., & Wang, J. (2008). The implementation and application of iptv supported on pull mode of peer-to-peer, *International Symposium on Knowledge Acquisition and Modeling*, ISBN : 978-0-7695-3488-6 , Wuhan, China, pp. 371–374, December 2008.

Matei, R., Iamnitchi, A. & Foster, P. (2002). Mapping the Gnutella network, *Internet Computing*, IEEE , Vol.6, No.1, January – February 2002, pp. 50-57, ISSN: 1089-7801.

Maymounkov, P. & Mazieres, D. (2002). Kademlia: A Peer-to-Peer Information System Based on the XOR Metric, *In International Workshop on Peer-to-Peer Systems, 2002.* Springer-Verlag, ISBN:3-540-44179-4, Cambridge, MA, USA, pp 53-65, March 2002.

Mazzini, G., & Rovatti, R. (2008). Peer-to-Peer distribution on asymmetric channels, *IEEE Communication Letters*, Vol. 12, No. 9, September 2008, pp. 699–701, ISSN: 1089-7798.

Merlanti D. and Mazzini G. (2009). Peer-to-peer distribution on radio channel, *Proceedings of the 17th international conference on Software, Telecommunications and Computer Networks. 24-26 Sept. 2009*, ISBN: 978-1-4244-4973-6, Hvar, pp.106-110, September 2009.

Papandreou, N. & Antonakopoulos, T. (2003). Cooperative bit-loading and fairness bandwidth allocation in adsl systems, *Circuits and Systems, 2003. ISCAS '03. Proceedings of the 2003 International Symposium on*, ISBN: 0-7803-7761-3, Bangkok, II-352 - II-355 vol.2, May 2003.

Proakis, J. (15-th August 2000), Digital Communications 4th Edition, McGraw-Hill, ISBN: 978-0072321111, New York.

RFC 793 (1981), Transmission Control Protocol DARPA, Internet Program Protocol Specification, Information Sciences Institute University of Southern California 4676 Admiralty Way Marina del Rey, California 90291, September 1981.

RFC 791 (1981), Internet Protocol DARPA, Program Protocol Specification, Information Sciences Institute University of Southern California 4676 Admiralty Way Marina del Rey, California 90291, September 1981.

Soderstrom, T. & Stoica, P. (July 1989). System Identification, Prentice Hall, ISBN: 978-0138812362.

Tay, V. (2005). Massively multiplayer online game (MMOG) - a proposed approach for military application, *Cyberworlds, 2005. International Conference on Cyberworlds. 23-25 Nov. 2005. IEEE Computer Society*, ISBN: 0-7695-2378-1, Singapore, pp. 396-400, November 2005.

The Gnutella Protocol Specification v0.4, available on http://www.stanford.edu/class/cs244b/gnutella_protocol_0.4.pdf.

Tomoya, K., & Shigeki, Y. (2005). Application of peer-to-peer technology to marketing, *Proceedings of the 2003 International Conference on Cyberworlds (CW"03)*, ISBN: 0-7695-1922-9, Singapore, pp. 372–379, December 2003.

Wang, Y., Yun, X., Li, Y. (2007). Analyzing the Characteristics of Gnutella Overlays, *Information Technology, 2007. ITNG '07. Fourth International Conference on*, ISBN: 0-7695-2776-0, Las Vegas, Nevada, pp.1095-1100, April 2007.

Part 2

Multimedia and Wireless Networks

2

A Dynamic Link Adaptation for Multimedia Quality-Based Communications in IEEE_802.11 Wireless Networks

Ahmed Riadh Rebai and Mariam Fliss
Wireless Research Group, Texas A&M University at Qatar, Qatar

1. Introduction

Assuming that the IEEE 802.11 Wireless Local Area Networks (WLANs) are based on a radio/infrared link, they are more sensitive to the channel variations and connection ruptures. Therefore the support for multimedia applications over such WLANs becomes non-convenient due to the compliance failure in term of link rate and transmission delay performance. Voice and broadband video mobile transmissions (which normally have strict bounded transmission delay or minimum link rate requirement) entail the design of various solutions covering different research aspects like service differentiation enhancement (Rebai et al., 2009), handoff scheme sharpening (Rebai, 2009a, 2009b, 2010) and physical rate adjustment. The core of this chapter focuses on the last facet concerning the link adaptation and the Quality of Service (QoS) requirements essential for successful multimedia communications over Wi-Fi networks. In fact, the efficiency of rate control diagrams is linked to the fast response for channel variation. The 802.11 physical layers provide multiple transmission rates (different modulation and coding schemes). The original 802.11 standard operates at 1 and 2 Mbps (IEEE Std. 802.11, 1999). Three high-speed versions were added to the original version. The 802.11b supports four physical rates up to 11 Mbps (IEEE Std. 802.11b, 1999). The 802.11a provides eight physical rates up to 54 Mbps (IEEE Std. 802.11a, 1999). The last 802.11g version, maintains 12 physical rates up to 54 Mbps at the 2.4 GHz band (IEEE Std. 802.11g, 2003). As a result, Mobile Stations (MSs) are able to select the appropriate link rate depending on the required QoS and instantaneous channel conditions to enhance the overall system performance. Hence, the implemented link adaptation algorithm symbolizes a vital fraction to achieve highest transmission capability in WLANs. "When to decrease and when to increase the transmission rate?" are the two fundamental matters that we will be faced to when designing a new physical-rate control mechanism. Many research works focus on tuning channel estimation schemes to better detect when the channel condition was improved enough to accommodate a higher rate, and then adapt their transmission rate accordingly (Habetha & de No, 2000; Qiao et al., 2002). However, those techniques usually entail modifications on the current 802.11 standard. In (del Prado Pavon & Choi, 2003), authors presented a motivating rate adaptation algorithm based on channel estimation without any standard adjustment. However, this scheme supposes that all the transmission failures are due to channel errors and not due to multi-user collisions.

Another way to perform link control is based on local Acknowledgment (Ack) information for the transmitter station (Qiao & Choi, 2005). Consequently, two new techniques (Chevillat et al., 2003; Kamerman & Monteban, 1997) where accepted by the standard due to their efficiency and implementation simplicity. In fact, the source node tries to increase its transmission rate after successive successful Ack responses, and therefore they do not involve any change for the 802.11 standard. Moreover and as it was demonstrated by (Sangman et al., 2011) a fine and excellent physical link adjustment will carry out a quality-aware and robust routing for mobile multihop ad hoc networks. A good study (Galtier, 2011) was recently addressed regarding the adaptative rate issues in the WLAN Environment and highlighted the high correlation between the Congestion Window (CW) of the system, and the rate at which packets are emitted. The given analytical approach opens the floor and shows that the different mechanisms that have been implemented in the MAC systems of WLAN cards have strong correlations with other transmission parameters and therefore have to be redesigned with at least a global understanding of channel access problems (backoff and collisions) and rate adaptation questions.

In this chapter we propose a new dynamic time-based link adaptation mechanism, called MAARF (Modified Adaptive Auto Rate Fallback). Beside the transmission frame results, the new model implements a Round Trip Time (RTT) technique to select adequately an instantaneous link rate. This proposed model is evaluated with most recent techniques adopted by the IEEE 802.11 standard: ARF (Auto Rate Fallback) and AARF (Adaptive ARF) schemes. Thus, we are able to achieve a high performance WLAN transmission. Consequently, we can extend this approach in various Wi-Fi modes to support multimedia applications like voice and video tasks.

The rest of the chapter is organized as follows. Section 2 offers a literature survey on related link-adjustment algorithms and the actual used ones. Section 3 is dedicated to the new proposed MAARF method and its implementation details. Simulation results will be given in Section 4 to illustrate the link quality improvement of multimedia transmissions over Wi-Fi networks and to compare its performance with previous published results (Kamerman & Monteban, 1997; Lacage et al.,2004). We show how the proposed model outperforms previous approaches (ARF and AARF) because of its new time-based decision capability in addition to Ack count feature.

2. Review of the current rate-control approaches

First we recall that the standard IEEE802.11 (IEEE Std. 802.11a, 1999; IEEE Std. 802.11b, 1999; IEEE Std. 802.11g, 2003) includes various versions a/b/g and allows the use of multiple physical rates (from 1Mbps to 54Mbps for the 802.11g). Therefore several studies have been made to develop mechanisms which lead to adapt transmission attempts with the best physical available rate depending on the estimated channel condition to avoid transmission failures with Wi-Fi connections. The most important issues that should be taken into account and are responsible for the design of a reliable rate adaptation mechanism are:

- The channel condition variation due to a packet transmission error which results to multiple retransmissions or even a transmission disconnection.
- The channel sensitivity against interferences (Angrisani et al., 2011) due to disturbing incidences, additive random noises, electromagnetic noises, the Doppler effect, an accidental barrier or natural phenomena.

- The packet emissions latency which affects the autonomy of mobile stations in case of transmission error (since the communication duration is extended and the energy consumption becomes more important).
- The MSs Mobility leads to a distances change, hence, to an appropriate mobility management protocol over Wi-Fi connections.

Depending on the instantaneous channel quality, a rate adjustment will be always needed to achieve better communication performance with respect for multimedia QoS requirements.

Since WLAN systems that use the IEEE802.11g (IEEE Std. 802.11g, 2003) physical layer offer multiple data rates ranging from 1 to 54 Mb/s, the link adaptation can be seen as a process of switching or a dynamic choosing mechanism between different physical data rates corresponding to the instantaneous channel state. In other words, it aims to select the 'ideal' physical rate matching the actual channel condition. The best throughput can be larger or smaller than the current used one. The adequate rate will be chosen according to the instantaneous medium conditions. There are two criteria to properly evaluate this adaptation/adjustment: the first is the channel quality estimation; secondly is the adequate rate selection.

The estimation practice involves a measurement of the instantaneous channel states variation within a specific time to be able to predict the matching quality. This creates a large choice of indicator parameters on the medium condition that may include the observed Signal to Noise Ratio (SNR), the Bit Error Rate (BER), and the Received Signal Strength Indicator (RSSI). Those various physical parameters express instantaneous measurements operated by the 802.11 PHY card after completion of the last transmission.

Regarding the rate selection formula, it entails a first-class exploitation of channel condition indicators to better predict the medium state and then fit/adjust the suitable physical rate for the next communication. Consequently, this process will reduce packets' retransmissions and the loss rate. Bad channel-quality estimation would result in performance degradation. Thus, inaccurate assessments resulting from a bad choice of medium state indicators give rise to inappropriate judgments on the instantaneous conditions and cause deterioration on the observed performance. Therefore, this estimation is essential to better support multimedia services and maximize performance and the radio channel utilization.

Accordingly, during packets transmission, the corresponding MS may increase or decrease the value of its physical rate based on two different approaches:

a. With the help of accurate channel estimation, the MS will know precisely when the medium conditions are improved to accommodate a higher data rate, and then adapt its transmission rate accordingly. However, those techniques (Habetha & de No, 2000; Qiao et al., 2002) require efforts to implement incompatible changes on the 802.11 standard. Another research work (del Prado Pavon & Choi, 2003) have presented a very interesting data rate adapting plan based on RSSI measurements and the number of transmitted frames for an efficient channel assessment without any modification on the standard. On the other hand, this plan operates under the assumption that all transmission failures are due to channel errors. Thus, it will not work efficiently in a multi-user environment where multiple transmissions may fail due to collisions and not only to the channel quality.

b. The alternative way for the link adaptation is to carry out decisions based exclusively on the information returned by the receiver. In 802.11 WLANs, an acknowledgment (ACK) is sent by the receiver after the successful data recovery. Only after receiving an ACK frame the transmitter announces a successful transmission attempt. On the other hand, if an ACK is either incorrect or not received, the sender presumes a data transmission failure and reduces its actual data rate down to the next available physical rate-slot. In addition, the transmitter can increase its transmission rate after assuming a channel condition enhancement by receiving a specific number of consecutive positive ACKs. These approaches (Qiao & Choi, 2005; Chevillat et al., 2003) do not require changes on the actual Fi-Wi standard and are easy to deploy with existing IEEE 802.11 network cards.

Various additional techniques have been proposed in the literature to sharpen the accuracy of the rate adaptation process and improve the performance of IEEE 802.11 WLANs. The authors in (Pang et al., 2005) underlined the importance of MAC-layer loss differentiation to more efficiently utilize the physical link. In fact, since IEEE 802.11 WLANs do not take into account the loss of frames due to collisions, they have proposed an automatic rate fallback algorithm that can differentiate between the two types of losses (link errors and collisions over the wireless link). Moreover it has been shown in (Krishnan & Zakhor, 2010) that an estimate of the collision probability can be useful to improve the link adaptation in 802.11 networks, and then to increase significantly the overall throughput by up to a factor of five.

In (Xin et al., 2010) the authors presented a practical traffic-aware active link rate adaptation scheme via power control without degrading the serving rate of existing links. Their basic idea consists to firstly run an ACK based information exchange to estimate the upper power bound of the link under adaptation. Then by continuously monitoring the queue length in the MAC layer, it would be easy to know whether the traffic demand can be met or not. If not, the emitting power will be increased with respect to the estimated power upper-bound and will switch to a higher modulation scheme. A similar strategy was presented in (Junwhan & Jaedoo, 2006) that provides two decisions to estimate the link condition and to manage both the transmission rate and power.

Several research works (Haratcherev et al., 2005; Shun-Te et al., 2007; Chiapin & Tsungnan, 2008) have implemented a cross-layer link adaptation (CLLA) scheme based on different factors as: the number of successful transmissions, the number of transmission failures, and the channel information from the physical layer to determine actual conditions and therefore to adjust suitably transmission parameters for subsequent medium accesses. As well in (Chen et al., 2010) a proper-designed cross application-MAC layer broadcast mechanism has been addressed, in which reliability is provided by the application layer when broadcasting error corrections and next link rate adaptations (resulting from the MAC layer).

Another approach (Jianhua et al., 2006) has been developed where both packet collisions and packet corruptions are analytically modeled with the proposed algorithm. The models can provide insights into the dynamics of the link adaptation algorithms and configuration of algorithms parameters. On the other hand, in (An-Chih et al., 2009) the authors presented a joint adaptation of link rate and contention window by firstly considering if a proper backoff window has been reached. Specifically, if the medium congestion level can be reduced by imposing a larger backoff window on transmissions, then there may be no need to decrease the link rate, given that the Signal to Interference-plus-Noise Ratio (SINR) can be sustained.

In the rest of this section we decide to provide details and discuss only the two main currently-implemented techniques.

2.1 Auto Rate Fallback (ARF)

Auto Rate Fallback (Kamerman & Monteban, 1997) was the first rate-control algorithm published and quickly adopted/integrated with the Wi-Fi standard. It was designed to optimize the physical rate adjustment of the second WLANs generation (specifically for 802.11a/g versions which allow multi-hop physical rates). The ARF technique is based simply on the number of ACKs received by the transmitting MS to determine the next rate for the next frame transmission. This method does not rely on hidden out-layer information, such as a physical channel quality measurement like (i.e. the SNR value). Thus, it was easy to implement and fully compatible with the 802.11 standard. In fact, after a fixed number of successful transfers equal to 10 or the expiration of a timer T initially launched the ARF increments the actual physical transmission rate from R_i to a higher rate R_{i+1} among those allocated by the standard. In other words, the ARF mechanism decides to increase the data rate when it determines that channel conditions have been improved. Unlike other algorithms reported in the literature, the ARF detection is not based on Physical layer measurements upon a frame delivery. Basically it simply considers the medium status improvement by counting the number of consecutive successful transmissions made or the timer (T) timeout. This timer is defined as the maximum waiting delay which will be launched by the MS each time it switches between the given data rates. Once this timer ends without any rate swap the MS will be testing a higher available rate. This practical implementation is considered as second alternative to adapt the best transmission rate since it covers the case that medium conditions are excellent and favorable to adopt a higher rate and the counter of consecutive successful transmissions will never reach the desired value (10) due to other failures. This case is very common in such wireless networks where a transmission failure is not only due to an inadequate rate.

In addition, the next transmission must be completed successfully immediately after a rate increase otherwise the rate will be reduced instantaneously (back to the old smaller value), and the timer T will be reset. In fact, the mechanism has estimated that the new adopted rate is not adequate for next network transmissions.

Also after any two consecutive failures the algorithm automatically reduces its actual rate until it reaches again a number of 10 consecutive ACKs or the expiration of timer T. In this way, ARF detects the deterioration of the channel quality based on two consecutive failed transmissions, and chooses to back out to the previous rate. Figure 1 summarizes the operation of the ARF and shows the corresponding flow diagram.

While ARF increases the transmission rate at a fixed frequency (each 10 consecutive ACKs) to achieve a higher system throughput, this model has two main drawbacks:

- Firstly, this process can be costly since a transmission failure (produced by an unsuitable rate increasing decision made by the ARF mechanism) reduces the overall throughput. Specifically, for a steady channel status (stable characteristics) ARF will try periodically to switch to a higher rate by default which leads to unnecessary frame transmission failure and reduces the algorithm efficiency.

- Secondly, ARF is unable to stabilize the rate variations. In fact if the channel conditions deteriorate suddenly, the ARF mechanism will be unable to respond fast to these changes and to suit the current state. It will carry out numerous transmission failures so that it reaches the desired rate value. Therefore, this algorithm cannot cope with rapid medium status changes.

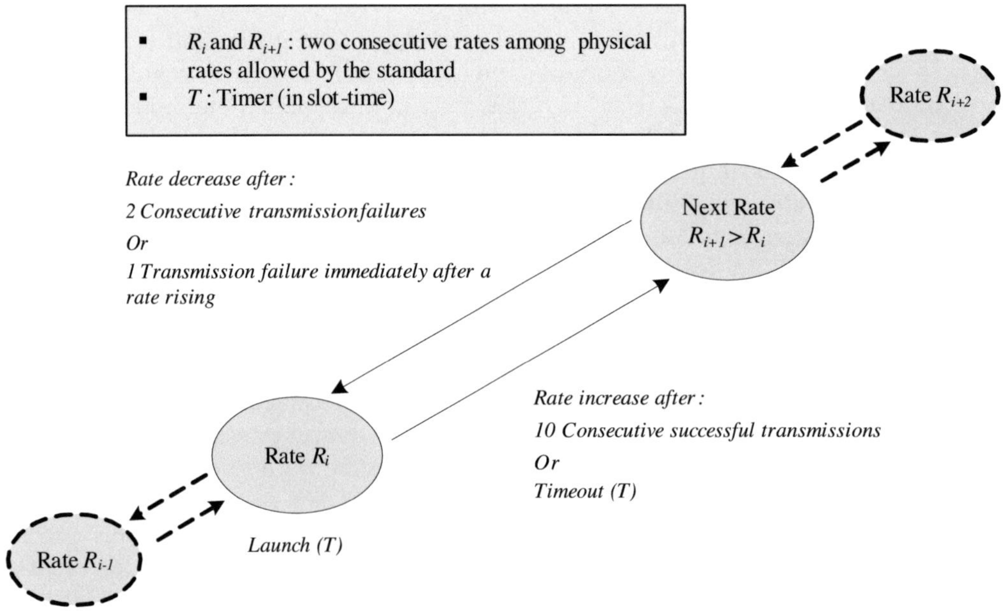

Fig. 1. The ARF flow diagram

2.2 Adaptive Auto Rate Fallback (AARF)

To overcome the given shortcomings, a new approach called Adaptive Auto Rate Fallback (AARF), was proposed (Lacage et al., 2004). It is based on the communication history and aims to reduce unnecessary rate variations caused by a misinterpretation of the channel state. Thus, this method controls the time-making process by using the Binary Exponential Backoff (BEB) technique (the same used by the CSMA/CD and CSMA/CA access mechanisms).

Therefore, when a packet transmission fails just after a rate increase, a lower rate is chosen for next transmission attempts. In addition, the number of consecutive successful transmissions n required for the next rate-switching decision will be multiplied by two (with a limit of $n_{max} = 50$). Similar to the old version in a rate decrease caused by two consecutive frames transmission errors, this value is reset to $n_{min} = 10$. The flow diagram in Figure 2 briefly explains the operation of AARF.

Consequently, this new version dynamically controls the number of positive ACKs needed for the rate control. Thus, AARF overcomes the old ARF version in case of a long steady channel conditions by eliminating needless and continuous rate-rising attempts. However it keeps the same disadvantage of the old implementation in case of rapid changes produced on the channel state.

Figure 3 illustrates the behavior of both ARF and AARF approaches for a time period equal to 0.4s needed for 230 data frames. Various physical rates were adopted in this experiment (1, 2, 5.5 and 11Mbps for 802.11b). During this experimentation, we set channel conditions supporting the use of the physical rate R_3 (5.5Mbps) for data transmission. We note that the period between two successive attempts is increased using the AARF technique while the ARF mechanism is trying regularly to increment the current rate to a higher value each ten successive successful transmissions. For example, within the time interval [0.2s, 0.25s] AARF doesn't create any unnecessary rate-switching effort, while ARF carries out three attempts. Likewise, the AARF algorithm considerably has reduced the number of produced errors due to bad decisions (3/4 of errors were removed compared to those generated by the ARF mechanism).

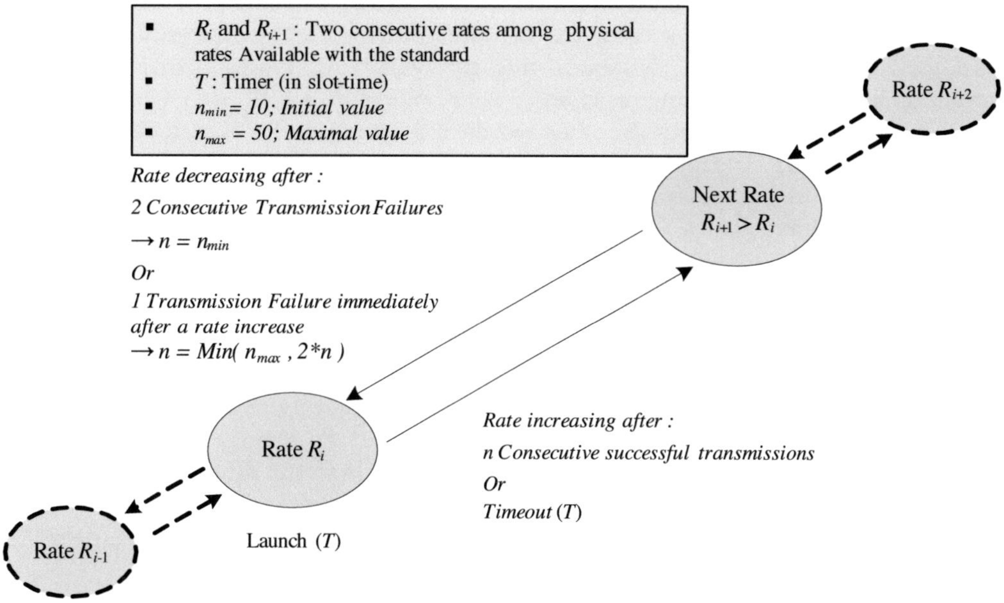

Fig. 2. The AARF flow diagram

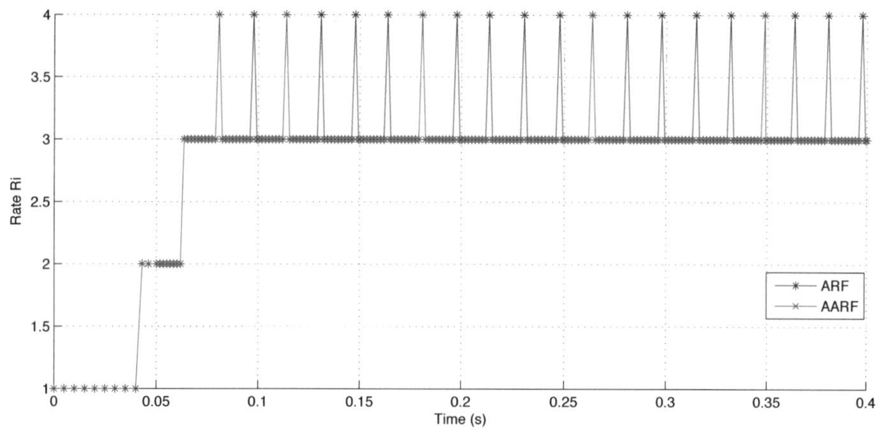

Fig. 3. ARF and AARF performance evaluation

2.3 Discussion

We have shown in the above study that the actual rate selection algorithms ARF and AARF do not conduct to an accurate decision when the channel is relatively noisy. Despite the given transmission enhancements both models still need improvement and refinement since they cannot react instantly to sudden changes of the channel state. In addition, an interval of time is needed to reach the maximum throughput in case of 'ideal' medium condition. Thus, these mechanisms do not represent optimal solutions for the physical link adaptation in noisy and 'ideal' environments.

Indeed, at a slow channel quality variation AARF is more suitable than ARF as it proceeds to the elimination of unnecessary rate increases. And thereafter, it decreases greatly the number of lost packets while relying on already rate exchanges made previously. However, this improvement is still insufficient since the decision criterion depends only on the nature of acknowledgments (ACKs), whereas this parameter no longer provides sufficient information about the instantaneous channel state. As result AARF need a high latency to reach the maximum throughput. In other words, a negative ACK (or lack of transmission success) is interpreted only by medium quality deterioration. However, this phenomenon may be caused by other networks anomalies (destination not reachable, collision occurred with another data frame, bad CRC, etc.).

It is also observed that when the competing number of stations is high, packet collisions can largely affected the performance of ARF and make ARF operate with the lowest data rate, even when no packet corruption occurs. This is in contrast to the existing assumption that packet collision will not affect the correct operation of ARF and can be ignored in the evaluation of ARF. Therefore, ARF and AARF can only passively react to the signal quality experienced at the receiver. In some occasions, we need to actively improve the signal quality in order to make the transmission rate to meet the traffic demand, even when the link length is a little large. This enhancement will optimize the overall performance and typically will demonstrate a practical effectiveness for multimedia transmissions over Wi-Fi WLANs.

Accordingly, in the next section we propose a new rate adaptation technique to improve the decision based on instantaneous channel conditions while respecting and still complying with the 802.11 standard. In addition, the new approach will be compared with those currently deployed. Simulation results will be also presented to demonstrate the enhancement of the proposed technique compared to those currently presented. Also parameters optimization of the new mechanism will be carried out to be then considered during next scenario simulations.

3. Proposed adaptive rate control technique

The main idea of the proposed method is to introduce a new channel status assessment parameter which cooperates with the number of ACKs to provide an efficient and accurate prediction of instantaneous channel conditions and subsequently to improve the actual rate adjustment mechanism. A logical way to cope with the slow accommodation characteristics of statistics-based feedback methods is to look for methods that use faster feedback, i.e., feedback that quickly provides up-to-date information about the channel status. Such a feedback — the RTT — has been theoretically discussed in (Rebai et al., 2008), but so far, to our knowledge, it has not been used in a practical implementation. We use this RTT measurement in the proposed 802.11 radio to enhance multimedia performance, and also to provide feedback information about the channel conditions that the MAC layer requires. In this section, we first define the new parameter which will be required for the system design. Next, we will describe its implementation and the principle of operation.

3.1 Round Trip Time (RTT)

Reliable transport protocols such as Transport Control Protocol (TCP) (Tourrilhes, 2001) were initially designed to operate in 'traditional' and wired networks where packet losses are mainly due to congestion. However, wireless networks introduce additional sorts of errors caused by uncontrolled variations of the medium.

Face to the congestion problems, TCP responds to each loss by invoking congestion control algorithms such as *Slow Start*, *Congestion Avoidance* and *Fast Retransmission*. These techniques have been introduced in different versions of the TCP protocol (TCP Reno, TCP Tahoe, etc.).. These proactive algorithms consist to control the Congestion Window (CW) size based on observed errors. Another TCP-Vegas version has been proposed by (Kumar & Holtzman, 1998; Mocanu, 2004) and rapidly has been adopted by the TCP protocol since it includes an innovative solution designed for preventive systems. In fact, it performs a CW size adjustment based on a fine connection status estimation achieved by a simple measurement of the TCP segment transmission delay. This delay is called Round Trip Time (RTT) and represents (as illustrated in Figure 4) the time period between the instant of issuing a TCP segment by the source noted t_e and the reception time of the corresponding ACK noted t_r.

If the measured RTTs will have larger values, the TCP protocol infers network congestion, and reacts accordingly by reducing the congestion window size (symbolized by the number of sent frames and their size). If the values of observed RTTs become smaller, the protocol concludes an improvement on the medium conditions and that the network is not overloaded anymore. Therefore, it proceeds dynamically to increment the CW size, and thus a good operating performance will be achieved based on the new Vegas-version technique.

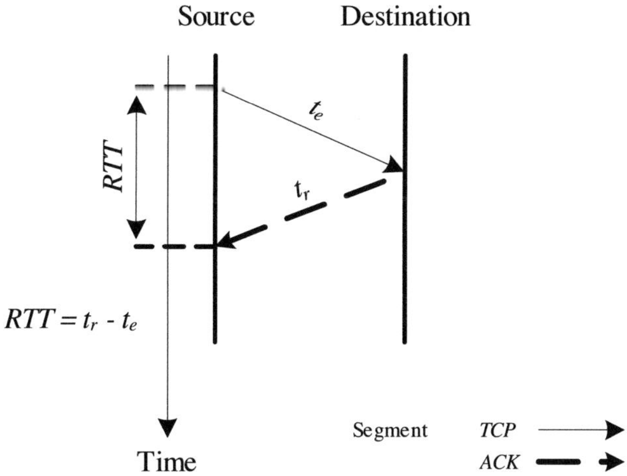

Fig. 4. The RTT delay computation

3.2 The RTT parameter integration

An interesting information and immediate channel observation will be deducted after each data frame transmission by means of RTT measurement and calculation. This feature represents the innovative part of the new control algorithm to adjust the data rate based on the channel capacity. A first integration attempt has been presented in (Rebai et al., 2008) and a rate adaptation design has been proposed. In this chapter, we implement an enhanced mechanism called *Modified Adaptive Auto Rate Fallback* (MAARF) which aims to predict the medium conditions and minimize the unnecessary loss of data. It chooses the appropriate rate value needed for the next transmission according to the measured RTT value. In fact, it performs a match between the observed value of RTT and the physical rate selection.

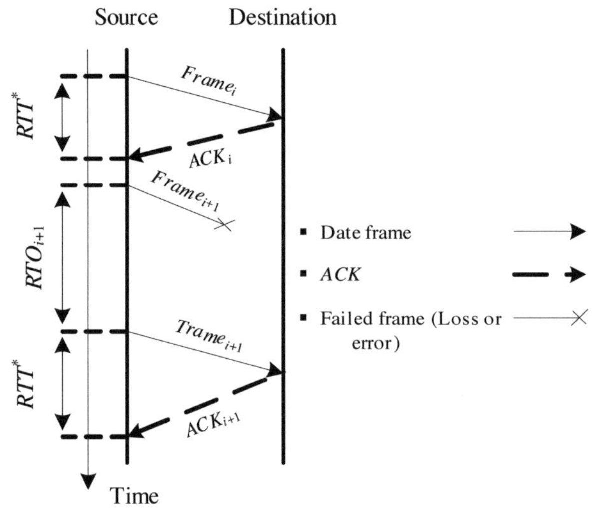

Fig. 5. The date frames transmissions

Furthermore we define two types of RTT. The first variety is the observed value directly measured from the channel following the frame sending and called instantaneous RTT denoted by RTT^*. The second, denoted by RTT_i, is a theoretical value computed based on the sending rate R and the data frame size. During a successful transmission of a frame i resulting the receipt of the associated ACK_i, a value of RTT^* is calculated. We introduce an associated recovery timer, called "Retransmission Time Out" and noted RTO_i, which will detect receipt/loss of a data frame. Based on this parameter, the transmitter detects the loss of a frame i in case of no receipt of the corresponding ACK_i till the expiration of the RTO_i timer. In this case, the last issued frame i will be retransmitted (see Figure 5).

Similarly, we introduce an interval defined by $[\, RTT_i^+ \,, RTT_i^- \,]$ adjacent to the theoretical value RTT_i corresponding to the rate R_i. If the observed value of RTT^* belongs this interval (i.e. close enough to the theoretical expected value RTT_i) the channel conditions will be considered insignificant and do not require change of the current rate R_i for next transmissions. In other words, if the value of RTT^* belongs the interval $[\, RTT_i^+ \,, RTT_i^- \,]$ the link quality is assumed stable and therefore it is suitable that the MS will transmit using the same current rate R_i since the measured RTT^* is considered close to the expected RTT_i value. Outside this window, channel changes are presumed:

- Improved, if the RTT^* value is less than RTT_i^+ since the corresponding ACK frame was received earlier than expected and therefore channel conditions had got better.
- Degraded, if the RTT^* value is greater than RTT_i^- since the received ACK frame was delayed and then we assume that the risk of data loss increases.

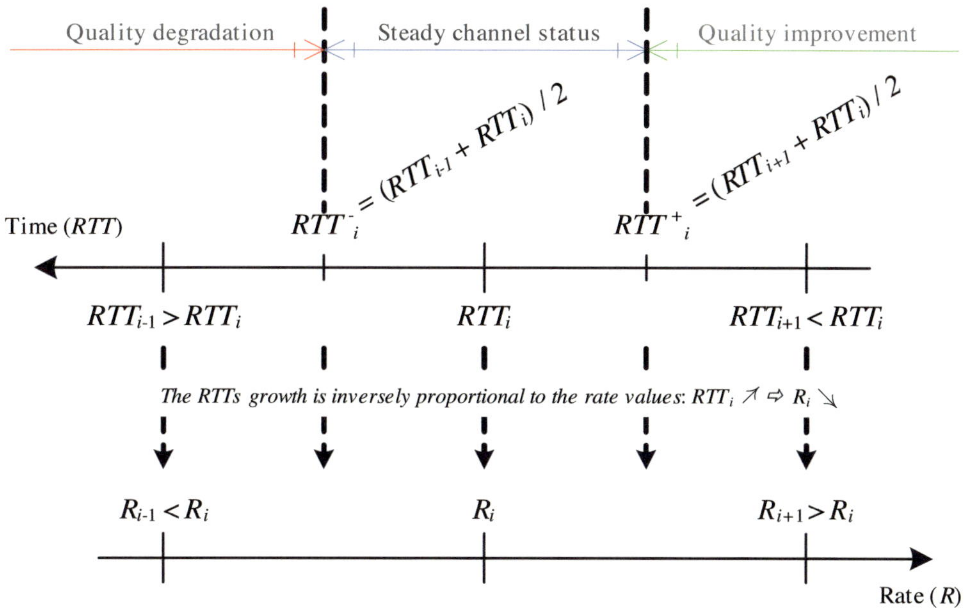

Fig. 6. The algorithm parameters set

In both cases, the MS must then change its emission rate and adapt it according to these instantaneous channel state interpretations. We point that $RTT_i^+ < RTT_i^-$ based on the statement $RTT_{i+1} < RTT_i < RTT_{i-1}$ since $R_{i+1} > R_i > R_{i-1}$. The calculation of the parameters values RTT_i^+ and RTT_i^- is associated to the RTT_i value as defined in the Equation 1 and 2.

$$RTT_i^- = (RTT_{i-1} + RTT_i)/2 \quad (1)$$

$$RTT_i^+ = (RTT_{i+1} + RTT_i)/2 \quad (2)$$

As stated in Figure 6 the RTT_i^- value will be the middle of the interval [RTT_{i-1}, RTT_i], and similarly, RTT_i^+ will have the center value of the interval [RTT_{i+1}, RTT_i].

3.3 Modified Adaptive Auto Rate Fallback (MAARF): Principle of operation

Subsequent to each successful frame transmissions, we compare the variation between instantaneous RTT^* and theoretical RTT_i values. More specifically, we test if the value of RTT^* has exceeded RTT_i^+ and RTT_i^- bounds or no. However, the according rate adjustment decision will be taken after several observations of RTT^* samples:

- As the number of consecutive successful transmissions did not reach a value of n (required as in AARF algorithm for the next rate-switching decision – it is initially initialized to n_{min}) we perform the following tests:
  - If the observed RTT^* value is less than RTT_i^+ ($RTT^* < RTT_i^+$) during h successive transmissions and the maximum speed (54 Mbps) is not yet acquired, then the instant RTT^* is considered smaller than the RTT_i value and rather close to the RTT_{i+1} one. Subsequently, the MAARF technique switches to a higher bit rate R_{i+1} starting the next attempt (since an improvement of the channel characteristics was interpreted).
  - If the value of RTT^* is greater than RTT_i^- ($RTT^* > RTT_i^-$) for the last g transmission attempts and the lower rate (6 Mbps) is not yet reached, this implies that the instantaneous RTT^* value is larger than the expected RTT_i and relatively close to RTT_{i-1}. Thus, MAARF detect an early deterioration of the link quality and therefore we reduce the current rate R_{i-1} for future communications.
  - If the value of RTT^* remains between the two theoretical bounds $[RTT_i^+, RTT_i^-]$ (i.e. $RTT_i^+ < RTT^* < RTT_i^-$) then the rate will be kept and stay invariant R_i (MAARF assumes a steady state for subsequent network transmissions).
- Similar to the AARF algorithm, when the number of consecutive successful transmissions reaches the desired value (which can be at any given time 10, 20, 40 or 50), we switch to a higher throughput without consideration of the observed RTT^* values.

Analogically, when a transmission fails (no acknowledgment received within the RTO_i value) MAARF modifies values of the decision-making parameters (n, h and g) as follows:

- If a transmission error is occurred just after a rate increase, it will be then decremented. In addition, as shown in Equation 3 the number of successful transmissions n that should be attained for the next rise will be doubled with a limit value equal to n_{max}.

$$n = Min(2 * n; n_{\max}) \tag{3}$$

- If two consecutive errors are detected the MAARF mechanism reduces the current rate, while resetting the value of successful transmissions to the minimum one ($n = n_{min}$) for the next rising attempt.
- The same backoff control technique used for the parameter n adaptation is employed as well for the parameters h and g adjustment. In fact, these two variables will be dynamically adapted and will vary between the upper and lower limits to maintain a rigorous decision to increment/decrement the data rate.
  - When a transmission error occurs just after a rate increase decision caused by an interpretation of the RTT^* value, the current rate will be reduced and the h value (as shown in Equation 4) will be multiplied by two as the upper limit h_{max} is not reached.

$$h = Min(2 * h; h_{\max}) \tag{4}$$

  - In other words, during successful transmissions the condition ($RTT^* < RTT_i^+$) should verified using the new value of h to be able to increment the rate.

- Likewise, if a transmission error was detected immediately after a rate decrease decision based on comparisons between RTT^* and RTT_i^- values. Then the rate will be raised to its old value and the responsible g parameter (see Equation 5) will be doubled if its value does not reach g_{max}.

$$g = Min(2 * g;\, g_{\max}) \tag{5}$$

- This means that the condition $RTT^* > RTT_i^-$ should be established using the new value of g during subsequent transmissions to be able to decrease again the rate.
- Both of the above parameters will also be reset identically to the parameter n after two consecutive transmission failures as follows:

$$h = h_{min};\ g = g_{min}$$

3.4 The MAARF setting

In this section we detail the new parameters designed for the MAARF algorithm. The IEEE 802.11 standard defines within its 802.11a and 802.11g versions, different physical rate values which can reach 54Mbps. Thus, we setup:

- R_i: the current data rate that varies from the following shown values {6, 9, 18, 12, 24, 36, 48, 54}Mbps.
- RTT^*: is the observed value when sending a frame (measured from the transmission channel after receiving the corresponding ACK).
- RTT_i: the theoretical time computed between the frame sending time to the ACK receipt instant. It reflects the channel occupation and does not include the waiting time to access the medium by the transmitter. It is given by Equation 6 as follows:

$$RTT_i = t_{em.Frame} + t_{propag} + t_{treat.Receiver} + SIFS + t_{em.ACK} + t_{propag} + t_{treat.Emitter} \tag{6}$$

- with, t_{em} is the emission time (Data Frame or ACK), t_{propag} is the propagation time over the transmission medium and t_{treat} is the treatment time of each received frame

In practice, this value will be represented only by the data frame transmission delay as shown in Equation 7. This approximation is made because of the negligibility of the other delays compared to the chosen value.

$$RTT_i \approx t_{em.Frame} = \frac{Frame.size}{R_i} \tag{7}$$

- RTO_i (Retransmission Time Out): is a recovery controlling timer after a frame loss. Its value is assigned based on RTT_i (see Equation 8).

$$RTO_i = 2 * RTT_i \tag{8}$$

- RTT_i^+ and RTT_i^- : the two decisional parameters (the RTT_i borders) which their values are chosen for each used rate R_i as defined in Equations 1 and 2.

- h: is the rate-increase responsible variable and it belongs to the interval $[h_{min}, h_{max}] = [4, 16]$.
- g: is the rate-decrement responsible variable and it belongs to the interval $[g_{min}, g_{max}] = [2, 8]$.
- n: is the already used parameter by the AARF technique. It represents the number of successive successful transmissions and belongs to the interval $[n_{min}, n_{max}] = [10, 50]$.

Finally, we illustrate the detailed MAARF functioning in Figure 7.

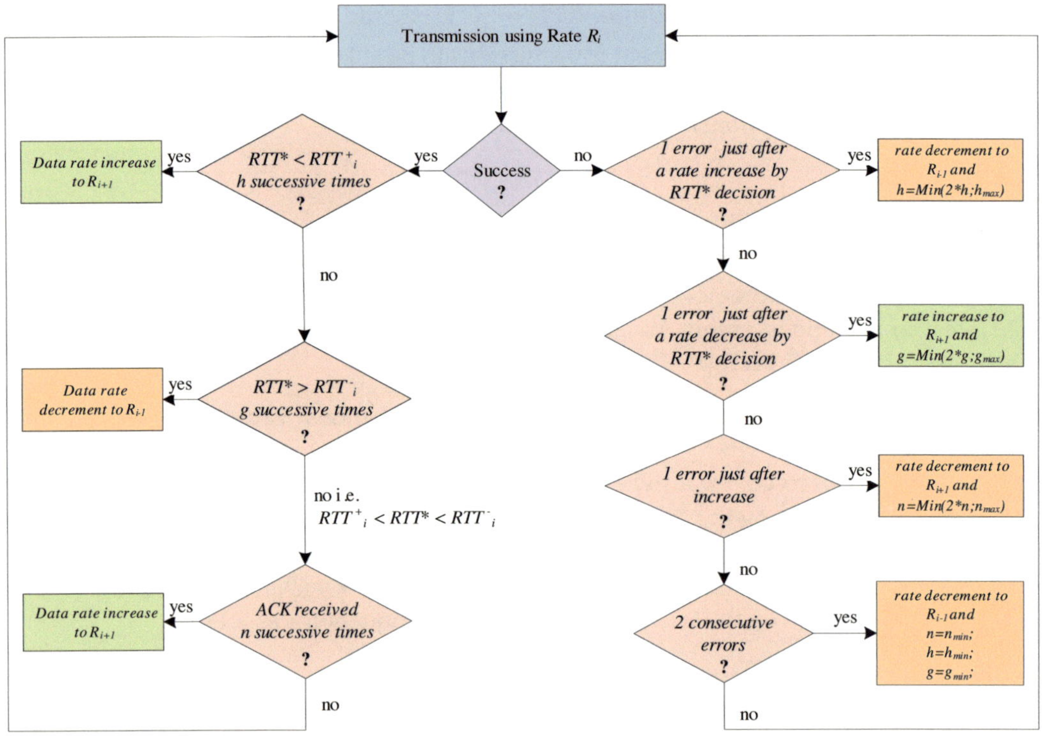

Fig. 7. The Transition diagram of the new MAARF algorithm

4. Results and performance evaluation

The algorithms were implemented using the C language on a Unix based operating-system environment (gcc/terminal MAC) to be then easily integrated into the network simulator.

We conducted various tests using the following configuration:

- The number of sent frames is 100 frames (approximately 0.5 seconds).
- The size of each data frame is equal to the 802.11g minimum frame size (=1200 bytes).
- An initial data rate of R_i is 6Mbps (up to 54Mbps).
- Failure of an ACK return reflects a transmission failure: packet loss, RTO expired or error detected by the CRC.
- A returned ACK by the receiver indicates a successful transmission only if it is received before the RTO expiration.
- The current value of RTT (RTT^*) is read/measured after each ACK reception.

Several scenarios have been considered to evaluate the performance of the proposed algorithm compared to the other versions (ARF and AARF).

4.1 Optimization of algorithm parameters

This first experiment is designed to study and optimize the decision-making parameters of the new algorithm: h (counting the number of successive times in which $RTT^* < RTT_i^+$) and g (reflecting the number of consecutive times that $RTT^* > RTT_i^-$). We discuss the values of h_{min} and g_{min}. In Figure 8, we show the implementation results of different MAARF algorithm configurations for various parameters values. These results express the chosen physical rate for each transmitted frame in the network.

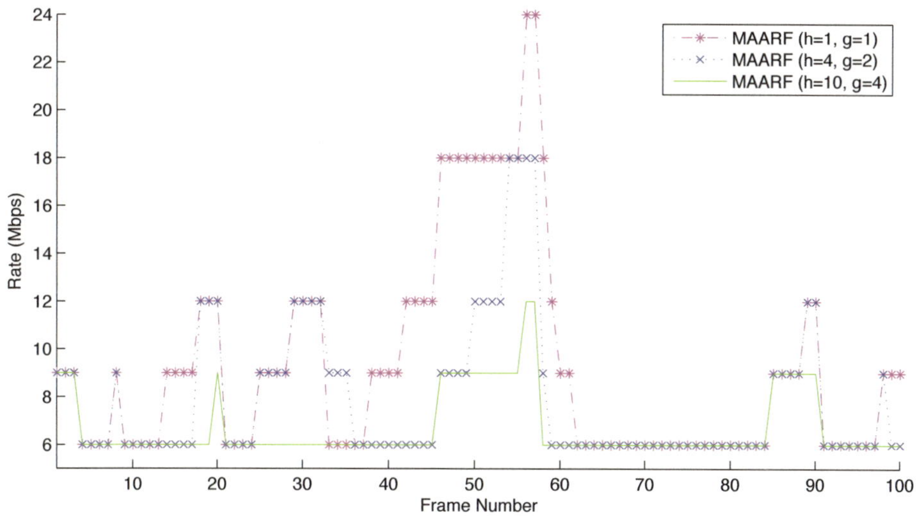

Fig. 8. Rate adaptation for different MAARF configurations

We note that by choosing low values of g and h ($h_{min} = g_{min} = 1$), MAARF makes quick decisions to increment and decrement the physical rate. In fact, it becomes sensitive for channel variations and adapts sinusoidal regime. On the other hand, by choosing large initial values of the g and h parameters (h_{min}=10 and g_{min}=4) the algorithm does not respond effectively to significant quality deviations and reacts as AARF. Therefore, we point out that the best initial and rigorous values of g and h with which MAARF gives the best results are respectively 4 and 2.

4.2 Test regimes

4.2.1 Unbalanced channel state

We compare now the new scheme against the AARF technique (currently used by the 802.11 WLANs) during unstable channel conditions (random improvement/degradation of the medium state). In Figure 9, we present the corresponding results graph and we clearly notice an efficient reaction of the MAARF technique against channel changes. In fact, the new algorithm detects faster the medium availability by adjusting its physical rate value starting from the 4th frame, while AARF reacts only from the 10th frame. We also note the

MAARF ability to dynamically respond against medium interferences dissimilar to the AARF mechanism. In addition, we conclude a significant improvement that has been reached (about 26%) regarding the mean value of recorded rates. In fact, we measure 6.1Mbps and 7.6Mbps respectively for the AARF and MAARF techniques.

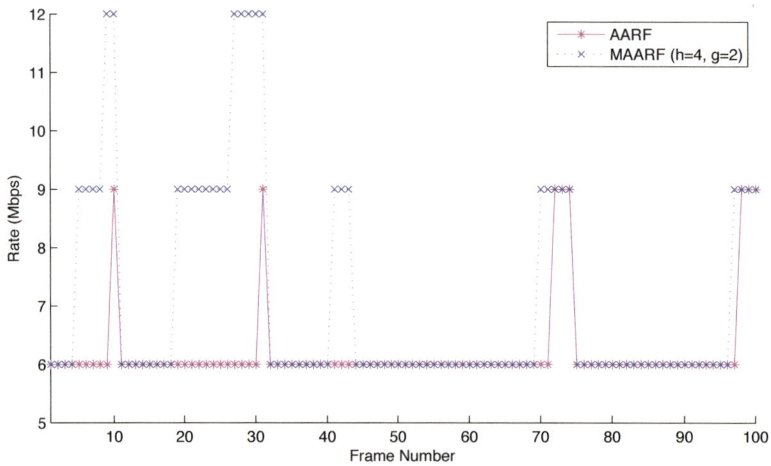

Fig. 9. Rate adaptation in transitory regime

4.2.2 Steady channel state

We assume in this case that only positive acknowledgments will be returned to the transmitter following the frame sending (packet transmissions without losses). Thus RTT^* values recorded from the medium will be close to those of the theoretical corresponding RTT_i values.

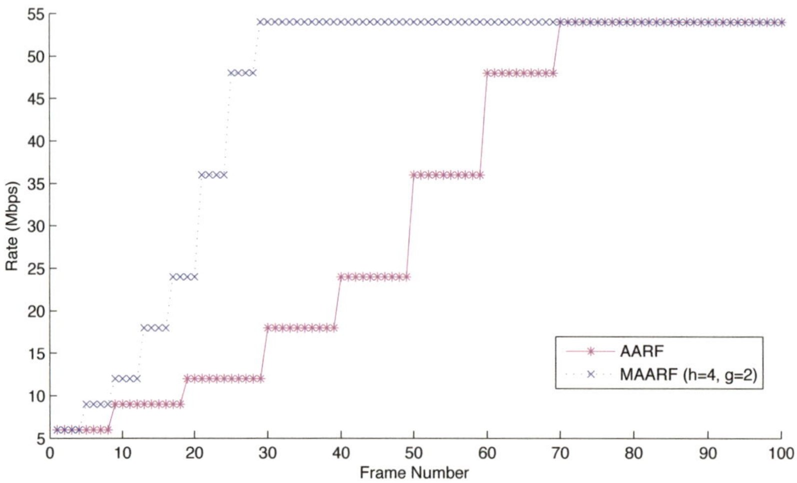

Fig. 10. Rate adaptation within steady regime

This first scenario shows a huge variation in terms of selected physical data rate and the overall mean value between the two techniques. In fact, a clear throughput enhancement is obtained (41%) since we traced as a mean rate value during the simulation time, 32.04Mbps for the AARF and 45.48Mbps for the new algorithm.

According to the results in Figure 10, the maximum data rate (54Mbps) is reached earlier by the new algorithm as it detects the channel condition improvement (from frame No. 28) and thus takes advantage of the large possible rate values. However the AARF technique reaches the maximum rate later on (only from the frame No. 70). This was caused by the fact that AARF is required to wait at least 10 positive acknowledgments at each rate hop.

4.2.3 Mobile environment situation

A fourth simulation on the rate adaptation is conducted within a variable channel regime. In the case of 802.11 WLAN the medium quality variations are very fast and totally random. This is reflected by intervals where the channel conditions improve rapidly, separated by those where the medium state deteriorates suddenly. We note from Figure 11 that the new technique adapts the same rate as obtained by AARF; however MAARF is more agile and predictive of the medium communication conditions for the data rate rise decision. When transmission errors take place, both methods pass at a lower rate almost at the same time.

The average rate value obtained for both AARF and MAARF mechanisms is equal, respectively, to 6.72Mbps and 7.89Mbps. As a result, an improvement of 17% was reached due to the responsive capability and the fast adaptability of the new link control mechanism.

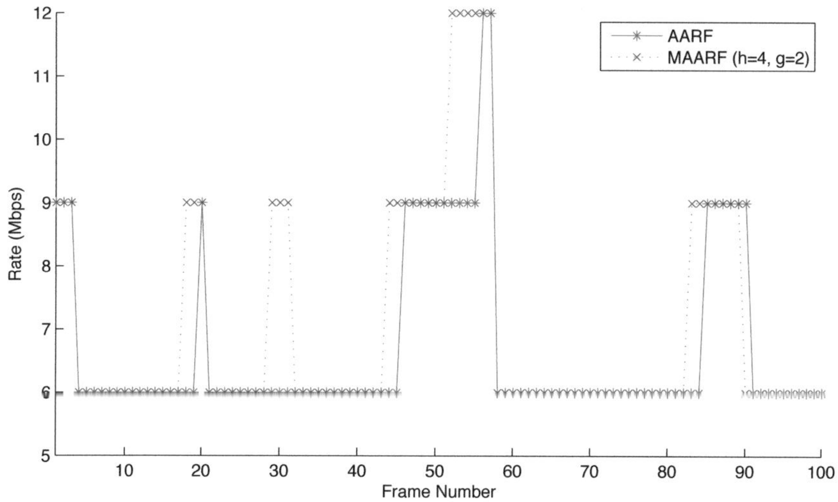

Fig. 11. Rate adaptation for instantaneous and unpredictable channel conditions

4.3 Network simulations under NS-2 platform

The results obtained during the new MAARF algorithm implementation have shown that it is possible:

- To estimate the channel conditions through the observed RTT^* values.
- To detect/avoid packet losses before they happen.
- To take the necessary decisions faster than current mechanisms.

We have revealed in this study that it is no longer necessary to wait 10 or more consecutive ACKs to adjust the theoretical rate as it was deployed by classical algorithms. We compare in Figures 12 and 13 the results obtained by applying the new MAARF mechanism and the current AARF for the same channel conditions. These results are reflecting, respectively, the computed rate mean value and the number of frames errors depending on the transmitted packets number.

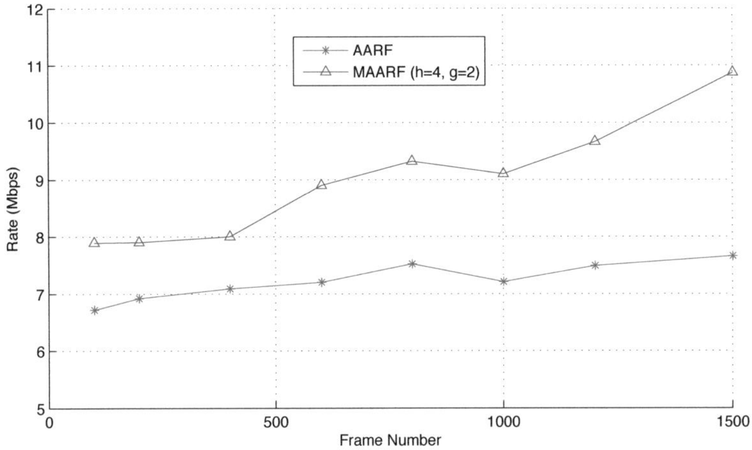

Fig. 12. Observed throughput for both AARF and MAARF mechanisms

Parameter	Value
WLAN version	802.11b
Radio propagation model	Two Ray Ground
Transmission range	250 meters
Number of Mobile Stations	2
Available physical rates	1Mps to 11Mbps
Routing protocol	Ad-hoc On demand Distance Vector
Slot Time	16 µs
SIFS Time	8 µs
DIFS Time	40 µs
Packet size	1000 Bytes
Traffic	CBR / UDP
Simulation time	80s (starting t=10s)
Simulation grid	745x745 meters

Table 1. NS-2 simulation parameters

We show based on the conducted experimentations, the improvements are distinguished and very clear in terms of the overall throughput and packet errors. We also confirm the MAARF algorithm performance by simulating the new technique on the Network Simulator NS-2 platform (Network Simulator-II, 1998). Figure 14 outlines various simulation arrangements performed on NS-2. We easily confirm the initial results by varying the bit error rate. The simulation parameters are summarized in Table 1.

First we note that the chosen traffic for the carried simulations was Constant Bit Rate (CBR) over the Transport-layer User Datagram Protocol (UDP). In fact, the CBR service category is

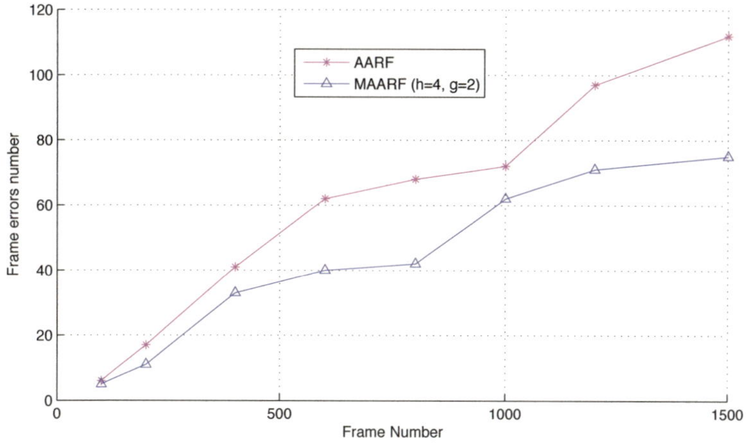

Fig. 13. Number of frame errors compared to the number of transmitted frames

used for connections that transport traffic at a constant bit rate, where there is an inherent reliance on time synchronization between the traffic source and destination. CBR is tailored for any type of data for which the end-systems require predictable response time and a static amount of bandwidth continuously available for the life-time of the connection. These applications include services such as video conferencing, telephony (voice services) or any type of on-demand service, such as interactive voice and audio.

The obtained results verify the initial theoretical observations and validate the efficiency and adaptability of the new mechanism for both slow and rapid fluctuations of the transmission channel quality. In absence of errors (as shown in Figure 14.a.), MAARF reacts quickly and rises the higher allowed rate before the current techniques. While varying the Bit Error Rate (BER) value during simulation scenarios (Figures 14.b., 14.c. and 14.d.) the physical rate adjustment corresponding to MAARF is more suitable and faster than other tested algorithms. This outcome is clearly confirmed in Figures 14.e. and 14.f. by measuring the achieved throughput for two different BER values. Accordingly, we note an enhanced response from MAARF against the channel quality variations compared to the other two techniques.

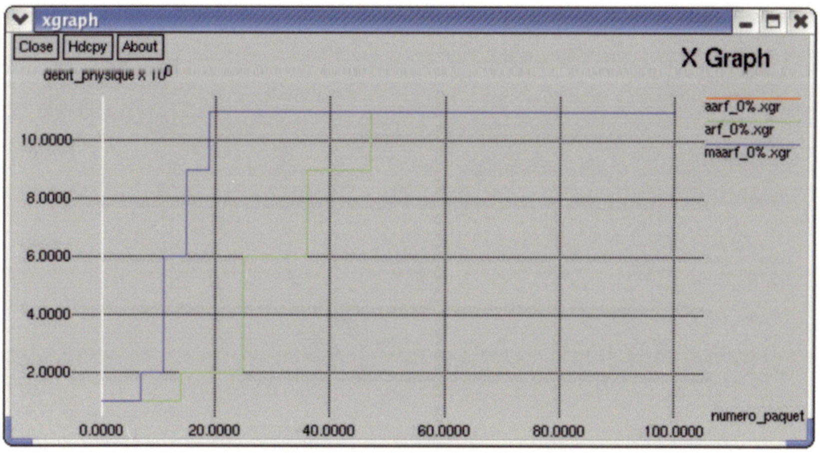

a. Physical rate tuning for ideal channel

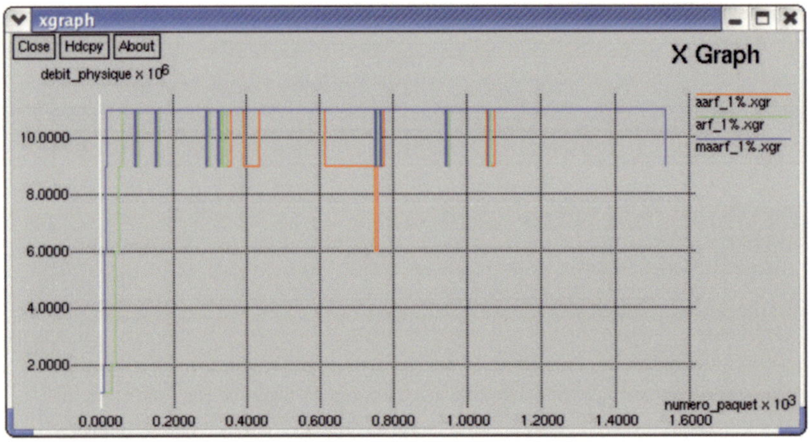

b. Physical rate tuning with BER=1%

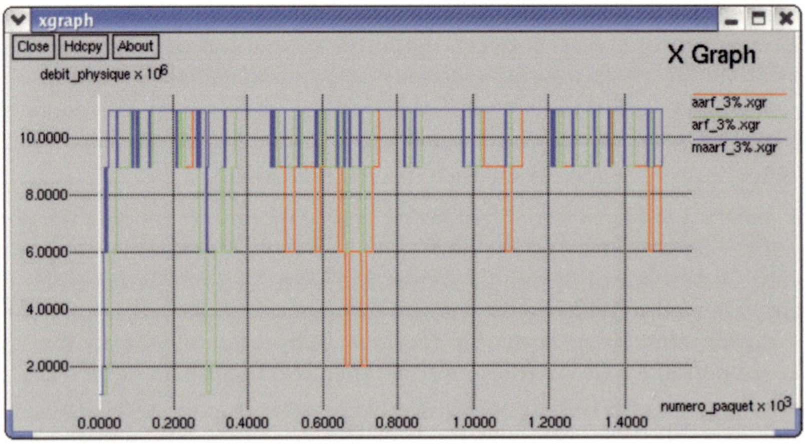

c. Physical rate tuning with BER=3%

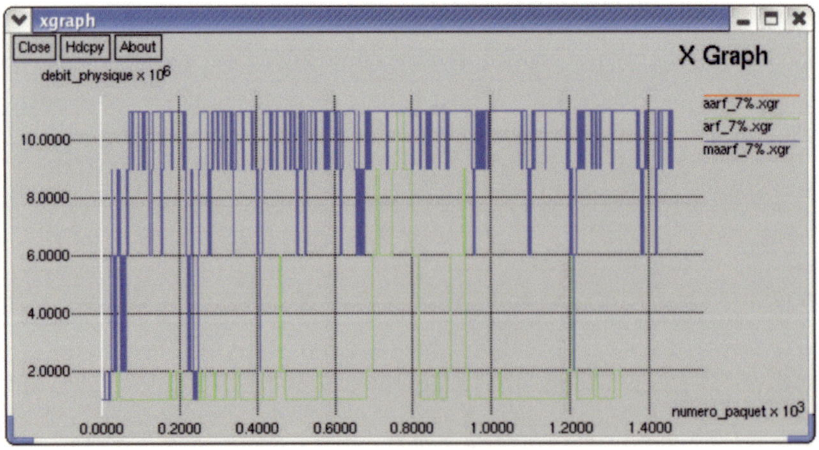

d. Physical rate tuning with BER=7%

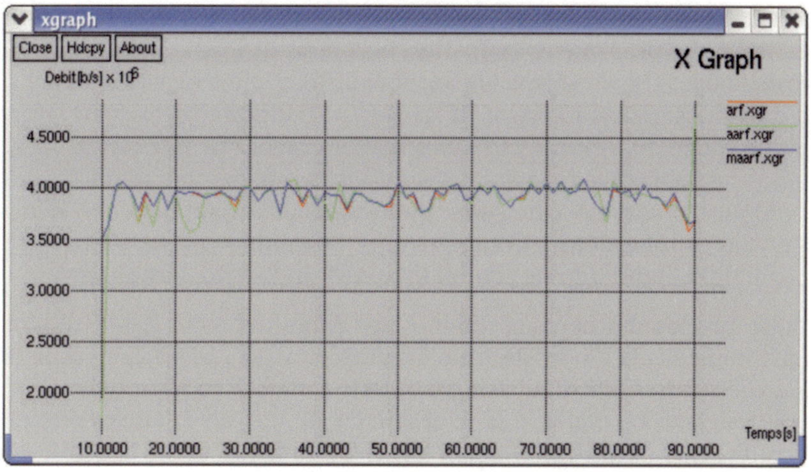

e. Measured throughput with BER=1%

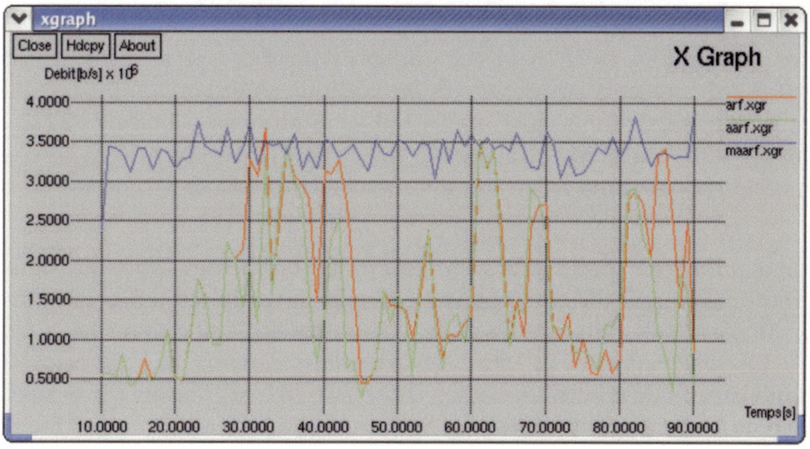

f. Measured throughput with BER=5%

Fig. 14. Experimental NS-2 simulation results by varying the BER value

5. Conclusions

5.1 General remarks

The IEEE 802.11 standard defines several MAC-level parameters (settings) that are available for tuning at the side of the Wireless Network Interface Card (NIC). The most important parameter available for adjustment is the transmit rate. Each rate corresponds to a different modulation scheme with its own trade-off between data throughput and distance between the MSs. In order to decide which rate is optimal at each specific moment, a control algorithm needs information about the current link conditions. Since it is difficult to get these information directly, most of the MAC rate-control algorithms use statistics-based feedbacks, for example, ACK count. We have shown, through a deep study of the currently-used rate control mechanisms, that the main disadvantage of this indirect feedback is that it is inherently slow, causing communication failures when the link conditions degrade rapidly (e.g., when the user moves fast). The short-term dropouts are normally handled by frame retransmissions. This is acceptable for download applications whose key requirement is a flagrant data throughput. However it leads to a significant increase in (average) packet delay and in the jitter due to the variations in the number of retransmissions. Streaming applications are very sensitive to long packet delays and high jitter, and less sensitive to the overall throughput (of course when this throughput is larger than the minimum value required by the application). Consequently, streaming applications achieve poor performances under a standard rate control (like ARF and AARF techniques).

Hence, we have proposed a new algorithm noted Modified Auto Rate Fallback (MAARF). This technique implements a new decisional variable called Round Trip Time (RTT) which complies and cooperates with the basic parameter (number of returned ACKs). This new parameter is designed to make a good estimate of the instantaneous channel quality (observation of the channel state after each transmitted frame), and choose the adequate rate accordingly.

Based on the simulation results we have shown a remarkable improvement in data throughput and physical rate control. In fact, the proposed MAARF mechanism provides higher values (about 17% to 58%) in comparison with those resulting from conventional algorithms. Table 2 presents an observed throughput summary of the MAARF scheme compared to existing algorithms (ARF and AARF) and gives an overview on the rate control enhancement for different BERs. The overall throughput observed within MAARF is much higher than other mechanisms when the BER reaches high values (12 times when the error rate is 10%).

In conclusion simulation experiments were performed on the new dynamic time-based link adaptation mechanism and the corresponding results have shown the quality improvement on the transmission link. The results also demonstrated that the proposed mechanism outperforms the basic solution in terms of providing support to both acknowledgment-based and time-based rate control decisions. Therefore MAARF meets the desired objectives by being able to reduce errors resulting from bad rate adjustment and then satisfy the transmission of multimedia applications in terms of required QoS.

Observed throughput in 10^6 Mbps				*Enhancement in %*
BER	*ARF*	*AARF*	*MAARF*	*MAARF / AARF*
0%	*4.0335*	*4.0339*	*4.0461*	*0.3%*
1%	*3.8930*	*3.8877*	*3.9225*	*0.8%*
3%	*3.5419*	*3.3612*	*3.6719*	*9%*
5%	*1.6992*	*1.4564*	*3.3826*	*>80%*
7%	*0.4914*	*0.4914*	*3.0195*	*>80%*
10%	*0.0774*	*0.7740*	*1.8273*	*>80%*

Table 2. Enhancement ratio of the MAARF technique

5.2 The MAARF working out performance for real-time video streaming

In the context of the Voice-over-IP and real-time video streaming (Video conferencing) which represent the most end-user demanded multimedia streaming applications to be supported over wireless connections, the proposed technique is supposed to enhance the video quality transmission by keeping the same compression degree, and so, avoiding the cross layer design implemented by (Haratcherev et al., 2005) which involves an interaction between the application and MAC layers by assuming that the video encoder can also adapt to the link quality by changing the compression degree for example, and thus modifying the data rate. This so-called Coupled scheme is based on a cross-layer signaling by letting the rate control loops - of the MAC-layer and the Video coder - be mutually associated. In such way, the video coder will poll frequently for the current and predicted rate. For performance evaluation purpose, the same real experiment as performed in (Haratcherev et al., 2005) was carried out by streaming a video file between two laptops, both running Linux. The 802.11a cards used are based on the Atheros AR5000 chipset, and the card driver implements the discussed rate control algorithms. One of the laptops had a fixed position and the other one is following a predetermined track. The track consists of three parts: reaching from the room to a specific start position in the hallway, and waiting until certain time elapses (10s). Then keep moving with the laptop three times up and down the hallway (60s). Finally we back again into the room, where the fixed laptop lies (20s). We have evaluated four cases: ARF, AARF, MAARF and a Coupled version of the hybrid rate control (responsive MAC-adaptation using radio-SNR and packet loss statistics) as described in (Haratcherev et al., 2004). Each experiment took 90 seconds and we have compared the quality of the received videos using the Peek-Signal-to-Noise-Ratio (PSNR), a commonly used metric in video compression.

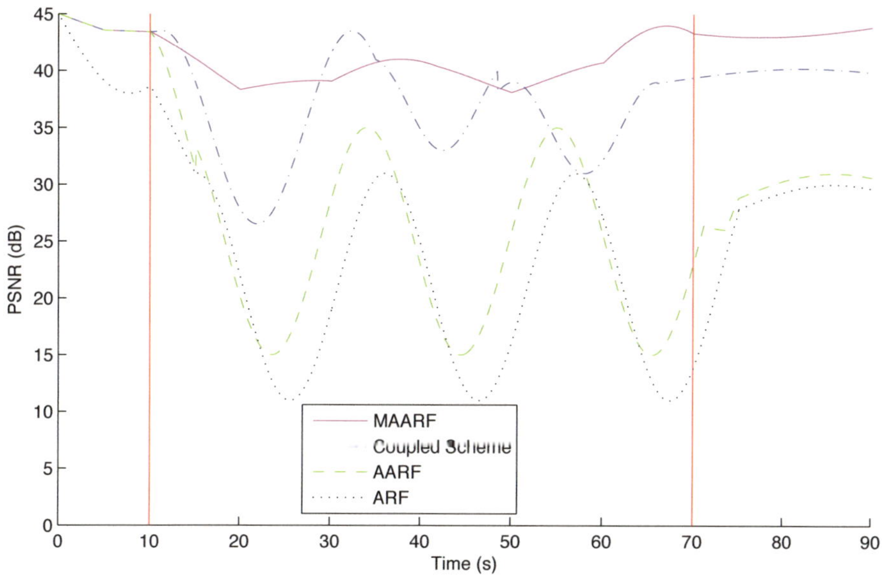

Fig. 15. PSNR measurements during the 90s real-time video streaming experiments

Algorithm	*# Skipped Frames*	*# Lost Packets*	*PSNR*	*PSNR Middle*
MAARF	*63*	*15*	*41.41*	*40.4*
Coupled Scheme	*50*	*13*	*37.9*	*36.23*
AARF	*182*	*16*	*28.19*	*25.32*
ARF	*205*	*21*	*24.95*	*21.74*

Table 3. Summary of algorithms results

In Figure 15 the quality (PSNR) is shown for the whole experiment (90s). In the left part (0–10s) the channel conditions are excellent since a high quality was fulfilled with all cases. The middle part is best described as having continuous variation. The right part has good channel conditions again. As we can notice, the MAARF case has a higher PSNR in almost all cases. Table 3 summarizes the number of skipped frames (by the encoder), the number of lost packets, the average PSNR and the average PSNR in the unstable period (between 10 and 70s). Although the lost packets counts are not the same in the four cases, it does not justify the difference in PSNR values. In the ARF and AARF cases, the total number of skipped frames is much higher, as we expected. Looking at the average PSNR in the 10–70s period, we conclude that MAARF outperforms the other techniques based on an enhanced channel assessment. As a result, the proposed video streaming experiments better illustrate the improvement made using MAARF by reducing the number of lost packets and skipped frames. Both effects resulted in a high visual quality opposed to the cases of ACK-based rate control algorithms. Meanwhile the Coupled cross-layer signaling scheme had also very encouraging results in terms of packets loss and skipped frames which let us consider a warning concept between the video encoder and the MAARF decision in the MAC layer. Therefore, a second version of the MAARF technique including a cross-layer signaling solution will be investigated in the next research step. This extended adaptation would be able to further avoid packet losses and especially to prevent skipped frames of the emerging voice/video streaming services. Of course, it would have an adverse effect on the visual quality of the decoded video however we will need to further carry out real streaming video experiments over a wireless 802.11 link between MSs to conclude if the cross-layer signaling between the MAC-layer and the video coder will lead to a visual quality increase in term of measured PSNR.

6. References

Angrisani, l.; Napolitano, A. & Sona, A. (2011). VoIP over WLAN: What about the Presence of Radio Interference?, *VoIP Technologies, Shigeru Kashihara (Ed.)*, ISBN: 978-953-307-549-5, InTech, pp. 197-218, Feb. 2011

An-Chih, L.; Ting-Yu, L. & Ching-Yi, T. (2009). ARC: Joint Adaptation of Link Rate and Contention Window for IEEE 802.11 Multi-rate Wireless Networks, *The 6th Annual IEEE Communications Society Conference on Sensor, Mesh and Ad Hoc Communications and Networks SECON '09*, Rome, Italy, July 2009.

Chen, X.; Wan, Y. & Lu, J. (2010). Cross-layer link rate adaptation for high performance multimedia broadcast over WLANs, *in Proc. IEEE GLOBECOM Workshops GC-Workshops'10*, pp. 965-969, Miami, FL, USA, Dec. 2010

Chevillat, P.; Jelitto, J.; Barreto, A. N. & Truong, H. (2003). A Dynamic Link Adaptation Algorithm for IEEE 802.11a Wireless LANs, *in Proc. IEEE International Conference on Communication ICC'03*, Anchorage, AK, May 2003

Chiapin W. & Tsungnan L. (2008). A Cross-Layer Link Adaptation Algorithm for IEEE 802.11 WLAN with Multiple Nodes, *in Proc. IEEE Asia-Pacific Services Computing Conference APSCC '08*, pp. 1161-1167, Yilan, Taiwan, Dec. 2008

del Prado Pavon, J. & Choi, S. (2003). Link Adaptation Strategy for IEEE 802.11 WLAN via Received Signal Strength Measurement, *in Proc. IEEE International Conference on Communication ICC'03*, Anchorage, AK, May 2003

Galtier, J. (2011). Adaptative Rate Issues in the WLAN Environment, *Advances in Vehicular Networking Technologies, Miguel Almeida (Ed.)*, ISBN: 978-953-307-241-8, InTech, pp. 187-201, April 2011

Habetha, J. & de No, D. C. (2000). New Adaptive Modulation and Power Control Algorithms for HIPERLAN/2 Multihop Ad Hoc Networks, *in Proc. European Wireless (EW'2000)*, Dresden, Germany, Sept. 2000

Haratcherev, I.; Langendoen, K.; Lagendijk, I. & Sips, H. (2004). Hybrid Rate Control for IEEE 802.11. *In ACM International Workshop on Mobility Management and Wireless Access Protocols MobiWac'04*, pp. 10–18, Philadelphia, USA, Oct. 2004

Haratcherev, I.; Taal, J.; Langendoen, K.; Lagendijk, I. & Sips, H. (2005). Fast 802.11 link adaptation for real-time video streaming by cross-layer signaling, *In Proc. IEEE International Symposium on Circuits and Systems ISCAS'05*, pp. 3523-3526, Vol. 4, Kobe, May 2005

IEEE Standard 802.11 (1999), Part 11: Wireless LAN Medium Access Control (MAC) and Physical Layer (PHY) Specifications, *IEEE Standard 802.11*, 1999

IEEE Standard 802.11a (1999), Supplement to Part 11: Wireless LAN Medium Access Control (MAC) and Physical Layer (PHY) specifications: High-speed Physical Layer in the 5 GHz Band, *IEEE Std. 802.11a-1999*, Sept. 1999

IEEE Standard 802.11b (1999), Supplement to Part 11: Wireless LAN Medium Access Control (MAC) and Physical Layer (PHY) specifications: Higher-speed Physical Layer Extension in the 2.4 GHz Band, *IEEE Std. 802.11b-1999*, 1999

IEEE Standard 802.11g (2003), Supplement to Part 11: Wireless LAN Medium Access Control (MAC) and Physical Layer (PHY) specifications: Further Higher Data Rate Extension in the 2.4 GHz Band, *IEEE Std. 802.11g-2003*, June 2003

Jianhua, H.; Kaleshi, D.; Munro, A. & McGeehan, J. (2006). Modeling Link Adaptation Algorithm for IEEE 802.11 Wireless LAN Networks, *The 3rd International Symposium on Wireless Communication Systems ISWCS '06*, pp. 500-504, Sep. 2006

Junwhan, K. & Jaedoo, H. (2006). Link Adaptation Strategy on Transmission Rate and Power Control in IEEE 802.11 WLANs, *in Proc. IEEE Vehicular Technology Conference VTC'06*, Montreal, QC, Canada, Sept. 2006

Kamerman, A. & Monteban, L. (1997). WaveLAN-II: A High-Performance Wireless LAN for the Unlicensed Band, *Bell Labs Technical Journal*, pp. 118–133, Summer 1997

Krishnan, M. N. & Zakhor, A. (2010). Throughput Improvement in 802.11 WLANs Using Collision Probability Estimates in Link Adaptation, *in Proc. IEEE Wireless Communications and Networking Conference WCNC'10*, Sydney, Australia, April 2010

Kumar, A. & Holtzman, J. (1998). Performance analysis of versions of TCP in WLAN, *Indian Academy of Sciences Proceedings in Engineering Sciences*, Sadhana, Feb. 1998

Lacage, M.; Manshaei, M. H. & Turletti, T. (2004). IEEE802.11 Rate Adaptation: A Practical Approach. *INRIA Research Report*, number 5208, May 2004

Mocanu, S. (2004). Performance Evaluation of TCP Reno and Vegas. *Technical report* CR256, Laboratoire d'Automatique de Grenoble, Département Télécom, July 2004

Network Simulator II (1998), ns-2, available from http://www.isi.edu/nsnam/ns/

Pang, Q.; Leung, V.C.M. & Liew, S.C. (2005). A rate adaptation algorithm for IEEE 802.11 WLANs based on MAC-layer loss differentiation, *in Proc. International Conference on Broadband Networks BroadNets'05*, pp. 659-667, Vol. 1, Boston, MA, USA, Oct. 2005

Qiao, D.; Choi, S. & Shin, K. G. (2002). Goodput Analysis and Link Adaptation for IEEE 802.11a Wireless LANs, *IEEE Transactions on Mobile Computing*, vol. 1, pp. 278–292, Oct. 2002

Qiao, D. & Choi, S. (2005). Fast-Responsive Link Adaptation for IEEE 802.11 WLANs, *in Proc. IEEE International Conference on Communication ICC'05*, Sept. 2005

Rebai, A. R.; Alnuweiri, H.; Hanafi, S. (2009). A novel prevent-scan Handoff technique for IEEE 802.11 WLANs, *in Proc. International Conference on Ultra Modern Telecommunications & Workshops ICUMT '09*, St. Petersburg, Russia, Oct. 2009

Rebai, A. R.; Fliss, M.; Jarboui, S. & Hanafi, S. (2008). A new Link Adaptation Scheme for IEEE 802.11 WLANs, *in Proc. IEEE New Technologies, Mobility and Security NTMS'08*, Nov. 2008

Rebai, A. R.; Haddar, B.; Hanafi, S. (2009). Prevent-scan: A novel MAC layer scheme for the IEEE 802.11 handoff, *In Proc. International Conference on Multimedia Computing and Systems ICMCS '09*, pp. 541-546, Ouarzazate, Morocco, April 2009

Rebai, A. R.; Hanafi, S.; Alnuweiri, H. (2009). A new inter-node priority access enhancement scheme for IEEE_802.11 WLANs, *in Proc. International Conference on Intelligent Transport Systems Telecommunications ITST'09*, pp. 520-525, Lille, France, Oct. 2009

Rebai, A. R.; Rebai, M. F.; Alnuweiri, H.; Hanafi, S. (2010). An enhanced heuristic technique for AP selection in 802.11 handoff procedure, *In Proc. IEEE International Conference on Telecommunications ICT'10*, pp. 576-580, Doha, Qatar, April 2010

Sangman, M.; Moonsoo, K. & Ilyong, C. (2011). *Link Quality Aware Robust Routing for Mobile Multihop Ad Hoc Networks, Mobile Ad-Hoc Networks: Protocol Design, Xin Wang (Ed.)*, ISBN: 978-953-307-402-3, InTech, pp. 201-216, Jan. 2011

Shun-Te, W.; Wu, J.-L.C.; Chung-Ching, D. & Chun-Yen, H. (2007). An adaptation scheme for quick response to fluctuations in IEEE 802.11 link quality, *in Proc. IEEE Region 10 Conference TENCON'07*, Taipei, Oct. 2007

Tourrilhes, J. (2001). Fragment Adaptive Reduction: Coping with Various Interferers in Radio Unlicensed Bands", *in Proc. IEEE International Conference on Communication ICC'01*, Helsinki, Finland, July 2001

Xin, A.; Shengming, J. & Lin T. (2010). Traffic-aware active link rate adaptation via power control for multi-hop multi-rate 802.11 networks, *in Proc. IEEE International Conference on Communication Technology ICCT'10*, pp. 1255-1259, Nanjing, Nov. 2010

3

A Multimedia and VoIP-Oriented Cell Search Technique for the IEEE 802.11 WLANS

Ahmed Riadh Rebai[1], Mariam Fliss[1] and Saïd Hanafi[2]
[1]Texas A&M University at Qatar – Doha,
[2]University of Valenciennes et du Hainaut-Cambrésis,
[1]Qatar
[2]France

1. Introduction

With the development and widespread of diverse wireless network technologies such as wireless local area networks (WLANs), the number of mobile internet users keeps on growing. This rapid increase in mobile internet users records a phenomenal growth in the deployment of the IEEE 802.11 WLANs (IEEE Std 802.11, 1999) in various environments like universities (Corner et al., 2010; Hills & Johnson, 1996), companies, shopping centers (Bahl et al., 2001) and hotels. This category of networks then will be the underlying basis of ubiquitous wireless networks by decreasing infrastructure costs and providing stable Internet connectivity at anytime and anywhere (Kashihara et al., 2011; Kunarak & Suleesathira, 2011). Hence many believe that are expected to be part of the integrated fourth generation (4G) network. At the same time, voice over IP (VoIP) is expected to become a core application in the ubiquitous wireless networks, i.e., the next generation cell-phone. Recently, many users have easily used VoIP communication such as Skype (Skype, 2003) in wireless networks. However, in the mobility context WLANs become not appropriate to the strict delay constraints placed by many multimedia applications, and Mobile Stations (MSs) cannot seamlessly traverse the 802.11 Access Points (APs) during VoIP communication due to various factors such as the inherent instability of wireless medium and a limited communication area. MSs are required to find and then to associate with another AP with acceptable signal quality whenever they go beyond the coverage area of the currently associated AP. The overall process of changing association from one AP to another is called *handoff* or *handover* process and the latency involved in the process is termed as handoff latency.

Thus, even if an MS can avoid communication termination at handoff, the following problems must also be resolved to maintain VoIP communication quality during movement. First, the timing to initiate handover is also a critical issue. In fact, late handover initiation severely affects VoIP communication quality because the wireless link quality suddenly degrades. Second, how to recognize which AP will be the best choice among available APs is an issue of concern. Thus, to meet the lofty goal of integrating the next generation networks and to maintain VoIP communication quality during movement, the above requirements must be satisfied.

In fact, in 802.11 networks, the handoff process is partitioned into three phases: *probing* (scanning), *re-authentication* and *re-association*. According to (Mishra et al., 2003; Bianchi et al., 1996) the handoff procedure in IEEE 802.11 normally takes hundreds of milliseconds, and almost 90% of the handoff delay is due to the search of new APs, the so-called *probe delay*. This rather high handoff latency results in play-out gaps and poor quality of service for time-bounded multimedia applications. Other than the latency concern, the MS association with a specific AP is based only on the Received Signal Strength Indicator (RSSI) measurement of all available APs. This naïve procedure needs to be tuned since it leads to undesirable results (many MSs are connected to a few overloaded APs). The handoff process should take into account other context-based parameters, i.e. the load of APs.

In this chapter, we propose an optimized VoIP-oriented version of the Prevent Scan Handoff Procedure (PSHP) scheme (Rebai et al., 2009a, 2010, 2011) that will decrease both handoff latency and occurrence by performing a seamless prevent scan process and an effective next-AP selection. Basically, the IEEE 802.11 PSHP technique reduces the *probe phase* and adapts the process latency to support most of multimedia applications. In fact, it decreases the delay incurred during the discovery phase significantly by inserting a new Pre-Scan phase before a poor link quality will be reached. The available in range APs are kept in a dynamic list which will be periodically updated. As a complementary proposition, the authors in (Rebai et al., 2009b) integrated an effective AP selection based on Neighbor Graph (NG) manipulation and a new heuristic function that employs multiple-criteria to derive optimized search. Furthermore so far, to our knowledge, no adaptive techniques with crosslayering approach have been addressed, on transmitting real-time applications during a handover process. However various cross-layer adaptive rate control methods coupled with the MAC link adaptation have been presented for voice/video applications. Analyzing the opportunity from the literature, this research study focuses on IEEE802.11 handoff optimization using codec adaptation mechanism based on both parameters: codec type and packet size. Through real experiments and performance evaluation, we show effectiveness of the optimized PSHP draft which accomplishes a VoIP transmission over an 802.11 link without interruptions when altering between available APs. The rest of the chapter is organized as follows. Section 2 presents overview of handoff procedure performed in IEEE 802.11 WLANs and discusses related works. We present in section 3 operation details and several simulation results of PSHP Medium Access Control (MAC)-Layer handoff method (Rebai et al., 2011). The new VoIP-oriented PSHP technique and its experimental analysis are shown in section 4 followed by concluding remarks in section 5.

2. Backgrounds and related works

2.1 The Handoff Process in IEEE 802.11

Typically the 802.11 WLAN was originally designed without the consideration of mobility support, MAC layer handoff mechanism enables MSs to continue their communication between multiple nearby APs. However, in regard to the mobility in the WLAN, there exists a problem to support the VoIP applications. When a MS performs handoff to the other AP, it should suffer from significant handoff latency causing the service degradation of the VoIP service where the typical VoIP application requires maximum 20~50ms packet arrival time. First we define the following terms: the coverage area of an AP is termed by Basic service set (BSS). Extended service set (ESS) is an interconnection of BSSs and wired LANs via distributed system (DS) as shown in Figure 1.

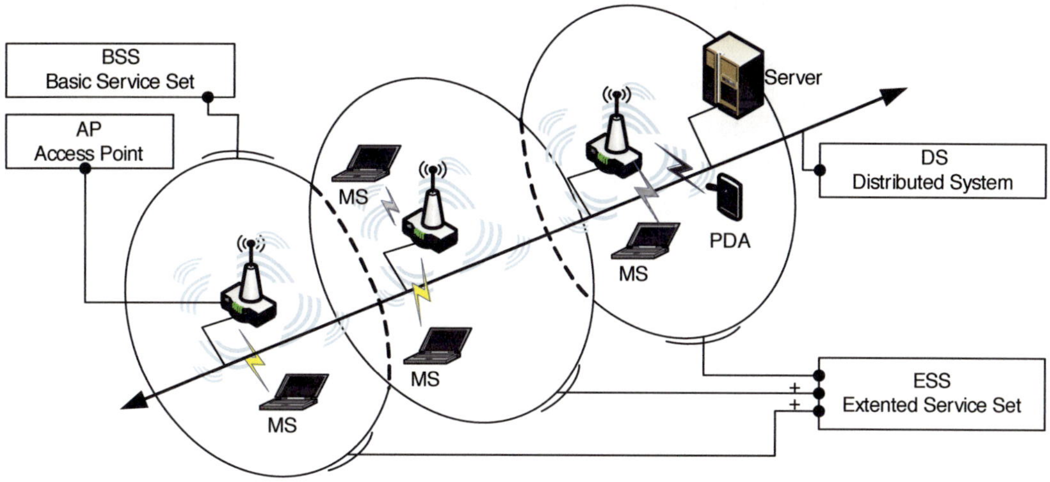

Fig. 1. The IEEE 802.11 infrastructure mode

The inter-cell commutation can be divided into three different phases: *detection*, *probing* (scanning) and *effective handoff* (including *authentication* and *re-association*). In order to make a handoff, the MS must first decide when to handoff. A handoff process in IEEE 802.11 is commonly initiated when the Received Signal Strength (RSS) from current AP drops below a pre-specified threshold, termed as handoff threshold in the literature (Mishra et al., 2003; Raghavan et al., 2005). Using only current AP's RSS to initiate handoff might force the MS to hold on to the AP with low signal strength while there are better APs in its vicinity. As shown in Figure 2, when a handoff is triggered, an AP discovery phase begins and a MAC layer function called scan is executed. A management frame called *De-authentication* packet is sent, either by the mobile station before changing the actual channel of communication which allows the access point to update its MS-affiliation table, either by the AP which requests the MS to leave the cell. Since there is no specific control channel for executing the scan, the MS has to search for new APs from channel to channel by temporarily interrupting its association with the old AP. The scan on each channel can be performed by either passively listening to beacon signals or actively exchanging probe messages with new APs. After a new AP is found and its RSS exceeds Delta-RSS over the old AP, the MS will change its association to the new AP and a *re-authentication* phase begins. During the passive scan mode the MS listens to the wireless medium for beacon frames which provide the MS with timing and advertising information. Current APs have a default beacon interval of 100ms (Velayos & Karlsson, 2004). Therefore, the passive scan mode incurs significant delay. After scanning all available channels, the MS performs a *Probe* phase (used in active mode) only for the selected AP. As mentioned the polled AP is elected only based on RSSI parameter. The 802.11k group (IEEE Std. 802.11k, 2003) works on improving the choice of the next AP taking into account the network. In the active scan mode, the MS sends a *Probe Request* packet on each probed channel and waits *MinChannelTime* for a *Probe Response* packet from each reachable AP. If one packet at least is received, the MS extends the sensing interval to *MaxChannelTime* in order to obtain more responses and the channel is declared *active*. Thus, the waiting time on each channel is irregular since it is controlled by two *timers* (not as passive scan). The selected AP exchanges IEEE 802.11 authentication messages with the MS.

During this phase one of the two authentication methods can be achieved: *Open System Authentication* or *Shared Key Authentication*. Detailed authentication packets exchange has been addressed in (Rebai et al., 2011). After that the MS is authenticated by the AP, it sends *Re-association Request* message to the new AP. At this phase, the old and new APs exchange messages defined in Inter Access Point Protocol IAPP (IEEE Std. 802.11F, 2003). Furthermore, once the MS is authenticated, the association process is triggered. The Cell's information is exchanged: the ESSID and supported transmission rates.

During these various steps, the MS will be not able to exchange data with its AP. Based on values defined by the IEEE 802.11 standard, it is observed that the *re-authentication* which comprises an authentication and an association spends no more than 20ms on average, but a scanning delay may take between 350 and 500 ms and increase considerably the overall *handoff latency* (Mishra et al., 2003; Bianchi et al., 1996). An additional process is involved when the MS needs to change its IP connectivity (Johnson et al., 2004). In such a scenario, the MS needs to find a new access router. Also, the address binding information has to be updated at the home agent and corresponding agent (Cornall et al., 2002).

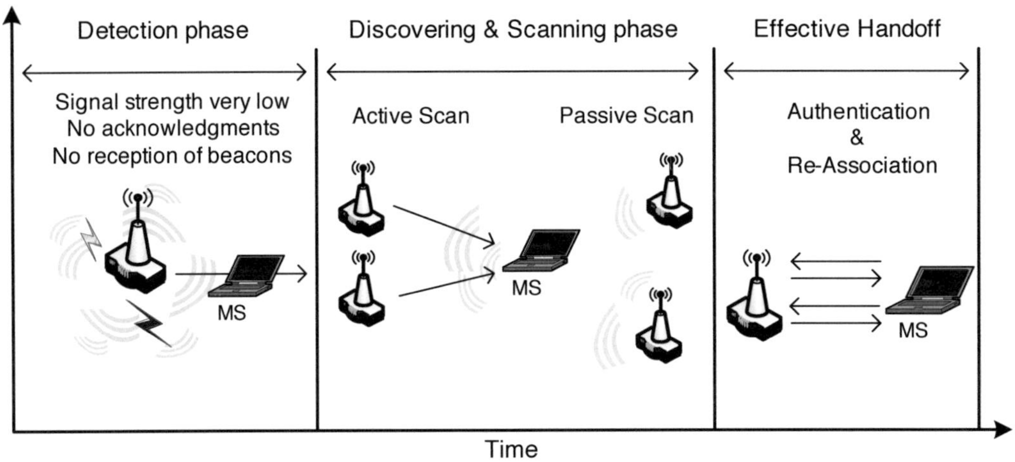

Fig. 2. The 802.11 handover phases

2.2 Literature survey

The *scan* phase of handover is the most costly in terms of time and traffic since it includes the *probe* and the *channel switching* sub-phases. Explicitly, the switching time is negligible and varies between 40 and 150µs as it was identified in (IEEE Std. 802.11i, 2004). Within the *passive* scan the interval between beacons is 100ms of IEEE 802.11b with 11 channels and 802.11a with 32 channels, the average latency will be respectively 1100ms and 3200ms. On the other hand, the time incurred with an *active* scan can be determined by the *MinChannelTime* and *MaxChannelTime* values. The *MinChannelTime* value should be large enough to not miss the *proberesponse* frames and obeys the formula given in Equation 1.

$$MinChannelTime \geq DIFS + (CW \times SlotTime) \tag{1}$$

where, *DIFS* is the minimum waiting time necessary for a frame to access to the channel. The backoff interval is represented by the contention window (*CW*) multiplied by *SlotTime*. Regarding the *authentication* and *authentication* phases latency are proportional to the number of messages exchanged between the AP and the MS and limited to the medium access time which depends on the traffic in the cell (such management frames have no special priority). In (Velayos & Karlsson, 2004) these delays are estimated to less than 4ms in absence of a heavy traffic in the new selected cell. Thus, numerous schemes have been proposed to reduce the handoff scan delay in the 802.11 WLANs.

An interesting handoff scheme, called *SyncScan*, is proposed (Ramani & Savage, 2005) to reduce the probe delay by allowing a MS to monitor continuously the nearby APs and to record RSSs from available channel. Essentially, this technique replaces the existing large temporal additional costs during the scan phase. The absence delay of the MS with its current channel is minimized by synchronizing short listening periods of other channels (see Figure 3). In fact, the MS synchronize its next channel probing with the transmission of other APs beacons on each channel. By switching regularly and orderly on each channel, the MS reduces its disconnection delay with its actual AP. However, the *SyncScan* process suffers from regular additional interruptions during the MS absence when exploring other channels. These errors are very costly in terms of packets loss and skipped frames for time-bounded applications. Moreover, this extra charge will affect all MSs even those that will never proceed to a handoff.

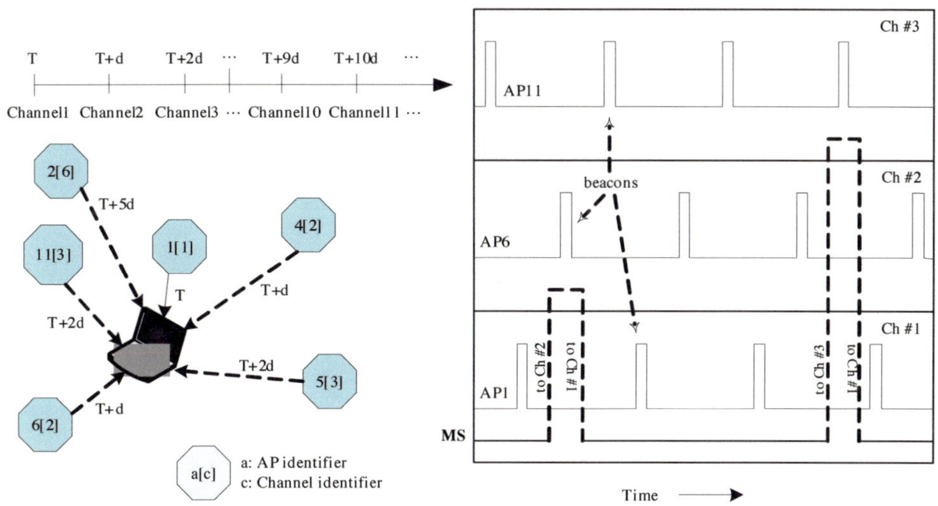

Fig. 3. The SyncScan mechanism

In (Waharte et al., 2004) authors propose an innovative solution to optimize the AP's exploration during the scan phase based on the use of sensors operating on the 802.11 network. As shown in Figure 4, these sensors are arranged in cells and spaced 50 to 150 meters. These sensors have a role to listen to the network using beacons sent periodically by in-range APs. When the MS should change its actual cell, it performs a pre-scan operation which involves the sending of a request query to the sensors. Only sensors that have received this request (in range of the MS) react by sending the list of APs that they have identified. We figure out that this solution is effective in terms of the next-AP choice and the consequent results have improved significantly the standard handoff scheme. However, it is very expensive and has an extra cost by causing an additional load of unnecessary network traffic due to the sensor use. Moreover, this method is a non compliant solution with the actual 802.11 networks and requires radical changes to adapt it.

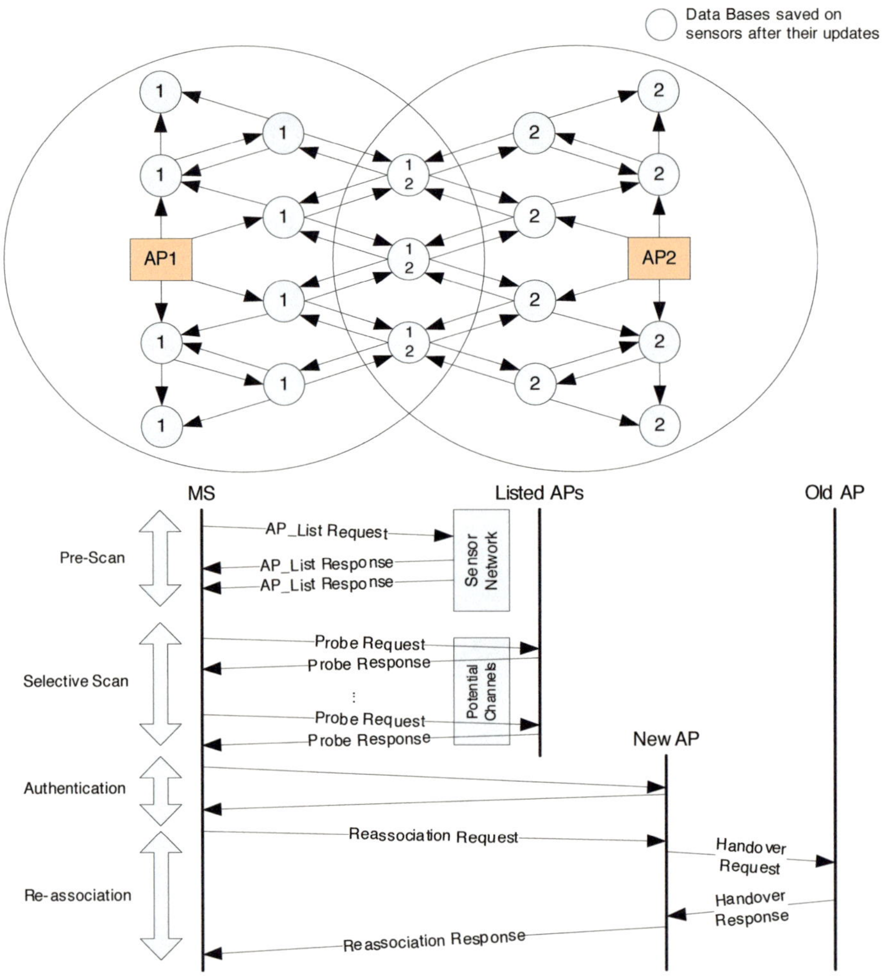

Fig. 4. Sensors-based scan handoff technique

In (Huang et al., 2006), the authors proposed a *selective scan* technique in the IEEE 802.11 WLAN contexts that support the IAPP protocol (IEEE Std. 802.11F, 2003) to decrease the handover latency. This mechanism, as shown in Figure 5, reduces the scan time of a new AP by combining an enhanced Neighbor Graph 'NG' (Kim et al., 2004) scheme and an enhanced IAPP scheme. If a MS knows exactly its adjacent APs - provided by the NG RADIUS server (Radius, RFC 2865 & 2866) - it can use selective scanning by unicast to avoid scanning all channels. They enhanced the NG approach by putting the MS to power-saving mode (PSM) to pre-scan neighboring APs. This solution reduces, in a remarkable way, the total latency of the handoff mechanism. On the other hand, it requires that the MS must have knowledge on the network architecture and its adjacent APs to be able to employ selective scan. In addition, we should take into account the number of packets added by the IAPP that may affect the current traffic. Moreover, we note that all data packets have been sent to the old AP and then routed to the new selected AP before the link-layer is updated, which corresponds to a double transmission of the same data frames in the network. Thus, it greatly increases both the collision and the loss rates in 802.11 wireless networks.

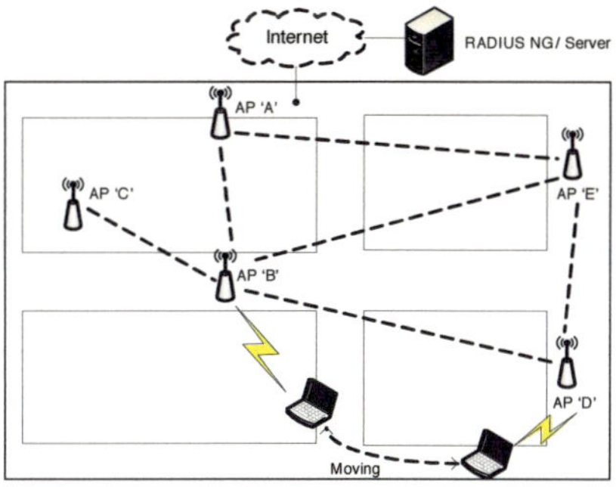

AP	*Neig.*	*Channel*	*# MSs*	*IP*	*BSSID*
A	*B*	6	2	192.168...	00:60:B3...
	E	6	6	192.168...	00:60:B3...
	D	11	7	192.168...	00:60:B3...
	...	...	...	...	...
B	*A*	1	3	192.168...	00:60:B3...
	C	11	1	192.168...	00:60:B3...
	D	11	7	192.168...	00:60:B3...
	...	...		192.168...	...
...	...	...	...	...	...

Fig. 5. The NG-based handover architecture

In (Chintala et al., 2007) the authors proposed two changes to the basic algorithm of IEEE 802.11 which reduce significantly the handover average latency using inter-AP communications during the scan phase. In the first proposed scheme (as shown in Figure 6), called Fast Handoff by Avoiding Probe wait (FHAP), additional costs incurred during this phase are reduced by forcing the potential APs to send their probe response packets to the old AP using the IAPP protocol and not to the MS which was sent the probe request. Therefore, the MS will avoid the long probe wait and then the packets loss is considerably reduced without any additional cost in the network. Consequently, during the probe phase the MS switches between channels and sends the probe request. Then it switches back to its actual AP to receive the probe responses.

However, based on this approach we note that the handover threshold should be adjusted so that the MS can communicate with its AP after the probe phase. Also, while the probe response packets are received via the current AP and not on their respective channels, the MS will not be able to measure the instantaneous values of RSSI and then evaluate the sensed channels quality.

In (Chintala et al., 2007; Roshan & Leary, 2009) the authors improved their first solution by proposing a new mechanism called Adaptive Preemptive Fast Handoff (APFH). The APFH method requires that the MS predetermines a new AP before the handover begins. Then, the handover threshold is reached, the MS avoids the discovery phase and triggers immediately the re-authentication phase. This process will reduce the total handover latency to the re-association/authentication delay. The APFH method splits the coverage area of the AP depending on the signal strength in three areas: safe zone, gray zone and handover zone. As its name indicates, the safe zone is the part of the coverage area where the MS is not under a handover threat. The gray area is defined as an area where the handover probability is high. Therefore the MS begins collecting information on a new best AP. This second mechanism removes the entire handover latency and respects the strict VoIP transmission constraints.

Many research works were done on the network-layer regarding the challenge to support the mobility in IP networks – i.e. IPv6 (Johnson et al., 2004; Cornall et al., 2002). A detailed review of the most relevant methods and a deep time study of the handoff process have been presented in (Rebai et al., 2009a, 2009b; Ramani & Savage, 2005).

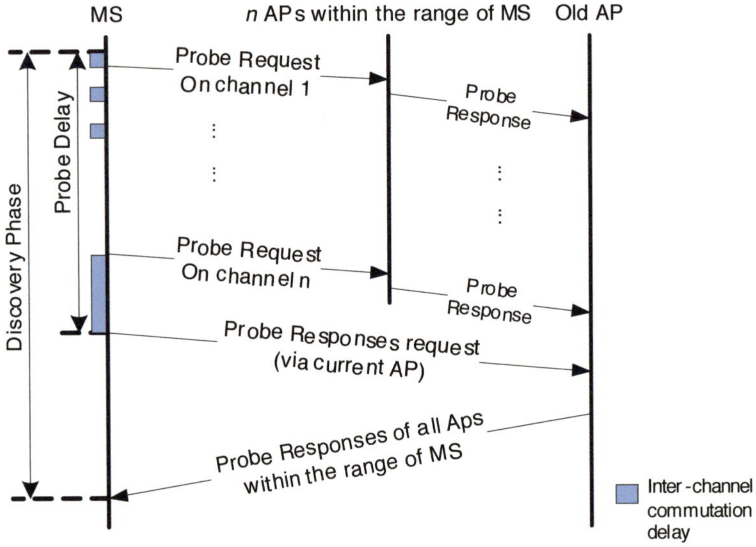

Fig. 6. The discovery phase of the FHAP method

3. Prevent-Scan Handoff Procedure (PSHP)

In (Aboba, 2003) it has showed that the typical handoff latency in IEEE 802.11b with IAPP network may take a probe delay of 40 to 300ms with a constant IAPP delay of 40ms. To allow the IAPP protocol to reduce this delay, we firstly have imposed (Rebai et al., 2009b) that the MS must authenticate with the first AP of the ESS. The IAPP based pre-authentication (Orinoco T.B., 2000) is achieved even before MS enters into the discovery state, thus it does not contribute to the handoff latency. Then we have proposed (Rebai et al., 2011) to define a new threshold other than the existing handoff threshold. It is called Preventive RSSI and termed by ($RSSI_{prev}$) and defined in the given Equation 2.

$$RSSI_{prev} = RSSI_{\min} + (RSSI_{\max} - RSSI_{\min})/2 \tag{2}$$

where, $RSSI_{max}$ indicates the best link quality measured between a MS and its AP. As its name implies, the $RSSI_{prev}$ is a value of the *link quality* above which the MS is not under the threat of imminent handoff. Starting from this threshold the proposed algorithm detects the mobility of a MS and triggers the next-AP search which can offer a better link quality.

A continuous *pre-scan* process is generated in which the MS should switch channels and wait for beacons from potential APs. Since the switching and waiting delays are greater than the maximum retransmission time of 802.11 frames (4ms), time-bounded packets may be dropped by the MS (not able to acknowledge them). To overcome this drawback, the algorithm let the MS announces a Power Saving Mode (PSM) before switching channels (Baek & Choi, 2008). This causes the AP to buffer packets until the MS returns to its channel and resets the PSM mode. These buffers will not be overfilled during the PSM mode (very short in duration). In addition the *pre-scan* is programmed so that it does not disturb the existing traffic flow between the MS and its AP. Figure 7 presents the new state machine for a MS showing the various amendments that we have added to the basic algorithm.

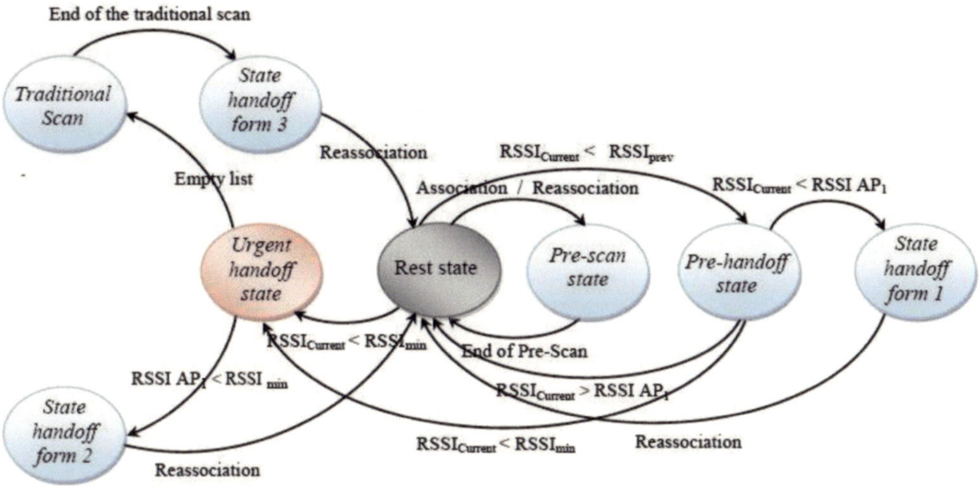

Fig. 7. State machine of the PSHP procedure performed by the mobile station

The major advantage of the proposed scheme resides in the periodicity of checking for a new AP offering a better quality of link for forthcoming transmissions. The pre-scan phase is launched each α defined by the following Equation 3:

$$\alpha = \left[(T_{switch} + MaxChannelTime) \times N \right] \times 1.5 \quad (3)$$

where, T_{switch} is the switching delay from one channel to another, and N is the number of available channels.

In the PSHP scheme we enumerate three forms of handoff that can be happened depending on network conditions. Initially, the MS is in standby state. If the RSSI value associated to the current AP degrades and reaches the $RSSI_{prev}$, then the MS switches to the pre-handoff state to check its dynamic list. It will try to find out a new AP with a corresponding RSSI value higher than the actual one. If such value exists, the MS switches to a 'handoff form1' state and performs a re-association procedure with the chosen AP. Otherwise, the MS returns to its standby state. If the measured RSSI value with the current AP is deteriorating suddenly and reaches the minimum bound (handover threshold), then the MS passes directly from the standby state to the 'urgent handover' state. In such state the MS must decide whether to perform the second or the third form of handover depending only on the instantaneous data of the dynamic list. If the first-listed AP has a value of RSSI greater than the handover threshold, then the MS switches to the 'handover form2' state. If such case does not exist, the MS switches to the 'handover form3' state in which it carries out a classical 802.11 handoff with a traditional scan procedure. We note that during the first two handoff occurrences (form1 and form2) the overall latency is equal only to the re-association delay, while using the 'handoff form3' is rare in practice (after carrying out pre-scan cycles).

3.1 Multiple-criteria AP selection technique

A second PSHP add-on mechanism for the AP selection was proposed initially in (Rebai et al., 2010). The proposed techniques aims to choose the most adapted AP from available APs for the next handover occurrence. The basic procedure is considering only the RSSI value as an indicator of the AP quality. This naïve procedure, leads to the undesirable result that many MSs are connected to a few APs, while other APs are underutilized or completely idle. In (Chou & Shin, 2005) the authors argued that the login data with the APs can reflect the actual situation of handovers given discrete WLAN deployment. As an example (see Figure 8), two WLANs may be very close to each other but separated by a highway or a river. Conversely, if the user is moving fast (e.g. in a train), handover may need to take place among WLANs that are far apart, i.e. among non-neighbor APs. Thus, the context user history allows us to better predict the probability of the user's next movement.

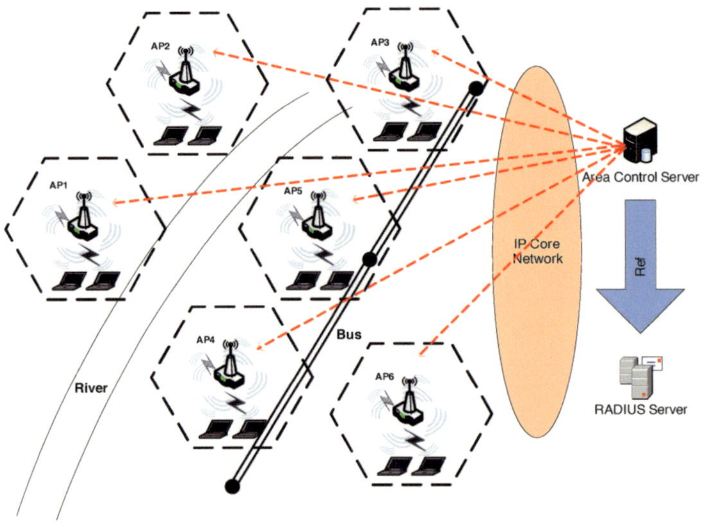

Fig. 8. Example of an IEEE 802.11 infrastructure-mode WLAN

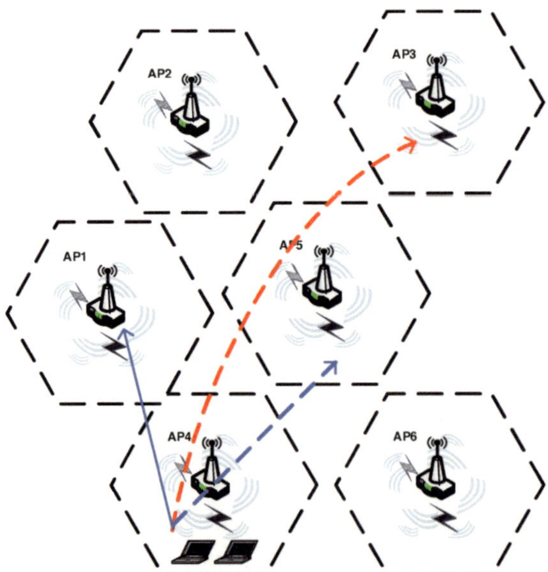

Fig. 9. Handoff scenario for a MS moving towards AP3

A new network-configuration method - that differs from the RSSI constrained process (Shin et al., 2004) – has been proposed by introducing three new network parameters to optimize the next-AP selection during a WLAN handoff procedure (Rebai et al., 2010). The first parameter reproduces the number of MSs associated with an AP to exploit the overload factor of APs. The second parameter counts the handoff occurrence between the actual AP and each potential AP, and so represents significant history-based information. This counter is incremented by one each time a handoff occurs between the corresponding two APs. It includes the location and other context-based information useful for the next AP-selection. The third parameter reproduces the number of neighbors APs of the next handover chosen AP. In other words, is reflects the number of 2-hop neighbors of the current AP through a potential AP. This "look-ahead" parameter is added to improve the choice of the next AP to maintain long-term connections. A full numerical optimization approach for the next-AP selection was discussed in (Rebai et al., 2010) as well as its application results.

To elucidate the concept further, Figure 9 shows a sample handoff situation for a mobile moving from AP4 towards AP3. The standard 802.11 approach would handoff the mobile station (MS) to AP1 based on RSSI strength only. Then after few attempts it may switch the mobile to AP5. The proposed approach would result in a handoff directly to AP5 based on better handoff history criteria between AP4 and AP5 (high occurrence because of the bus trail), and more 2-hop neighbors through AP5. As the number of MSs was increased, with a bias towards moving to AP3, this add-on heuristic technique demonstrates clear advantage over the simple RSSI only approach and reduces considerably the handovers over the WLAN.

3.2 PSHP simulation results

In this section, the performance of the proposed scheme PSHP is evaluated and compared to the basic handoff scheme (currently used by most network interface cards) and other significant works founded in (Velayos & Karlsson, 2004; Ramani & Savage, 2005; Chintala et al., 2007). The handoff latencies of all schemes for different traffic loads are presented. This is followed by discussion on the total amount of time spent on handoff for all schemes. The effect of the proposed schemes on real time traffic is explored and weighed against the basic handoff scheme. We used C++ to simulate the new 802.11 handoff versus other described techniques. The IEEE 802.11b (IEEE Std. 802.11b, 1999) networks are considered for testing the schemes. The total number of the probable channels is assumed to be 11 channels (number of all the legitimate channels used in USA for 802.11b). We employed a total of 100 APs and 500 MSs to carry out the simulations. The other parameters are outlined in Table 1.

Parameter	Value
Speed of MS	0.1 – 15 m/s
Mobility Model	Random Way Point
MinChannelTime / MaxChannelTime	7/11 ms
Switch Delay	5 ms
Handoff Threshold	-51 dB
Pre-Scan Threshold	-45 dB

Table 1. Simulation Parameters

In general, all the suggested solutions to optimize the handoff process aim to reduce the total latency below 50ms (International Telecom Union [ITU], 1988) mainly for multimedia applications. The proposed PSHP solution aims to be conforming to this restriction by reducing the total handoff delay incurred in 802.11 WLANs. We choose a free propagation model for the mobile stations. Thus, in performed simulations the received signal strength indicator value is based on the distance between a MS and its AP (RSSI-based positioning) as shown in (Kitasuka et al., 2005; Rebai et al., 2011). The adopted mobility model is based on the model of random mobility "Random Way Point Mobility Model" presented in (Boudec, 2005). The same moving model has been also adopted in other algorithms (Ramani & Savage, 2005; Huang et al., 2006; Kim et al., 2004; Chintala et al., 2007).

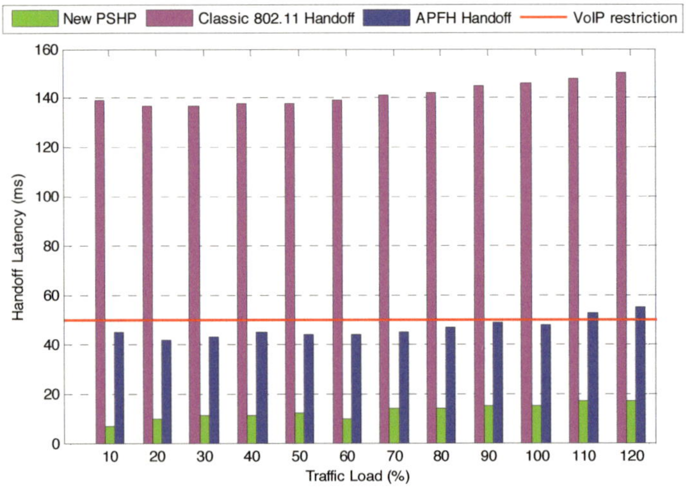

Fig. 10. Handoff Latency versus Traffic Loads

Figure 10 shows the average handoff latency against different traffic loads for the three tested schemes. The APFH scheme achieves 67.62% delay improvement while the new PSHP method attains 95.21% improvement versus the basic 802.11 handoff scheme. The handoff latency of the classical approach is consistent with the simulation results in (Velayos & Karlsson, 2004) with similar parameters. Also, we point out by observing Figure 8 that the average handoff latencies for the PSHP and APFH schemes are both under 50ms which is well within VoIP constraints. However, PSHP performs the best and the minimal handoff delay compared to the APFH (Chintala et al., 2007). This remarkable improvement is reached since the new procedure performs a cyclic pre-scan phase before carrying out a handoff and most of handoffs are accomplished early by detecting the premature quality deterioration. As in (Ramani & Savage, 2005; Chintala et al., 2007) the traffic load is computed by dividing the number of active MSs (the MSs having data to transmit) over the maximum number of MSs transmitting on one AP's cell. The maximum number of active MSs is equal to 32 in IEEE 802.11 WLANs.

Based on the given results in (Mishra et al., 2003; Ramani & Savage, 2005; Kim et al., 2004) of related handoff techniques, we draw the following Table 2 resuming the total handoff delays for corresponding proposed mechanisms. We figure out a significant reduction achieved by the new PSHP algorithm compared to other solutions, and more specifically with the basic handover mechanism. We also note that the *SyncScan* solution satisfies the time-bounded applications. However, the selective scanning method occasionally exceeds the required QoS limits. This result is due to the inefficacity of the NG graph technique to manage all network topology changes due to the continuous MS mobility. With PSHP the total latency is reduced to the re-authentication phase (≈11ms). This delay may reach 18ms because in some simulated cases a handoff occurrence is triggered during a pre-scan cycle.

Scan Technique	Total Latency
SyncScan (Ramani & Savage, 2005)	40±5ms
Selective Scan (Kim et al., 2004)	48±5ms
APFH (Chintala et al., 2007)	42±7ms
Traditional 802.11 handoff	from 112ms up to 366ms
Proposed PSHP	11±7ms

Table 2. Average latencies of different handoff procedures

Figures 11 and 12 evaluate the performance of the APFH technique – the best known solution in literature – and the new PSHP scheme against VoIP traffic. The packet inter-arrival time for VoIP applications is normally equal to 20ms (Chen et al., 2004), while it is also recommended that the inter-frame delay to be less than 50 ms (ITU, 1988; Chen et al., 2004). This restriction is depicted as a horizontal red line at 50ms in Figures 11 and 12. A node with VoIP inter-arrival time is taken and the corresponding delays are shown. The vertical green dotted lines represent a handoff occurrence. The traffic load for the given simulations was fixed to 50% and the number of packets sent to 600 (≈2.5s). We note that handoff occurrences are not simultaneous for the two simulated patterns. The MSs adopting the new PSHP algorithm detect the quality deterioration with their corresponding AP earlier than the APFH process. We note that both techniques respect the time constraint of real-time applications on recorded inter-frame delays without exceeding the required interval (50ms). However, this constraint is better managed by the new approach and the inter-packet periods are more regular and smaller. As discussed before, the PSHP handoff latency is only reduced to re-authentication delay if all handovers occur under form1 and 2. If PSHP form3 is performed, the latency is equal to the delay incurred in legacy 802.11 scanning all channels in addition to re-authentication delay.

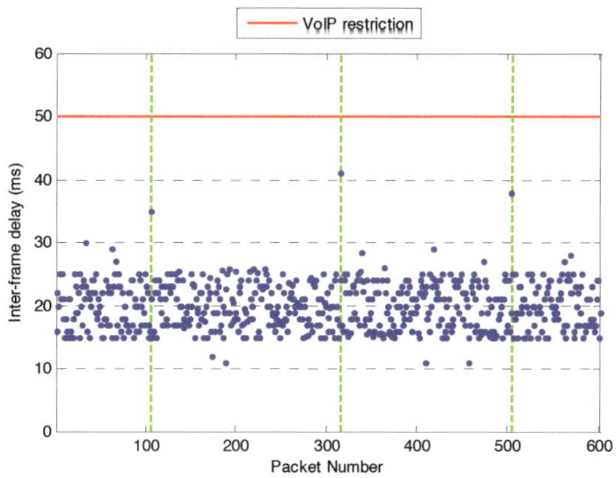

Fig. 11. Inter-frame delay in APFH (Chintala et al., 2007)

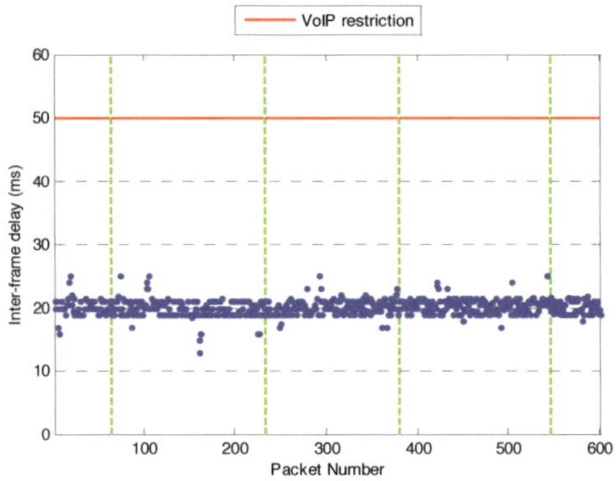

Fig. 12. Inter-frame delay in PSHP

To emphasize the last assertion we present in Figures 13 and 14, respectively, a count of handoff occurrences for both APFH and PSHP schemes according to the traffic load and the detailed number of the various handoff forms related to the new PSHP technique. We set the simulation time to 10s for each considered traffic load.

By comparing values obtained by the two algorithms in Figure 13, we easily point out that the APFH technique (Chintala et al., 2007) performs less handovers in the network than the proposed PSHP scheme. This result can be explained by the adoption of the new form of preventive Handover (termed form1). Using this new form, a MS will not wait for a minimum quality recorded equal to the handoff threshold to trigger a handover. This new technique detects early the link quality deterioration with its current AP and performs an AP-switching to potentially improve link conditions. Therefore, the periodic pre-scan adopted by the new technique offers new opportunities to enhance the link quality between a MS and its AP and a significant reduction of the total handover delay. Indeed, with the pre-scan cycle the MS can discover other APs that have a better value of RSSI than provided by the current AP and provide the means to make more intelligent choices before and during a handover. The new algorithm PSHP has a better choice for the next AP by collecting periodic RSSI measurement. Thus, the decision is earlier and more beneficial when a handover is performed (rather than relying on a single sample as in usual schemes). Consequently, the extra number of PSHP occurrences versus APFH procedure happenings is compensated by an early choice of next AP with a better offered quality.

In Figure 14, the vertical red lines represent the executed number of form1 handoffs. Blue lines represent the number of handoffs taken under the second and third form, i.e. urgent handoffs. Recall that handoff under the first form is started when the RSSI value degrades below the $RSSI_{prev}$ and above the handoff threshold. Handoffs of the second and third form start only if RSSI value is degraded below the handoff threshold. In Figure 14 we figure out for most traffic loads, urgent handoffs occur less frequently than handoffs of form1. We also state that the proposed algorithm presents true opportunity to improve link quality since most of handoff occurrences are executed before that the RSSI value degrades below the handoff threshold. Accordingly, we conclude that almost half of accomplished handoffs are done under the new first form, which explains the delay reduction of PSHP since the first form decreases the related latency considerably and improves the link quality between the MS and its current AP.

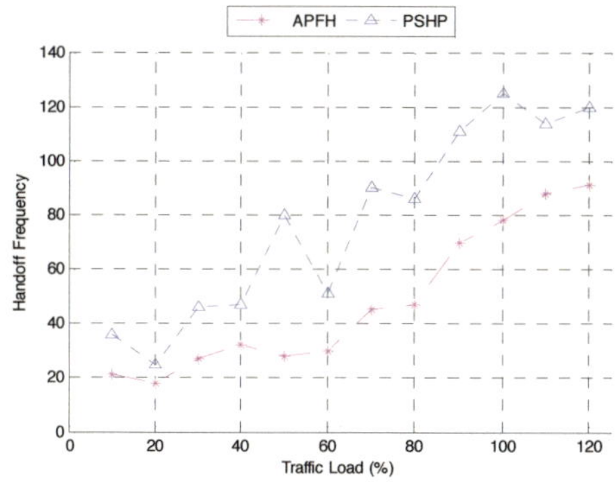

Fig. 13. Handoff Frequency

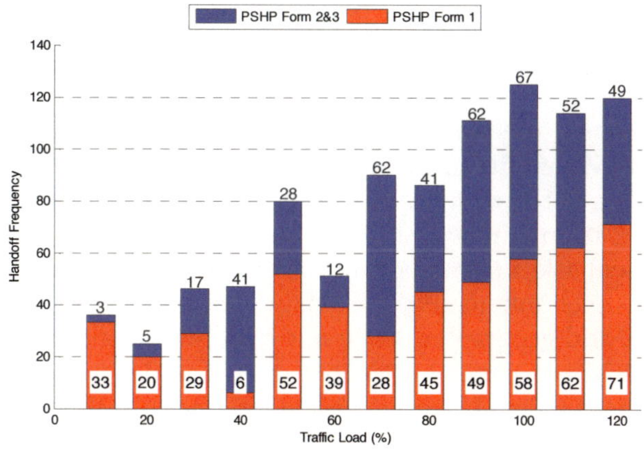

Fig. 14. Occurrence of Handoff forms in PSHP

Table 3 shows the average probability of data packets being dropped and caused mainly by handoff procedure for the three schemes (APFH, PSHP, and the classic 802.11 approach). We also add the obtained result in (Ramani & Savage, 2005; Kim et al., 2004) for *SyncScan* and *SelectiveScan*, respectively. For comparison purposes, the traffic load for all nodes is divided into real-time and non real-time traffic with a ratio of 7.5/2.5. Other than errors caused by handoff occurrences, the real-time data packets are dropped also if the inter-frame delay exceeds 50ms. The simulation time for each traffic type is 10s (equivalent to about 2500 frames). Clearly, PSHP outperforms the other three schemes and the basic 802.11 as long as the traffic load is limited. The loss probability value of the new PSHP technique is divided by two compared to these obtained by *SyncScan* and *SelectiveScan* methods and by three of that accomplished by the standard 802.11 scheme.

Scan Technique	Loss Probability
SyncScan (Ramani & Savage, 2005)	0.92 x1E-02
Selective Scan (Kim et al., 2004)	1.28 x1E-02
APFH (Chintala et al., 2007)	0.72 x1E-02
IEEE 802.11 handoff	1.62 x1E-02
New PSHP	0.53 x1E-02

Table 3. VoIP packet's loss

In conclusion, periodic scanning also provides the means to make more intelligent choices when to initiate handoff. The new PSHP can discover the presence of APs with stronger RSSIs even before the associated AP's signal has degraded below the threshold. In addition, the pre-scan phase does not affect the existing wireless traffic since the corresponding MS will carry out a pre-scan cycle after declaring the PSM mode to buffer related packets.

3.3 Evaluation of the new add-on AP-selection heuristic

As mentioned above we add new context-based parameters for the next AP choice when a handover is triggered in the network by a MS. The result technique is not dependent on the used handoff method. Thus, we integrate the new developed heuristic function with both the classic and the proposed switching algorithm. Specifically, in the standard 802.11 method the next AP selection will be performed after the scan phase on the found APs by choosing one based on the new objective function. Regarding the PSHP procedure this choice will be performed after each pre-scan cycle only on APs belonging the associated dynamic list. This function is also performed for both handoff form2 and form3. The only algorithm modification in PSHP form1 handoff process is that the objective function is performed only on listed APs that have an RRSI value greater than the actual RSSI measured between the MS and its actual AP. By adopting this condition we always maintain the main purpose of the PSHP which is an earlier selection of a new AP that offers a better link quality. Therefore, the modified PSHP will not choose automatically the first best AP in the list. However, it will select from existing AP that maximizes the objective function and also offers a better channel link quality. We set the same simulation parameters as given in Table 1. However, we add geographic constrains by influencing some MS-AP link qualities depending on AP initial positions and by introducing initial specific values for the CNX parameter to illustrate the already performed MS-journeys in the network and a random primary associations between MSs and the given set of APs. The simulated mobility model regarding the MS moves is no longer "Random Way Point". To be closer to realistic networks and to better assess our mechanism we switch to the "Random Direction" Mobility Model which forces mobile stations to travel to the edge of the simulation area before changing direction and speed. We choose this model because of its inclusion simplicity and instead of the "City Section" Mobility Model – which represents streets within a city. By including these constrain, we evaluated of the proposed heuristic combined with handoff schemes. In Figure 15 we resume the handoff occurrences for both classic and modified handoff schemes for the standard 802.11 and the PSHP techniques according to the traffic load. We set the simulation time to 10s for each considered traffic load. We point out a perceived reduction for handoff occurrences for both schemes when using the proposed heuristic procedure during the next AP selection. The produced results with the PSHP procedure are clearly enhanced in term of handoff count by integrating the new add-on heuristic technique. This result reflects the pay effect of the new objective function that accomplishes a better AP choice for the next inter-cell commutation, and consequently, improves the total number of handoff happening by reducing worse AP selections that was based only on RSSI-measurement decisions.

The detailed number of the various handoff forms related to the extended PSHP technique is shown in Figure 16. As well as in Figure 14, the vertical red and blue lines represent, respectively, the executed number of form1 handoffs and the count of handoffs taken under the second and third form (called also urgent handoffs). We figure out that handoffs form1 –

performed when the RSSI value degrades below the $RSSI_{prev}$ threshold – are more triggered using the modified PSHP. We note that the proposed algorithm detects earlier the MS path and direction based on supplementary context-based information, and as a result, chooses quicker the best AP that improves the link quality and offers a continuous channel connection. Accordingly, 72% of accomplished handoffs are done under the first form of PSHP that decrease considerably the total latency and improves the link quality. As discussed before, data packets are dropped mainly by the handoff procedure and the violation of VoIP restrictions. Table 4 summarizes the data loss average probability for both classic 802.11 and PSHP approaches. As settled before the simulation time is 10s. The traffic load for MSs is equally combining real-time and non real-time traffic. The given results are the average of simulated values by varying the traffic load (from lower to higher loads).

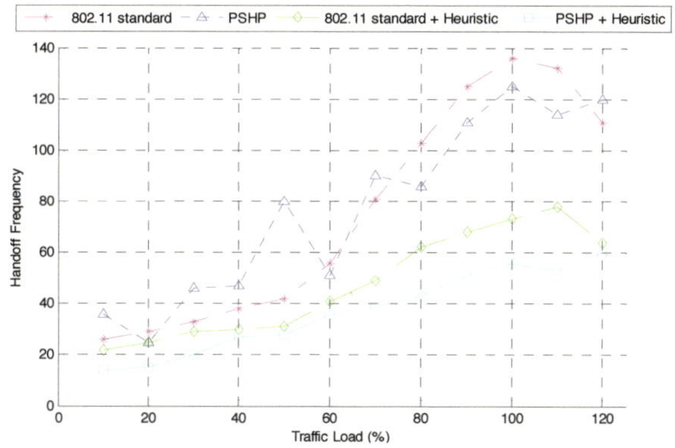

Fig. 15. WLAN Handoff's frequency

Scan Technique	Loss Probability
Standard 802.11 handoff	1.62 x1E-02
PSHP	0.53 x1E-02
IEEE802.11+heuristic selection	0.78 x1E-02
PSHP + heuristic selection	0.32 x1E-02

Table 4. Packet's loss with heuristic selection

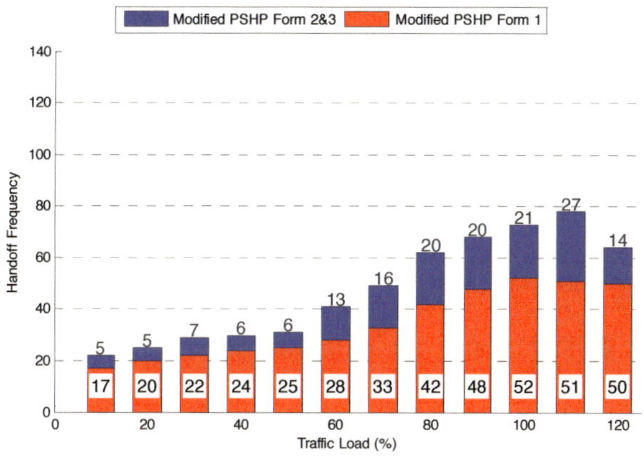

Fig. 16. Handoff Occurrence in PSHP

We note that the modified PSHP version is outperforming the standard scheme. The reduced number of handoffs and also the high percentage of form1 handoffs lead to minimize the packet loss caused by handoff procedures. Thus, we can conclude that the loss probability value obtained by the new PSHP integrating the heuristic technique includes mainly dropped packets associated to a higher traffic load and not linked to the lack of respect of QoS constrains.

In this section we have established that the proposed merit function used to evaluate network performance based on user preferences was adopted to find the best possible next-AP for the MS and to determine the optimal target AP based on a heuristic prediction process.

4. A new cross-layer signaling approach for VoIP-oriented PSHP mechanism

Although the layered architecture of the network model is designed for wired networks and it served that purpose well, it is still not efficient enough for wireless networks (Srivastava & Motani, 2005). Consequently, the wired network layering structure is not sufficient enough to support the objective of transmitting real-time applications over WLAN. There have been several methods and algorithms designed to improve the performance of wireless network for real-time transmission. However, some studies and surveys showed that cross-layer approach has a great impact on improving transmission performance of real-time traffic over wireless networks, and thus over WLAN. The concept of cross layer approach is that it allows the network layers to communicate and exchange information with each other for better performance (Ernesto et al., 2008). On the other hand, since no specific codec can work well in all network conditions (Karapantazis & Pavlidou, 2009), developing codec adaptive techniques have been proposed. Although developing this mechanism is still in its early stage (Myakotnykh & Thompson, 2009), different adapting codec rate schemes were proposed particularly for real-time applications in wired, wireless, or WLAN networks. Codec rate adaptation technique is defined as a technique that adjusts codec parameters or changes it to another codec with lower rate when the network gets congested. Codec parameters that can be considered in this technique are: packet size and compression rate (Myakotnykh & Thompson, 2009). Besides, adaptive rate approaches have been implemented using different constant bit-rate codec or variable bit-rate codec, such as AMR (Servetti & De Martin, 2003) and Speex (Sabrina & Valin, 2008). Moreover, it was shown that adaptive approaches perform better than constant bit rate (Servetti & De Martin, 2003; Sabrina & Valin, 2008). Table 5 (Karapantazis & Pavlidou, 2009), below illustrates parameters of different codecs. It was also concluded that for WLAN adapting the packet rate of a codec is sufficient with remaining the same codec type. Thus, changing packet size is an important parameter and would produce results of better quality (Myakotnykh & Thompson, 2009); hence it is considered in the approach.

Hence, our objective is to develop a cross-layering approach between MAC and Application layers. An agent will be designed and positioned as a mean of implementing the approach, which mainly aims to reduce VoIP delay and packet loss over WLAN, and therefore achieving better quality of VoIP. This section will focus on addressing a cross layer signaling technique in WLAN during handoff event by using the codec adaptive technique.

	G.711	G.726	G.729A	G.723.1
Bit rate (Kbps)	64	32	8	5.3
Bits per frame	8	4	80	159
Compression type	PCM	ADPCM	CS-ACELP	ACELP
Codec delay (ms)	0.25	0.25	25	67.5
MOS	4.1	3.85	3.7	3.6

Table 5. Voice codec Parameters

4.1 Cross Layer Adaptive Agent (CLAA)

In order to improve the QoS of VoIP during a handoff procedure, a cross-layer agent is proposed to allow the communication between MAC and Application layers. This new Cross Layer Adaptive Agent (CLAA) monitors the MAC handoff state changes and then adapts the suitable packet size and the codec type in the Application layer (Figure 17).

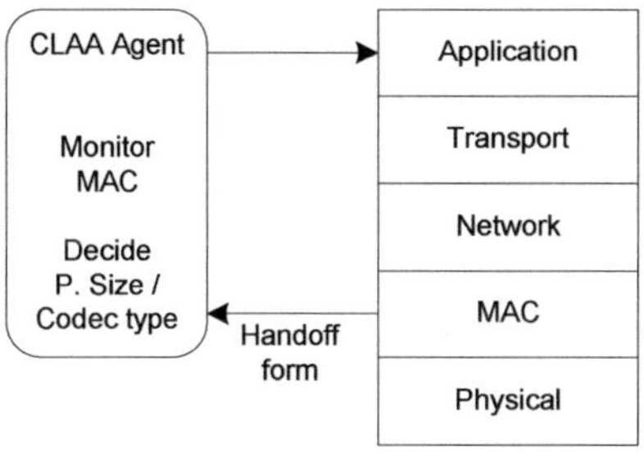

Fig. 17. Cross Layer Adaptive Agent (CLAA) model

The main function of the agent is to detect if there is a change in the PSHP state machine traced in the MAC layer. If such change occurs, it will inform the Application layer to act accordingly and better compensate either by the packet size at the codec algorithm in a dynamic manner in order to minimize channel congestion in WLAN or by codec type change. The other key point is that the agent tries to resolve congestion that the MS suffers locally firstly. If the congested MS condition is getting worse, then a second decision-phase will assist the agent to reduce the congestion.

We point that the CLAA agent is implemented only on local mode (sender side) since a global mode involves a collaboration between the sender and the receiver nodes. Such operations entail the receiver to send back to the sender information regarding the voice quality through its current AP which leads for extra network congestions during a handoff procedure. Figure 18 shows a descriptive flow chart of the local CLAA function.

Therefore, the agent chooses to resolve the handoff process issue locally at the sender side. This phase is in an open loop monitoring MAC layer and observes if any changes on the PSHP state/handover form occurred. If so, then the agent decides a new packet size/codec type and informs the Application layer to adjust. In fact, when MS detects a potential handoff (PSHP pre-handoff state) with one new cell (selected from the listed APs) offering a better quality, it initiates the handoff form1 state and simultaneously the CLAA agent decides to reduce the packet size to reduce congestion and packet loss during this short handoff period. However if a transition from pre-handoff state to an urgent handover state is triggered by the PSHP mechanism, the CLAA will change moderately the codec type. By doing so the resultant bit rate is lowered to prevent from large delay transmissions and enhance the overall received voice quality. Of course the codec type adaptation has a minor effect to decrease the received VoIP quality; however it will eliminate the RTP stream interruption on the receiver.

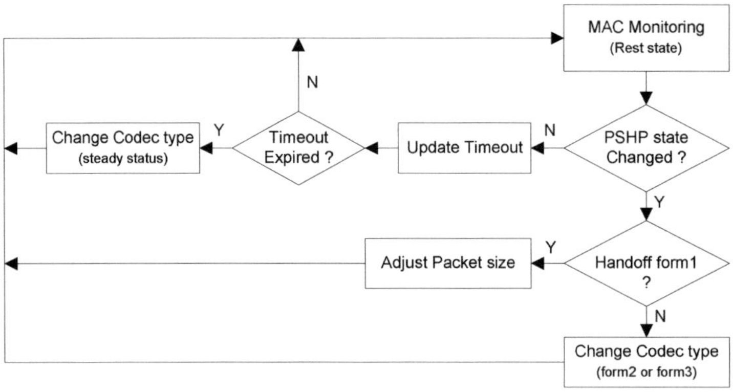

Fig. 18. CLAA flowchart and principle of operation

On the other hand, following to an inter-cell occurrence involving a codec alteration a threshold will be set, thus no consecutive changes will happen at the Application layer. If the agent detects a long steady status (Rest state in the PSHP state machine) within a pre-defined timeout, then codec type would be changed to a higher one with larger bit rate. The codec techniques are sorted based on their bit rate (as shown in Table 5) for the agent to select accordingly.

4.2 Performance evaluation and discussions

The testbed used in the performance tests of the proposed VoIP-oriented PSHP method is shown in Figure 19. The mobile client's 802.11b driver has been slightly modified to provide transport of the necessary cross-layer related information during handoffs. The Chariot Console [NetIQ] was used to measure the handoff performance under real-time and multimedia traffic. In all tests, three laptops (MS1 MS2, and MS3) were running VoIP sessions towards three different PC hosts (RTP Stream, Chariot G.711u script).

The measurements were taken for movements between different APs (a likelihood path is shown in Figure 19 using a dotted blue line). Both of MS1 and MS2 are implementing PSHP + the Heuristic function while MS3 uses only a standard PSHP driver. The MS1 includes also the designed VoIP-oriented CLAA Agent. All MSs were initially located in AP1, and then moved around the university lab rooms and the hallway following a predefined path and using a constant 1~2m/s speed over potential seven APs. The experiment consisted mainly to walk through the hallway (from a start point to a far end point), then to lab room#1 and finally back to the start point. In Figure 19 the red lines represent the physical separation between university rooms and the green dotted line corresponds approximately to the AP's coverage area. Several handoffs were performed over the network during multiple three-minute experimentations for each MS.

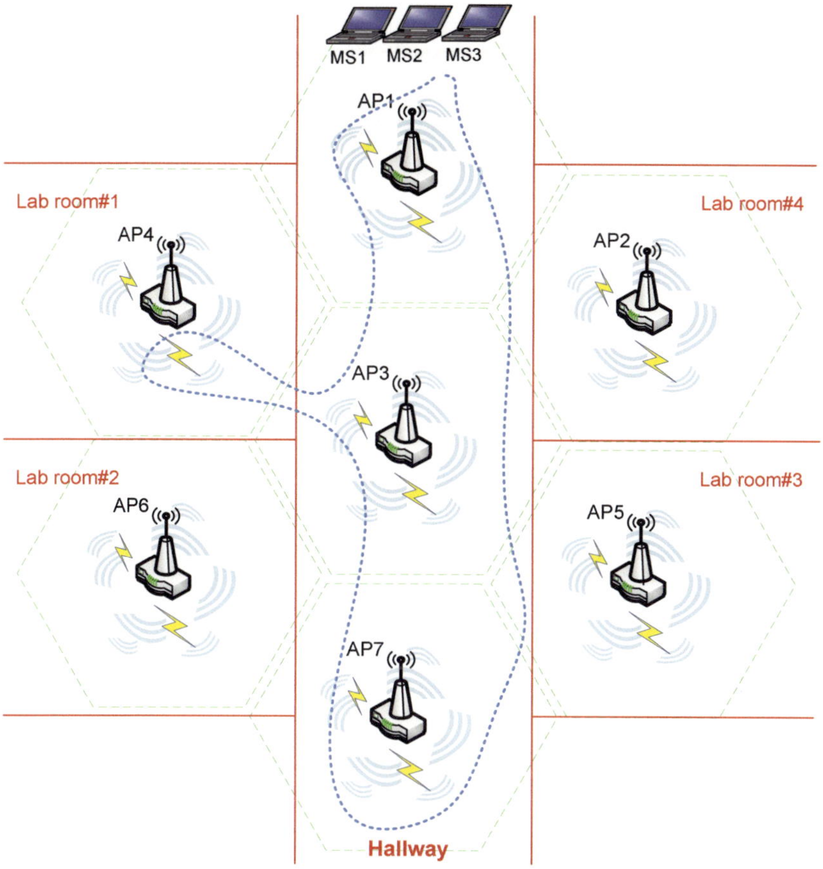

Fig. 19. Testbed for the MS's movement and network topology

The clients MS1 and MS2 roam between APs identically: from AP1 to AP3 at around 17th second in both tests, from AP3 to AP7 at around the 31st sec., from AP7 to AP4 at around 96th sec., and back to AP1 at around the 124th sec. Since MS3 was using a standard PSHP driver (without an enhanced heuristic AP selection), it performed dissimilar handoffs approximately as follows: from AP1 to AP2 at 21st sec., then from AP2 to AP5 at 35th sec., from AP5 to AP3 at 46th sec., from AP3 to AP7 at 58th sec., from AP7 to AP6 at 69th sec., back to AP7 at 72nd sec., then from AP7 to AP4 at 104th sec., from AP4 to AP3 at 126th sec., and finally to AP1 at 155th sec. It is important to note that the initial transmission rate and codec type values are set to 11Mbps and G.711 respectively for all simulated MSs.

What can be observed from Figures 20 and 21 are the very small one-way delay and the very small packet loss performance achieved by MS1 compared to the other mobile nodes. Indeed, the CLAA integration has reduced significantly the total packet delay (caused by handoffs) by 64.5% from the PSHP+Heuristic mechanism and by 87.9% from the standard PSHP method which affects considerably the overall quality of received voice streams. Analogically, the number of the lost packets decreases to just 247 (from 538 and 2067 resulted through PSHP+Heuristic and PSHP implementations, respectively) during the three-minute RTP streaming. The high number of lost frames accomplished by standard

PSHP arises from multiple handoff occurrences during the continuous MS movement between available APs.

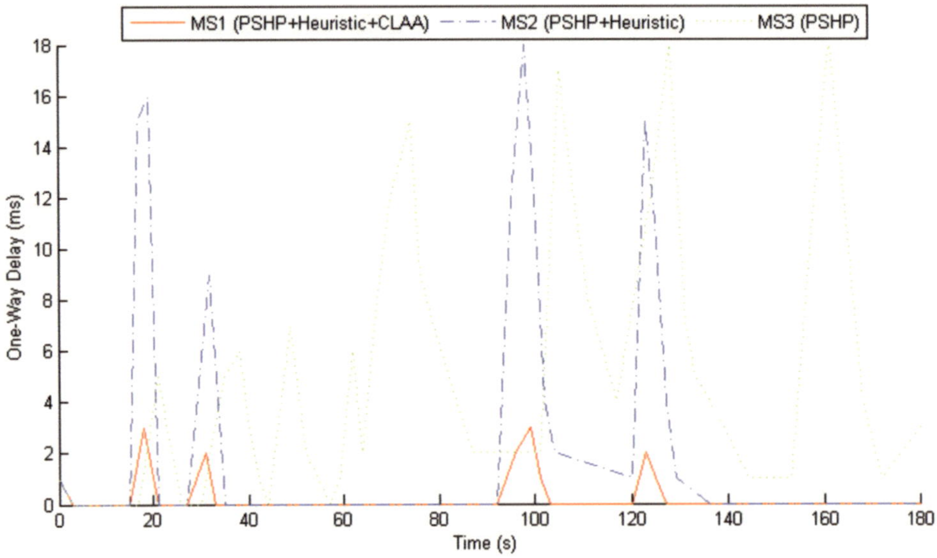

Fig. 20. Measured one-way delay from MS drivers

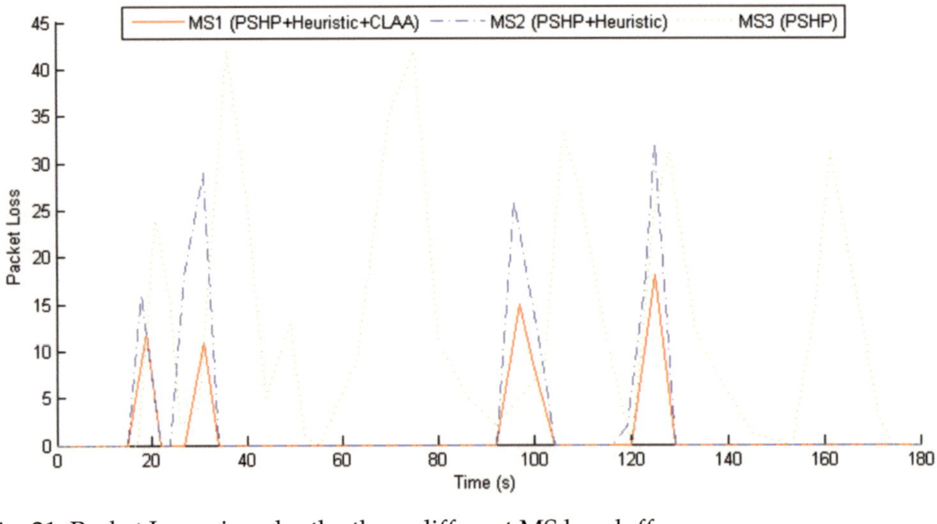

Fig. 21. Packet Loss given by the three different MS handoff

From the result given by Figure 22 the overall throughput attained by MS1 suffered a degradation of only ≈ 6.6% while values of 11.8% and 14.3% were accomplished by MS2 and MS3 respectively. To determine the quality of VoIP under packet loss, the most common metric is the Mean Opinion Score (MOS) (IUT, 1996), which evaluates the effect of bursty loss on VoIP perceived quality (the Overall Voice Quality). In a MOS test, the listeners rate audio clips by a score from 5 to 1, with 5 meaning Excellent, 4 Good, 3 Fair, 2 Poor, and 1

Bad. In fact, voice and video communications quality usually dictates whether the experience is a good or bad one. Therefore, besides the qualitative description we hear, like 'quite good' or 'very bad', there is a numerical method of expressing voice and video quality given by the MOS which provides a statistical indication of the perceived quality of the media received after being transmitted and eventually compressed using VoIP codecs.

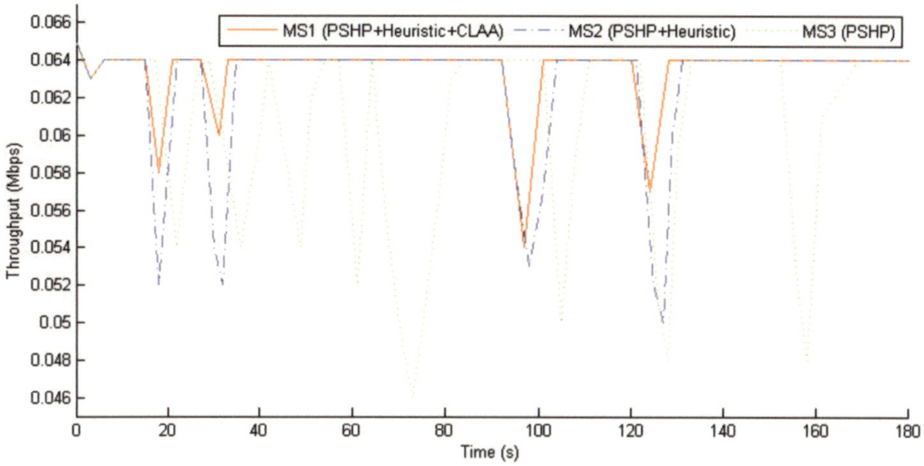

Fig. 22. Throughput measurements versus VoIP streaming elapsed time

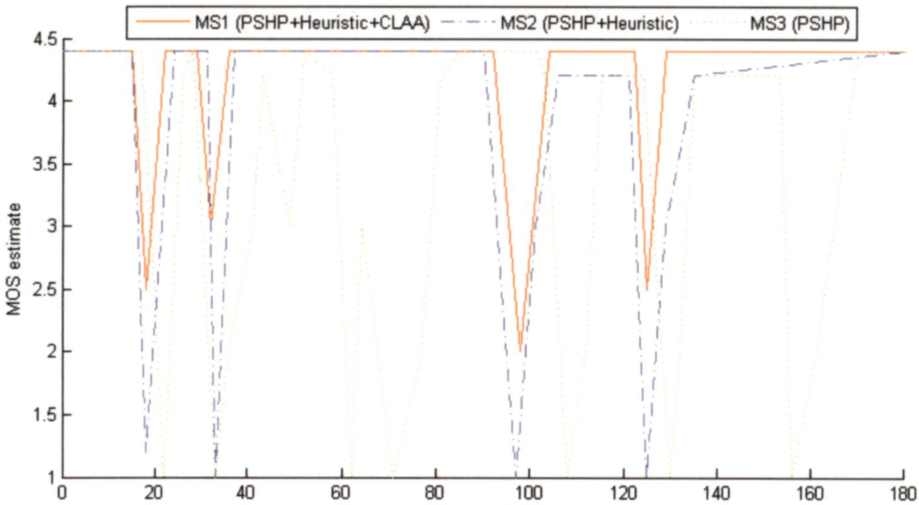

Fig. 23. MOS estimate of received voice quality

The MOS estimate of conducted test experiments shows in Figure 23 that the call was not interrupted with all MSs; It only suffered substantial quality degradation with a low peak at MOS=1, and quickly restored its initial quality (MOS=4).

Based on the above VoIP session experiments, we notice that MS1 (PSHP+Heuristic+CLAA) roams between different APs and all related test results are enhanced. In fact, the MOS mean values obtained by MS1, MS2 and MS3 handoff implementations are 3.86, 3.35 and 3.04 respectively; hence a considerable enhancement of 15.2% from PSHP+Heuristic and 28.6% from the standard PSHP was achieved by the new VoIP-oriented technique. This is due to the fact that the integrated CLAA agent cooperates between the MAC and Application layers and then contributes in shortening the total handoff latency during movements by adjusting the packet size and the codec type when needed. Thus, it preserves efficiently the VoIP session and maintains a satisfactory aggregate throughput. As also verified by the MOS estimate, the minimum measured MOS value during the MS1 test is equal to 2 (which match 'Poor' quality). This value was reached only one time (around the 98th second). However using the other two handoff versions a minimum MOS value of 1 (symbolizes Bad quality) was measured several times over the real streaming experiments.

5. Conclusions

VoIP over WLAN applications are rapidly growing due to the features they offer over the traditional public switched phones and their support symbolize at present an emerging challenge for 802.11-based WLANs. However, the integration of these two technologies still facing quality challenges to meet the quality obtained from the traditional telephony system. Besides, mobile stations in WLAN suffer the continuous inter-cell handoff issue, which affects the quality of the perceived voice. In order to keep a VoIP communication several commitments should be satisfied: eliminating communication termination, initiating appropriate handover based on reliable handover triggers and selecting the next AP with good link quality.

We firstly highlighted some of the technical challenges and related literature on the ongoing research force, especially focusing on approaches for enabling multimedia transit, as well as convenient and effective handover over IEEE802.11 mobile environments. Then we have revisited the PSHP handoff technique. As demonstrated, the continuous scanning PSHP technique offers significant advantages over other schemes by minimizing the time during which an MS remains out of contact with its AP and allowing handoffs to be made earlier and with more confidence. The result is a staggering 95% reduction of handoff latency compared to the typical procedure. As a second contribution we took into account additional network-based parameters to drive a better next-AP choice. This new add-on profit function is used to insert new factors reflecting resource availability, location, and other context-based information. Thus, the overall network performance is improved by electing from available APs, the one that increases the benefit of the next handoff occurrence.

In particular, this chapter presented another PSHP version satisfying between user requirement and network conditions and avoiding unnecessary handoffs as well. The policy is to minimize handoff delay for real time service and to reach an acceptable level for non-real time services. A pre-scanning phase is periodically activated to consider whether the handoff should be triggered. During the AP selection procedure, the heuristic function is adopted to find candidate APs satisfying preference of a user and minimizing the overall delay. PSHP is using four handoff metrics, RSS, (AP-extensibility) number of neighbors, (load) number of users per AP, and historical traffic (old occurred handoffs) as inputs to determine the optimal target network.

Furthermore, one of the challenges in the next generation of wireless communications is the integration of existing and future wireless technologies and supporting transparent and seamless vertical handoffs (between different networks standards and technologies) without degrading the QoS between these heterogeneous networks. Hence, this research work proposed a Cross-Layer Adaptive Approach (CLAA) in order to enhance the QoS of VoIP over WLAN with help of an agent. The Cross layering concept has been shown to have a great impact on the performance of the wireless networks. Adapting code parameters in the Application layer according to the network condition has also shown better performance of real-time applications. Thus, the new scheme would be easily extended to cover inter-networks handoff decision toward universal 4G ubiquitous access.

6. References

Aboba, B. (2003). Fast handoff issues. *IEEE-03-155rO-I, IEEE 802.11 Working Group*, Mars 2003

Baek, S. & Choi, B.D. (2008). Performance analysis of power save mode in IEEE 802.11 infrastructure WLAN. *International Conference on Telecommunications ICT 2008*, St. Petersburg, Russia, 2008

Bahl, P.; Balachandran, A. & Venkatachary, S. (2001). Secure Wireless Internet Access in Public Places. *IEEE International Conference on Communications*, vol.10, pp. 3271-3275, June 2001

Bianchi, G.; Fratta, L. & Oliveri, M. (1996). Performance Evaluation and Enhancement of the CSMA/CA MAC Protocol for 802.11 Wireless LANS. *The 7th International Symposium on Personal, Indoor and Mobile Radio Communications (PIMRC)*, vol. 2, pp. 392 – 396, 1996

Boudec, J.Y. (2005). On the Stationary Distribution of Speed and Location of Random Waypoint. *The IEEE Transactions on Mobile Computing*, vol. 4, pp. 404-405, July 2005

Chen, Y.; Smavatkul, N. & Emeott, S. (2004). Power management for VoIP over IEEE 802.11 WLAN. *The IEEE WCNC 2004*, vol.5, pp.1648–1653, March 2004

Chintala, V. M. & Zeng, Q.A. (2007). Novel MAC Layer Handoff Schemes for IEEE 802.11 Wireless LANs. *The IEEE Wireless Communications and Networking Conference, WCNC*, Mars 2007

Chou, C.T. & Shin, K.G. (2005). An Enhanced Inter-Access Point Protocol for Uniform Intra and Intersubnet Handoffs. *IEEE Transactions on Mobile Computer*, vol. 4, no. 4, July 2005

Cornall, T.; Pentland, B. & Khee, P. (2002). Improved Handover Performance in Wireless Mobile IPv6. *The 8th International Conference on Communication Systems (ICCS)*, vol. 2, pp. 857-861, Nov. 2002

Corner, D.; Lin, J. & Russo, V. (2010). An Architecture for a Campus-Scale Wireless Mobile Internet. *Technical Report* CSD-TR 95-058, Purdue University, Computer Science Department, 2010

Ernesto, E.; Nicolas, V. W.; Christophe, C. & Khalil, D. (2008). Introducing a cross-layer interpreter for multimedia streams, *Computer Networks*, Vol. 52 (6), pp. 1125-1141, April 2008

Huang, P.J.; Tseng, Y.C. & Tsai, K.C. (2006). A Fast Handoff Mechanism for IEEE 802.11 and IAPP Networks. *The 63rd IEEE Vehicular Technology Conference, VTC Spring*, 2006

Hills, A. & Johnson, D. (1996). A Wireless Data Network Infrastructure at Carnegie Mellon University. *IEEE Personal Communications*, vol. 3, pp. 56–63, Feb. 1996

IEEE Standard 802.11 (1999), Part 11: Wireless LAN Medium Access Control (MAC) and Physical Layer (PHY) Specifications, *IEEE Standard 802.11*, 1999

IEEE Standard 802.11b (1999), Supplement to Part 11: Wireless LAN Medium Access Control (MAC) and Physical Layer (PHY) specifications: Higher-speed Physical Layer Extension in the 2.4 GHz Band, *IEEE Std. 802.11b-1999*, 1999

IEEE Standard 802.11F (2003). IEEE Trial-use Recommended Practice for Multi-Vendor Access Point Interoperability via An Inter-access Point Protocol across Distribution Systems supporting IEEE 802.11 Operation. *IEEE Std 802.11F*, July 2003

IEEE Standard 802.11i (2004), Part 11. Wireless LAN Medium Access Control (MAC) and Physical Layer (PHY) Specifications: Medium Access Control (MAC) Security Enhancements. *Supplement to IEEE 802.11 Standard*, June 2004

IEEE Standard 802.11k (2003). Radio Ressource Management. *IEEE Standard 802.11*- 2003

International Telecommunication Union (1988). General Characteristics of International Telephone Connections and International Telephone Circuits. *ITU-TG.114*, 1988

International Telecommunication Union (1996). *Subjective performance assessment of telephone-band and wideband digital codecs, Recommendation P.830*, Telecommunication Standardization Sector of ITU, Geneva, Feb. 1996

Johnson, D.; Perkins, C. & Arkko, J. (2004). Mobility Support in IPv6. *RFC 3775 (Proposed Standard)*: ftp.rfc-editor.org in-notes rfc3775.txt, June 2004

Karapantazis, S. & Pavlidou, F. (2009). VoIP: A comprehensive survey on a promising technology, *Computer Networks*, Vol. 12, pp. 2050-2090, 2009

Kashihara, S.; Niswar, M.; Taenaka, Y.; Tsukamoto, K.; Yamaguchi, S. & Oie, Y. (2011). End-to-End Handover Management for VoIP Communications in Ubiquitous Wireless Networks, *VoIP Technologies, Shigeru Kashihara (Ed.)*, ISBN: 978-953-307-549-5, InTech, pp. 295-320, Feb. 2011

Kim, H.; Park, S.; Park, C.; Kim, J. & Ko, S. (2004). Selective Channel Scanning for Fast Handoff in Wireless LAN using Neighboor Graph. *ITC-CSCC*, July 2004

Kitasuka, T.; Hisazumi, K.; Nakanishi, T. & Fukuda, A. (2005). Positioning Technique of Wireless LAN Terminals Using RSSI between Terminals. *The 2005 International Conference on Pervasive Systems and Computing (PSC-05)*, pp. 47-53, Las Vegas, Nevada, USA, June 2005

Kunarak, S. & Suleesathira, R. (2011). Predictive RSS with Fuzzy Logic based Vertical Handoff Decision Scheme for Seamless Ubiquitous Access, *Mobile Ad-Hoc Networks:*

Protocol Design, Xin Wang (Ed.), ISBN: 978-953-307-402-3, InTech, pp. 261-280, Jan. 2011

Mishra, A.; Shin, M. & Arbaugh, W. (2003). An empirical analysis of the IEEE 802.11 MAC layer handoff process. *ACM SIGCOMM Computer Communication Review*, vol. 33: 93-102, April 2003

Mishra, A.; Shin, M.; Petroni, N.; Clancy, T. & Arbaugh, W. (2004). Proactive Key Distribution Using Neighbor Graphs. *IEEE Wireless Communications Magazine*, vol. 11, pp. 26-36, Feb. 2004

Myakotnykh, E. S. & Thompson, R. A. (2009). Adaptive Speech Quality Management in Voice-over-IP Communications, *Fifth Advanced International Conference on Telecommunications*, Venice, Italy, May 2009.

NetIQ Chariot Console, available at: http://www.netiq.com/products/chr/default.asp.

Orinoco (2000). Inter Access Point Protocol (IAPP). *Technical Bulletin TB 034/A*, Feb. 2000

Radius, RFC 2865 et 2866, *http www.ietf.org rfc rfc2865.txt, http www.ietf.org rfc rfc2866.txt*

Raghavan, M.; Mukherjee, A.; Liu, H.; Zeng, Q-A. & Agarwal, D. P. (2005). Improvement in QoS for Multimedia Traffic in Wireless LANs during Handoff. *The 2005 International Conference on Wireless Networks ICWN'05*, Las Vegas, USA, pp. 251-257, June 2005

Ramani, I. & Savage, S. (2005). SyncScan: Practical Fast Handoff for 802.11 Infrastructure Networks. *The IEEE Infocom'05*, vol. 1, pp. 675-684, March 2005.

Rebai, A. R.; Alnuweiri, H.; Hanafi, S. (2009). A novel prevent-scan Handoff technique for IEEE 802.11 WLANs, *in Proc. International Conference on Ultra Modern Telecommunications & Workshops ICUMT '09*, St. Petersburg, Russia, Oct. 2009

Rebai, A. R.; Haddar, B.; Hanafi, S. (2009). Prevent-scan: A novel MAC layer scheme for the IEEE 802.11 handoff, *In Proc. International Conference on Multimedia Computing and Systems ICMCS '09*, pp. 541-546, Ouarzazate, Morocco, April 2009

Rebai, A. R. & Hanafi, S. (2011). An Adaptive Multimedia-Oriented Handoff Scheme for IEEE 802.11 WLANs, *International Journal of Wireless & Mobile Networks IJWMN*, pp. 151-170, Vol. 3, No. 1, Feb. 2011

Rebai, A. R.; Rebai, M. F.; Alnuweiri, H.; Hanafi, S. (2010). An enhanced heuristic technique for AP selection in 802.11 handoff procedure, *In Proc. IEEE International Conference on Telecommunications ICT'10*, pp. 576-580, Doha, Qatar, April 2010

Roshan, P. & Leary, J. (2009). 802.11 Wireless LAN Fundamentals. *CISCO Press., ISBN No.1587050773*, 2009

Sabrina, F. & Valin, J.-M. (2008). Adaptive rate control for aggregated VoIP traffic, *in Proc. of GLOBECOM'08*, pp. 1405–1410, 2008

Servetti, A. & De Martin, J. C. (2003). Adaptive Interactive Speech Transmission Over 802.11 Wireless LANs". *In Proc. Int. Workshop on DSP in Mobile and Vehicular Systems*, Nagoya, Japan, April 2003

Shin, M.; Mishra, A. & Arbaugh, W. A. (2004). Improving the Latency of 802.11 Hand-offs using Neighbor Graphs. *The ACM MobiSys Conference*, Boston, MA, USA, pp. 70-83, June 2004

Skype Limited. (2003), available at: http://www.skype.com

Srivastava, V.; Motani, M. (2005). *Cross-Layer Design: A Survey and the Road Ahead, IEEE Communications Magazine*, Vol. 43, No. 12., pp.112-119, 2005

Velayos, H. & Karlsson, G. (2004). Techniques to Reduce IEEE 802.11b MAC Layer Handover Time. *IEEE ICC 2004*, vol. 7, pp. 3844-3848, June 2004

Waharte, S.; Ritzenthaler, K. & Boutaba, R. (2004). Selective active scanning for fast handoff in wlan using sensor networks. *IEEE International Conference on Mobile and Wireless Communication Networks (MWCN'04)*, Paris, France, October 2004

Part 3

Security Issues in Multimedia

4

A Novel Access Control Scheme for Multimedia Content with Modified Hash Chain

Shoko Imaizumi[1], Masaaki Fujiyoshi[2] and Hitoshi Kiya[2]
[1]*Chiba University*
[2]*Tokyo Metropolitan University*
Japan

1. Introduction

With the continuing growth in network technology, the exchange of digital images and audio as well as text has become very common regardless of whether the digital content is used for commercial purpose or not. Since such digital content is easily duplicated and re-distributed, protecting copyrights and privacy is an important issue. For the protection of digital content, *access control* based on naïve encryption (encrypting the whole content) (1) or media-aware encryption (2–6) has been studied widely.

A simple and straightforward way to realize versatile access control for multimedia content, consisting of several kinds of media to which several entities belong, is encrypting each entity individually. This approach, however, has to manage a large number of keys, given the large number of entities in multimedia content.

Scalable access control schemes have been proposed (2–6) for JPEG 2000 (7) coded images and/ or MPEG-4 fine granularity scalability (8) coded videos. These schemes control access to entities corresponding to hierarchical scalability assigned by coding technologies, so that the user can obtain an image or a video at the permitted quality from one common codestream. *Hash chain* (9; 10) has also been introduced to several schemes for reduction of managed keys and the keys delivered to each user (3–6).

Although a hash chain-based access control scheme has been proposed for multimedia content (11), the number of managed keys and that of delivered keys increase, depending on the kinds of media in the content.

In this chapter, we introduce an efficient access control scheme for multimedia content. The scheme assumes that multimedia content consists of several media and there is a scalable hierarchy on the quality in each or one medium. By introducing *modified* hash chains (MHCs), the number of managed keys is reduced to one and the number of delivered keys is also less than the conventional scheme (11). When a scalable hierarchy is in only one medium, the delivered key is particularly reduced to one. The managed key is not delivered to any user, providing security against key leakage. This scheme is also resilient to collusion attacks, in which malicious users illegally access the multimedia content at higher quality than that allowed by their access rights.

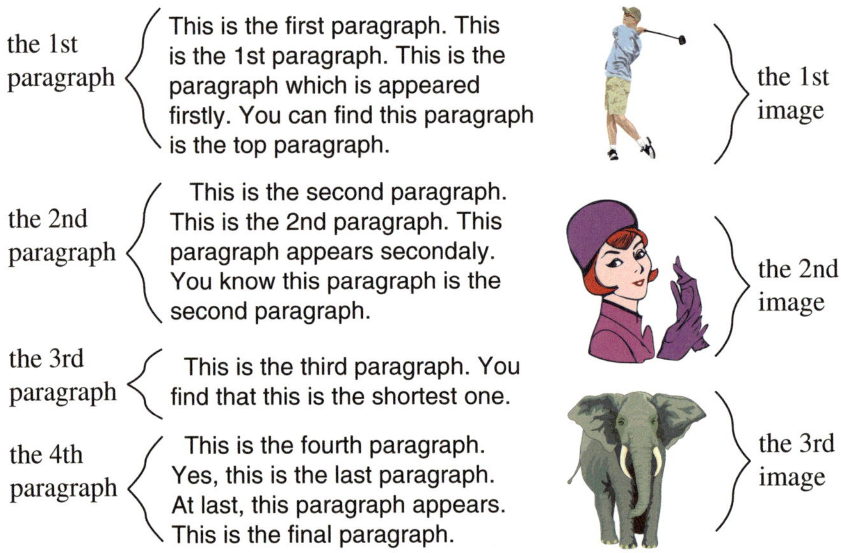

Fig. 1. An example of multimedia content (the number of media $M = 2$, the number of entities in the first medium $D_1 = 4$, and the number of entities in the second medium $D_2 = 3$).

This chapter is organized as follows. Section 2 mentions the conventional access control scheme for multimedia content and summarizes the requirements for access control. The new scheme is described in Section 3 and Section 4, and is analyzed in Section 5. Finally, conclusions are drawn in Section 6.

2. Access control for multimedia content

This section briefly describes the conventional access control scheme for multimedia content (11), and summarizes the requirements for access control to clarify the aim of this work.

2.1 Conventional scheme (11)

The conventional scheme (11) assumes that multimedia content consists of M different media (image, video, audio, text, and so on), in each of which a scalable hierarchy (image/video resolution, frame rate, audio quality, etc) exists; In the text medium, the appearing order of paragraphs has its own meaning, and it is referred to as a *semantic* hierarchy. The scheme uses a symmetric encryption technique.

For a particular multimedia content consisting of M different media, this scheme manages M keys. Figure 1 shows an example of multimedia content where $M = 2$. For the m-th medium where $m = 1, 2, \ldots, M$, all encryption keys are derived from managed key K_m^1. Encryption keys $K_m^{d_m}$'s are derived through an ordinary hash chain (OHC) (9) as

$$K_m^{d_m} = H^{d_m - 1}\left(K_m^1\right), \; d_m = 2, 3, \ldots, D_m + 1, \tag{1}$$

where $H^{\alpha}(\beta)$ represents a cryptographic one-way hash function $H(\cdot)$ applied to β recursively α times, and D_m represents the number of entities in the medium, i.e., the depth of the scalable hierarchy. The d_m-th entity in the m-th medium is encrypted with its corresponding encryption key, $K_m^{d_m}$.

Each user receives different set of M decryption keys due to which media/entities the user is allowed to access to, and also receives the common encrypted multimedia content. From the delivered keys, the user derives decryption keys $K_m^{\delta_m}$'s for accessible entities in accessible media through the same OHC as used in the encryption key derivation. That is,

$$K_m^{\delta_m} = H^{\delta_m - \Delta_m}\left(K_m^{\Delta_m}\right), \ \delta_m = \Delta_m + 1, \Delta_m + 2, \ldots, D_m, \tag{2}$$

where $K_m^{\Delta_m}$ is the delivered key for the m-th medium. It is noted that decryption keys $K_m^{\delta_m}$'s are the same as encryption keys $K_m^{d_m}$'s. By using Δ_m decryption keys, the user decrypts Δ_m entities from the first entity to the Δ_m-th entity.

A user who receives $K_m^{D_m+1}$ cannot access any entities in the m-th medium, because one-way property of $H(\cdot)$ prevents the user to derive any other valid keys for the m-th medium of the multimedia content. The conventional scheme introduced this *unusable key* concept in order to cope with medium-based access control.

2.2 Requirements

We describe three requirements for access control of multimedia content, i.e.,

- reduction of managed keys and delivered keys,
- protection of managed key,
- collusion attack resilience.

As mentioned in the previous section, the conventional scheme (11) encrypts entities in a medium independently of those in other media. This feature of the conventional scheme requires to manage and deliver the same number of keys as media in the multimedia content, i.e., M keys are managed and M keys are delivered to a user for the multimedia content consisting of M different media. This conventional scheme employs a simple OHC (9) rather than cross-way hash trees (10).

The conventional scheme (11) delivers the managed keys to users who are allowed to access at least one medium at the highest quality. The managed keys should not be delivered to any users and should be protected against key leakage.

A collusion attack is made by multiple users to obtain multimedia content with higher quality than that allowed by their access rights. For example, when a user who is allowed to display images and another user who is allowed to read text paragraphs share their keys, they can also obtain audio coupled with images and text paragraphs. Access control schemes must be resilient to collusion attacks.

In the next section, we introduce a new access control scheme for multimedia content. This scheme manages only one key for a particular multimedia content and delivers less key to each user than the conventional method (11), regardless of which media/entities in the content the user can access. The single managed key is not delivered to any user. It is also resistant to collusion attack.

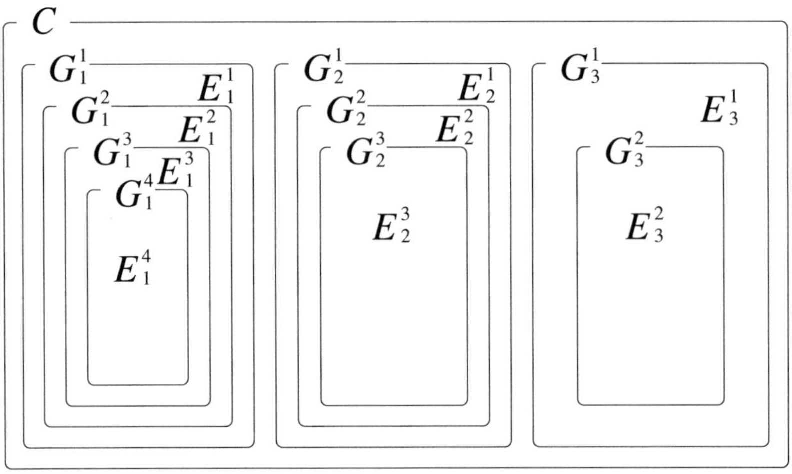

Fig. 2. An example of multimedia content conceptual diagram with a scalable hierarchy in each medium (the number of media $M = 3$ and the depths of each scalable hierarchy $D_1 = 4$, $D_2 = 3$, and $D_3 = 2$).

3. Access control for multimedia content with multiple hierarchies (12)

First, we assume that multimedia content C consists of M media and each medium has a hierarchical structure;

$$C = \left\{G_1^1, G_2^1, \ldots, G_m^1, \ldots, G_M^1\right\}, \tag{3}$$

$$G_m^1 \supset G_m^2 \supset G_m^3 \supset \cdots \supset G_m^{D_m}, \quad m = 1, 2, \ldots, M, \tag{4}$$

where G_m^1 represents the m-th medium itself, and D_m is the depth of the scalable hierarchy in the m-th medium. The complementary sets represent entities in medium G_m^1 as

$$E_m^{d_m} = G_m^{d_m} - G_m^{d_m+1}, \quad d_m = 1, 2, \ldots, D_m - 1, \tag{5}$$

and

$$E_m^{D_m} = G_m^{D_m}. \tag{6}$$

This scheme derives keys from single managed key K_C and encrypts multimedia content C by encrypting $E_m^{d_m}$'s using those corresponding keys.

Fig. 2 shows an example conceptual diagram of the assumed multimedia content, where multimedia content C consists of three media, G_1^1, G_2^1, and G_3^1, i.e., $M = 3$, and the depths of each scalable hierarchy in medium G_m^1 are four, three, and two ($D_1 = 4$, $D_2 = 3$, and $D_3 = 2$), respectively, i.e.,

$$G_1^1 \supset G_1^2 \supset G_1^3 \supset G_1^4, \tag{7}$$

$$G_2^1 \supset G_2^2 \supset G_2^3, \tag{8}$$

$$G_3^1 \supset G_3^2. \tag{9}$$

$E_m^{d_m}$'s are entities in medium G_m^1.

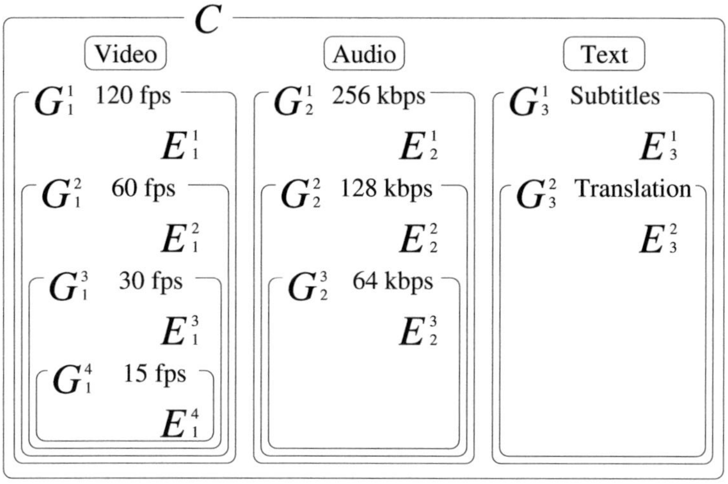

Fig. 3. A practical example of multimedia content with a scalable hierarchy in each medium (the number of media $M = 3$ and the depths of each scalable hierarchy $D_1 = 4$, $D_2 = 3$, and $D_3 = 2$).

For easy understanding, more practical example of Fig. 2 is given in Fig. 3. Multimedia content C in Fig. 3 consists of video G_1^1, audio G_2^1, and text G_3^1, i.e., $M = 3$, and each medium has a scalable hierarchy, whose depths are four, three, and two, i.e., $D_1 = 4$, $D_2 = 3$, and $D_3 = 2$, respectively.

3.1 Key derivation using a MHC

In the example based on Fig. 3, access control is provided based not only on media, but also on each scalable hierarchy in each medium. Keys for encryption are derived as shown in Fig. 4, and each key is used to encrypt and decrypt the corresponding entity. For example, $K_{E_1^1}$ is a key for entity E_1^1 which represents video frames decoded only at 120 frames per second (fps). $K_{E_1^2}$, $K_{E_1^3}$, and $K_{E_1^4}$ are similarly keys for E_1^2, E_1^3, and E_1^4, respectively. $K_{E_2^{d_2}}$ and $K_{E_3^{d_3}}$ are also keys for audio $E_2^{d_2}$ and text $E_3^{d_3}$ ($d_2 = 1,2,3$, $d_3 = 1,2$), respectively. It is noted that key K_C is the single managed key.

Firstly, key $K_{E_1^0}$ is derived from K_C as

$$K_{E_1^0} = H(K_C), \tag{10}$$

where $H(\cdot)$ is a cryptographic one-way hash function. Similarly, keys $K_{E_m^{d_m}}$'s are derived by

$$K_{E_m^{d_m}} = H^{d_m}\left(K_{E_m^0}\right),$$
$$d_m = 1,2,\ldots,D_m, \quad m = 1,2,3, \tag{11}$$

where keys $K_{E_2^0}$ and $K_{E_3^0}$ are given in the next paragraph. Eq. (11) represents OHCs (9), and the OHCs are shown with solid arrows in Fig. 4.

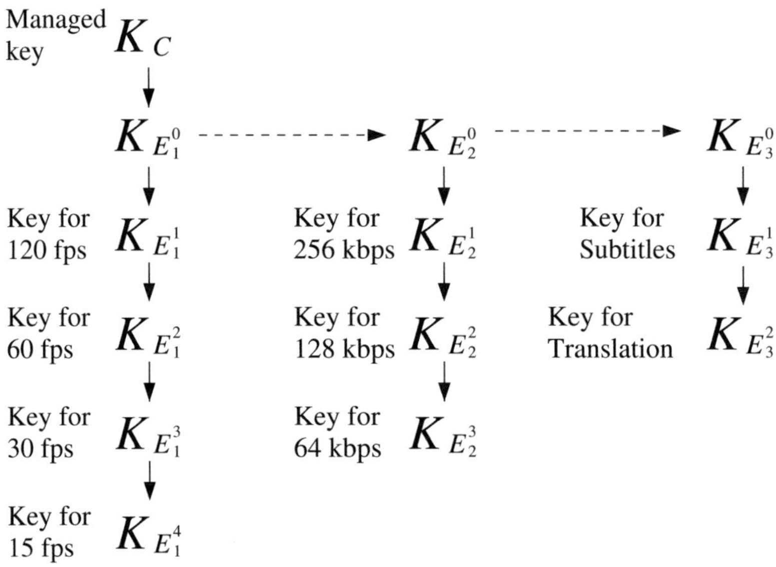

Fig. 4. Key derivation to control access to the multimedia content shown in Fig. 3. Solid arrows represent OHCs and dashed arrows represent a MHC.

Meanwhile, keys $K_{E_2^0}$ and $K_{E_3^0}$ are derived by a MHC. In this example, these keys are given as

$$\begin{aligned} K_{E_m^0} &= H\left(f\left(K_{E_{m-1}^0}, H\left(K_{E_{m-1}^0}\right)\right)\right) \\ &= H\left(f\left(K_{E_{m-1}^0}, K_{E_{m-1}^1}\right)\right), \\ m &= 2, 3, \end{aligned} \tag{12}$$

respectively, where $f(\cdot)$ is a function with two inputs and one output in which the length of inputs and output are identical. A bitwise exclusive or (XOR) operation is a simple example of function $f(\cdot)$. As shown in Eq. (12) which represents a MHC introduced in this scheme, keys given previously are repeatedly used to derive another hash chain that is different from the OHC. The MHC is shown with dashed arrows in Fig. 4.

3.2 Encryption and decryption

Each entity $E_m^{d_m}$ is encrypted using each corresponding key $K_{E_m^{d_m}}$, and then, multimedia content C is opened to public.

3.2.1 User allowed to access three media

A user allowed to access the whole multimedia content receives three keys $K_{E_1^1}$, $K_{E_2^1}$, and $K_{E_3^1}$ as shown in Fig. 5 (a). The user derives all keys needed to decrypt all entities, through OHCs. Each user allowed to access three media at arbitrary quality also receives three keys $K_{E_1^{d_1}}$, $K_{E_2^{d_2}}$, and $K_{E_3^{d_3}}$. A user allowed to access each medium at the lowest quality, i.e., video at 15 fps, audio at 64 kbps, and translation data, receives three keys $K_{E_1^4}$, $K_{E_2^3}$, and $K_{E_3^2}$ as shown in Fig. 5 (b). The user cannot, however, derive any keys from his/her delivered keys.

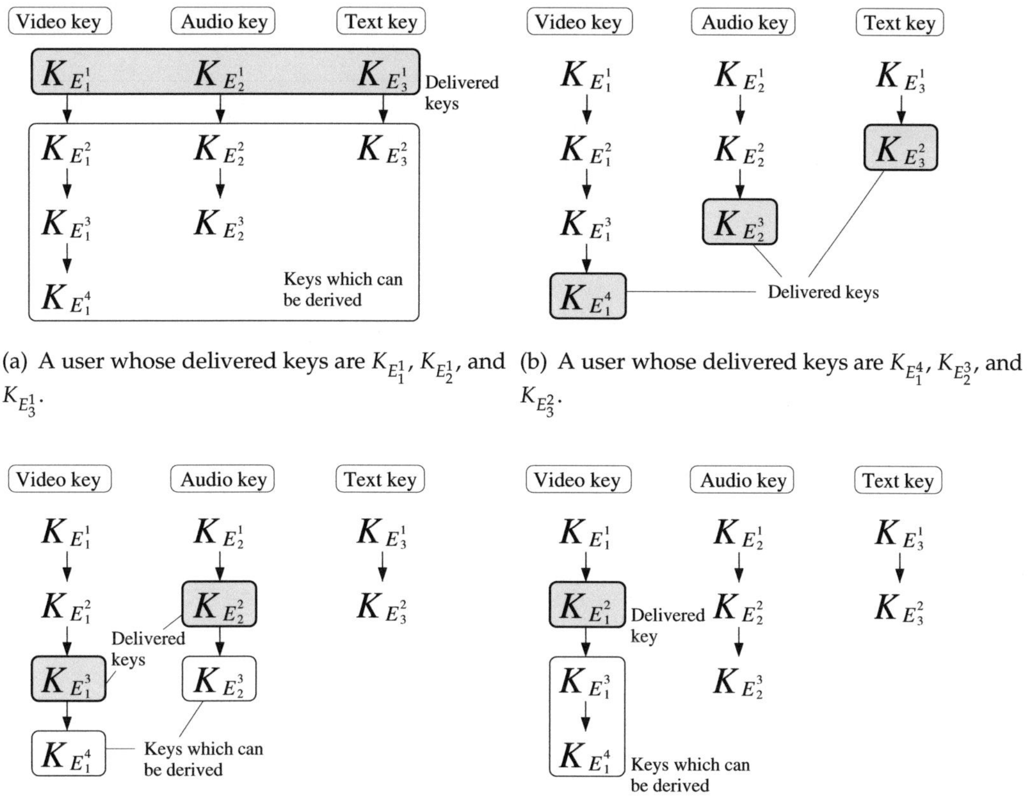

(a) A user whose delivered keys are $K_{E_1^1}$, $K_{E_2^1}$, and $K_{E_3^1}$.

(b) A user whose delivered keys are $K_{E_1^4}$, $K_{E_2^3}$, and $K_{E_3^2}$.

(c) A user whose delivered keys are $K_{E_1^3}$ and $K_{E_2^2}$.

(d) A user whose delivered key is $K_{E_1^2}$.

Fig. 5. Delivered keys and derived keys for each user.

3.2.2 User allowed to access two media

Fig. 5 (c) shows an example user allowed to access two of the three media. In this example, the user can access video at 30 fps and audio at 128 kbps. The user receives two keys $K_{E_1^3}$ and $K_{E_2^2}$, and derives keys $K_{E_1^4}$ for video and $K_{E_2^3}$ for audio, respectively.

3.2.3 User allowed to access a single medium

If a user can access only movie at 60 fps, the user receives single key $K_{E_1^2}$ and derives keys $K_{E_1^3}$ and $K_{E_1^4}$ dependently as shown in Fig. 5 (d). Each user who can access a single medium receives single key $K_{E_1^{d_1}}$, $K_{E_2^{d_2}}$, or $K_{E_3^{d_3}}$.

In this scheme, the number of keys which a user receives is equal to the number of media which he/she can decode. Each user uses only OHCs to derive keys from the delivered keys. Keys K_C, $K_{E_1^0}$, $K_{E_2^0}$, and $K_{E_3^0}$ are not delivered to any user.

3.3 Features

Three main features of the access control scheme are briefly summarized here. They have satisfied with the requirements described in Section 2.2.

This scheme, introducing a MHC, has reduced the number of managed keys to one. The number of delivered keys is less than the conventional scheme (11) which manages and delivers the same number of keys as media in the multimedia content.

Each key for each entity is derived from the single managed key. The managed key is not delivered to any user.

The scheme using a MHC can prevent malicious users to collude to decode multimedia content at higher quality than that allowed by their access rights. As shown in Fig. 5, although keys are derived from delivered keys through OHCs, the OHCs are isolated from each other. This structure provides collusion attack resilience.

It is noted that any arbitrary function and key combination can be used for a MHC. In addition, it is noted that any arbitrary key assignment can be used to properly control access to the multimedia content.

4. Access control for multimedia content with a single hierarchy (13)

In this section, we assume that multimedia content C consists of M media and only medium G_1^1 has a hierarchical structure which the depth is D_1, as

$$C = \left\{ G_1^1, G_2^1, \ldots, G_m^1, \ldots, G_M^1 \right\}, \tag{13}$$

$$G_1^1 \supset G_1^2 \supset G_1^3 \supset \cdots \supset G_1^{D_1}. \tag{14}$$

This scheme derives keys from single managed key K_C and encrypts multimedia content C by encrypting entities $E_m^{d_m}$'s using those corresponding keys $K_{E_m^{d_m}}$'s. In addition, each user receives only a single key regardless of his/her access right.

Fig. 6 shows an example conceptual diagram of the assumed multimedia content, where multimedia content C consists of three media, G_1^1, G_2^1, and G_3^1, i.e., $M = 3$, and the depth of the scalable hierarchy in medium G_1^1 is four ($D_1 = 4$), i.e.,

$$G_1^1 \supset G_1^2 \supset G_1^3 \supset G_1^4. \tag{15}$$

E_1^1, E_1^2, E_1^3, and E_1^4 are entities in medium G_1^1. More practical example is given in Fig. 7. Multimedia content C in Fig. 7 consists of video, audio, and text, i.e., $M = 3$, and video is four-tiered, i.e., $D_1 = 4$, in terms of frame rates. In this example, G_1^1 is video, and it is playable in several frame rates; 120, 60, 30, and 15 fps.

4.1 Key derivation using MHCs

For multimedia content C shown in Fig. 7, keys for encryption are derived as shown in Fig. 8, and each key is used to encrypt and decrypt the corresponding medium/entity. $K_{E_1^1}$ is a key for entity E_1^1 which represents video frames decoded only at 120 fps. $K_{E_1^2}$, $K_{E_1^3}$, and $K_{E_1^4}$ are

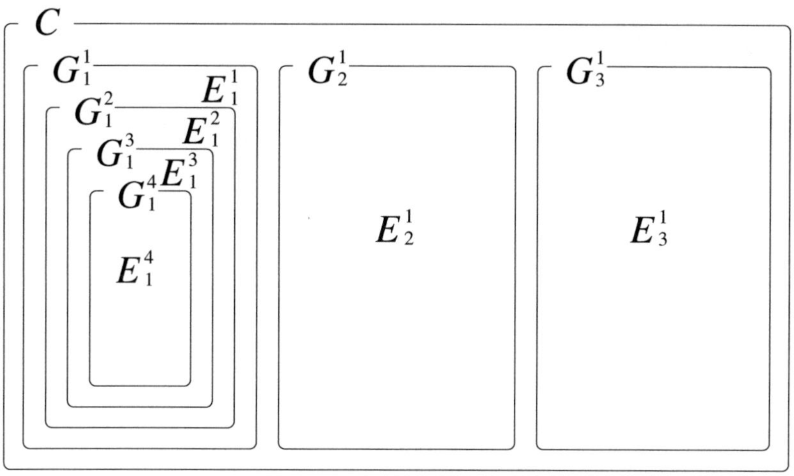

Fig. 6. An example of multimedia content conceptual diagram with a scalable hierarchy in the first medium (the number of media $M = 3$ and the depth of the scalable hierarchy $D_1 = 4$).

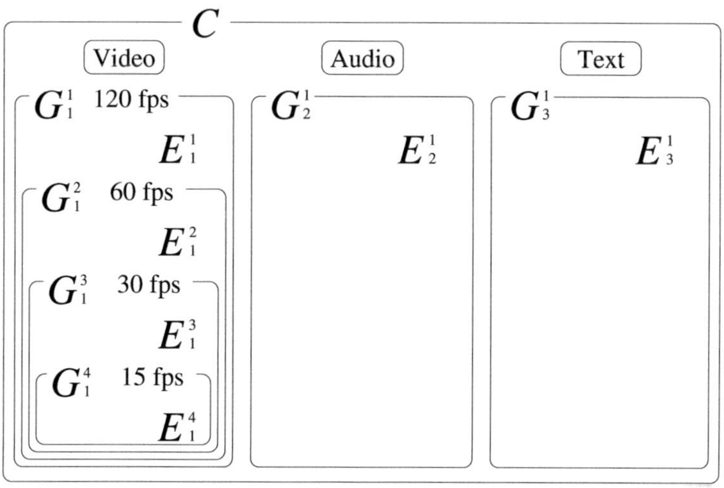

Fig. 7. A practical example of multimedia content with a scalable hierarchy in the first medium (the number of media $M = 3$ and the depth of the scalable hierarchy $D_1 = 4$).

similarly keys for E_1^2, E_1^3, and E_1^4, respectively. $K_{E_2^1}$ and $K_{E_3^1}$ are also keys for audio E_2^1 and text E_3^1, respectively. It is noted that key K_C is the single managed key.

Firstly, keys $K_{E_1^{d_1}}$ are derived from the managed key K_C as

$$K_{E_1^{d_1}} = H^{d_1}(K_C), \quad d_1 = 1, 2, \ldots, D_1, \tag{16}$$

where $H(\cdot)$ is a cryptographic one-way hash function. Eq. (16) represents an OHC (9), and the OHC is shown with solid arrows in Fig. 8.

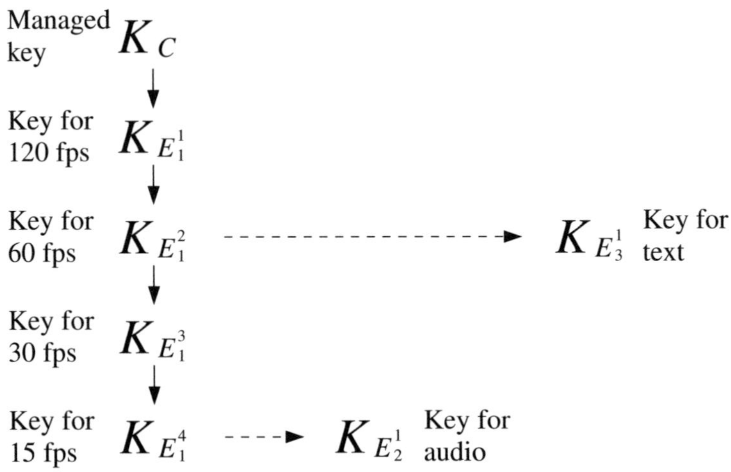

Fig. 8. Key derivation to control access to the multimedia content shown in Fig. 7. All users who are allowed to access video with any frame rates can access audio medium. Users who are allowed to access video with 120 or 60 fps can also view text paragraphs. Solid arrows represent an OHC and dashed arrows represent MHCs.

Meanwhile, keys $K_{E_2^1}$ and $K_{E_3^1}$ are derived by MHCs. In this example, these keys are given as

$$K_{E_2^1} = H\left(f\left(K_{E_1^4}, H\left(K_{E_1^4}\right)\right)\right), \tag{17}$$

$$\begin{aligned} K_{E_3^1} &= H\left(f\left(K_{E_1^2}, H\left(K_{E_1^2}\right)\right)\right) \\ &= H\left(f\left(K_{E_1^2}, K_{E_1^3}\right)\right), \end{aligned} \tag{18}$$

respectively, where $f(\cdot)$ is a function with two inputs and one output in which the inputs are the same length of the output. A simple example of function $f(\cdot)$ is a bitwise exclusive or (XOR) operation. As shown in Eqs. (17) and (18), keys given by Eq. (16) are repeatedly used to derive other hash chains that are different from the OHCs. The MHCs are shown with dashed arrows in Fig. 8.

4.2 Encryption and decryption

Each medium/entity $E_m^{d_m}$ is encrypted using corresponding key $K_{E_m^{d_m}}$, and multimedia content C is opened to public.

4.2.1 User allowed to access video, audio, and text

A user permitted to decode video frames at 120 or 60 fps receives $K_{E_1^1}$ or $K_{E_1^2}$ shown in Figs. 9 (a) and (b). Eq. (16) is the same as

$$K_{E_1^{d_1}} = H\left(K_{E_1^{d_1-1}}\right), \quad d_1 = 2, 3, \ldots, D_1. \tag{19}$$

The user can obtain $K_{E_1^{d_1}}$ $(d_1 = 2, 3, 4)$ using an OHC in Eq. (19).

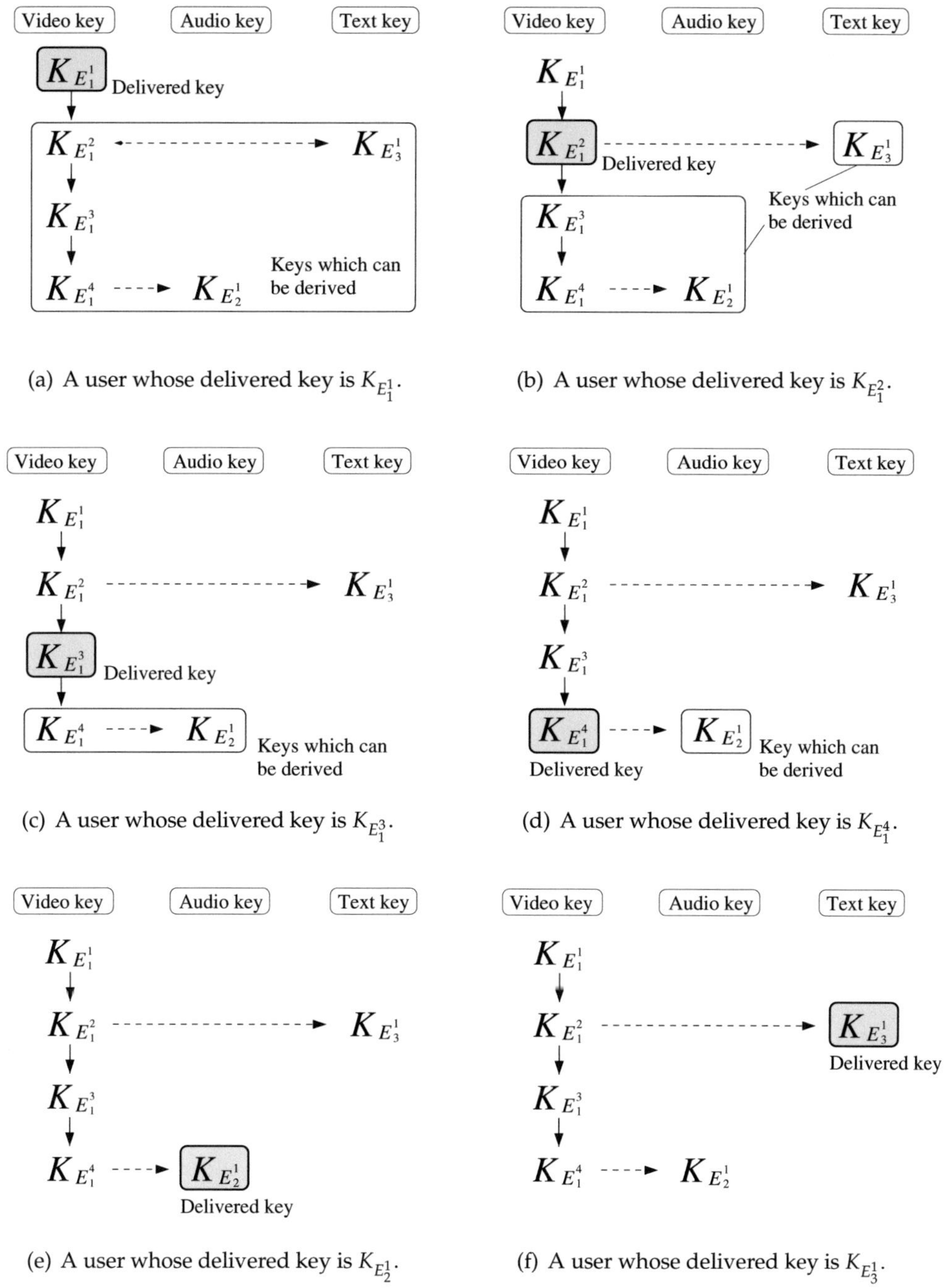

(a) A user whose delivered key is $K_{E_1^1}$.

(b) A user whose delivered key is $K_{E_1^2}$.

(c) A user whose delivered key is $K_{E_1^3}$.

(d) A user whose delivered key is $K_{E_1^4}$.

(e) A user whose delivered key is $K_{E_2^1}$.

(f) A user whose delivered key is $K_{E_3^1}$.

Fig. 9. A single delivered key and derived keys for each user.

As shown in Fig. 8, keys $K_{E_2^1}$ and $K_{E_3^1}$ for audio E_2^1 and text E_3^1 are derived from $K_{E_1^4}$ and $K_{E_1^2}$, respectively, using MHCs in Eqs. (17) and (18). Thus the user can also obtain $K_{E_2^1}$ and $K_{E_3^1}$ and play audio and read text in addition to watch the video.

4.2.2 User allowed to access video and audio

A user can access video frames decoded at 30 or 15 fps receives $K_{E_1^3}$ or $K_{E_1^4}$ as shown in Figs. 9 (c) and (d). The user obtains $K_{E_1^4}$, but cannot derive $K_{E_1^2}$. Thus the user cannot derive $K_{E_3^1}$ for text E_3^1, and can derive only $K_{E_2^1}$ for audio E_2^1 by Eq. (17) and play audio as well as the video.

4.2.3 User allowed to access audio

A user allowed to access only audio E_2^1 receives $K_{E_2^1}$ as shown in Fig. 9 (e). $K_{E_2^1}$ is a key derived by Eq. (17). Any keys cannot be derived from $K_{E_2^1}$.

4.2.4 User allowed to access text

A user allowed to access only text E_3^1 receives $K_{E_3^1}$ as shown in Fig. 9 (f). $K_{E_3^1}$ is a key derived by Eq. (18). $K_{E_3^1}$ can derive no other key.

4.3 Features

The following three features of the access control scheme have satisfied the requirements described in Section 2.2.

By introducing MHCs, the number of managed keys and that of delivered keys are reduces to one, respectively. In contrast, the conventional scheme (11) manages and delivers the same number of keys as media.

The single managed key is the basis of each key for each entity/medium. Any user do not receive the managed key.

This scheme also prevents collusion attacks. Even if any of the users shown in Fig. 9 collude to access multimedia content at higher quality than that allowed by their access rights, they cannot access the content beyond their rights.

It is noted that any arbitrary function and key combination can be used for a MHC. In addition, it is noted that any arbitrary key assignment can be used to properly control access to the multimedia content.

5. Evaluation

The MHC-based scheme is evaluated by comparing with the conventional scheme (11) which uses only OHCs. Evaluation is given in terms of the number of managed keys and that of delivered keys, protection of managed keys, and collusion attack resilience.

Table 1 shows the results of comparisons. The MHC-based scheme manages only a single key regardless of both the number of media and the depths of each scalable hierarchy in each medium, whilst the conventional scheme must manage M keys, which is the same number

	MHC-based	Conventional (11) (OHC-based)
The number of managed keys	1	M
The number of delivered keys	between 1 and M	M
Protection of managed keys	Yes	No
Collusion attack resilience	Yes	Yes

Table 1. Comparisons in terms of the number of managed keys and that of delivered keys, protection of managed keys, and collusion attack resilience.

of media in the multimedia content. The MHC-based scheme delivers the same number of keys as accessible media, while the conventional scheme should deliver M keys in any case. Particularly, when only a single medium has a hierarchical structure, the MHC-based scheme constantly delivers a single key to each user.

The single managed key is not delivered to any user in the MHC-based scheme, whereas the managed keys are delivered to users allowed to access at least one medium at the highest quality in the conventional scheme. The MHC-based scheme is also resilient to collusion attacks as the conventional scheme. The table brings out the effectiveness of the MHC-based scheme.

6. Conclusion

This chapter has introduced a new access control scheme for multimedia content, in which MHCs are employed. The scheme manages only a single key regardless of both the number of media and the depths of each scalable hierarchy in each medium. Each user also receives less keys than the conventional method. Particularly, when a hierarchical structure exists in only one medium, any user receives a single key. The single managed key is not delivered to any user, providing security against key leakage. This scheme also prevents collusion attacks, in which malicious users illegally access the multimedia content at higher quality than that allowed by their access rights.

7. References

[1] B. B. Zhu, M. D. Swanson, and S. Li, "Encryption and authentication for scalable multimedia: current state of the art and challenges," in *Proc. SPIE*, vol.5601, pp.157–170, 2004.

[2] Z. Shahid, M. Chaumont, and W. Puech, "Selective and scalable encryption of enhancement layers for dyadic scalable H.264/AVC by scrambling of scan patterns," in *Proc. IEEE ICIP*, pp.1273–1276, 2009.

[3] Y. Wu, D. Ma, and R.H. Deng, "Progressive protection of JPEG 2000 codestreams," in *Proc. IEEE ICIP*, pp.3447–3450, 2004.

[4] Y. G. Won, T. M. Bae. and Y. M. Ro, "Scalable protection and access control in full scalable video coding," in *Proc. IEEE IWDW*, vol.4283 of *LNCS*, pp.407–421, 2006.

[5] S. Imaizumi, M. Fujiyoshi, Y. Abe, and H. Kiya, "Collusion attack-resilient hierarchical encryption of JPEG 2000 codestreams with scalable access control," in *Proc. IEEE ICIP*, pp.II–137–II–140, 2007.

[6] S. Imaizumi, M. Fujiyoshi, and H. Kiya, "Efficient collusion attack-free access control for multidimensionally hierarchical scalability content," in *Proc. IEEE ISCAS*, pp.505–508, 2009.

[7] *Information technology — JPEG 2000 image coding system – Part 1: Core coding system.* ISO/IEC 15444–1, 2004.

[8] *Information technology — Coding of audio – Visual objects – Part 2: Visual.* ISO/IEC 14496–2, 2004.

[9] L. Lamport, "Password authentication with insecure communication," *Communications of the ACM*, vol.24, no.11, pp.770–772, 1981.

[10] M. Joye and S. M. Yen, "One-way cross-trees and their applications," in *Proc. IACR PKC*, vol.2274 of *LNCS*, pp.355–358, 2002.

[11] M. Fujiyoshi, W. Saitou, O. Watanabe, and H. Kiya, "Hierarchical encryption of multimedia contents for access control," in *Proc. IEEE ICIP*, pp.1977–1980, 2006.

[12] S. Imaizumi, M. Fujiyoshi, H. Kiya, N. Aoki, H. Kobayashi, "Derivation Scheme for Hierarchical Access Control to Multimedia Content," in *Proc. International Workshop on Advanced Image Technology*, 2012, to be published.

[13] S. Imaizumi, M. Fujiyoshi, and H. Kiya, "An efficient access control method for composite multimedia content," *IEICE Electronics Express*, vol.7, no.20, pp.1534–1538, 2010.

5

Multimedia Security: A Survey of Chaos-Based Encryption Technology

Zhaopin Su, Guofu Zhang and Jianguo Jiang
School of Computer and Information, Hefei University of Technology
China

1. Introduction

In the recent years, with the development of network and multimedia technology, multimedia data, especially image, audio and video data, is used more and more widely in human society. Some multimedia data, including entertainment, politics, economics, militaries, industries, education etc, are necessary to be protected by providing confidentiality, integrity, and ownership or identity. In this regard, to protect multimedia contents, cryptology, which appears to be an effective way for information security, has been employed in many practical applications.

However, number theory or algebraic concepts based traditional ciphers, such as Data Encryption Standard (DES) (Tuchman, 1997), Advanced Encryption Standard (AES) (Zeghid et al., 1996), International Data Encryption Algorithm (IDEA) (Dang & Chau, 2000), and the algorithm developed by Rivest, Shamir and Adleman (RSA) (Cormen et al., 2001), most of which are used for text or binary data, appear not to be ideal for multimedia applications, and the reasons are:

(1) As multimedia data, especially image and video data, are usually very large-sized and bulky, encrypting such bulky data with the traditional ciphers incurs significant overhead, and it is too expensive for real-time multimedia applications, such as video conference, image surveillance, which require real-time operations, such as displaying, cutting, copying, bit-rate control or recompression.

(2) In the case of digital image, adjacent pixels often have similar gray-scale values and strong correlations, or image blocks have similar patterns, while for video data, consecutive frames are similar and most likely only few pixels would differ from frame to frame. Such an extremely high data redundancy of multimedia makes the conventional ciphers fail to obscure all visible information (Furht et al., 2005).

(3) For many real-life multimedia applications, it is very important that very light encryption should be made to preserve some perceptual information. For example, video pay-per-view system (Ballesté, 2004) in which a degraded but visible content could potentially influence a consumer to order certain paid services. This is impossible to achieve with traditional ciphers alone, which most likely degrade the data to a perceptually unrecognizable content.

Very recently, an increasing attention has been devoted to the usage of chaotic theory to implement the encryption process (Alligood et al., 1997; Alvarez et al., 2004; Devaney, 2003; He et al., 2010; Solak, 2005; Yang et al., 1997). The main advantage of these encryptions lies in the observation that a chaotic signal looks like noise for non-authorized users ignoring the mechanism for generating it. Secondly, time evolution of the chaotic signal strongly depends on the initial conditions and the control parameters of the generating functions: slight variations in these quantities yield quite different time evolutions. In other words, this means that initial states and control parameters can be efficiently used as keys in an encryption system. What's more, generating of chaotic signal is often of low cost, which makes it suitable for the encryption of large bulky data (Alvarez & Li, 2006).

Due to these recognized potential benefits, chaos-based multimedia encryption algorithms are of high interest up to now, and have made great progress (Chen et al., 2004; Gao et al., 2006; Li et al., 2002; Lian, 2009; Su et al., 2010; Wang et al., 2011). This chapter focuses on a survey of chaos-based encryption algorithms for image, video and audio respectively.

The organization of this chapter is as follows. In Section 1, backgrounds of chaos-based multimedia encryption technology are first given. Section 2 describes some special requirements of multimedia encryption. To evaluate the performance of multimedia encryption algorithms, Section 3 gives some generic evaluation methods. In Section 4, 5 and 6, the existing chaos-based encryption algorithms are analyzed for image, video and audio, respectively. The last section concludes the chapter.

2. Requirements of multimedia encryption

Due to special characteristics of multimedia data, such as large data volumes, high redundancy, interactive operations, and requires real-time responses, sometimes multimedia applications have their own requirements like security, invariance of compression ratio, format compliance, transmission error tolerance, demand of real-time. In this section, some special requirements of multimedia encryption are summarized.

2.1 Security

For multimedia encryption, security is the primary requirement, thus the usage of chaotic maps should guarantee the security of a multimedia datum. Generally speaking, an encryption algorithm is regarded as secure if the cost for cracking it is no smaller than the one paid for the authorization of video content. For example, in broadcasting, the news may be of no value after an hour. Thus, if the attacker can not break the encryption algorithm during an hour, then the encryption algorithm may be regarded as secure in this application (Lian et al., 2008). Security of an encryption usually consists of its perceptual security, its key space, key sensitivity, and its ability against potential attacks.

(1) Perceptual security: when we use a method to encrypt a multimedia datum, for example an image, if the encrypted image is not perceptual recognized, the encryption is secure in perception.

(2) Key space: it is generally defined as the number of encryption keys that are available in the cryptosystem. Assume k_i denotes a key and K represents a finite set of possible keys, the key space can be expressed as $K = \{k_1, k_2, ..., k_r\}$, where r is the number of key. For

chaos-based encryptions, the chaotic sequence generator should produce chaotic ciphers with good randomness, which can be tested by long period, large linear complexity, randomness and proper order of correlation immunity (Rueppel, 1986).

(3) Key sensitivity: an ideal multimedia encryption should be sensitive with respect to the secret key i.e. the change of a single bit in the secret key should produce a completely different encrypted result, which is called key sensitivity. Generally, key sensitivity of a chaotic cipher refers to the initial states sensitivity and control parameters sensitivity of chaotic map.

(4) Potential attacks: here, we just introduce the common used attacks as following:
   - Ciphertext-only attack: it is an attack with an attempt to decrypt ciphertext when only the ciphertext itself is available. The opponent attempts to recover the corresponding plaintext or the encryption key.
   - Known-plaintext attack: when having access to the ciphertext and an associated piece of plaintext, the opponent attempts to recover the key.
   - Chosen-plaintext attack: it is an attack where the cryptanalyst is able to choose his own plaintext, feed it into the cipher, and analyze the corresponding ciphertext.
   - Brute-force attack: it is a form of attack in which each possible key is tried until the success key is obtained. To make brute-force attack infeasible, the size of key space should be large enough.
   - Differential attack: it is a chosen-plaintext attack relying on the analysis of the evolution of the differences between two plaintexts.

Therefore, a secure encryption algorithm should be secure in perception, have large key space, high key sensitivity, and resist potential attacks.

2.2 Other requirements

Besides security, there are many other requirements as follows.

(1) Computational complexity: compared with texts, multimedia data capacity is horrendously large. For example, a common 16-bit true-color image of 512-pixel height and 512-pixel width occupies $512 \times 512 \times 16/8 = 512KB$ in space. Thus, a one-second motion picture will reach up to about 13 MB. If a cryptographic system encrypts all of the multimedia data bits equally in importance, the computational complexity may be high, which has often proved unnecessary. As human vision or audition has high robustness to image or audio degradation and noise, only encrypting those data bits tied with intelligibility can efficiently accomplish multimedia protection with low computational complexity.

(2) Invariance of compression ratio: an encryption algorithm with invariance of compression ratio can preserve the size of a multimedia datum, and maintain the same storage space or transmission bandwidth. However, in some practical applications, the encryption stage is allowed to slightly increase the size of a bit stream. In this case, multimedia encryption algorithms should not change compression ratio or at least keep the changes in a small range (Su et al., 2011).

(3) Format compliance: due to the huge amount of multimedia data and their very high redundancy, the data are often encoded or compressed before transmission, which produces the data streams with some format information. The format information will be used by the decoder to recover the multimedia data successfully. Thus, directly encrypting multimedia data as ordinary data will make file format conversion impossible. It is desired that the encryption algorithm preserves the multimedia format. This property of an encryption algorithm is often called format compliance. Generally, encrypting the data except the format information will keep the multimedia format. This will support some direct operations(decoding, playing, bit-rate conversion, etc.) and improve the error robustness in some extent.

(4) Demand of real-time: real-time performance is often required for many multimedia applications, e.g. video conferencing, image surveillance. However, bulk capacity of multimedia data also makes real-time encryption difficult. Therefore, the main challenge is how to bring reasonable delay of encryption and decryption to meet the requirements of real-time applications.

(5) Multiple levels of security: in some image or video applications, multiple levels of security may be needed for the ability to perform more complex multimedia processing. For example, in video pay-per-view system, only those users who have paid for the service can have access to large-size images or video with high resolution, and the others may be able to get some small-size images or video with low resolution and little business value. Most available cryptographic systems are fully or partially scalable, in the sense that one can choose different security levels. Scalability is usually achieved by allowing variable key sizes or by allowing different number of iterations, or rounds. A higher level of security is achieved with larger key sizes or larger number of rounds.

(6) Transmission error tolerance: since the real-time transport of multimedia data often occurs in noisy environments, which is especially true in the case of wireless channels (Gschwandtner et al., 2007; Lin, Chung & Chen, 2008), the delivered multimedia data is prone to bit errors. So, a perfect encryption algorithm should be insensitive and robust to transmission errors.

3. Evaluation methods of multimedia encryption

Generally speaking, a multimedia encryption algorithm is often evaluated by security analysis, time analysis, compression ratio and error robustness.

3.1 Security analysis

Security of an algorithm is generally evaluated by the perceptual experiments, key space analysis, key sensitivity analysis, and the ability against attacks.

The perceptual experimental result is achieved by a group of comparison between the original multimedia data and the encrypted. Besides, some works decrypt the encrypted data to examine the effects of their algorithms.

Key space can be obtained by analyzing the number of key used in the encryption process. For example, a 20-bit key would have a key space of 2^{20}.

Key sensitivity of a chaotic cipher refers to the initial states sensitivity and control parameters sensitivity of chaotic map. Take image encryption as an example, a typical key sensitivity test is performed according to the following steps:

Step 1. First, an original image is encrypted by using the secret key "K1=0123456789ABCDEF", and the resulting image is referred to as encrypted image A.

Step 2. Then, the same image is encrypted by making the slight modification in the secret key i.e. "K2=1123456789ABCDEF", which changes the least significant bit of K1. The resultant image is referred to as encrypted image B.

Step 3. Finally, the above two encrypted images, encrypted by K1 and K2 respectively, are compared, and cross-correlation curve between the two encrypted images is analyzed.

A good cipher can avoid potential attacks. In general, brute-force attack is analyzed by key apace analysis. Known-plaintext attack and chosen-plaintext attack can be tested by comparing the original data and the decrypted. Differential attack test can be achieved through measuring the percentage p of different pixel numbers (see Equation 1 and Equation 2) between two encrypted images, I_1 and I_2 (the width and height is W and H, respectively), whose corresponding plain-images have only one pixel's difference. And the bigger p is, the stronger the ability of the encryption to resist differential attack.

$$p = \frac{\sum_{i,j} D(i,j)}{W \cdot H} \cdot 100\%, i = 0,1,\cdots,W-1 j = 0,1,\cdots,H-1 \tag{1}$$

$$D(i,j) = \begin{cases} 0, I_1(i,j) = I_2(i,j) \\ 1, \text{otherwise} \end{cases} \tag{2}$$

3.2 Time analysis

The encryption time analysis is measured in the following three manners:

(1) Absolute encryption time: it refers to the assumed time for encrypting a multimedia datum on a certain running platform, and its measuring unit is second.

(2) Relative encryption time ratio: it refers to the time ratio between encryption and compression.

(3) Computation complexity: it depends on the cost of the chaos-based cipher and the multimedia data volumes to be encrypted.

If the computational cost or assumed time of a multimedia encryption scheme is very little compared with their compression, it is considered to be suitable for real-time applications.

3.3 Compression ratio test

In general, the compression ratio is tested by comparing the original compressed data volumes and encrypted and compressed data volumes. Considering that the compression encoder often produces the data stream with a given bit-rate, the compression ratio test may be measured by the video quality under certain bit rate.

The common measurement of image and video quality is $PSNR$ (Peak Signal-to-Noise Ratio) shown as Equation 3 and Equation 4, where B is the sampling frequency, I and I' represent an original $m \times n$ image and the encrypted one, respectively.

$$PSNR = 10 \cdot \log_{10}\left(\frac{(2^B - 1)^2}{MSE}\right) \tag{3}$$

$$MSE = \frac{1}{m \cdot n} \cdot \sum_{i=0}^{m-1}\sum_{j=0}^{n-1}\left[I(i,j) - I'(i,j)\right]^2 \tag{4}$$

The common measurement of audio quality is $segSNR$ (Segmented Signal-to-Noise Ratio) shown as Equation 5, where M is the number of frames in the audio file, $s(i)$ is the ith frame of the original audio, $sn(i)$ is the ith frame of the encrypted audio.

$$segSNR = \frac{10}{M} * \log_{10}\frac{sum[s(i)]^2}{sum[sn(i) - s(i)]^2} \tag{5}$$

From Equation 3, Equation 4 and Equation 5, big $PSNR$ and $segSNR$ would appear to indicate that the encryption has good performance and high security.

3.4 Error-robustness test

If an encryption scheme does not change file format, and a slight change in one pixel does not spread to others, it is called transmission error robustness.

The general test method for error-robustness is analyzing the relationship (usually expressed by a curve) between the quality ($PSNR$ for image and video, $segSNR$ for audio) of the decrypted frames and the number of bit-error happened in the encrypted frames. Besides, error-robustness can be tested through correct decryption of an encrypted data, even if a frame or some bytes are corrupted or lost in its transmission.

4. Chaos-based image encryption algorithms

So far, many chaos-based image encryption methods have been proposed. According to the percentage of the data encrypted, they are divided into full encryption and partial encryption (also called selective encryption). Moreover, with respect to the encryption ciphers, the two encryption methods above can also be further classified into block encryption and stream encryption, where compression-combined encryption and non-compression encryption are discussed according to the relation between compression and encryption.

4.1 Full encryption

In the full encryption scheme shown as Fig.1, image as binary large objects or pixels are encrypted in their entirety. Full encryption can offer a high level of security, effectively prevent unauthorized access, and is widely used nowadays. For image encryption, full encryption is often operated without any compression process. Some algorithms have been proposed based on chaotic block ciphers, and some based on chaotic stream ciphers.

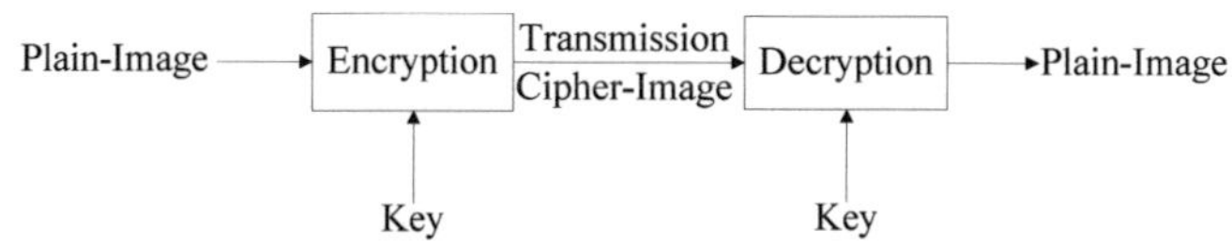

Fig. 1. The process of full encryption for a image

4.1.1 Algorithms based on chaotic block ciphers

A chaotic map based chaotic block cipher is a type of symmetric-key encryption algorithm that transforms a fixed-length group of plain-text bits into a group of ciphertext bits of the same length. The fixed-length group of bits is called a block, and the fixed length is the block size. A block cipher encryption algorithm for image might take (for example) a 128-bit block of plain-image as input, and output a corresponding 128-bit block of cipher-image, that is, a plain-image is encrypted block by block. Many algorithms of this kind have been proposed in (Cokal & Solak, 2009; Fridrich, 1997; Guan et al., 2005; Lian et al., 2005a;b; Mao et al., 2004; Salleh et al., 2003; Wang et al., 2011; Xiao et al., 2009). In this section, we just discuss the representative ones.

Fridrich (Fridrich, 1997) presented a symmetric block encryption technique based on two-dimensional chaotic map, such as the standard map, cat map and baker map shown in Equation 6, Equation 7 and Equation 8 (Lian et al., 2005b) (henceforth called B2CP). The B2CP, shown in Fig.2, consists of two parts: chaotic confusion and pixel diffusion, where the former process permutes a plain-Standard image with a two-dimensional chaotic map, and the latter process changes the value of each pixel one by one. In the confusion process, the parameters of the chaotic map serve as the confusion key. In addition, in the diffusion process, such parameters as the initial value or control parameter of the diffusion function serve as the diffusion key. However, security analysis are not efficiently given in their work. Lian et al (Lian et al., 2005b) studied the performance of Fridrich's algorithm and its security against statistical attack, known-plaintext attack, select-plaintext attack, and so on. Furthermore, they proposed some enhancement means to improve the focused cryptosystem, and gave some advices to select suitable chaotic map, diffusion function and iteration time.

$$\begin{cases} x_{j+1} = (x_j + y_j) \bmod N \\ y_{j+1} = (y_j + k \sin \frac{x_{j+1}N}{2\pi}) \bmod N \end{cases} \tag{6}$$

$$\begin{bmatrix} x_{j+1} \\ y_{j+1} \end{bmatrix} = \begin{bmatrix} 1 & u \\ v & uv+1 \end{bmatrix} \begin{bmatrix} x_j \\ y_j \end{bmatrix} (\bmod N) \tag{7}$$

$$\begin{cases} x_{j+1} = \frac{N}{k_i}(x_j - N_i) + y_j \bmod \frac{N}{k_i} \\ y_{j+1} = \frac{k_i}{N}(y_j - y_j \bmod \frac{N}{k_i}) + N_i \end{cases} \text{with} \begin{cases} k_1 + k_2 + \cdots + k_t = N \\ N_i = k_1 + k_2 + \cdots + k_{i-1} \\ N_i \le x_j < N_i + k_i \\ 0 \le y_j \le N \end{cases} \tag{8}$$

Mao et al (Mao et al., 2004) proposed a three-dimensional chaotic baker map based image encryption scheme (henceforth called BCBP), which contains confusion and diffusion stage, and aims to obey traditional block cipher's principles. In BCBP (see Fig.3), the standard two-dimensional baker map is first extended to be three-dimensional, and then it is used to speed up image encryption while retaining its high degree of security. Comparing with

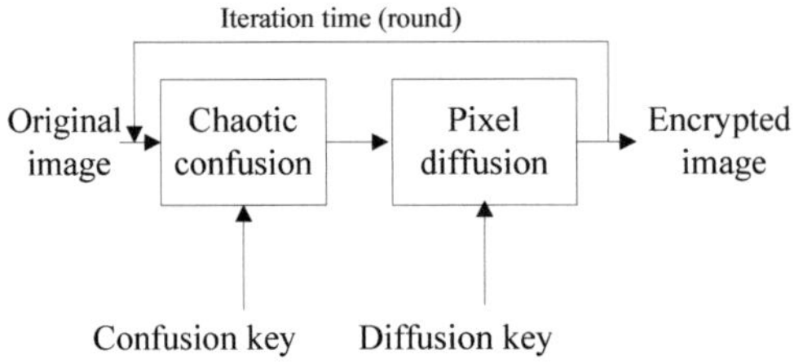

Fig. 2. The image encryption scheme in (Fridrich, 1997)

existing similar schemes which are designed on the two-dimensional baker map, the BCBP has higher security and faster enciphering/deciphering speeds, which makes it a very good candidate for real-time image encryption applications.

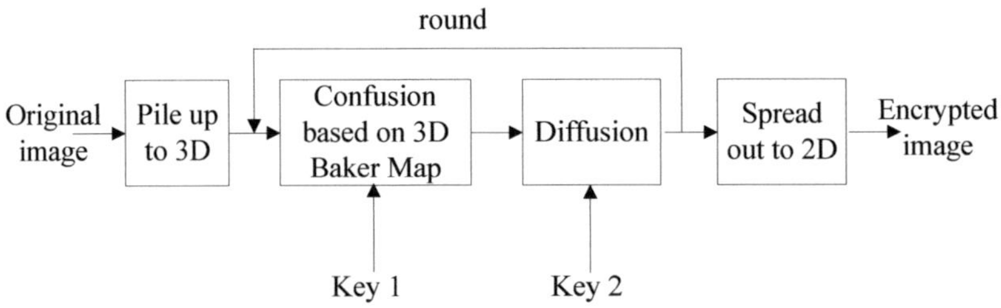

Fig. 3. The image encryption scheme in (Mao et al., 2004)

Lian et al (Lian et al., 2005a) proposed a block image cipher, which is composed of three parts: a chaotic standard map based corner-pixels confusion process which consists of the random-scan process and the chaotic permutation process, a diffusion function realized by a logistic map (Su et al., 2009) (see Equation 9) based diffusion function that spreads changes from one pixel to another, and a chaotic skew tent map (see Equation 10) (Brock, 1986) based key generator, which are used to generate the keys of the confusion process, the random-scan process and the diffusion process, respectively (henceforth called BCDG). The BCDG is of high key-sensitivity, and high security against brute-force attack, statistical attack and differential attack.

$$x_{j+1} = 1 - \mu {x_j}^2 \tag{9}$$

$$x_{j+1} = \begin{cases} \frac{x_j}{h}, 0 < x_j \leq h \\ \frac{1-x_j}{1-h}, h < x_j \leq 1 \end{cases} \tag{10}$$

In the above three algorithms, chaotic confusion and pixel diffusion are operated separately, which makes the encryption algorithms require at least two image-scanning processes. Thus, these algorithms may waste time on image-scanning.

Wang et al (Wang et al., 2011) improved these algorithms and proposed a fast image encryption algorithm with combined permutation and diffusion (henceforth called BCPD). In BCPD (see Fig.4) , the image is first partitioned into blocks of 8×8 pixels. Then, the pseudorandom numbers, generated from the nearest-neighboring coupled-map lattices (NCML) shown as Equation 11 (Kaneko, 1989), are used to change the pixel values in the blocks. Meanwhile, the blocks are relocated according to the lattice values of the NCML. The generation of pseudorandom numbers from NCML can avoid time-consuming operations such as multiplication and conversion from floating points to integers, which greatly increases the encryption speed. In addition, the combination of the permutation and diffusion stages makes the image scan required only once in each encryption round, which also improves the encryption speed. Besides, the algorithm can well resist brute-force attack, statistical attack, differential attack, known/chosen-plaintext attacks.

$$x_{n+1}(i) = (1-\varepsilon)f(x_n(i)) + \varepsilon f(x_n(i+1)) \tag{11}$$

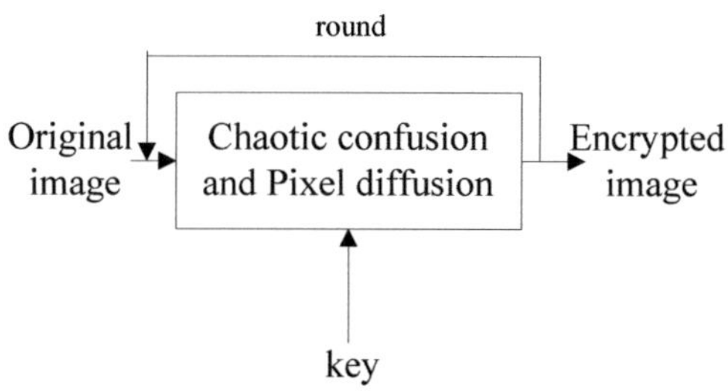

Fig. 4. The image encryption scheme in (Wang et al., 2011)

4.1.2 Algorithms based on chaotic stream ciphers

A chaotic stream cipher is a pseudorandom cipher bit stream (keystream) generated by a chaotic map, which is used to encrypt a plaintext bit by bit (typically by an XOR operation). For image, many algorithms have been proposed (Chen et al., 2004; Gao et al., 2006; Gao & Chen, 2008a;b; Kwok & Tang, 2007; Zhang et al., 2005).

Chen et al (Chen et al., 2004) designed a fast and secure symmetric image encryption scheme based on 3D cat map (see Fig.5) (henceforth called S3CP). In S3CP, 3D cat map is employed to shuffle the positions (and, if desired, grey values as well) of pixels in the image, and a chaotic logistic map based diffusion process among pixels is performed to confuse the relationship between cipher-image and plain-image. Besides, Chen's chaotic system (see Equation 12) (Chen & Ueta, 1999) is employed in key scheming to generate a binary sequence of 128 bits, which guarantees the high security of S3CP.

$$\begin{cases} \dot{x} = a(y-x) \\ \dot{y} = (c-a)x - xz + cy \\ \dot{z} = xy - bz \end{cases} \tag{12}$$

Gao and Chen proposed two image encryption algorithms in (Gao & Chen, 2008a;b)

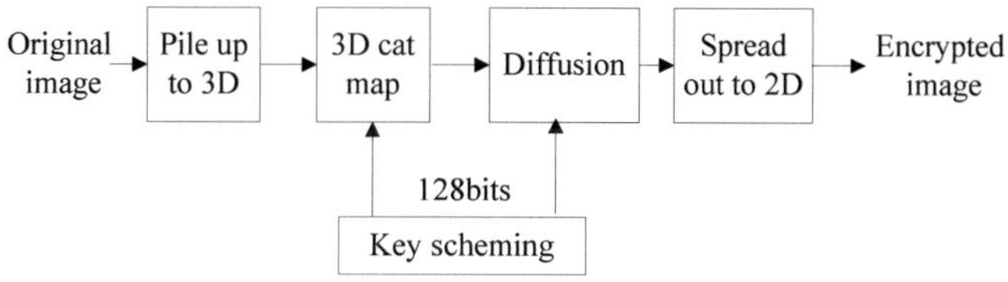

Fig. 5. The image encryption scheme in (Chen et al., 2004)

(henceforth called SGC). In both papers they shuffled the image based on total image shuffling matrix generated by using logistic map, then encrypted the shuffled image with a keystream generated from one or two chaotic systems. The difference between the two encryption schemes is that in (Gao & Chen, 2008a) the keystream is generated by the systems of both Lorenz (see Equation 13) and Chen (see Equation 12) (Chen & Ueta, 1999), while in (Gao & Chen, 2008b) it is generated only by one hyper-chaotic system (see Equation 14). However, researchers in (Rhouma & Belghith, 2008) and (Arroyo & C. Li, 2009) point out that the two algorithms present weakness, and a chosen-plaintext attack and a chosen-ciphertext attack can be done to recover the ciphered-image without any knowledge of the key value.

$$\begin{cases} \frac{dx}{dt} = \sigma(y - x) \\ \frac{dy}{dt} = rx - zx - y \\ \frac{dz}{dt} = xy - bz \end{cases} \tag{13}$$

$$\begin{cases} \dot{x}_1 = a(x_2 - x_1) \\ \dot{x}_2 = -x_1x_3 + dx_1 + cx_2 - x_4 \\ \dot{x}_3 = x_1x_2 - bx_3 \\ \dot{x}_4 = x_1 + k \end{cases} \tag{14}$$

Zhang et al (Zhang et al., 2005) applied discrete exponential chaotic map in image encryption (henceforth called SDEC). In SDEC, shown in Fig.6, a permutation of the pixels of plain-image is designed, and "XOR plus mod" operation is used. Besides, time varied-parameter piece-wise linear map (TVPPLM) (Qiu & He, 2002) is chosen to generate keystream, which may resist statistic attack, differential attack, and linear attack.

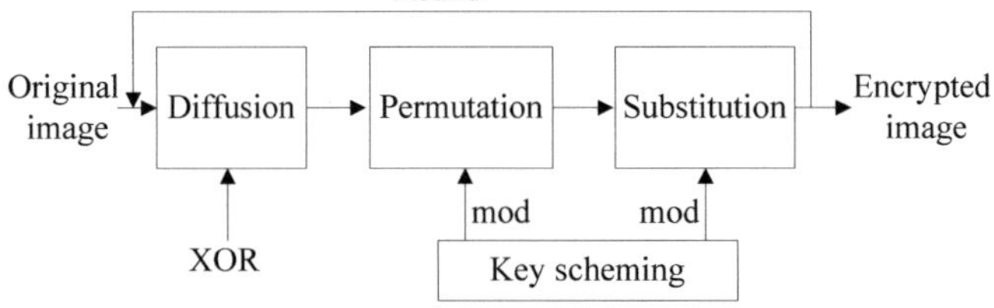

Fig. 6. The image encryption scheme in (Zhang et al., 2005)

Kwok and Tang (Kwok & Tang, 2007) proposed a fast image encryption system based on high-dimensional chaotic maps with finite precision representation (henceforth called SFPR). The core of the encryption system is a pseudo-random keystream generator formed by two chaotic maps (a skewed tent map and high-dimensional cat map), which not only achieves a very fast throughput, but also enhances the randomness even under finite precision implementation. Their experiments show that the SFPR is of high speed, high security, and can be applied in fast real time encryption applications.

Gao et al (Gao et al., 2006) presented an image encryption algorithm based on a new nonlinear chaotic algorithm (see Equation 15) (henceforth called SNCA) which uses power function and tangent function instead of linear function. In addition, the SNCA is a one-time-one password system, that is, it encrypts image data with different keys for different images. Thus the SNCA is secure against statistic attack, brute-force attack, and chosen/known-plaintext attacks.

$$x_{n+1} = \lambda \cdot tg(\alpha x_n)(1 - x_n)^{\beta} \quad (15)$$

Apart from the aforementioned algorithms, there are many other researchers doing the image encryption algorithms based on chaotic stream ciphers, such as Wong (Wong et al., 2009), Tong (Tong & Cui, 2008), Li (Li et al., 2009), Socek (Socek et al., 2005), and so on.

4.2 Partial encryption

Partial encryption, which is also called selective encryption, only encrypts part of the data. As shown in Fig.7, a plain-image is partitioned into two parts: sensitive data and insensitive data. Only the sensitive data are encrypted, and the other is unprotected.

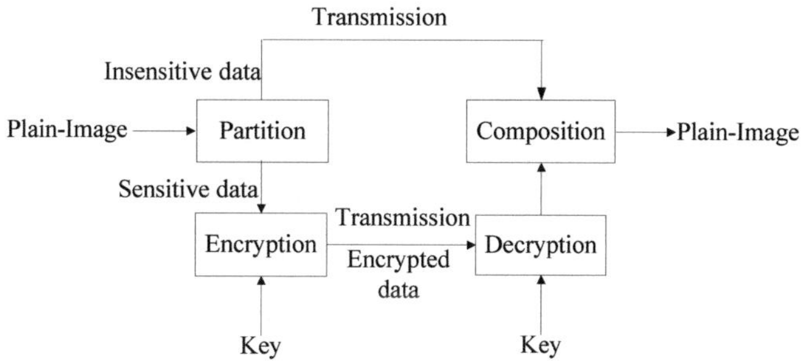

Fig. 7. The process of partial encryption for a image

Considering that image encryption emphasizes on content protection, the focused problem is how to select sensitive data, which is highly sensitive to the understandability of an image. Researchers have proposed many encryption algorithms, such as (Cheng & Li, 2000; Droogenbroeck & Benedett, 2002; Pommer & Uhl, 2003). However, these algorithms are mostly non-chaotic except (El-Khamy et al., 2009; Lian et al., 2004; Lin, Mao & Wang, 2008; Xiang et al., 2007), which are all based on chaotic stream ciphers.

Lian et al (Lian et al., 2004) proposed a partial image encryption algorithm by combining chaotic neural networks with JPEG2000 codec (henceforth called PCNN), which is a compression-combined encryption scheme. In PCNN, sensitive bitstreams, the subband with the lowest frequency, the significant bit-planes, and the cleanup pass, are selected from different subbands, bit-planes or encoding-passes. Besides, they are encrypted by a chaotic sequence in a chained encryption mode. The PCNN is secure against brute-force attack, known-plaintext attack or replacement attack. Additionally, it is time-efficient, does not change compression ratio, supports direct bit-rate control, and keeps the original error-robustness.

Xiang et al (Xiang et al., 2007) proposed a partial gray-level image encryption scheme based on a one-way coupled map lattice (CML, see Equation 16) (henceforth called PCML). The PCML first splits each pixel of image into $n(n < 8)$ significant bits and $(8 - n)$ less significant bits, and then only encrypts the n significant bits by the key-stream generated from CML, which is based on a chaotic skew tent map. The PCML is secure when $n = 4$. However, for an image which has a high correlation between adjacent pixels, the PCML is not secure and can not resist known-plaintext attack. Besides, as PCML is a non-compression encryption, it can not keep compression ratio and format compliance.

$$x_{t+1}^{i} = (1 - \varepsilon)g(x_t^i) + \varepsilon g(x_t^{i-1}) \tag{16}$$

Lin et al (Lin, Mao & Wang, 2008) presented a partial image encryption scheme based on a chaotic skew tent map (henceforth called PSTP). The PSTP integrates chaotic encryption into the process of bit stream generation by an SPIHT (Set Partitioning In Hierarchical Tree) encoder. As structure bits are used for synchronizing the encoding and the decoding in the construction of spatially oriented tree, and more sensitive than the data bits, they are only encrypted so that only few overheads are introduced to the image coder. Meanwhile, the PSTP has good key sensitivity and can well resist the brute-force attack and the known-plaintext attack. However, as PSTP encrypts the format information, it may change the image format.

El-Khamyl et al (El-Khamy et al., 2009) proposed a partial image encryption scheme based on discrete wavelet transform (DWT) and ELKNZ chaotic stream cipher (El-Zein et al., 2008) (henceforth called PDEC, shown in Fig.8). In PDEC, the image first goes through a single-level 2-dimensional discrete wavelet transform (2D DWT) resulting in four coefficient matrices: the approximation (*ca*), horizontal (*ch*), vertical (*cv*), and diagonal (*cd*) matrices. Only *ca* matrix, as the lowest frequency sub-band of the image, is encrypted using the ELKNZ cipher, and the other sub-bands ch, cv, cd are scrambled. The encrypted *ca* matrix and the scrambled ch, cv, cd matrices then undergo 2D inverse discrete wavelet transform (2D IDWT) to produce the encrypted image. The PDEC can provide complete perceptual encryption in the spatial and transform domains, and it is secure against known/chosen plaintext attacks.

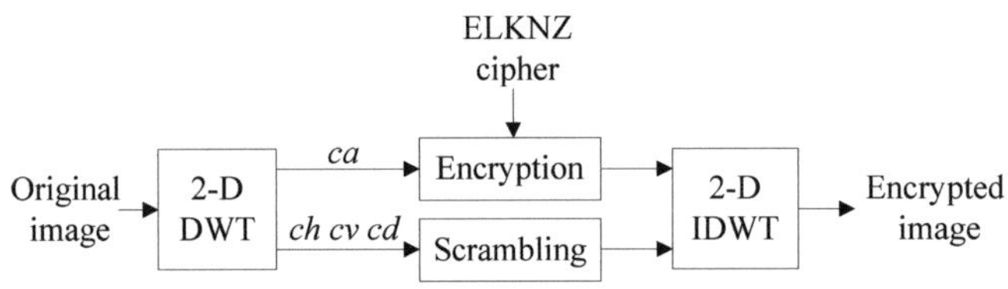

Fig. 8. The image encryption scheme in (El-Khamy et al., 2009)

4.3 Performance comparison

In this section, we compare the performance of different image encryption algorithms mentioned in Section 4.1 and 4.2. Here, various aspects listed in Section 2 are considered, and contrast results are shown in Table 1.

From Table 1, we conclude as follows:

(1) No matter chaos-based image encryption algorithms belong to full encryption or partial encryption, they can guarantee large key space and high key sensitivity, which make them resist brute-force attack. And they can confuse the pixels of an image completely so that the encrypted image is not perceptual recognized, that is, they are secure against ciphertext-only attack.

(2) As full encryption algorithms encrypt an image entirely and treat each bits equally, they have higher computational complexity than partial encryption, and do not provide

	BFA	KPA	CPA	COA	DA	CC	ICR	FC	RT	MLS	TET
B2CP (Fridrich, 1997)	Y	Y	Y	Y	N	H	N	N	N	N	N
BCBP (Mao et al., 2004)	Y	Y	Y	Y	Y	H	N	N	Y	N	Y
BCDG (Lian et al., 2005a)	Y	N	N	Y	Y	H	N	N	N	N	N
BCPD (Wang et al., 2011)	Y	Y	Y	Y	Y	H	N	N	Y	N	N
S3CP (Chen et al., 2004)	Y	N	N	Y	Y	M	N	N	Y	N	N
SGC (Gao & Chen, 2008a;b)	Y	Y	N	Y	N	M	N	N	Y	N	N
SDEC (Zhang et al., 2005)	Y	N	N	Y	Y	M	N	N	N	N	Y
SFPR (Kwok & Tang, 2007)	Y	Y	Y	Y	N	M	N	N	Y	N	N
SNCA (Gao et al., 2006)	Y	Y	Y	Y	N	M	N	N	Y	N	N
PCNN (Lian et al., 2004)	Y	Y	N	Y	Y	L	Y	Y	Y	N	Y
PCML (Xiang et al., 2007)	Y	N	N	Y	N	L	N	N	N	N	N
PSTP (Lin, Mao & Wang, 2008)	Y	Y	N	Y	N	L	Y	N	N	N	N
PDEC (El-Khamy et al., 2009)	Y	Y	Y	Y	N	L	N	N	N	N	N

BFA: against brute-force attack; KPA: against known-plaintext attack
CPA: against chosen-plaintext attack; COA: against ciphertext-only attack
DA: against differential attack; CC: computational complexity; FC: format compliance
ICR: invariance of compression ratio; RT: real-time
TET: transmission error tolerance; MLS: multiple levels of security
Y: yes; N: no; L: low; M: middle; H: high

Table 1. Comparison of chaos-based image encryption algorithms

multiple levels of security. Moreover, they are often operated with any compression process, so they can not keep invariance of compression ratio and format compliance.

(3) If an encryption scheme (such as PCNN) is combined with image compression or coding process, as it only encrypts a small part of image data and does not change statistical characteristics of DCT coefficients, it can keep invariance of compression ratio. Moreover, since it does not encrypt any format information, it can keep format compliance.

(4) Although the block cipher is usually considered faster than stream cipher, it may provide worse security than stream cipher.

(5) Different chaotic maps have different key space, key sensitivity and computational complexity. For example, Table 2 lists the differences among cat map, baker map and standard map. Comparing to cat map and standard map, baker map has the lowest computational complexity, middle key space, and middle key sensitivity. Thus, baker map is preferred as a tradeoff between security and computing complexity.

(6) Although the above image encryption algorithms can not fulfill all the requirements listed in Section 2, they still provide very promising methods that can demonstrate superiority over the conventional encryption methods.

	cat map	baker map	standard map
key space	L	M	H
key sensitivity	H	M	L
computational complexity	M	L	H

Table 2. The differences among cat map, baker map and standard map

5. Chaos-based video encryption algorithms

According to the relation between compression process and encryption, this section partitions chaos-based video encryption algorithms into three types: encrypting the raw video data, encrypting the video data in compression process, and encrypting the compressed video data. As to encrypting the video data in compression process, it means realizing encryption in the encoding process before entropy coding. Encrypting the compressed video data means realizing encryption after entropy-encoding and before package.

5.1 Encrypting the raw video data

In the type of encrypting the raw video data, some algorithms encrypt the raw data completely without considering region-of-interest, and others consider the region-of-interest partially or selectively.

5.1.1 Encryption without considering region-of-interest

Encryption without considering interest regions means to encrypt the video data frame by frame and does not consider the video objects or any other semantic information. Thus, it treats the regions fairly without special considerations.

Li et al (Li et al., 2002) proposed a chaotic video encryption scheme (CVES) for real-time digital video based on multiple digital chaotic systems. In CVES, each plain-block is first XORed by a chaotic signal, and then substituted by a pseudo-random S-box based on multiple chaotic maps. The CVES is secure against brute-force attack, known/chosen-plaintext attacks. Moreover, it is of low computational complexity, and thus it can be realized easily by both hardware and software.

Ganesan et al (Ganesan et al., 2008) described a public key encryption (PKVE) of videos based on chaotic maps. In PKVE, if the number of frames is too large, they first use phase scrambling (see Fig.9) (Nishchal et al., 2003) to scramble the video data, and then encrypt the data using chebyshev maps (Bergamo et al., 2005) (see Equation 17). Otherwise, they encrypt each frame by Arnold scrambling (Prasad, 2010). The PKVE is secure against known/chosen-plaintext attacks, and has high key sensitivity. In particular, it is very efficient in real-time applications for 64×64 and 128×128 pixel size videos.

$$\begin{cases} T_n(x) = 2 \cdot x \cdot T_{n-1}(x) - T_{n-2}(x), n \geq 2 \\ T_0(x) = 1 \\ T_1(x) = x \end{cases} \tag{17}$$

Kezia and Sudha (Kezia & Sudha, 2008) used a high dimensional Lorenz chaotic system to

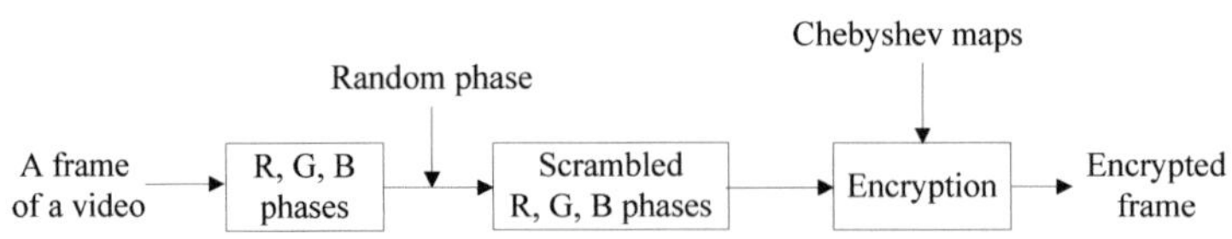

Fig. 9. The video encryption scheme in(Ganesan et al., 2008)

encrypt each frame of a video by confusing the position of the pixels (henceforth called LCVS).

In LCVS, each frame is encrypted by a unique key instead of changing the key for a particular number of frames. The LCVS can resist brute-force attack and differential attack, and it is robust to transmission error and much suitable for real-time transmission.

5.1.2 Encryption considering regions-of-interest

In many practical applications, it is not necessary or suitable to encrypt all video data, while just regions of interest. For the video data, a region of interest means human video objects or any other kind of regions of semantic information. In this issue, researchers have proposed some encryption algorithms according to the mode shown in Fig.10.

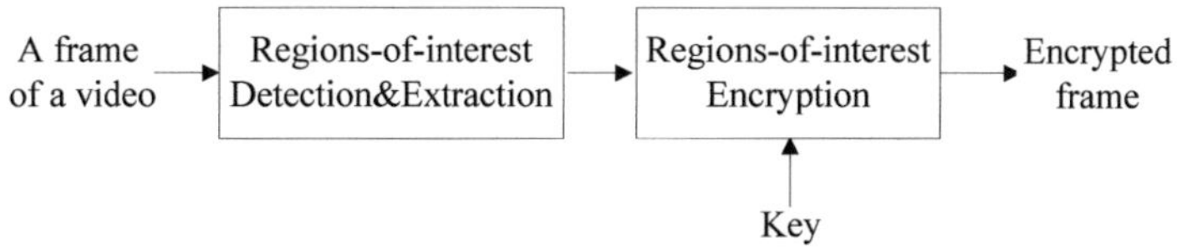

Fig. 10. The encryption mode considering regions-of-interest

Tzouveli et al (Tzouveli et al., 2004) proposed a human video object encryption system (henceforth called HVOE) based on logistic map. In HVOE, face regions are first efficiently detected, and afterwards body regions are extracted using geometric information of the location of face regions. Then, the pixels of extracted human video objects are encrypted based on logistic map. The HVOE can resist brute-force attack, different-key attack and differential attack, and it is efficient in computational resources and running time.

Ntalianis and Kollias (Ntalianis & Kollias, 2005) proposed a video object based chaotic encryption system (henceforth called VOCE). First, in VOCE video objects are automatically extracted based on the appropriate fusion of color information. Next, for each video object, multi-resolution decomposition is performed and the pixels of the lowest resolution level are encrypted using a complex product cipher combining a chaotic stream cipher and two chaotic block ciphers. Finally, the encrypted regions are propagated to the higher resolution levels and the encryption process is repeated until the highest level is reached. The VOCE presents robustness against brute-force attack and known cryptanalytic attack.

5.2 Encrypting the video data in compression process

Encrypting the video data in compression process means realizing encryption in the encoding process before entropy coding, such as Context-adaptive variable-length coding (CAVLC), Context-adaptive binary arithmetic coding (CABAC), variable length coding (VLC), run length coding (RLC), Golomb, Huffman, and so on. This section just discusses the most representative schemes for MPEG or H.26x.

Yang and Sun (Yang & Sun, 2008) proposed a chaos-based video encryption method in DCT domain (henceforth called CVED). In CVED, only I-frames are selected as encryption objects. First, they use a double coupling logistic maps (see Equation 18) to scramble the DCT coefficients of I-frames, and then encrypt the DCT coefficients of the scrambled I-frames by using another logistic map (see Equation 9). In CVED, five keys are introduced in the whole process, and thus the key space is large enough to resist brute-force attack. Besides, only encrypting the DCT coefficients of I-frames consumes little time, and is feasible for real-time applications. However, considering that there are some macro blocks in B-frames or P-frames, which are encoded without referring to I-frames, these blocks will be left unprotected. Therefore, some video contents may be intelligible and the CVED is not secure enough.

$$\begin{cases} x_{n+1} = \mu_x x_n(1 - x_n) \\ y_{n+1} = \mu_y y_n(1 - y_n) \end{cases} \tag{18}$$

Lian (Lian, 2009) constructed an efficient chaos-based selective encryption scheme for image/video (henceforth called CSVE) shown in Fig.11. In CSVE, only the DC (direct current coefficient) and the ACs (signs of the alternating current coefficients) of each frame are encrypted using the 2D coupled map lattice (2D CML). The encryption is operated after pre-encoding (namely, color space transformation), block partitioning (each block is in 8×8 size), DCT transformation and quantization, and before post-encode (i.e., zig-zag scan and VLC). The CSVE has high key sensitivity and is secure in perception. Moreover, its encryption operation does not change the compression ratio a lot, and incurs little computational cost compared with video compression. The cryptographic security of CSVE depends on the randomness of the chaotic sequences generated by the 2D coupled map lattice.

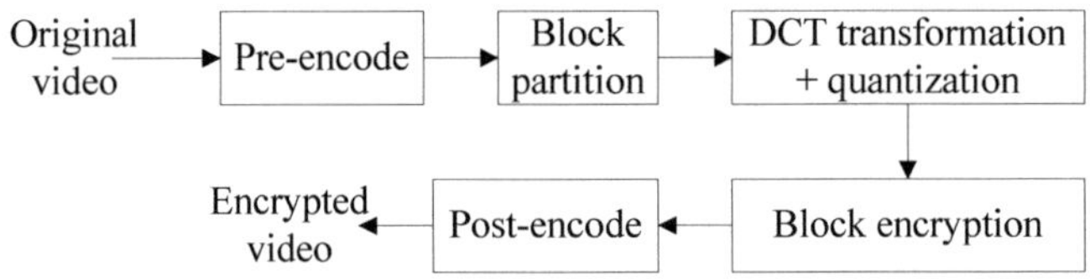

Fig. 11. The video encryption scheme in (Lian, 2009)

Chiaraluce et al (Chiaraluce et al., 2002) presented a selective encryption algorithm for the H.263 videos (henceforth called SEHV), in which the cipher operations have been seamlessly integrated into the H.263 encoding process, i.e., before RLC and packaging. In SEHV, only the most significant bit in the DC coefficients of DCT , the AC coefficients of I-MB (intra macro blocks), the sign bit of the AC coefficients of the PMB (predicted macro blocks), and the sign bit of the motion vectors are encrypted by using three suitably arranged different chaotic functions, namely, the skew tent map, saw-tooth likewise map, and logistic map. The key space (2^{512}) of SEHV is large enough to resist brute-force attack. The SEHV changes the key every 30 frames, and thus it is secure against known/chosen-plaintext attacks. Besides, it introduces a modest additional processing time and is suitable for "real time" or "almost real time" applications.

5.3 Encrypting the compressed video data

Encrypting the compressed video data means realizing encryption after entropy-encoding and before package (shown as Fig.12.). The representative works are done by Lian et al (Lian, Liu, Ren & Wang, 2007; Lian, Sun & Wang, 2007) and Qian et al (Qian et al., 2008).

Lian et al (Lian, Sun & Wang, 2007) proposed an efficient partial video encryption scheme based on a chaotic stream cipher generated by a discrete piecewise linear chaotic map (henceforth called VESC). In VESC, both the intra-macroblocks (all the macroblocks in I-frame and some intra-encoded macroblocks in P/B-frame) and the motion vectors' signs are

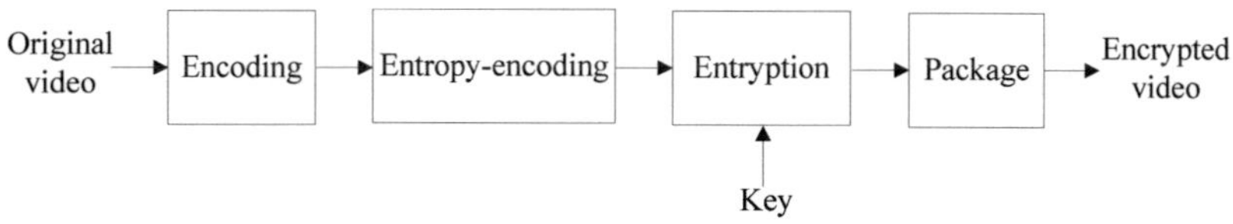

Fig. 12. The mode of encrypting the compressed video data

encrypted, and the encryption process is achieved after VLC and before packaging. The VECS has large key space, and high key sensitivity. Besides, it can keep invariance of compression ratio, format compliant and is robust to transmission error.

In (Lian, Liu, Ren & Wang, 2007), Lian et al proposed a fast video encryption scheme for MPEG-4 (henceforth called VEM4). In VEM4, the file format information, such as file header, packet header, and so on, are left unencrypted in order to support such operation as bit-rate control, and the motion vectors, subbands, code blocks or bit-planes are partially encrypted by a stream cipher based on a modified chaotic neural network (Lian et al., 2004). Moreover, for each encoding-pass, the chaotic binary sequence is generated from different initial-condition based on logistic map. Thus, if one encoding-pass cannot be synchronized because of transmission errors, the other ones can still be decrypted correctly. The VEM4 is of high security in perception, of low computation complexity, and secure against brute-force attack, statistic attack or differential attack. It keeps compression ratio and file format unchanged, supports direct bit-rate control, and keeps the error-robustness unchanged.

Qian et al (Qian et al., 2008) proposed a multiple chaotic encryption system (MCES) for MPEG-2. In MCES, three chaotic or hyperchaotic maps, namely logistics map, 2-D baker map and 4-D hyperchaotic map (Li et al., 2005), are introduced for stream partial encryptions, block permutation, confusion after block permutation, respectively. Moreover, stream ciphers encrypt only DC coefficients. The MCES is secure, efficient, of low computational complexity, and nearly brings no data expansion.

5.4 Performance comparison

In this section, we compare the performance of different encryption algorithms mentioned above. Here, various aspects listed in Section 2 are considered, and contrast results are shown in Table 3.

From Table 3, we get the following conclusions:

(1) The CVES, PKVE and LCVS encrypt the video data completely without considering interest regions. Their security depends on the proposed chaotic ciphers, and as long as the ciphers are well-designed, they are often of higher security and higher complexity than other types, and thus are more suitable for secure video storing.

(2) The HVOE and VOCE encrypt only the regions of interest, and leave the rest (such as background) unprotected. They are of lower computation complexity, and more suitable for real-time applications. Their cryptographic security depends on the adopted chaotic cipher and the region selection.

(3) The algorithms that encrypt the video data in compression process belong to partial or selective encryption, and are often of lower complexity than those encrypt the raw video data directly. However, some of them, such as CVED and SEHV, change the compression

	BFA	KPA	CPA	COA	DA	CC	ICR	FC	RT	MLS	TET
CVES (Li et al., 2002)	Y	Y	Y	Y	N	M	N	N	Y	N	N
PKVE (Ganesan et al., 2008)	Y	Y	Y	Y	N	H	N	N	Y	N	N
LCVS (Kezia & Sudha, 2008)	Y	N	N	Y	Y	M	N	N	Y	N	N
HVOE (Tzouveli et al., 2004)	Y	N	N	Y	Y	L	N	N	Y	N	N
VOCE (Ntalianis & Kollias, 2005)	Y	N	N	Y	N	L	N	N	Y	Y	Y
CVED (Yang & Sun, 2008)	Y	N	N	N	N	L	N	Y	Y	N	N
CSVE (Lian, 2009)	Y	N	N	Y	N	L	Y	Y	Y	N	N
SEHV (Chiaraluce et al., 2002)	Y	Y	Y	Y	N	L	N	Y	Y	N	N
VESC (Lian, Sun & Wang, 2007)	Y	N	N	Y	N	L	Y	Y	Y	N	Y
VEM4 (Lian, Liu, Ren & Wang, 2007)	Y	N	N	Y	Y	L	Y	Y	Y	N	Y
MCES (Qian et al., 2008)	Y	N	N	Y	N	L	Y	Y	Y	N	N

Table 3. Comparison of chaos-based video encryption algorithms

ratio because they change the statistical characteristics of DCT coefficients. Interestingly, some of them can keep file format unchanged, and thus support direct bit rate control, that is, they permit to re-compress the encoded and encrypted video before decrypting it firstly, and save much time for secure transcoding. Therefore, they are more suitable for real-time applications, such as wireless multimedia network or multimedia transmission over narrow bands.

(4) The algorithms that encrypt the compressed video data can not only preserve invariance of compression ratio and format compliance, but also be of low overhead. Additionally, they are of low-cost and easy to be realized, and thus are suitable for real-time required applications, such as video transmission or video access. However, as the video stream after entropy encoding may have a certain structure or syntax, they may destroy the structure of the video stream, furthermore, they may bring error spreading when the transmission error happens because they do not consider the rules of package before transmission.

6. Chaos-based audio encryption algorithms

Comparing to image and video, the work for audio or speech encryption is sadly lacking at present. Therefore, this section will deal with not only the chaos-based methods, but also other audio encryption technologies. In general, according to the percentage of the audio data encrypted, the existing audio encryption algorithms are mostly divided into full encryption and partial encryption.

6.1 Full encryption

For full encryption, there are two fundamentally distinct approaches to achieve audio security: analogue audio encryption and digital audio encryption.

6.1.1 Analogue audio encryption

Analogue audio encryption contains four main categories, namely, frequency domain scrambling, time domain scrambling, two-dimensional scrambling which combines the frequency domain scrambling with the time domain scrambling, and amplitude scrambling.

Sridharan et al (Sridharan et al., 1990; 1991) and Borujeni (Borujeni, 2000) proposed scrambling approach using orthogonal transformation like discrete fourier transform (DFT), fast fourier transform (FFT), DCT, respectively. Lin et al (Lin et al., 2005) proposed a modified time domain scrambling scheme with an amplitude scrambling method, which masks the speech signal with a random noise by specific mixing. Andrade et al (Andrade et al., 2008) presented a two-dimensional scrambling method combining the frequency domain scrambling with the time domain scrambling for AMR (adaptive multi-rate) speech. Sadkhan et al (Sadkhan et al., 2007) proposed analog speech scrambler based on parallel structure of wavelet transforms.

Mosa et al (Mosa et al., 2009) proposed a chaos based speech encryption system in transform domains (henceforth called SETD). The SETD consists of two stages: substitution and permutation. First, the stream of speech segments is divided and reshaped into two fixed size blocks and the elements are permutated by chaotic map technique, then substituted to different values by DCT and then permutated another time. The SETD is of low-complexity, and secure against brute-force attack, statistical attack and noise attack.

These analogue audio encryption techniques are simple and have following advantages (Sridharan et al., 1990):

- they provide excellent voice recognition or voice recovery.
- The quality of the recovered speech is independent of the language and speaker.
- It is possible to acoustically couple the encryption device to the handset which enables the device to be used with any handset.
- The system does not require speech compression or modems.
- The system is less sensitive to errors in synchronization.
- The system generates scrambled speech without any residual intelligibility.

However, these techniques do not change the redundancy of speech greatly, which leads to the intelligibility of the encrypted analog signal, and thus analogue audio encryption has poor security.

6.1.2 Digital audio encryption

In digital encryption, the analogue signal is first digitised and compressed to generate a data signal at a suitable bit rate. The bit stream is then encrypted.

Gnanajeyaraman et al (Gnanajeyaraman et al., 2009) proposed an audio encryption scheme (shown in Fig.13) based on a look-up table which is generated by using higher dimensional cat map (henceforth called AELT). The AELT has the characteristic of sensitive to initial condition, and resists brute-force attack and chosen/known-plaintext attacks.

Liu et al (Liu et al., 2008) proposed a block encryption algorithm for digital speech codes (henceforth called BEDS). The BEDS encrypts message with chaotic sequences which randomly come from chaotic model database using logistic map (see Equation 9) and henon map (see Equation 19). The BEDS has large key space, and partially solves the problem of decryption for receiver when some data packages are lost during real-time transportation.

$$\begin{cases} x_{i+1} = 1 + by_i - ax_i^2 \\ y_{i+1} = x_i \end{cases} \tag{19}$$

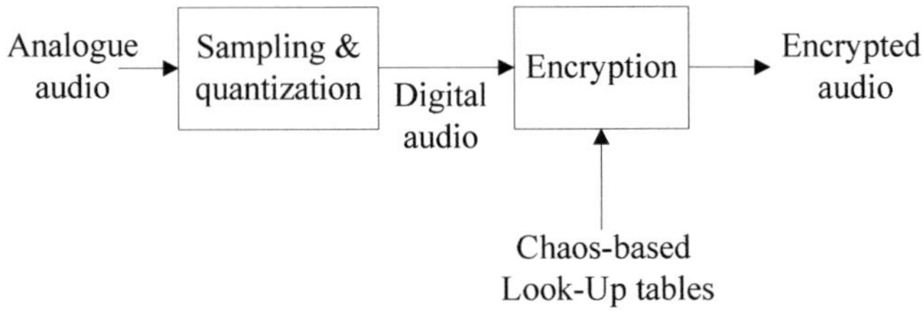

Fig. 13. The audio encryption scheme in (Gnanajeyaraman et al., 2009)

Sheu (Sheu, 2011) presented a two-channel chaos-based speech encryption using fractional Lorenz system for speech communication (henceforth called TCSE). The TCSE can achieve large key space, high key sensitivity, and the ability to resist chosen plaintext/ciphertext attack.

Full encryption can offer a high level of security and effectively prevent unauthorized access, however, is computationally demanding, and not effectively applied to power-constrained, real-time multimedia applications.

6.2 Partial encryption

Partial encryption, which is often operated on a certain audio coding standard, such as G.723, G.729 and MP3, only encrypts the sensitive subset of an audio data.

Wu and Kuo (Wu & Kuo, 2001) presented a fast selective encryption method for G.723 (henceforth called FSEM), where the most significant 37 bits of all important coefficients are encrypted. As the FSEM does not select any of the pulse position coefficients, it can be applied directly to bit rate modes. Moreover, it distorts speech totally, and is secure against ciphertext-only attack, brute-force attack, known/chosen-plaintext attacks.

Servetti and Martin (Servetti & Martin, 2002) proposed a perception based partial encryption scheme for G.729 (henceforth called LPPE). In LPPE, speech signals are first partitioned into two classes based on perception, where the mostly perceptually relevant bits are encrypted and the others are left unprotected. The LPPE can achieve content protection which is equivalent to full encryption. However, there are still remaining some comprehensible bit steams structures which might leak some information for attackers and reduce security to an extent.

Servetti et al (Servetti et al., 2003) presented a frequency-selective partial encryption for MP3 (henceforth called FPEM). In FPEM, only a part of the stop-band coefficients are encrypted. The FPEM is combined with low-pass filtering in the compressed domain, which makes the FPEM against statistical attack and offers good content protection. Moreover, the FPEM is of low-complexity and format compliance.

Su et al (Su et al., 2010) improved the LPPE and presented a group of chaos-based hierarchical selective encryption schemes (henceforth called CHSE) which can obtain a good tradeoff between high security and low computational cost. In CHSE, speech bit streams are partitioned into two parts according to the bit sensitivity where the sensitive bits are encrypted by a strong cipher and the remaining are encrypted by a lightweight cipher.

6.3 Performance comparison

In this section, we just compare the performance of SETD, AELT, BEDS, TCSE, LPPE, CHSE, FPEM and FSEM. Here, various aspects listed in Section 2 are considered, and contrast results are shown in Table 4.

	BFA	KPA	CPA	COA	DA	CC	ICR	FC	RT	MLS	TET
SETD (Mosa et al., 2009)	Y	N	N	Y	N	M	N	N	N	N	N
AELT (Gnanajeyaraman et al., 2009)	Y	Y	Y	Y	N	H	N	N	N	N	N
BEDS (Liu et al., 2008)	Y	N	N	Y	N	H	N	N	Y	N	Y
TCSE (Sheu, 2011)	Y	N	Y	Y	N	H	N	N	N	N	N
FSEM (Wu & Kuo, 2001)	Y	Y	Y	Y	N	L	Y	Y	Y	N	N
LPPE (Servetti & Martin, 2002)	Y	N	N	Y	N	L	N	Y	Y	N	N
FPEM (Servetti et al., 2003)	Y	N	N	Y	N	L	N	Y	Y	N	N
CHSE (Su et al., 2010)	Y	Y	Y	Y	Y	L	Y	Y	Y	Y	N

Table 4. Comparison of audio encryption algorithms

From Table 4, we can we get the following conclusions:

(1) As partial encryption only encrypts a subset of audio data, it has lower computational complexity than full encryption. Thus, audio encryption algorithms of this category can be used to meet the real-time demand for power-constrained devices and narrow bandwidth environments.

(2) As partial encryption is generally used for compressed audio data, it can keep the audio format compliance.

(3) Compared with analogue encryption, digital encryption can give lower residual intelligibility and higher cryptanalytic strength, and thus it is the main technique for audio encryption at present. However, analogue encryption also has its advantage in analogue telephone, satellite and mobile communication systems without the use of a modem.

7. Conclusions

Multimedia encryption becomes more and more important with the development of network and multimedia technology in today's world. To tackle the problem, many encryption algorithms have been proposed. Although there does not seem to be any multimedia encryption algorithm that can fulfill all aforementioned requirements in Section 2, chaos-based multimedia encryptions provide a class of very promising methods which can demonstrate superiority over the conventional encryption methods and can be used as the foundation of future research. However, chaos-based multimedia encryption is not yet mature and more efforts are needed for its further development toward practical applications with high security, low computational complexity, invariance of compression ratio, format compliance, real-time, multiple levels of security, and strong transmission error tolerance.

8. References

Alligood, K. T., Sauer, T. & Yorke, J. A. (1997). *Chaos: an introduction to dynamical systems*, Springer-Verlag, New York.

Alvarez, G. & Li, S. (2006). Some basic cryptographic requirements for chaos-based cryptosystems, *International Journal of Bifurcation and Chaos* Vol.16(No.7): 2129–2151.

Alvarez, G., Montoya, F., Romera, M. & Pastor, G. (2004). Breaking two secure communication systems based on chaotic masking, *IEEE Transaction on Circuit and Systems II: Express Briefs* Vol.51(No.10): 505–506.

Andrade, J., Campos, M. & Apolinario, J. (2008). Speech privacy for modern mobile communication systems, *Proceedings of IEEE Int. Conf. on Acoustics, Speech, and Signal Processing*, IEEE Press, Nevada, U.S.A., pp. 1777 – 1780.

Arroyo, D. & C. Li, S. Li, G. A. W. A. H. (2009). Cryptanalysis of an image encryption based on a new total shuffling algorithm, *Chaos, Solitons & Fractals* Vol.41(No.5): 2613–2616.

Ballesté, A. M. (2004). *Real-time pay-per-view of protected multimedia content v:2.0*, Ph.D. Dissertation, Universitat Polit'ecnica de Catalunya, Barcelona.

Bergamo, P., D'Arco, P. & Santis, A.and Kocarev, L. (2005). Security of public key cryptosystems based on chebyshev polynomials, *IEEE Transactions on Circuits and Systems-I* Vol.52: 1382–1393.

Borujeni, S. (2000). Speech encryption based on fast fourier transform permutation, *Proceedings of ICECS 2000*, IEEE Press, Jounieh , Lebanon, pp. 290 – 293.

Brock, W. A. (1986). Distinguishing random and deterministic systems: Abridged version, *Journal of Economic Theory* Vol.1986(No.40): 168–195.

Chen, G., Mao, Y. & Chui, C. K. (2004). A symmetric image encryption scheme based on 3d chaotic cat maps, *Chaos, Solitons & Fractals* Vol.21(No.3): 749–761.

Chen, G. & Ueta, T. (1999). Yet another chaotic attractor, *Int J Bifurcat Chaos* Vol.9(No.7): 1465–1466.

Cheng, H. & Li, X. (2000). Partial encryption of compressed images and videos, *IEEE Transactions on Signal Processing* Vol.48(No.8): 2439–2451.

Chiaraluce, F., Ciccarelli, L., Gambi, E., Pierleoni, P. & Reginelli, M. (2002). A new chaotic algorithm for video encryption, *IEEE Transactions on Consumer Electronics* Vol.48(No.4): 833–844.

Cokal, C. & Solak, E. (2009). Cryptanalysis of a chaos-based image encryption algorithm, *Phys. Lett. A* Vol.373(No.15): 1357–1360.

Cormen, T. H., Leiserson, C. E., Rivest, R. L. & Stein, C. (2001). *Introduction to algorithms (2nd edition)*, MIT Press, McGraw-Hill Cambridge.

Dang, P. P. & Chau, P. M. (2000). Implementation idea algorithm for image encryption, *Proceedings of SPIE*, SPIE Press, San Diego, CA, pp. 1–9.

Devaney, R. L. (2003). *An introduction to chaotic dynamical systems(2nd edition)*, Westview Press, San Francisco.

Droogenbroeck, M. & Benedett, R. (2002). Techniques for a selective encryption of uncompressed and compressed images, *Proceedings of ACIVS 2002*, IEEE Press, Ghent, Belgium, pp. 90–97.

El-Khamy, S., El-Nasr, M. & El-Zein, A. (2009). A partial image encryption scheme based on the dwt and elknz chaotic stream cipher, *MASAUM Journal of Basic and Applied Sciences* Vol.1(No.3): 389–394.

El-Zein, A., El-Khamy, S. & El-Nasr, M. (2008). The chaotic stream cipher "elknz" for high security data encryption, *Proceedings of URSIGA'2008*, URSI Press, Chicago, USA, pp. 1105–1110.

Fridrich, J. (1997). Image encryption based on chaotic maps, *Proceedings of IEEE Conf. on Systems, Man, and Cybernetics*, IEEE Press, Florida, USA, pp. 1105–1110.

Furht, B., Muharemagic, E. & Socek, D. (2005). *Multimedia encryption and watermarking*, Springer-Verlag, New York.

Ganesan, K., Singh, I. & Narain, M. (2008). Public key encryption of images and videos in real time using chebyshev maps, *Proceedings of the 2008 Fifth International Conference on Computer Graphics, Imaging and Visualisation*, IEEE Computer Society, Washington DC, USA, pp. 211–216.

Gao, H., Zhang, Y., Liang, S. & Li, D. (2006). A new chaotic algorithm for image encryption, *Chaos, Solitons & Fractals* Vol.29(No.2): 393–399.

Gao, T. & Chen, Z. (2008a). Image encryption based on a new total shuffing algorithm, *Chaos, Solitons and Fractals* Vol.1(No.38): 213–220.

Gao, T. & Chen, Z. (2008b). A new image encryption algorithm based on hyper-chaos, *Physics Letters A* Vol.372: 394–400.

Gnanajeyaraman, R., Prasadh, K. & Ramar, D. (2009). Audio encryption using higher dimensional chaotic map, *International Journal of Recent Trends in Engineering* Vol.1(No.2): 103–107.

Gschwandtner, M., Uhl, A. & Wild, P. (2007). Transmission error and compression robustness of 2d chaotic map image encryption schemes, *EURASIP Journal on Information Security* Vol.2007(No.1): 1–16.

Guan, Z., Huang, F. & Guan, W. (2005). Chaos-based image encryption algorithm, *Physics. Letters A* Vol.346(No.1-3): 153–157.

He, J., Qian, H., Zhou, Y. & Li, Z. (2010). Cryptanalysis and improvement of a block cipher based on multiple chaotic systems, *Mathematical Problems in Engineering* Vol.2010: 14 Pages.

Kaneko, K. (1989). Pattern dynamics in spatiotemporal chaos: pattern selection, diffusion of defect and pattern competition intermittency, *Physica D* Vol.34(No.1-2): 1ĺC41.

Kezia, H. & Sudha, G. F. (2008). Encryption of digital video based on lorenz chaotic system, *Proceedings of the 16th International Conference on Advanced Computing and Communications*, IEEE Computer Society, Tamilnadu India, pp. 40–45.

Kwok, H. & Tang, W. (2007). A fast image encryption system based on chaotic maps with finite precision represention, *Chaos, Solitons & Fractals* Vol.32(No.4): 1518–1529.

Li, C., Li, S., Chen, G. & Halang, W. A. (2009). Cryptanalysis of an image encryption scheme based on a compound chaotic sequence, *Image and Vision Computing* Vol.27(No.8): 1035–1039.

Li, S., Zheng, X., Mou, X. & Cai, Y. (2002). Chaotic encryption scheme for real-time digital video, *Proceedings of SPIE*, SPIE Press, San Jose, CA, pp. 149–160.

Li, Y. X., Tang, W. K. S. & Chen, G. R. (2005). Generating hyperchaos via state feedback control, *Int. J. of Bifurcation and Chaos* Vol.15(No.10): 3367–3375.

Lian, S. (2009). Efficient image or video encryption based on spatiotemporal chaos system, *Chaos, Solitons & Fractals* Vol.40(No.5): 2509–2519.

Lian, S., Chen, G., Cheung, A. & Wang, Z. (2004). chaotic-neural-network-based encryption algorithm for jpeg2000 encoded images, *Proceedings of ISNN 2004-II*, Springer-Verlag, Praha, Czech Republic, pp. 627–632.

Lian, S., Liu, Z., Ren, Z. & Wang, H. (2007). Secure media distribution scheme based on chaotic neural network, *Proceedings of ISNN 2007*, IEEE Computational Intelligence Society, Nanjing, China, pp. 79–87.

Lian, S., Sun, J., Liu, G. & Wang, Z. (2008). Efficient video encryption scheme based on advanced video coding, *Multimed Tools Appl* Vol.38(No.1): 75–89.

Lian, S., Sun, J. & Wang, Z. (2005a). A block cipher based on a suitable use of chaotic standard map, *Chaos, Solitons & Fractals* Vol.26(No.1): 117–129.

Lian, S., Sun, J. & Wang, Z. (2005b). Security analysis of a chaos-based image encryption algorithm, *Phys Lett A* Vol.351(No.2-4): 645–661.

Lian, S., Sun, J. & Wang, Z. (2007). A chaotic stream cipher and the usage in video protection, *Chaos, Solitons & Fractals* Vol.34(No.1): 851–859.

Lin, C., Chung, C. & Chen, Z. (2008). A chaos-based unequal encryption mechanism in wireless telemedicine with error decryption, *Wseas Transactions On Systems* Vol.7(No.2): 75–89.

Lin, Q., Yin, F. & Liang, H. (2005). Blind source separation-based encryption of images and speeches, *Lecture Notes in Computer Science-Advances in Neural Networks* Vol.3497: 544–549.

Lin, R., Mao, Y. & Wang, Z. (2008). Chaotic secure image coding based on spiht, *Proceedings of ChinaCom 2008*, IEEE press, Hangzhou, China, pp. 149–160.

Liu, J., Gao, F. & Ma, H. (2008). A speech chaotic encryption algorithm based on network, *Proceedings of IIHMSP '08*, IEEE press, Harbin, China, pp. 283–286.

Mao, Y., Chen, G. & Lian, S. (2004). A novel fast image encryption scheme based on the 3d chaotic baker map, *Int J Bifurcat Chaos* Vol.14(No.10): 3613–3624.

Mosa, E., Messiha, N. & Zahran, O. (2009). Chaotic encryption of speech signals in transform domains, *Proceedings of ICCES 2009*, IEEE Press, Cairo, pp. 300–305.

Nishchal, N. K., Joseph, J. & Singh, K. (2003). Fully phase based encryption using fractional fourier transform, *Opt.Eng* Vol.42: 1583–1588.

Ntalianis, K. S. & Kollias, S. D. (2005). Chaotic video objects encryption based on mixed feedback, multiresolution decomposition and time-variant s-boxes, *Proceedings of ICIP (2) 2005*, IEEE press, Genoa, Italy, pp. 1110–1113.

Pommer, A. & Uhl, A. (2003). Selective encryption of wavelet-packet encoded image data: efficiency and security, *Multimedia Systems* Vol.9(No.3): 279–287.

Prasad, V. V. R.and Kurupati, R. (2010). Secure image watermarking in frequency domain using arnold scrambling and filtering, *Advances in Computational Sciences and Technology* Vol.3(No.2): 236–244.

Qian, Q., Chen, Z. & Yuan, Z. (2008). Video compression and encryption based-on multiple chaotic system., *the 3rd International Conference on Innovative Computing Information and Control*, IEEE computer society, Washington, DC, USA, pp. 561–564.

Qiu, Y. & He, C. (2002). Construction and analysis of one class chaotic running key generator, *J Shanghai Jiaotong Univ* Vol.136(No.3): 344–347.

Rhouma, R. & Belghith, S. (2008). Cryptanalysis of a new image encryption algorithm based on hyper-chaos, *Phys. Lett. A* Vol.372(No.38): 5973–5978.

Rueppel, R. A. (1986). *Analysis and design of stream ciphers*, Springer-Verlag, New York.

Sadkhan, S., Abdulmuhsen, N. & Al-Tahan, N. (2007). A proposed analog speech scrambler based on parallel structure of wavelet transforms, *Proceedings of NRSC 2007*, IEEE Press, Cairo, pp. 1–12.

Salleh, M., Ibrahim, S. & Isnin, I. F. (2003). Image encryption algorithm based on chaotic mapping, *Jurnal Teknologi* Vol.39(No.D): 1–12.

Servetti, A. & Martin, J. (2002). Perception-based partial encryption of compressed speech, *IEEE Transactions on Speech and Audio Processing* Vol.10(No.1): 637–643.

Servetti, A., Testa, C. & Martin, J. (2003). Frequency-selective partial encryption of compressed audio, *Proceedings of ICASSP '03*, IEEE Press, Hongkang, China, pp. 668–671.

Sheu, L. (2011). A speech encryption using fractional chaotic systems, *Nonlinear Dyn* Vol.65(No.1-2): 103–108.

Socek, D., Li, S., Magliveras, S. & Furht, B. (2005). Enhanced 1-d chaotic key-based algorithm for image encryption, *Proceedings of SecureComm 2005*, IEEE Press, Athens, Greece, pp. 406–408.

Solak, E. (2005). Cryptanalysis of observer based discrete-time chaotic encryption schemes, *International Journal of Bifurcation and Chaos* Vol.2(No.15): 653–658.

Sridharan, S., Dawson, E. & Goldburg, B. (1990). Speech encryption in the transform domain, *Electronics Letters* Vol.26(No.10): 655–657.

Sridharan, S., Dawson, E. & Goldburg, B. (1991). Fast fourier transform based speech encryption system, *Proceedings of the Int. Conf. on Communications, Speech and Vision*, IEEE Press, Anchorage, AK, pp. 215–223.

Su, Z., Jiang, J. & Lian, S. (2009). Selective encryption for g.729 speech using chaotic maps., *Proceedings of International Conference on Multimedia Information Networking and Security*, IEEE computer society, Wuhan , China, pp. 488–492.

Su, Z., Jiang, J. & Lian, S. (2010). Hierarchical selective encryption for g.729 speech based on bit sensitivity, *Journal of Internet Technology* Vol.5(No.11): 599–607.

Su, Z., S., L., Zhang, G. & Jiang, J. (2011). *Chaos-based video encryption algorithms*, Springer-Verlag, New York.

Tong, X. & Cui, M. (2008). Image encryption with compound chaotic sequence cipher shifting dynamically, *Image and Vision Computing* Vol.26(No.6): 843–850.

Tuchman, W. (1997). *A brief history of the data encryption standard*, ddison-Wesley Publishing, New York.

Tzouveli, P., Ntalianis, K. & Kollias, S. (2004). Security of human video objects by incorporating a chaos-based feedback cryptographic scheme, *Proceedings of MULTIMEDIA '04*, ACM Press, New York, USA, pp. 10–16.

Wang, Y., Wong, K. W., Liao, X. & Chen, G. (2011). A new chaos-based fast image encryption algorithm, *Applied Soft Computing* Vol.11(No.1). 514–522.

Wong, K., Kwok, B. & Yuen, C. H. (2009). An efficient diffusion approach for chaos-based image encryption, *Chaos, Solitons & Fractals* Vol.41(No.5): 2652–2663.

Wu, C. & Kuo, C. J. (2001). Fast encryption methods for audiovisual data confidentiality, *Proceedings of SPIE4209*, SPIE Press, Boston, MA, USA, pp. 284–295.

Xiang, T., Wong, K. & Liao, X. (2007). Selective image encryption using a spatiotemporal chaotic system, *Chaos* Vol.17(No.2): 2191–2199.

Xiao, D., Liao, X. & Wei, P. (2009). Analysis and improvement of a chaos-based image encryption algorithm, *Chaos Solitons & Fractals* Vol.2009(No.40): 2191–2199.

Yang, S. & Sun, S. (2008). A video encryption method based on chaotic maps in dct domain, *Progress in natural science* Vol.18(No.10): 1299–1304.

Yang, T., Wu, C. W. & Chua, L. O. (1997). Cryptography based on chaotic systems, *IEEE Transactions on Circuits and Systems I: Fundamental Theory and Applications* Vol.5(No.44): 469–472.

Zeghid, M., Machhout, M. & Khriji, L. (1996). A modified aes based algorithm for image encryption, *International Journal of Computer Science and Engineering* Vol.1(No.11): 70–75.

Zhang, L., X, L. & X., W. (2005). An image encryption approach based on chaotic maps, *Chaos Soliton Fract* Vol.24(No.11): 759–765.

6

Polynomial-Time Codes Against Averaging Attack for Multimedia Fingerprinting

Hideki Yagi and Tsutomu Kawabata
The University of Electro-Communications
Japan

1. Introduction

With rapid advances of information technologies, a large amount of digital contents, especially multimedia, can be processed by electronic devices such as computers and smartphones. Protecting the copyrights of digital contents is of paramount importance, and *digital fingerprinting* has attracted a lot of attention for this purpose. In digital fingerprinting, a user's ID called a *fingerprint* is embedded into an original content with a watermarking technique, and then the fingerprinted contents are distributed to users.

Digital fingerprinting requires robustness against *collusion attacks*, in which more than one illicit user colludes to forge illegal contents. In the context of multimedia fingerprinting, well-known collusion attacks are the *interleaving attack* (Boneh & Shaw, 1998; Fernandez & Soriano, 2004; Silverberg et al., 2003; Staddon et al., 2001) and the *averaging attack* (Trappe et al., 2003; Wu et al., 2004). The averaging attack is particularly effective when fingerprint's watermark is embedded into host multimedia via the *spread spectrum* technique. Trappe et al. have devised collusion-secure codes, called *anti-collusion* (AC) codes, against the averaging attack based on block designs (Trappe et al., 2003). The AC codes given by Trappe et al. are also called AND-AC codes. Subsequently, several studies have proposed a method for increasing coding rates of AC codes based on a various class of block designs and related methods. Some examples are based on group-divisible design (Kang et al., 2006), finite geometries and low-density matrices (Yagi et al., 2009), and cover-free families of sets (Li et al., 2009). In order to further increase the coding rate, concatenated coding in which an outer error correcting code is concatenated with an inner AC code, has been proposed (Yagi et al., 2007). This method seems attractive since any AND-AC codes can be used as the inner codes. Whereas the concatenated codes given by (Yagi et al., 2007) greatly improve the coding rates of AC codes, the codes need *exponential-time* complexity in the code length for decoding (detecting the colluders).

In this chapter, we consider a method for constructing AC codes with *polynomial-time* encoding and decoding algorithms based on concatenated coding. We give a sufficient condition on outer error correcting codes assuring that the concatenated AC codes have a designed resilience. A polynomial-time decoding algorithm is proposed based on the list-decoding of error correcting codes. A key idea is that after the inner decoding, from the set of candidate outer symbols, we randomly create a sequence, which is input to the list-decoding of the outer code. If the outer code's parameters satisfy the derived condition, the list-decoding algorithm can output at least one colluder's codeword correctly. We repeat this procedure until *all* the colluders' codewords are found. The proposed coding method guarantees the perfect detection of *all* the colluders in the absence of noise. Although, for fixed code length and resilience, the number of codewords of the proposed concatenated codes is smaller than that of codes in (Yagi et al., 2007), it asymptotically approaches the exponential order in the overall code length, resulting in a greater number of codewords than those of the AC codes in (Trappe et al., 2003) and (Yagi et al., 2009). In the proposed concatenated coding, any AC codes can be used as the inner code. Using AC-codes given by (Kang et al., 2006) and (Li et al., 2009) as the inner codes, we obtain analogous results.

In related work, some coding and decoding methods have been proposed for the interleaving attack (also known as the attack based on the *marking assumption*), in which one of colluders i-th codeword symbol is selected as the i-th codeword symbol of the forged fingerprint (e.g., (Boneh & Shaw, 1998; Staddon et al., 2001)). In (Silverberg et al., 2003) and (Fernandez & Soriano, 2004), the list decoding of fingerprinting codes is used. This work assures that at least one of the colluders is identified with polynomial time complexity in the code length. It seems that, in our problem setting, i.e., against the averaging attack, the realization of efficient coding is much easier because the forged fingerprint can have more information under the averaging attack. This is true in the sense that we can identify all the colluders with AC codes. However, the code construction is rather hard in terms of coding rate, since the use of orthogonal sequences in AC codes (Trappe et al., 2003; Wu et al., 2004) prevents the code size from growing exponentially in the code length. In this chapter, we aim at realizing the polynomial-time complexity in the code length as well as increasing the code size greatly based on concatenated coding and list decoding of outer codes.

The proposed method is attractive in the sense that we can construct it in a deterministic way for given parameters and implement encoding and decoding with polynomial-time complexity in the code length. However, its code size still grows *semi-exponential* in the code length. This means that the *coding rate* of this code, which is defined as the logarithm of the code size per codeword symbol, goes to zero as the code length tends to infinity. Recently, it has been pointed out by (Koga, 2010) that there exist AC codes with a strictly positive coding rate although the way of constructing such codes is still unknown. In the last part of this chapter, we show that there exist polynomial-time AC codes with a strictly positive coding rate, based on the argument given by (Koga, 2010).

2. Fingerprinting model

2.1 Digital fingerprinting

When distributing a digital content to users, a codeword (*fingerprint*) corresponding to each user is embedded into the original content by a watermarking technique. Some illicit users may collude and attempt to forge their fingerprints (*collusion attack*) so that their fingerprints are not revealed from an illegally utilized content. The detector of colluders estimates colluders' fingerprints from the forged fingerprint.

Let $\Gamma = \{1, 2, \ldots, |\Gamma|\}$ be the set of users of a digital content, where $|\cdot|$ expresses the cardinality of its argument set. We denote a codeword of user $j \in \Gamma$ by $\boldsymbol{b}_j = (\boldsymbol{b}_j^{(1)}, \boldsymbol{b}_j^{(2)}, \ldots, \boldsymbol{b}_j^{(N)}) \in$

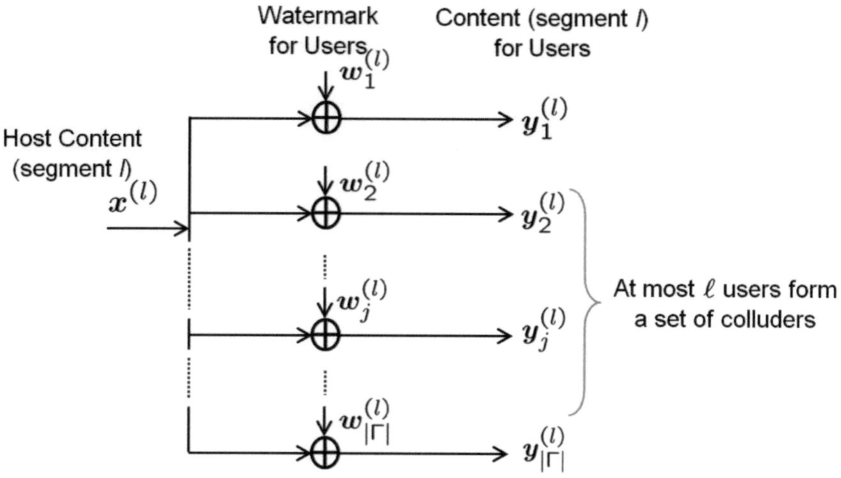

Fig. 1. A encoding procedure for multimedia fingerprinting using the spread spectrum technique. $\oplus$ denotes the real number addition of $w_j^{(l)}$ with the host content x.

$\{0,1\}^{n\times N}$ where $b_j^{(l)} = (b_{j1}^{(l)}, b_{j2}^{(l)}, \ldots, b_{jn}^{(l)})^{\mathrm{T}} \in \{0,1\}^n$ for $l = 1, \ldots, N$ (T denotes the transposition). Let

$$\{u_i \in \mathcal{R}^M \mid ||u_i||^2 = 1, i = 1, 2, \ldots, n\} \tag{1}$$

be a set of n orthogonal sequences of unit power. The fingerprint watermark $w_j = (w_j^{(1)}, w_j^{(2)}, \ldots, w_j^{(N)})$ is created via the *spread spectrum* technique in which $w_j^{(l)}$ is generated by $\{u_i \in \mathcal{R}^M \mid i = 1, 2, \ldots, n\}$ and $b_j^{(l)}$ as

$$w_j^{(l)} = \sum_{i=1}^{n} (2b_{ji}^{(l)} - 1) u_i. \tag{2}$$

Note that there always exists a set of n orthogonal sequences for every $M \geq n$. Then the created watermark signal is embedded into a host signal. Denoting the host signal by $x = (x^{(1)}, \ldots, x^{(N)}) \in \mathcal{R}^{M\times N}$, the distributed content to user $j \in \Gamma$ is[1] $y_j = x + w_j \in \mathcal{R}^{M\times N}$. A encoding procedure is illustrated in Fig. 1.

Since fingerprints are embedded with a watermark technique, any user cannot detect their own fingerprint w_j from the watermarked content y_j. Therefore illicit users may collude to disturb their fingerprints by creating a forged content from their distributed contents.

2.2 Assumed collusion attack

We consider a set of colluders of size $h \geq 1$, denoted by $\mathcal{S}_c \subseteq \Gamma$, and without loss of generality, we assume $\mathcal{S}_c = \{1, 2, \ldots, h\}$. The attacked host signal by a set of colluders $\mathcal{S}_c$ is expressed as

[1] More precisely, each w_j is multiplied by some value called Just-Difference Noticeable (JDN) coefficient (Podilchuk & Zeng, 1998), before it is added to the host signal.

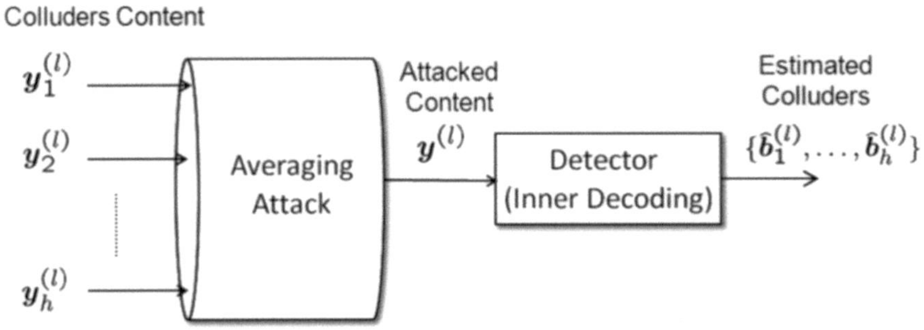

Fig. 2. Illustration of the averaging attack at segment l conducted by $\mathcal{S}_c = \{1,2,\ldots,h\}$. The sequence $\hat{\boldsymbol{b}}_j^{(l)}$ is an estimate which corresponds to $\boldsymbol{b}_j^{(l)}$.

$\boldsymbol{y} = (\boldsymbol{y}^{(1)}, \boldsymbol{y}^{(2)}, \ldots, \boldsymbol{y}^{(N)})$ such that

$$\boldsymbol{y}^{(l)} = \frac{1}{h}\sum_{j=1}^{h} \boldsymbol{y}_j^{(l)} \tag{3}$$

for $l = 1,2,\ldots,N$. From (2) and the relation $\boldsymbol{y}_j^{(l)} = \boldsymbol{x}^{(l)} + \boldsymbol{w}_j$, (3) can also be expressed as

$$\boldsymbol{y}^{(l)} = \boldsymbol{x}^{(l)} + \frac{1}{h}\sum_{j=1}^{h}\sum_{i=1}^{n}(2b_{ij}^{(l)} - 1)\boldsymbol{u}_i, \tag{4}$$

for $l = 1,\ldots,N$. The detector of the colluders estimates the set of colluders $\mathcal{S}_c$ from the attacked host signal $\boldsymbol{y} \in \mathcal{R}^M$. This attack is called the *averaging attack*, which is an effective collusion attack in multimedia fingerprinting (Trappe et al., 2003; Wu et al., 2004). Figure 2 illustrates the averaging attack at segment l conducted by $\mathcal{S}_c = \{1,2,\ldots,h\}$.

In practical situations, additive noise $\boldsymbol{z} \in \mathcal{R}^{M\times 1}$ is added to $\boldsymbol{y}^{(l)}$ in (4). However, we assume the absence of noise for the time being to focus on designing codes as in (Trappe et al., 2003). Later, some extension will be discussed to deal with noise.

2.3 Concatenated anti-collusion code

In this chapter, we consider concatenated coding, which increases the coding rates of AC codes in (Trappe et al., 2003), (Yagi et al., 2009), etc. In concatenated coding, we use two kinds of codes, namely an *outer code* and an *inner code* (Forney, 1966).

Let $\mathcal{C}^o \subseteq \mathrm{GF}^N(q)$ be a q-ary linear (N,K,D) error correcting code of length N, the number of information symbols, K, and minimum distance D (Lin & Costello, 2004), which is used as the outer code. We denote any codeword by $\boldsymbol{c}_j = (c_j^{(1)}, c_j^{(2)}, \ldots, c_j^{(N)}) \in \mathcal{C}^o$.

The encoder first generates a codeword of the outer code $\mathcal{C}^o$, and then each symbol $c_j^{(l)} \in \mathrm{GF}(q)$ for $l = 1,2,\ldots,N$ is mapped into a codeword $\boldsymbol{b}_j^{(l)} \in \mathcal{B}$, where $\mathcal{B} \subseteq \{0,1\}^{n\times 1}$ is a binary AC code (Trappe et al., 2003) of length n (Fig. 3). The mapping of a symbol $c_j^{(l)} \in \mathrm{GF}(q)$ to a

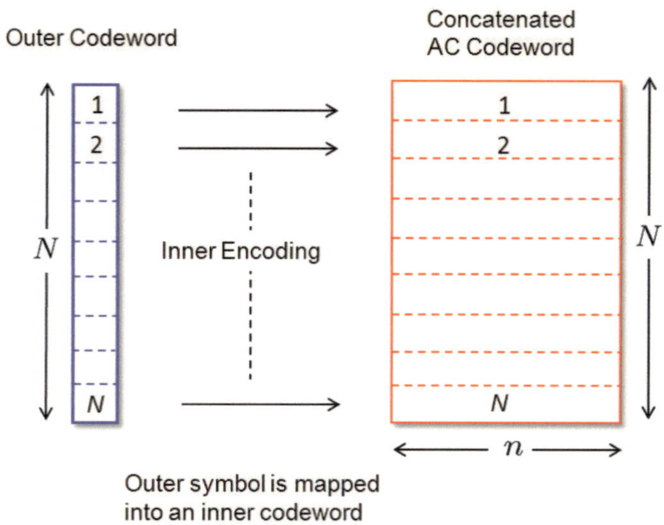

Fig. 3. Encoding procedure for a concatenated AC code. A codeword of the outer code is first generated, and each symbol is mapped into a codeword of the inner code. The total length of the concatenated AC code is $N_0 = Nn$, where N and n are the code length of the outer code and the inner code, respectively.

codeword $\boldsymbol{b}_j^{(l)} \in \mathcal{B}$ is unique and pre-determined. The code $\mathcal{B}$ is used as the inner code $\mathcal{C}^i$. We assume that $|\mathcal{B}| \geq q$ for one-to-one correspondence between q symbols of the outer code and a subset of codewords of $\mathcal{B}$. The mapped codeword is $\boldsymbol{b}_j = (\boldsymbol{b}_j^{(1)}, \ldots, \boldsymbol{b}_j^{(N)}) \in \{0,1\}^{n \times N}$. We denote the binary *concatenated code* of length $N_0 := Nn$ by $\mathcal{C} \subseteq \{0,1\}^{n \times N}$. After generating $\boldsymbol{b}_j \in \mathcal{C}$, we compute a watermark of each inner codeword $\boldsymbol{b}_j^{(l)} \in \mathcal{B}$, denoted by $\boldsymbol{w}_j^{(l)}$, by (2). If we use a trivial error correcting code, namely the (1,1,1) error correcting code, then this concatenated code reduces to the AC code in (Trappe et al., 2003) or (Yagi et al., 2009).

3. Inner codes and outer codes

3.1 Inner codes: AC codes based on finite geometries

Trappe et al. (Trappe et al., 2003) have devised anti-collusion (AC) codes, which are used as inner codes in our concatenated coding scheme. For the purpose of simple explanation, we assume $N = 1$ in this subsection. First, we give the definition of the AC codes.

Definition 1. Assume the *non-blind* scenario, in which the host signal $\boldsymbol{x}$ is known to the detector. If a set of colluders $\mathcal{S}_c$ satisfies $h \leq \ell$ for some positive integer $\ell \geq 2$, the code which can find all the colluders in $\mathcal{S}_c$ is referred to as an *ℓ-resilient AC code*. The parameter ℓ is called the *resilience* of the AC codes. □

Lemma 1 (Yagi et al., 2009)**.** *Assume that a binary matrix satisfies (i) the Hamming weight of each column is at least k, and (ii) any pair of distinct two columns has at most t 1-components in common.*

Then, the AC code whose codewords are all column vectors of this matrix is a $(\lceil k/t \rceil - 1)$*-resilient AC code. i.e., if* $h \leq \lceil k/t \rceil - 1$*, any set of colluders* $\mathcal{S}_c$ *can be uniquely detected*[2]. □

Remark 1. Let $\mathcal{Q}(\mathcal{S}_c)$ be the set of symbol positions where all of the fingerprints in $\mathcal{S}_c$ take the 0-component. Then an ℓ-resilient AC code in (Trappe et al., 2003) and (Yagi et al., 2009) uniquely identifies the set $\mathcal{Q}(\mathcal{S}_c)$ for any $\mathcal{S}_c$ with $h \leq \ell$. □

From Remark 1, since an ℓ-resilient AC code uniquely identifies $\mathcal{Q}(\mathcal{S}_c)$ for any $\mathcal{S}_c$ of size less than or equal to ℓ, the code reveals the set of colluders $\mathcal{S}_c$. For a detailed procedure of the inner decoding, refer to (Trappe et al., 2003).

In (Yagi et al., 2009), an algebraic construction of ℓ-resilient AC codes has been proposed based on finite geometries. We will use these AC codes as the inner code in concatenated coding for a comparison purpose though any AC codes can also be used. For a prime p and two positive integers m and s ($m \geq 2, s \geq 1$), the m-dimensional *Euclidean geometry* $\mathrm{EG}(m, p^s)$ over a Galois field $\mathrm{GF}(p^s)$ consists of *points, lines,* and *hyperplanes.* Any points in $\mathrm{EG}(m, p^s)$ are p^{ms} m-dimensional vectors over $\mathrm{GF}(p^s)$, and they form an m-dimensional vector space V over $\mathrm{GF}(p^s)$. For μ such that $0 \leq \mu \leq m$, a μ-dimensional hyperplane (generally, called a *μ-flat*) is a μ-dimensional subspace of V and its cosets, and any μ-flat contains $p^{\mu s}$ points. Points correspond to 0-flats. Any pair of two μ-flats, (F_1, F_2), has at most one $(\mu - 1)$-flat in common, which implies F_1 and F_2 have at most $p^{(\mu-1)s}$ points in common. In a Euclidean geometry $\mathrm{EG}(m, p^s)$, there are

$$f_{\mathrm{EG}}(\mu) = p^{(m-\mu)s} \prod_{i=1}^{\mu} \frac{p^{(m-i+1)s} - 1}{p^{(\mu-i+1)s} - 1} \tag{5}$$

μ-flats in total.

Letting $n_0 = f_{\mathrm{EG}}(0)$, consider an $n_0 \times f_{\mathrm{EG}}(\mu)$ matrix $B_\mu = (b_{ij})$. An element b_{ij} in a matrix B_μ takes $b_{ij} = 1$ if point i is contained in μ-flat j, or takes $b_{ij} = 0$ otherwise. This matrix B_μ is called the *incident matrix of μ-flats over points* in $\mathrm{EG}(m, p^s)$. Allocating the j-th column vector $\boldsymbol{b}_j$ of B_μ to the j-th user's fingerprint, the obtained code $\mathcal{B}_\mu = \{\boldsymbol{b}_j\}$ is called the *μ-th order EG-AC code.*

Lemma 2 (Yagi et al., 2009). *For given* $\mathrm{EG}(m, p^s)$*, the μ-th order EG-AC code* $\mathcal{B}_\mu$ *is a* $(p^s - 1)$*-resilient AC code of length* $n_0 = p^{ms}$ *and the number of codewords* $f_{\mathrm{EG}}(\mu)$*.* □

We mention parameters of EG-AC codes (Yagi et al., 2009). Let μ^* express dimension μ that maximizes $f_{\mathrm{EG}}(\mu)$. The number of codewords is $f_{\mathrm{EG}}(\mu^*) = \nu n_0^{\frac{1}{4}(m+2)}$ with some $1 \leq \nu < 2^{\frac{m}{2}}$. This means that the number of codewords increases in polynomial order $\Theta(n_0^{\frac{1}{4}(m+2)})$ of code length n_0.

3.2 Outer codes: Existing condition on error correcting codes

We state a previous condition on outer error-correcting codes (Yagi et al., 2007).

[2] $\lceil v \rceil$ expresses the minimum integer not less than v.

We define the Hamming distance between a sequence and a sequence set. Let $\boldsymbol{c}_j = (c_j^{(1)}, c_j^{(2)}, \ldots, c_j^{(N)}) \in \mathcal{C}^o$ such that $c_j^{(l)} \in \mathrm{GF}(q)$ for $l = 1, 2, \ldots, N$ be a codeword of the outer code $\mathcal{C}^o$. We define the following sets:

$$\mathcal{Y}^{(l)} = \{c_j^{(l)} \mid j \in \mathcal{S}_c\}, \tag{6}$$

and

$$\mathcal{Y} = \mathcal{Y}^{(1)} \times \mathcal{Y}^{(2)} \times \cdots \times \mathcal{Y}^{(N)} = \prod_{l=1}^{N} \mathcal{Y}^{(l)}. \tag{7}$$

The set $\mathcal{Y}^{(l)}$ expresses the set of symbols over $\mathrm{GF}(q)$ which give $\boldsymbol{y}^{(l)}$ (recall that there is one-to-one correspondence between symbols over $\mathrm{GF}(q)$ and a subset of inner codewords). We define the Hamming distance between a symbol $v \in \mathrm{GF}(q)$ and the set $\mathcal{Y}^{(l)}$ as

$$\delta(v, \mathcal{Y}^{(l)}) = \begin{cases} 0, & \text{if } v \in \mathcal{Y}^{(l)}; \\ 1, & \text{otherwise.} \end{cases} \tag{8}$$

We define the Hamming distance between a codeword $\boldsymbol{c}_j = (c_j^{(1)}, c_j^{(2)}, \ldots, c_j^{(N)}) \in \mathcal{C}^o$ such that $c_j^{(l)} \in \mathrm{GF}(q), l = 1, 2, \ldots, N$, and the set $\mathcal{Y}$ as

$$d_H(\boldsymbol{c}_j, \mathcal{Y}) = \sum_{l=1}^{N} \delta(c_j^{(l)}, \mathcal{Y}^{(l)}). \tag{9}$$

Definition 2. For a set of colluders $\mathcal{S}_c$ such that $h \leq \ell$ and any codeword $\boldsymbol{c}_j \in \mathcal{C}^o$ with $j \in \Gamma \setminus \mathcal{S}_c$, if at least r codewords $\boldsymbol{c}_i$ such that $i \in \mathcal{S}_c$ satisfy

$$d_H(\boldsymbol{c}_i, \mathcal{Y}) < d_H(\boldsymbol{c}_j, \mathcal{Y}), \tag{10}$$

then the concatenated code $\mathcal{C}$ is called the *(ℓ, r)-resilient concatenated AC (CAC) code* for $\mathcal{Y}$. □

The following theorem states a condition on the outer code $\mathcal{C}^o$ assuring that a concatenated code $\mathcal{C}$ becomes an (ℓ, h)-resilient AC code.

Theorem 1 (Yagi et al., 2007). *Assume that we use an ℓ-resilient AC code $\mathcal{B}$ as the inner code. If $h \leq \ell$ and a q-ary (N, K, D) error-correcting code such that*

$$D > N\left(1 - \frac{1}{\ell}\right) \tag{11}$$

is used as the outer code, the concatenated code $\mathcal{C}$ is an (ℓ, h)-resilient CAC code for $\mathcal{Y}$. □

The (ℓ, r)-resilient CAC codes enable us to detect at least r colluders in $\mathcal{S}_c$ by simply calculating the Hamming distance after obtaining each $\mathcal{Y}^{(l)}$ for $l = 1, 2, \ldots, N$ via the inner decoding. However, we need to exhaustively search codewords in $\mathcal{C}^o$, and a decoding algorithm requires exponential time complexity in outer code length N, i.e., $O(q^N)$. In (Yagi et al., 2007), the use of the Reed-Solomon (RS) codes is suggested as the outer codes. The RS code is an instance of the maximum distance separable (MDS) codes which meet Singleton's bound

$D \leq N - K + 1$ with equality, and $N = q - 1$ for a prime power q (Lin & Costello, 2004). In this case, the decoding complexity is expressed as $O(2^{N \log N})$. Further, $N_0 = \Theta(N^{\frac{m+6}{m+2}})$ since $n = \Theta(N^{\frac{4}{m+2}})$. Therefore, the overall decoding complexity[3] is $O(2^{N_0 \log N_0})$.

4. Polynomial-time concatenated AC codes

4.1 Condition on outer codes with ℓ-resilience

A main idea to give polynomial-time decodable concatenated codes is that after the inner decoding, we randomly create a sequence from the candidate symbol set $\mathcal{Y}$. Upon input of this sequence, a list-decoding algorithm for the outer code outputs at least one colluder's codeword. Like this, we consider iterating the following procedure:

(i) Set $\tau := 1$ and $\mathcal{Y}_0^{(l)} := \mathcal{Y}^{(l)}$ for each $l = 1, \ldots, N$.

(ii) Randomly pick a symbol $\tilde{y}_\tau^{(l)}$ from $\mathcal{Y}_{\tau-1}^{(l)}$ for each $l = 1, \ldots, N$, and set $\tilde{\mathcal{Y}}_\tau^{(l)} := \{\tilde{y}_\tau^{(l)}\}$ and $\tilde{\boldsymbol{y}}_\tau := (\tilde{y}_\tau^{(1)}, \ldots, \tilde{y}_\tau^{(N)})$.

(iii) Find all $j \in \Gamma$ such that

$$d_H(\boldsymbol{c}_j, \tilde{\boldsymbol{y}}_\tau) \leq N(1 - 1/\ell), \tag{12}$$

and the set of found colluders is denoted by $\mathcal{S}_{c,\tau}$. We define $\mathcal{Y}_\tau^{(l)}$ and $\mathcal{Y}_\tau$ in a similar way to (6) and (7), respectively, by replacing $\mathcal{S}_c$ with $\mathcal{S}_c \setminus \bigcup_{i=1}^{\tau} \mathcal{S}_{c,i}$ (notice that $|\mathcal{Y}_\tau^{(l)}| \leq |\mathcal{Y}_{\tau-1}^{(l)}|$ for every $l = 1, \ldots, N$).

(iv) Set $\tau := \tau + 1$, and go to step (ii). We repeat this procedure until there are no codewords satisfying (12).

Proposition 1. *Assume that the inner code is an ℓ-resilient AC code $\mathcal{B}$. If $h \leq \ell$ and a q-ary (N, K, D) error-correcting code such that*

$$D > N\left(1 - \frac{1}{\ell^2}\right) \tag{13}$$

is used as the outer code, the concatenated code $\mathcal{C}$ is an (ℓ, h_τ)-resilient CAC code for each $\tilde{\mathcal{Y}}_\tau$, where $h_\tau = |\mathcal{S}_{c,\tau}|$.

(Proof) Let $\boldsymbol{c}_j = (c_j^{(1)}, c_j^{(2)}, \ldots, c_j^{(N)}) \in \mathcal{C}^o$ such that $c_j^{(l)} \in \mathrm{GF}(q)$ for $l = 1, 2, \ldots, N$ be the j-th users' outer codeword. By the definition of $\mathcal{S}_{c,\tau}$, there are h_τ colluders whose $\boldsymbol{c}_i, i \in \mathcal{S}_{c,\tau}$, satisfy $d_H(\boldsymbol{c}_i, \tilde{\boldsymbol{y}}_\tau) \leq N(1 - 1/\ell)$. On the other hand, since any fingerprint $\boldsymbol{c}_j, j \in \Gamma \setminus \mathcal{S}_c$, agrees at most $(N - D)$ symbols with each fingerprint $\boldsymbol{c}_i, i \in \mathcal{S}_{c,\tau}$, any $\boldsymbol{c}_j$ agrees at most $\ell(N - D)$ symbols with $\tilde{\boldsymbol{y}}_\tau$. Therefore we have

$$\begin{aligned} d_H(\boldsymbol{c}_j, \tilde{\boldsymbol{y}}_\tau) &= N - \ell(N - D) \\ &> N - \ell N + \ell N\left(1 - \frac{1}{\ell^2}\right) = N\left(1 - \frac{1}{\ell}\right). \end{aligned} \tag{14}$$

[3] The complexity of encoding is $O(N_0^2)$ in the concatenated coding.

Since $d_H(c_i, \tilde{y}_\tau) \leq N(1-1/\ell)$, (14) implies $d_H(c_j, \tilde{y}_\tau) > d_H(c_i, \tilde{y}_\tau)$. Therefore we can correctly detect h_τ colluders in $\mathcal{S}_{c,\tau}$ by comparing the Hamming distance from $\tilde{y}_\tau$. □

The condition (13) is the same as the condition of ℓ-traceability (TA) codes against the interleaving attack (Staddon et al., 2001; Silverberg et al., 2003), which identify at least one colluder in $\mathcal{S}_c$ of size less than or equal to ℓ. The condition (13) is weaker than (11) in the sense that (13) is sufficient to satisfy (11).

By Singleton's bound, the minimum distance of a linear error correcting code satisfies $D \leq N - K + 1$. Since it is desirable to make D as large as possible, we may well use the RS code satisfying $D = N - K + 1$ as the outer code. For given prime power q, there always exists a lengthened/shortened RS code for every $N \leq q$ if $K \geq 1$ and $D = N - K + 1$. Other promising candidates for the outer code are algebraic geometry (AG) codes or near-MDS expander codes in (Guruswami, 2004), which asymptotically meet Singleton's bound. All these codes can be decoded by the Guruswami-Sudan (GS) list-decoding algorithm (Guruswami, 2004), which corrects up to $N(1-\sqrt{(K-1)/N})$ errors with the polynomial time complexity in N (Silverberg et al., 2003).

4.2 Decoding algorithm for concatenated AC codes

We propose a polynomial-time decoding algorithm for a concatenated code C base on Proposition 1. As in (Fernandez & Soriano, 2004) and (Silverberg et al., 2003) for ℓ-TA codes against the interleaving attack, we employ a code C^o that can be decoded by the GS list-decoding algorithm. The detail decoding procedure is described as follows:

[Proposed Decoding Algorithm]

(1) For each $y^{(l)}, l = 1, \ldots, N$ given by (4), find all the members in $\mathcal{Y}^{(l)}$ via the decoding of the inner AC code.

(2) Set $\tau_{\max} := \max_{1 \leq l \leq N} |\mathcal{Y}^{(l)}|$, $\tau := 1$ and $\mathcal{Y}_0^{(l)} := \mathcal{Y}^{(l)}$ for each $l = 1, \ldots, N$.

(3) Randomly pick $\tilde{y}_\tau^{(l)} \in \mathcal{Y}_{\tau-1}^{(l)}$ for each $l = 1, \ldots, N$, and set $\tilde{y}_\tau := (\tilde{y}_\tau^{(1)}, \ldots, \tilde{y}_\tau^{(N)})$.

(4) Execute the GS list-decoding algorithm for $\tilde{y}_\tau$, and find the set $\mathcal{S}_{c,\tau}$.

(5) Set $\mathcal{Y}_\tau^{(l)}$ for $l = 1, \ldots, N$ as

$$\mathcal{Y}_\tau^{(l)} := \begin{cases} \mathcal{Y}^{(l)} \setminus \bigcup_{i=1}^{\tau-1} \mathcal{Y}_i^{(l)}, & \text{if } \mathcal{Y}^{(l)} \neq \bigcup_{i=1}^{\tau-1} \mathcal{Y}_i^{(l)}, \\ \mathcal{Y}^{(l)}, & \text{otherwise,} \end{cases} \tag{15}$$

and set $\mathcal{Y}_\tau := \prod_{l=1}^{N} \mathcal{Y}_\tau^{(l)}$.

(6) If $\tau = \tau_{\max}$ or $|\bigcup_{i=1}^{\tau} \mathcal{S}_{c,i}| = \tau_{\max}$, then output $\bigcup_{i=1}^{\tau} \mathcal{S}_{c,i}$ as colluders and halt the algorithm. Otherwise, set $\tau := \tau + 1$ and go to step (3).

We note that in step (1), which corresponds to the inner decoding, $\mathcal{Y}^{(l)}$ for $l = 1, \ldots, N$ are correctly found although we cannot see $\mathcal{S}_c$ itself. We show that if the outer code satisfies the condition (13), then $\mathcal{S}_{c,\tau}$ is correctly found at step (4) in each iteration by the following lemmas:

Lemma 3. *If $h \leq \ell$ and an outer code satisfying (13) is concatenated with an ℓ-resilient AC code, there is some $l \in \{1, \ldots, N\}$ such that $|\mathcal{Y}^{(l)}| = h$. i.e., the maximum number of iterations of the proposed decoding algorithm is $\tau_{\max} = h$.*

(Proof) If $h = 2$, then there is at least D positions such that $|\mathcal{Y}^{(l)}| = 2$ because the Hamming distance of any two outer codewords is at least D. For the case $h \geq 3$, the symbols of user 1's codeword $\boldsymbol{c}_1$ and user 2's codeword $\boldsymbol{c}_2$ are different in at least D positions and we denote this position set by $\mathcal{D}$. Then user 3's codeword $\boldsymbol{c}_3$ cannot agree more than $N - D$ symbols with each of $\boldsymbol{c}_1$ and $\boldsymbol{c}_2$ in the position indexed by $\mathcal{D}$. i.e.,

$$|\{i|c_{ji} = c_{3i}, i \in \mathcal{D}\}| \leq N - D, \ \text{for } j = 1, 2. \tag{16}$$

Therefore, there are at least $D - 2(N - D)$ positions in which all three codewords disagree. When we consider the forth codeword $\boldsymbol{c}_4$, the same argument gives at least $D - (2+3)(N - D)$ positions in which all four codewords disagree. By induction, among $\{\boldsymbol{c}_1, \boldsymbol{c}_2, \ldots, \boldsymbol{c}_\nu\}$ such that $\nu \leq h$, the number of positions in which all the codewords $\boldsymbol{c}_1, \ldots, \boldsymbol{c}_\nu$ disagree is at least

$$D - (2 + 3 + \cdots + (\nu - 1))(N - D)$$
$$> D - \frac{1}{2}(\ell - 2)(\ell + 1)(N - D). \tag{17}$$

Since (13) is satisfied, the r.h.s. of (17) is further bounded by

$$\frac{N}{2}\left(1 + \frac{1}{\ell}\right) \tag{18}$$

from below. Equation (18) implies that the lemma holds. □

Lemma 4. *If $h \leq \ell$ and the outer code satisfies (13), all the codewords satisfying (12) for given $\tilde{\boldsymbol{y}}_\tau$ are correctly found at step (4).*

(Proof) If (13) is satisfied, then we can easily check

$$N(1 - 1/\ell) < N\left(1 - \sqrt{(K-1)/N}\right) \tag{19}$$

where the r.h.s. expresses the correcting radius of the GS list-decoding algorithm (Silverberg et al., 2003). Therefore all the codewords satisfying (12) are found in step (4). □

The next theorem states the number of colluders captured by the proposed decoding algorithm in the absence of noise.

Theorem 2. *If $h \leq \ell$ and we use an ℓ-resilient AC code $\mathcal{B}$ as the inner code and an (N, K, D) error correcting code satisfying (13) as the outer code, then the proposed decoding algorithm finds all the colluders in $\mathcal{S}_c$.*

(Proof) In the first iteration $\tau = 1$, obviously there is at least one colluder's codeword $\boldsymbol{c}_j \in \mathcal{C}^o$ which is in the distance $d_H(\boldsymbol{c}_i, \tilde{\boldsymbol{y}}_1) \leq N(1 - 1/\ell)$ and can be decoded by the GS list-decoding. This implies that all the colluders can be found if $h = 2$.

Let some $h, 3 \leq h \leq \ell$, be given, and we first assume that in each iteration only one colluder's codeword is found before iteration $\tau, 2 \leq \tau \leq h$. In iteration τ, we assume that the colluders found so far are denoted by $\tilde{c}_1, \ldots, \tilde{c}_{\tau-1}$ for simplicity. Let a function $\Delta(\tau)$ be defined as

$$\Delta(\tau) = D - (\tau - 1)(N - D) \tag{20}$$

Since any two codewords agree in at most $N - D$ positions, each of remaining $\tilde{c}_\tau, \ldots, \tilde{c}_h$ agrees at least $\Delta(\tau)$ positions with $\mathcal{Y}_{\tau-1}$, which has been calculated at step (5) in iteration $\tau - 1$. By using (13), $\Delta(\tau)$ is bounded as

$$\Delta(\tau) > N(1 - \tau/\ell^2). \tag{21}$$

When randomly picking $\tilde{y}_\tau$ at step (3) in iteration τ, there is at least one codeword among $\tilde{c}_\tau, \ldots, \tilde{c}_h$ which agrees greater than or equal to $\Delta(\tau)/(h - \tau + 1)$ positions with $\tilde{y}_\tau$, which is bounded as

$$\Delta(\tau)/(h - \tau + 1) > N(1 - \tau/\ell^2)/(h - \tau + 1). \tag{22}$$

The r.h.s. of (22) is greater than N/ℓ since

$$\begin{aligned} \frac{N}{h - \tau + 1}\left(1 - \frac{\tau}{\ell^2}\right) - \frac{N}{\ell} &= \frac{N\{\ell(\ell - h) + \ell\tau - \ell - \tau\}}{(h - \tau + 1)\ell^2} \\ &\geq \frac{N(h\tau - h - \tau)}{(h - \tau + 1)\ell^2}, \end{aligned} \tag{23}$$

where we substitute $h = \ell$ to obtain the last inequality. The r.h.s. of (23) is apparently greater than zero for $h \geq 3$ and $\tau \geq 2$. This in turn implies that there is at least one codeword $c_j, \tau \leq j \leq h$, such that $d_H(c_j, \tilde{y}_\tau) \leq N(1 - 1/\ell)$ and it can be found by the GS-list decoding algorithm.

The case where in some iteration $\tau' < \tau$, more than one colluder's codeword is found can be proved in a similar way. □

We state the time complexity of the proposed decoding algorithm by assuming an RS code is used as the outer code. As for the inner decoding (step (1)), we conduct the exhaustive search of all the combinations of ℓ or less inner codewords. The number of inner codewords is $q = O(N)$, so the time complexity for each inner decoding is $O(N^\ell)$, which is polynomial time in code length N_0. In each iteration, we execute the GS list-decoding algorithm for the outer code, which requires the time complexity of $O(N^{15})$ for iteration $\tau = 1$ when $h = \ell$ and of $O(N^4)$ for iteration $\tau \geq 2$ (or $\tau \geq 1$ when $h < \ell$). Since the maximum number of iteration is ℓ, the overall decoding complexity is bounded by $\max\{O(N^{\ell+1}), O(N^{15})\}$ when $h = \ell$. When $h < \ell$, we can also show that the overall decoding complexity is bounded by $\max\{O(N^{\ell+1}), O(hN^4)\}$.

4.3 Coding rates of concatenated AC codes

As for the inner code $\mathcal{C}^i = \mathcal{B}$, we require only the condition that $|\mathcal{B}| \geq q$, where q is the number of symbols of an outer code $\mathcal{C}^o$. If $|\mathcal{B}|/q > 1$, we can divide the CAC codes into several groups. Define $g = \lfloor |\mathcal{B}|/q \rfloor$. We first divide an inner code $\mathcal{B}$ into g disjoint subsets $\mathcal{B}^{(1)}, \mathcal{B}^{(2)}, \ldots, \mathcal{B}^{(g)}$ such that $|\mathcal{B}^{(i)}| \geq q, i = 1, 2, \ldots, g$. By using each $\mathcal{B}^{(i)}$ as the inner codes, we obtain g disjoint concatenated codes, denoted by $\mathcal{C}^{(1)}, \mathcal{C}^{(2)}, \ldots, \mathcal{C}^{(g)}$. The overall code $\mathcal{C} =$

$\bigcup_{i=1}^{g} \mathcal{C}^{(i)}$ is an ℓ-resilient CAC code with size $F_0 := gq^K$ if each concatenated code $\mathcal{C}^{(i)}$ is an ℓ-resilient AC code. Coding rate R_0 of $\mathcal{C}$ is given by $R_0 = (\log_2 gq^K)/N_0$.

Example 1. We show the numbers of codewords of five CAC codes $\mathcal{C}$ which consist of EG-AC inner codes $\mathcal{C}^i = \mathcal{B}$ and MDS outer codes $\mathcal{C}^o$ (shortened RS codes (Lin & Costello, 2004)). For comparison, we show conventional EG-AC codes $\mathcal{B}_\mu$ (Yagi et al., 2007) with the same resilience and the code length. Table 1 shows the parameters of original and concatenated EG-AC codes and Table 2 shows the logarithm of the number of codewords for each code. From Table 2, it can be found that the CAC codes is effective. In particular, as the code length becomes large, the effectiveness of the CAC codes is enhanced. □

We now analyze the asymptotic number of codewords by assuming an (N, K, D) RS code satisfying (13) and an EG-AC code of the maximal order μ^* are used as the outer code and the inner code, respectively. For simplicity, we assume $q = N$, which means that the lengthened RS code is used. The EG-AC code of the maximal order μ^* satisfies $f_{\mathrm{EG}}(\mu^*) = \nu n^{\frac{1}{4}(m+2)}$ with some $\nu, 1 \leq \nu < 2^{\frac{m}{2}}$ (Yagi et al., 2009). There exists an $m > 3$ such that $\nu n^{\frac{1}{4}(m+1)} < q \leq \nu n^{\frac{1}{4}(m+2)}$, and hence

$$\nu n^{\frac{1}{4}(m+1)} < N \leq \nu n^{\frac{1}{4}(m+2)} \tag{24}$$

from $N = q$. Note that the condition (13) is equivalent to $K < N/\ell^2 + 1$ since $K = N - D + 1$, but there always exit RS codes with $K \geq N/\ell^2$ (this can be confirmed by setting $D = \lceil N(1 - 1/\ell^2) \rceil$). Then the total number of codewords $F_0 := q^K = N^K$ satisfies

$$F_0 \geq 2^{N \log N/\ell^2}. \tag{25}$$

Since the overall length of the concatenated code is $N_0 = Nn$ where $n \leq (N/\nu)^{\frac{4}{m+1}}$ from (24), we have $N \geq (N_0 \nu^{\frac{4}{m+1}})^{\frac{m+1}{m+5}}$, and (25) becomes

$$F_0 \geq 2^{\nu' \cdot \frac{m+1}{(m+5)} \cdot \frac{\log N_0}{\ell^2} \cdot N_0^{\frac{m+1}{(m+5)}}} \tag{26}$$

where $\nu' = \nu^{\frac{4}{m+5}}$. Furthermore, by carefully investing the parameters of EG-AC codes, we find

$$m^2 + 6m + 2m \log_{\ell+1} 2 = 4 \log_{\ell+1} N_0, \tag{27}$$

resulting in $m = \Theta(2(\log_{\ell+1} N_0)^{\frac{1}{2}})$. We have $m \to \infty$ as $N_0 \to \infty$ and $\nu' \geq 1$. Thus, for any $\epsilon, 0 < \epsilon < 1$, there exists a concatenated AC code such that

$$F_0 \geq 2^{\frac{(1-\epsilon) N_0^{1-\epsilon} \log N_0}{\ell^2}} \tag{28}$$

with sufficiently large N_0. Equation (28) implies that the number of codewords increases arbitrarily closely in the exponential order of $N_0 \log N_0/\ell^2$, which is equal to a single RS code of length N_0. Thus, the number of codewords of the proposed concatenated codes is much greater than those of the AC codes in (Yagi et al., 2009).

No.	EG-AC code $\mathcal{B}_\mu$		Concatenated EG-AC code $\mathcal{C}$			
			Inner Code $\mathcal{C}^i$		Outer Code $\mathcal{C}^o$	
	(m, p^s)	n	(m, p^s)	n	(N, K, D)	q
(i)	$(4, 3^1)$	81	$(2, 3^1)$	9	$(9, 3, 7)$	11
(ii)	$(6, 3^1)$	729	$(3, 3^1)$	27	$(27, 7, 21)$	32
(iii)	$(7, 3^1)$	2187	$(4, 3^1)$	81	$(27, 7, 21)$	81
(iv)	$(8, 3^1)$	6561	$(4, 3^1)$	81	$(81, 21, 61)$	81
(v)	$(6, 2^2)$	4096	$(3, 2^2)$	64	$(64, 8, 57)$	64

Table 1. Parameters of original and concatenated EG-AC codes

No.	Resilience ℓ	Code length Nn	# of Information Symbols	
			$\log_2 \lvert\mathcal{B}_\mu\rvert$	$\log_2 \lvert\mathcal{C}\rvert$
(i)	2	81	10.19	10.38
(ii)	2	729	19.80	35.00
(iii)	2	2187	26.16	44.38
(iv)	2	6561	32.52	133.14
(v)	3	4096	24.52	48.00

Table 2. Examples of the number of codewords of original and concatenated EG-AC codes

4.4 Conditions of outer codes with ℓ-resilience and e-error correcting capability

The ℓ-resilient AC codes in Sect. 3.1 do not have error-correcting capability. On the other hand, with concatenated coding, we can make ℓ-resilient CAC codes have such capability. In the presence of noise in (4), i.e.,

$$y^{(l)} = 1/h \sum_{j=1}^{h} y_j^{(l)} + z \tag{29}$$

where $z \in \mathcal{R}^{n\times 1}$ is a vector of additive noise, this is particularly important because some of inner decoders may result in mis-correction (Trappe et al., 2003). For some non-negative integer e, we derive conditions on an outer code $\mathcal{C}^o$ assuring that a concatenated code $\mathcal{C}$ have an (ℓ, r)-resilience and e-error correcting capability[4].

Proposition 2. *Assume that an ℓ-resilient AC code $\mathcal{B}$ is used as the inner code, and an (N, K, D) error correcting code satisfying*

$$D > N\left(1 - \frac{1}{\ell^2}\right) + \frac{(\ell+1)e}{\ell^2} \tag{30}$$

is used as the outer code. If $h \le \ell$ and the number of inner decoders whose outputs are in error is less than or equal to e, the concatenated code $\mathcal{C}$ is an (ℓ, h_τ)-resilient CAC code for each $\tilde{\mathcal{Y}}_\tau$ (defined in Sect. 4.1), where $h_\tau = |\mathcal{S}_{c,\tau}|$.

(Proof) Let $c_j = (c_j^{(1)}, c_j^{(2)}, \ldots, c_j^{(N)}) \in \mathcal{C}^o$ such that $c_j^{(l)} \in \mathrm{GF}(q)$ for $l = 1, 2, \ldots, N$ be the j-th users' outer codeword. There are h_τ colluders such that each of $c_i, i \in \mathcal{S}_{c,\tau}$ agrees at least

[4] We can introduce *erasure* symbols instead of error symbols as in (Fernandez & Soriano, 2004), which was introduced against the interleaving attack.

$(N-e)/\ell$ symbols in $\tilde{\mathcal{Y}}_\tau$, i.e., we have

$$d_H(\mathbf{c}_i, \tilde{\mathcal{Y}}_\tau) \le N - (N-e)/\ell. \quad (31)$$

On the other hand, any fingerprint $\mathbf{c}_j, j \in \Gamma \setminus \mathcal{S}_c$ agrees at most $\ell(N-D)+e$ symbols in $\tilde{\mathcal{Y}}_\tau$. We have

$$\begin{aligned} d_H(\mathbf{c}_j, \tilde{\mathcal{Y}}_\tau) - d_H(\mathbf{c}_i, \tilde{\mathcal{Y}}_\tau) &\ge N - \ell(N-D) - e \\ &\quad -(N-(N-e)/\ell) > 0, \end{aligned} \quad (32)$$

for $\ell \ge 2$. Therefore the condition (10) is satisfied. □

Theorem 3. *Assume that we use an ℓ-resilient AC code $\mathcal{B}$ as the inner code and an (N, K, D) error correcting code satisfying (30) as the outer code. If the number of inner decoders whose outputs are in error is less than or equal to e, then the proposed decoding algorithm finds all the colluders in $\mathcal{S}_c$.* □

It follows from (13) and (30) that the e-error correcting capability requires a more stringent condition on D by $(\ell+1)e/\ell^2$. In this case, we can also use an MDS or a near-MDS code as the outer code $\mathcal{C}^o$.

5. Existence of polynomial-time AC codes with a positive rate

The proposed method given in the previous section is of importance from the fact that we can construct it in a deterministic way for given parameters and implement encoding and decoding with polynomial-time complexity in n. Theorem 2 indicates that the size of the concatenated AC codes still grows *semi-exponential* in the code length, and the *coding rate* of this code goes to zero as n tends to infinity. Recently, it has been pointed out by (Koga, 2010) that there exist AC codes with a strictly positive coding rate although it is not clear how to construct such codes. Here, we show that there exist polynomial-time AC codes with a strictly positive coding rate, based on the argument given by (Koga, 2010).

First, we review a result on the coding rate of ℓ-resilient AC codes shown by (Koga, 2010).

Theorem 4 (Koga, 2010). *For given $\ell \ge 2$, there exists at least one ℓ-resilient AC code with the coding rate*

$$R = \frac{1}{4^\ell + 1}. \quad (33)$$

for sufficiently large n. □

Theorem 4 is an " existence theorem" which indicates only the existence of good AC codes but does not imply how to construct such codes. In addition, encoding and decoding complexity is in the exponential order of n, which seems impractical even though such codes can be obtained. The next theorem shows the existence of ℓ-resilient AC codes that can be encoded and decoded with polynomial order complexity in n.

Theorem 5. *For given $\ell \ge 2$, there exists at least one ℓ-resilient concatenated AC code that can encoded and decoded with polynomial order complexity in n with the coding rate*

$$R = \frac{1}{\ell^2(4^\ell + 1)}. \tag{34}$$

for sufficiently large n.

(Proof) This theorem can be easily proven by noticing that the coding rate is decreased by the factor of $1/\ell^2$ if concatenated coding is used. □

From Theorem 5, we can reduce the encoding and decoding complexity to a great extent by allowing the coding rate decreases by the factor of $\frac{1}{\ell^2}$. However, it is guaranteed that the existence of an ℓ-resilient concatenated AC code whose coding rate is still strictly positive for all $\ell \geq 2$.

6. Conclusion

In this chapter, for multimedia fingerprinting, concatenated coding in which the outer code is a near-MDS error correcting code and the inner code is a class of AC codes in (Trappe et al., 2003) and (Yagi et al., 2009), was proposed. Using AC codes given by (Kang et al., 2006) and (Li et al., 2009) as the inner codes, a similar result can be obtained. Based on list-decoding for the outer code, we proposed a polynomial-time decoding algorithm. Furthermore, we derived a condition assuring that concatenated AC codes have e-error correcting capability.

In the last part of this chapter, we have shown the existence of AC codes that can be encoded and decoded with polynomial time complexity and have a positive rate. It is of interest to investigate how to construct such codes in a deterministic way.

7. References

Boneh, D. & Shaw, J. (1998). Collusion-secure fingerprinting for digital data, *IEEE Trans. Inform. Theory*, vol. 44, pp. 1897–1905.

Guruswami, V. (2004). *List Decoding of Error-Correcting Codes* (Lecture Notes in Computer Science, vol. 2282) Springer Berlin/Heidelberg.

Fernandez, M. & Soriano, M. (2004). Soft-decision tracing in fingerprinted multimedia content, *IEEE Multimedia*, vol. 11, no. 2, pp. 38–46.

Forney, Jr., G. D. (1966). *Concatenated Codes*, MIT Press, Cambridge, MA.

Kang, I. K. Sinha, K. & Lee, H. K. (2006). New digital fingerprint code construction scheme using group-divisible design, *IEICE Trans. Fundamentals*, vol. E89-A, no. 12, pp. 3732-3735.

Koga, H. (2010). On the capacity of the AND anti-collusion fingerprinting codes, (in Japanese) *IEICE Technical Report*, vol. 109, no. 444, pp. 439–444.

Li, Q. Wang, X. Li, Y. Pan, Y. & Fan, P. (2009). Construction of anti-collusion codes based on cover-free families, *Proc. Sixth International Conference on Information Technology: New Generations, ITNG 2009*, Las Vegas, USA.

Lin, S. & Costello Jr., D. J. (2004). *Error Control Coding: Fundamentals and Applications, 2nd ed.*, Prentice-Hall, Upper Saddle River.

Podilchuk, C. & Zeng, W. (1998). Image adaptive watermarking using visual models, *IEEE J. Select. Areas Commun.*, vol. 16, pp. 525–540.

Silverberg, A. Staddon, J. & Walker, J. L. (2003). Applications of list decoding to tracing traitors, *IEEE Trans. Inform. Theory*, vol. 49, no. 5, pp. 1312–1318.

Staddon, J. N. Stinson, D. R. & Wei, R. (2001). Combinatorial properties of frameproof and traceability codes, *IEEE Trans. Inform. Theory*, vol. 47, no. 3, pp. 1042–1049.

Trappe, W., Wu, M., Wang, Z. J. & Liu, K. J. R. (2003). Anti-collusion fingerprinting for multimedia, *IEEE Trans. Signal Processing*, vol. 51, pp. 1069–1087.

Wu, M., Trappe, W., Wang, Z. J. & Liu, K. J. R. (2004). Collusion-resistant fingerprinting for multimedia, *IEEE Signal Processing Magazine*, vol. 21, pp. 15–27.

Yagi, H. Matsushima, T. & Hirasawa, S. (2007). Short concatenated fingerprinting codes for multimedia data, *Proc. of 45th Annual Allerton Conference*, pp.1040–1045, Illinois, USA.

Yagi, H. Matsushima, T. & Hirasawa, S. (2009). Fingerprinting codes for multimedia data against averaging attack, *IEICE Trans. Fundamentals*, vol.E-92, no.1, pp.207–216.

7

Evaluation of Multimedia Fingerprinting Image

Kang Hyeon RHEE
College of Electronics and Information Engineering, Chosun University, Dept. of Electronics Engineering, Gwangju, Korea

1. Introduction

It would observe an enormous growth about a use and distribution of multimedia content in Internet, and an illegal copy and redistribution of multimedia content are also increased with a serious proclivity for a wrongdoer.

Among multimedia content specially, a digital image has been widely used in a variety of applications, from web, digital camera photography, military information and digital art to medical diagnosis and personal blog. As like this, digital image is more and more important media in an information society. Therefore, a necessity for a reliable multimedia content has been rising rapidly in recent years. How to protect the original creator's Intellectual Property Rights (IPR) and integrity of digital products is a realistic problem urgently needing to be solved [1]. Accordingly, the copyright of a content creator has to be protectable for IPR and discriminate between the original from an illegal copy.

Furthermore, a tracing of an illegal distribution has to be a necessary for a copyright protection and a cutoff of an illegal copy of multimedia content. The methods to prevent from an illegal reproduction and distribution are categorized into two ways. The one is enable to use and transmit within a boundary of admitted limitation for authorized users, and the other is to trace how people reproduce and redistribute the content illegally, when they are found to be illicit in contact with an unauthorized content [2].

In the early, the studies of content copyright protective are limited in application by encryption method, a watermarking technology introduced by the alternative.

Watermarking method inserts the original owner information to content. After piracy, the watermarking information is extracted from content, and then it compares with the original watermarking information [3]. So this method could be proving the original owner. But, watermarking method can only confirm the copied illegal content, and it never confirms the illegal distributor and the distributed path.

Digital watermarking method indicates the copyright which is made with a provider's self information and directly inserted into multimedia content. This orientation of technology comes from an intention to protect a copyright because multimedia contents on a web are easy to redistribute. Fig. 1 and 2 show the process of the watermark insertion and watermark detection.

According to the developed technology of watermarking, multimedia fingerprinting technology [4-6] was rising also. Multimedia fingerprinting technology includes owner's and user's information of content so that multimedia fingerprinting technology is to solve these problems. Colluders try to remove the inserted fingerprinting code in content then they regenerate the collusion codes and can redistribute illegally the pirated content by insert the collusion code. Thus, multimedia fingerprinting code has to be generated in order to be robust in this kind of the collusion attack by the colluders.

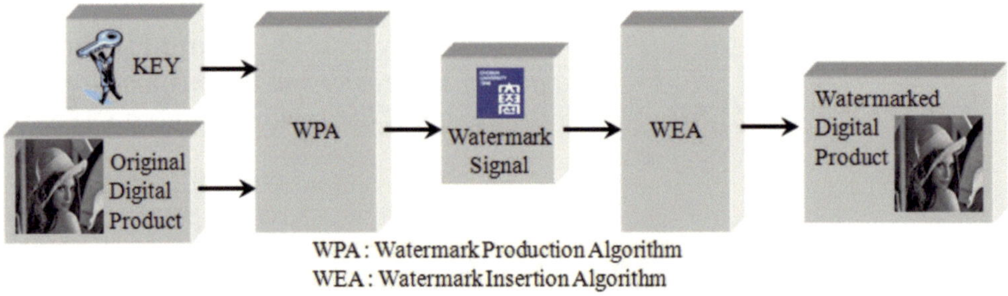

Fig. 1. Watermark insertion

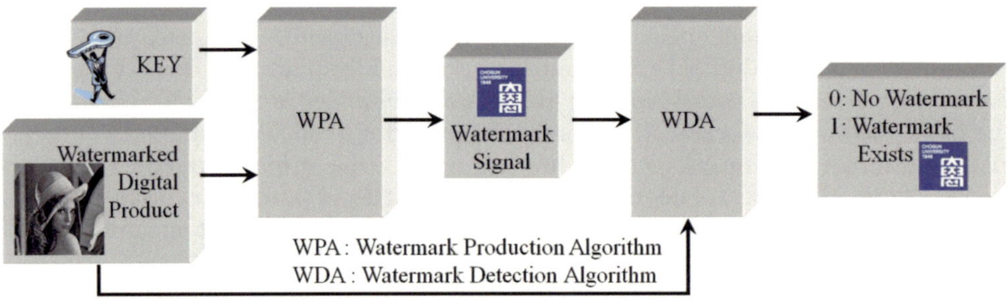

Fig. 2. Watermark detection

So, that would be robustness in this collusion attack into multimedia fingerprinting code should be created [7]. For the fingerprinting code of multimedia content protection, application of BIBD (Balanced Incomplete Block Design) code that satisfies the specification of ACC (Anti-Collusion code) was studied in several papers [8-16].

1.1 Prior art

The resistances of digital watermark to linear collusion attacks have been studied recently [16-18]. W. Trappe [16] presented a fingerprinting system using BIBD code derived from combinatorial design system proposed by D. R. Stinson [20], which proposed a fingerprint code system that satisfies "Frame-proof code" by using combinational design theory first time.

When a copyright infringement has been occurred, copyrighters can choose to insert the watermark into their content to acknowledge who is responsible for the original contents.

One of the first collusion resistant fingerprints was proposed by [4] for generic data. The watermarks were assumed to satisfy the marking assumption, that is, the users cannot change the state of an undetected mark without rendering the object useless [11].

Also, multimedia fingerprinting is a technology for copyright protection of the content's creators. It is a process of insertion in a distinct set of marks into a given host signal to produce a set of fingerprinted signals that each appears identical to use. If an illegal copy is detected, it's possible to trace the dishonest users. However, colluders may get together comparing their copies and make a new copy to avoid being incriminated, known as collusion attack [10].

For the multimedia content protection, BIBD code that satisfies the characteristics of ACC, so the application of BIBD code on the fingerprinting code was progressed in many researches [8-16]. The BIBD matrix is modified to form fingerprinting codes that had collusion resistant, even if all the users collude [8]. And ACC was proposed to accommodate more users while providing collusion-resistance [16].

Accordingly, a multimedia fingerprinting technology was rising. The insertion method of fingerprinting code to multimedia content was variously studied. When it inserts fingerprinting code in content, the robustness of orthogonal modulation technology is limited on Averaging attack by colluders, but a code modulation technology has robustness for Averaging attack.

Thus, a resilience code is used to fingerprinting code [16], which is derived from BIBD code, but this method is difficult to define the threshold value according to the change of the threshold setting value by the number of colluders when the collusion code is detected from an illegal content on used Averaging attack [12].

1.2 Article organization

In this article, the collusion code generated using a fingerprinting code based on BIBD is estimated and PSNR of the experimental images according to BIBD v value is computed also. The kind of collusion attacks used for the evaluation method of the considered collusion code generation is an average computing (Averaging) and logical operations (AND, OR and XOR).

It now summarizes the main focus and contributions of this article.

1. Fingerprinting code generation based on BIBD code.
2. Collusion code generation of Logic operation (AND, OR and XOR) and Averaging.
3. Evaluation of the generated collusion codes for an effect increasing of anti-collusion, and elimination of the useless collusion codes.
4. In consideration of image quality, evaluation of fingerprinting code length by the measurement of the PSNR.
5. Computation of fingerprinting code length by image transforms.

The rest of the article is organized as follows. In Section 2, the theoretical background of BIBD characteristic and collusion attack are introduced, and the evaluation algorithm of the collusion code is proposed in Section 3. Then in Section 4, the detection range of colluder by effect of the collusion code was computed and evaluated, and also fingerprinting code length is evaluated by image PSNR values. Lastly, the conclusion is drawn in Section 5.

2. Theoretical background

2.1 BIBD property

In this section, BIBD property is briefly introduced as for a requirement of multimedia fingerprinting code. Multimedia fingerprinting is content's security technology based on watermarking technology. To improve the weak point that illegal content distribution process remains an unknown, fingerprinting technology has been being researched.

The theory of block designs is a field of mathematics that has found application in the construction of error correcting codes and the statistical design of experiments.

Compounding a problem of BIBD {***v*,*b*,*r*,*k*** and **λ**}, which is using a matrix model to produce code satisfied with constraints.

Where *v*: points, number of elements of *X*.
k: number of points in a block.
b: number of blocks.
r: number of blocks containing a given point (*k*<*v*).
λ: number of blocks containing 2 (or more generally *t*) points.

Upper 5 parameters are satisfying following two limitation conditions.

$$vr = bk \tag{1}$$

$$r(k-1) = \lambda(v-1) \tag{2}$$

BIBD is simply able to express with {***v*, *k*, λ**}.

$$b = \frac{v(v-1)\lambda}{k(k-1)} \tag{3}$$

$$r = \frac{\lambda(v-1)}{k-1} \tag{4}$$

b=*v* or *r*=*k* then BIBD is symmetrical.

If $X = \{X_i\}_{i=1}^{v}$ and $A = \{A_j\}_{j=1}^{b}$, then BIBD's incidence matrix becomes ***M*** as Eq. (5).

Therefore, ***M*** satisfies Eq. (6).

$$m_{ij} = \begin{cases} 1\, if & x_i \in A_j \\ 0 & otherwise \end{cases} \tag{5}$$

$$\boldsymbol{MM}^{t} = (r-\lambda)I + \lambda J \tag{6}$$

For example, when {***v*,*k*,λ**} are {7,3,1}, ***M*** is presented in (7).
In block design, In Eq. (7), when {***v*, *k*, λ**} is {7,3,1} is shown the incidence matrix ***M*** of BIBD.

The reader can be found more specific information in [19].

All row vectors of the incidence matrix ***M*** in BIBD became a multimedia fingerprinting code and then authorize users. This ***M*** can be used like ACC in (7).

For example, BIBD code for multimedia fingerprinting is also appeared in (7). The author can have gained the incidence matrix ***M*** about one of the block designs based on BIBD when {*v*, *k*, λ} are {7,3,1}. This code requires 7 bits for 7 users and 1-resilience since any two column vectors share a unique pair of 1 bit.

In Eq. (7), v_n's row vector (n=1~7) will be *User n*'s fingerprinting code for his purchased media content.

$M =$ (7)

m_{ij}	b_1	b_2	b_3	b_4	b_5	b_6	b_7
v_1	0	1	0	1	0	1	0
v_2	1	0	0	1	1	0	0
v_3	0	0	1	1	0	0	1
v_4	1	1	1	0	0	0	0
v_5	0	1	0	0	1	0	1
v_6	1	0	0	0	0	1	1
v_7	0	0	1	0	1	1	0

2.2 Collusion attack

An early work on digital fingerprinting code design and collusion attacks were proposed in [4], which assumed that the colluders can detect a specific fingerprint code bit if it takes different values between their fingerprinted copies and can change it to any value [21].

In here, let's see how to make collusion code by some colluders using Averaging attack. If 3 colluders use their user's fingerprinting code from the row the incidence matrix $\boldsymbol{M}$ of {7,3,1} BIBD code as an ACC, 3 colluders can add their user's fingerprinting code, then the added values are on an average. Therefore, the reader can know that 3 illegal users have collusion attack according to the only their user's fingerprinting code by adding and averaging [1].

For example, if $User_2$, $User_4$, and $User_6$ intend collusion attack by Averaging with each one code from (7):

$User_2$ =(1 0 0 1 1 0 0), $User_4$ =(0 1 0 0 1 0 1) and $User_6$ =(1 0 0 0 0 1 1)

The generated a new collusion code(or new User's code) is (0 1 0 1 0 0 1). This is illustrated figured in Fig. 3, which shows the collusion attack [16] of Averaging.

In Fig. 3, the new collusion code (1 0 0 0 1 0 1) is no row vector in BIBD's incidence matrix $\boldsymbol{M}$ in (7). Once the new user code is detected, it knows $User_2$, $User_4$, and $User_6$ would be colluders as like corrupt users. So this collusion-secure fingerprinting scheme may resist collusion attack of 3 users ably, for example. In here, according to the varied threshold value, the generated collusion code would be a variety result.

The code efficiency, as well as the averaging resistance, is an important factor for the fingerprinting code design. The code efficiency refers to the number of recipients that can be handled by code length. The higher code efficiency, the better content fidelity can be achieved since fewer bits of information are inserted as well as better robustness [12]. And some papers [12,16] attempt the incidence matrix $\boldsymbol{M}$ to the bit-complement matrix $\boldsymbol{C}$ for increasing the resilience. In (7), if $\boldsymbol{M}$ has the bit-complement to {7,4,2} $\boldsymbol{C}$ afterwards the resilience is increased 1 to 2. Thus, the effect of anti-collusion is increased. $\boldsymbol{C}$ from (7) is shown in (8) by bit-complement.

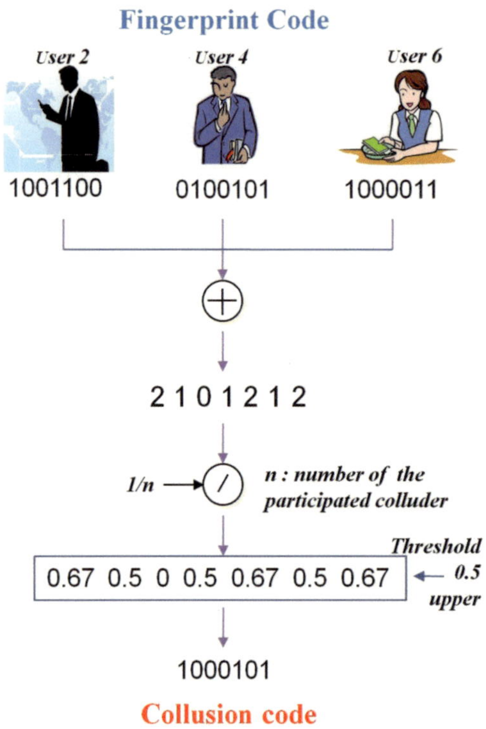

Fig. 3. Collusion attack by Averaging

M is transformed to the bit-complement matrix ***C*** then all row vectors of ***C*** will be fingerprinting code of each user. ***C*** can be used like ACC (Anti-Collusion code), which is presented in (8), in here row vectors (***n***=1~7) will be *User* ***n***'s each fingerprinting code and 2-resilience since any two column vectors share a unique pair of 2 bits for his purchased media content too.

$C =$ (8)

m_{ij}	b_1	b_2	b_3	b_4	b_5	b_6	b_7
v_1	1	0	1	0	1	0	1
v_2	0	1	1	0	0	1	1
v_3	1	1	0	0	1	1	0
v_4	0	0	0	1	1	1	1
v_5	1	0	1	1	0	1	0
v_6	0	1	1	1	1	0	0
v_7	1	1	0	1	0	0	1

2.3 Color model [32,33]

Color space is a complicated topic. Colors don't really exist, like dust does. We human being use colors to describe what we see. The most common way to describe what we see in terms of color is using combination of red, green and blue, which is referred as RGB color space.

2.3.1 RGB color space

The RGB color space consists of the three additive primaries: red, green and blue. Spectral components of these colors combine additively to produce a resultant color.

The RGB model is represented by a 3-dimensional cube with red green and blue at the corners on each axis which is shown in Fig. 4. Black is at the origin. White is at the opposite end of the cube. The gray scale follows the line from black to white. In a 24-bit color graphics system with 8 bits per color channel, then red is (255, 0, 0) green is (0, 255, 0) and blue is (0, 0, 255). On the color cube, red is (1, 0, 0), green is (0, 1, 0) is (0, 0, 1).

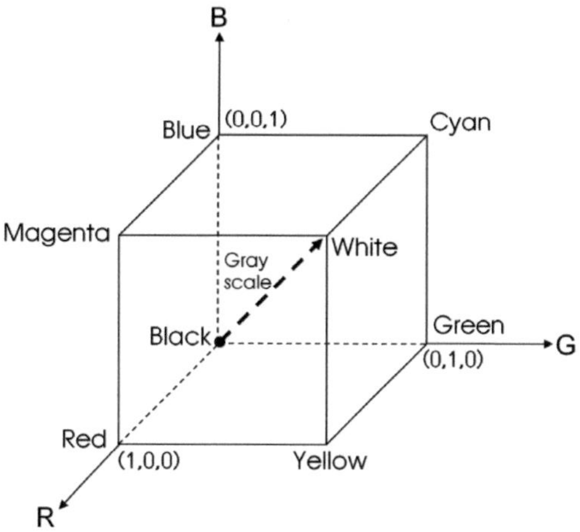

Fig. 4. RGB color cube

2.3.2 Grayscale

It converts RGB to grayscale values by forming a weighted sum of the R, G and B components as Eq. (9) below.

$$\text{Grayscale} = 0.2989R + 0.587G + 0.114B \tag{9}$$

2.3.3 YCbCr color space

A color space is simply a model of representing what we see in tuples. YCbCr is one of the popular color space in computing. It represents colors in terms of one luminance component/luma (Y), and two chrominance components/chroma(Cb and Cr).

Human eyes are sensitive to luminance, but not so sensitive to chrominance.

YCbCr color space has been defined in response to increasing demands for digital algorithms in handling video information, and has since become a widely used model in a digital video.

It belongs to the family of television transmission color spaces. The family includes others such as YUV and YIQ. YCbCr is a digital color system, while YUV and YIQ are analog spaces for the respective PAL and NTSC systems. These color spaces separate RGB (Red-Green-Blue) into luminance and chrominance information and are useful in compression applications however the specification of colors is somewhat unintuitive.

The YCbCr image can converted to/from RGB image. There're several standards defined for the conversion at different context. The conversion below is based on the conversion used in JPEG image compression.

The conversion can be expressed as Eq. (10) and (11) below.
From 8-bit RGB to 8-bit YCbCr :

$$\begin{aligned} Y &= 0.299R + 0.587G + 0.114B \\ Cb &= -0.16874R - 0.33126Green + 0.5B \\ Cr &= 0.5R - 0.41869G - 0.08131B \end{aligned} \tag{10}$$

From 8-bit YCbCr to 8-bit RGB :

$$\begin{aligned} R &= Y + 1.402Cr \\ G &= Y - 0.34414Cb - 0.71414Cr \\ B &= Y + 1.772Cb \end{aligned} \tag{11}$$

The YCbCr color space is widely used for digital video. In this format, luminance information is stored as a single component (Y), and chrominance information is stored as two color-difference components (Cb and Cr). Cb represents the difference between the blue component and a reference value. Cr represents the difference between the red component and a reference value.

Application of YCbCr is a commonly used color space in digital video domain. Because the representation makes it easy to get rid of some redundant color information, it is used in image and video compression standards like JPEG, MPEG1, MPEG2 and MPEG4.

3. Proposed evaluation algorithm of fingerprinting scheme

As introduced Section 1, most research had attempted multimedia fingerprinting for ACC on Averaging attack [12,15,16]. And in [16,22-28], AND-ACC is dealt with AND attack considered to ACC. On the author's opinion about using $\boldsymbol{C}$ from $\boldsymbol{M}$ ((7) and (8) in Section 2.2), if a number of resilient code increases for ACC, thus the effect of ACC would be increased.

Because of this reason, the author utilizes different logical operations such as OR-ACC and XOR-ACC along with the conventional AND-ACC. Clearly, if the factor of resilient code increases, then occurrence frequency of same collusion code will be increased also. These same code causes an attending colluder to be a non-attending user lucratively or a non-attending user to be an attending colluder unfortunately.

Thus, the author would like to reduce the same some collusion code keeping a lower resilient factor and the effect of ACC. It must adopt several logical operations as like AND, OR and XOR if have a lower resilient factor. Then the number of same collusion codes will be decreased and no necessary to change from the incidence matrix $\boldsymbol{M}$ to bit-complete $\boldsymbol{C}$.

In this article, according to the author adopts these criteria of the requirements, the evaluation algorithm of multimedia fingerprinting using BIBD code is proposed and shown in Fig. 5.

For the evaluation of multimedia fingerprinting in this article, the proposed system design can be classified in into 3 steps, namely the generation of the BIBD code as multimedia fingerprinting code on ① in Fig. 5. After then, the collusion code is generated by Logic operations and Averaging in which, there are occurred in case of the bitstream all '1' bit codes, all '0' bit codes and the same user fingerprinting codes. These codes are useless for collusion code because down to the effect of anti-collusion.

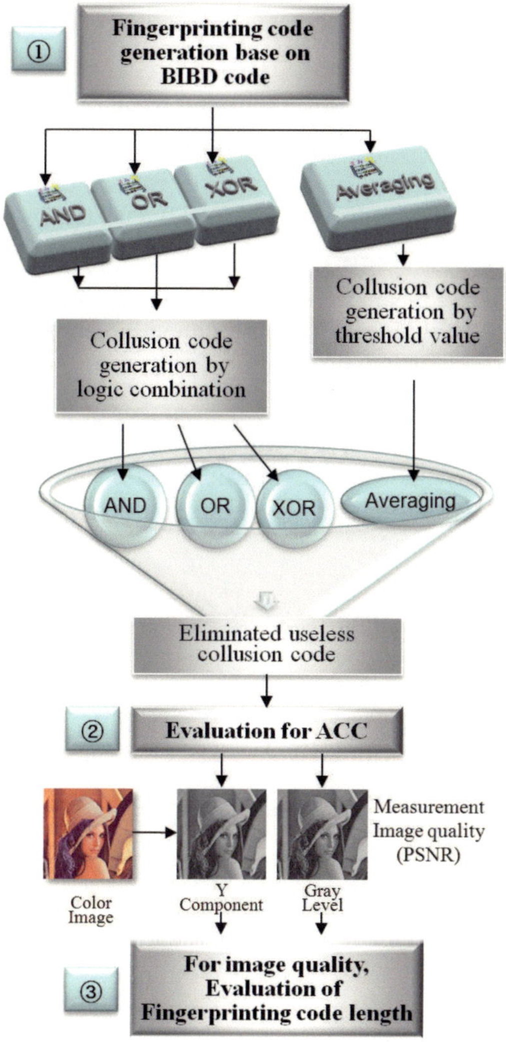

Fig. 5. The proposed evaluation algorithm of the collusion codes of the multimedia fingerprinting based on BIBD

After the useless collusion codes are eliminated, then on ② in Fig. 5, the rest of collusion codes is useful and must evaluate truly as anti-collusion code for the detection and the trace of the colluders which must satisfy for fingerprinting criteria.

And lastly, the useful fingerprinting codes will be inserting into digital images for the measurement of image quality PSNR on ③ in Fig. 5, in which Y component and gray level of color image are experimental image. The transform of Y component and gray level from color images is a very important transformation in image signal processing area. So these 2 kinds of transformation methods are adopts for the experiment of PSNR measurement.

In this article, the evaluation criterion is put in force 2 kinds of an effect of anti-collusion and fingerprinting code length in Section 4.

4. Experimental results

4.1 Evaluation of fingerprinting and anti-collusion code based on BIBD

The evaluation algorithm of the collusion code which are generated by Logical combinations (AND, OR and XOR) and Averaging for the effect increasing of anti-collusion. And also the collusion code will be separating for the definition of the usable or useless attack code.

In the theoretical collusion attack, BIBD {7,4,2} code able to make 119 numbers of collusion codes, and n-1 or fewer users have attended with collusion attack. Now, let it be counting the useless collusion code existed, and then they must be eliminated about each attack for the effect increasing of anti-collusion. Firstly, Averaging attack would be experimented.

On Averaging attack, Table 1 and Fig. 5 show the number of the collusion codes with BIBD {7,4,2} code, in which they cann't use according to the threshold value. Among 119 codes which would be to collude, the useless collusion codes are 56 least at threshold value 0.34~0.39 in Fig. 6. Eq. (12) computes to decide the number of the useless collusion codes about Averaging attack.

$$Averaging\_attack_{useless\_code} = Threshold \cdot \frac{1}{n} U_i code \tag{12}$$

where $Threshold$: 0.34~0.39

k: number of the colluders.

$U_i code$: colluder's user fingerprinting code based on BIBD code.

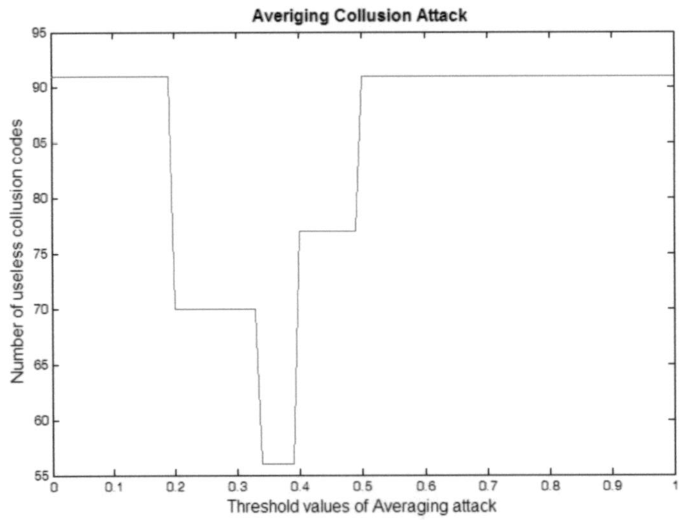

Fig. 6. Number of useless collusion codes by threshold value of Averaging attack

Threshold values of the average collusion attack	Number of the useless collusion codes
0~0.19	91
0.2~0.33	70
0.34~0.39	*56*
0.40~0.49	77
0.5~1	91

Table 1. Number of the useless collusion codes by threshold value of Averaging attack with BIBD {7,4,2} code

And secondly, Logical operation attacks would be experimented. On Logical operation attack with AND, OR and XOR, there are some same codes are appeared as like bitstream all '0' and all '1' codes by AND, OR and XOR attack. According to these results, the number of useless collusion codes is shown in Table 2 about Logical operation attack.

Number of the useless collusion codes		
AND collusion attack	**OR collusion attack**	**XOR collusion attack**
Useless codes caused by all '0' codes and user fingerprinting codes.	Useless codes caused by all '1' codes and user fingerprinting codes.	Useless codes caused by all '0' and '1' codes and user fingerprinting codes.
91	**63**	**49**

Table 2. Number of the useless collusion codes by AND, OR and XOR attacks with BIBD {7,4,2} code

For more number of content's users, if BIBD parameter v value is increased, and then a number of colluders is increased too. Thus, the proprietor of content must be knowing the number of useless collusion codes by v value and the number of attendable colluders.

In the experimental results, the fingerprinting code based on BIBD code proposed in this article is generated and evaluated for the effect of anti-collusion. Threshold value in Eq. (12) is using 0.34~0.39 for a minimum number of useless collusion code. This choice is that although the effect of anti-collusion is decreasing, which is not decrease and would be keeping their effect because another Logical operation(AND, OR and XOR) is performed with Averaging operation for the improving performance of anti-collusion.

According to Table 1 and 2, the efficiency ratio of useful collusion code is shown in Table 3 for anti-collusion.

Collusion attack kinds	Efficiency ratio of usable collusion code(%)
AND	23.5
OR	47.1
XOR	58.8
Averaging	47.1
Average	**44.13**

Table 3. Efficiency ratio of usable collusion code by the type of attacks

According to the kind of collusion operation and the number of the colluders, the number of the useless collusion codes Y_c is formed like Eq. (13)~(15). In here c is 3 kinds of Logic operations(AND, OR and XOR).

$$y_{AND-useless\_code} = 0.88c_n^{\ 4} - 12.25c_n^{\ 3} + 51.63c_n^{\ 2} - 54.25c_n - 14 \tag{13}$$

$$y_{OR-useless\_code} = 2.63c_n^{\ 4} - 43.75c_n^{\ 3} + 256.38c_n^{\ 2} - 614.25c_n - 511 \tag{14}$$

$$y_{XOR-useless\_code} = 0.58c_n^{\ 4} - 8.17c_n^{\ 3} + 37.92c_n^{\ 2} - 65.33c_n - 35 \tag{15}$$

where, c_n : number of colluders.

The number of the traceable colluders is n-1 with the effect 44.13% of collusion code with only 1-resilience BIBD code (7) not 2-resilience BIBD code (8). Table 4 is shown the compared performance of the number of the traceable colluders between the conventional scheme and the proposed algorithm.

Fingerprinting schemes	**Method**	**Possible to trace the number of colluders.**
Dittman[29]	d-detecting	2
Boneh [4]	c-secure	2
Trappe [16]	AND ACC	2
Domingo_Ferrer [30]	3-secure	3
This article	**AND, OR, XOR and Averaging attacks**	***n*-1**

(n: number of the total users)

Table 4. Compared performance of the number of the traceable colluders between the conventional scheme and the proposed algorithm.

4.2 Image quality measurement

The PSNR of real image is measured by the length of the inserted fingerprinting code based on BIBD code. The evaluation and measurement of image quality PSNR by the fingerprinting code is the main focus of this section on 4 kinds of the collusion attack. In here collusion code is inserted into Y component of color image and gray level image. The choice purpose of Y component and gray level images is that it is very important transform in an image processing area for the compression and pre-processing of multimedia communication, etc.

For the experiment of the used real 3 images are Lena, Korean woman and Thai woman. And the numerous fingerprinting code in this article is applied to 128x128, 256x256 and 512x512 color images. The 7~127bits fingerprinting code length was inserted in Y component and gray level image of 3 original color images, and then each image quality PSNR was measured. Fig. 7 is shown the original images which used in an experiment. Fig. 8 (a)~(c) are shown Y component images of original color images, and (d)~(f) are shown the images of the inserted 39bits fingerprinting code. Fig. 9 (a)~(c) are shown the gray level images of original color images, and also (d)~(f) are shown the images of the inserted 39bits fingerprinting code. And Table 3 and 4 represent PSNR measured values of Y component and gray level images according to the fingerprinting code length.

Fig. 7. Original images(256x256)

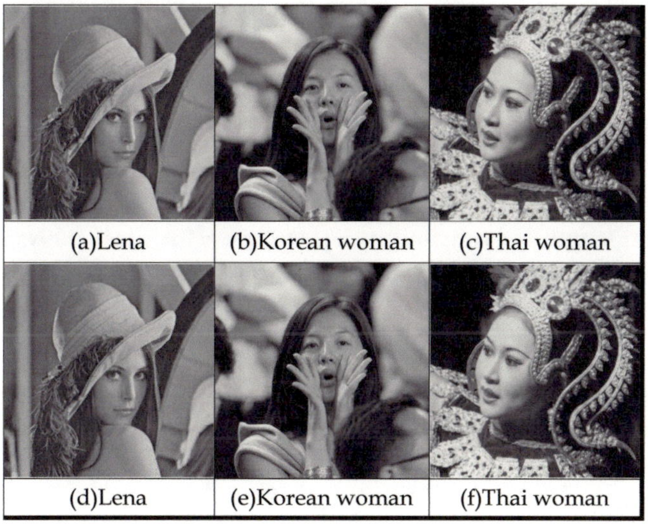

Fig. 8. (a)~(c): Y Component images of original images; (d)~(f): inserted fingerprinting code images

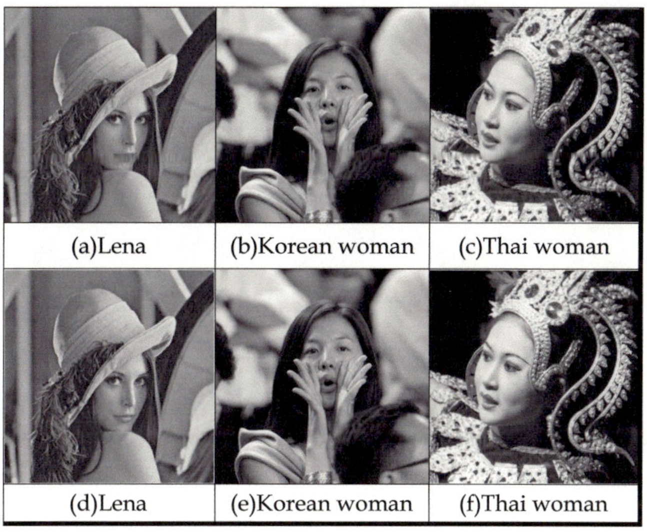

Fig. 9. (a)~(c): Gray level images of original images; (d)~(f): inserted fingerprinting code images

In Table 5 and 6, 2nd~4th columns are measured individually PSNR of Y component and gray level images about 3 kinds of 256x256 images by fingerprinting code length 7~127bits. And 5th~7th columns are shown the average PSNR of 3 images about 3 sizes.

At the consideration of fingerprinting code length is 7bits, the measured PSNRs of Y component images are 85.26, 90.63 and 97.13 on 3 kinds of image size. When a length is 39bits, PSNRs are 77.75, 83.37 and 90.11dB, and also length is 127bits, PSNRs are 72.64, 78.37 and 84.29dB by 3 kinds of image size individually.

And also, consider PSNR values of gray level image under the same condition too, the measured PSNRs are 84.35, 91.70 and 99.72 on 3 kinds of image size. When a length is 39bits, PSNRs are 78.08, 84.03 and 88.85dB, and also length is 127bits, PSNRs are 72.28, 78.06 and 84.86dB by 3 kinds of image size individually.

In these results, the variation of PSNR value is not proportional to same fingerprinting code length under the different images of Y component and gray level each. The author would be making a close examination in Eq. (16).

And also with the measured PSNR values in Table 5 and 6, polynomial expression of fingerprinting code length is evaluated in Eq. (16) by regression analysis of the measured PSNR values. And polynomial coefficients are represented in Table 7. As the evaluation of the fingerprinting code length, 3 polynomial coefficients a_n and a constant C are existed in Eq. (16) for Y component and gray level each.

This expression can be shown to predict a fingerprinting code length by a measured PSNR of Y component or gray level image.

$$Fingerprinting_{Code\_lenght} = a_3x^3 + a_2x^2 + ax + C \tag{16}$$

where x: PSNR value

Fingerprinting Code Length (bit)	Lena	Korea_ woman	Thai_ woman	Average		
	Image size			Image size		
	256x256			128x128	256x256	512x512
7	93.3	89.3	89.3	85.26	90.63	97.13
11	87.8	87.3	87.8	82.31	87.63	94.58
15	88.5	85.9	86.8	81.75	87.07	93.64
19	87.3	87.8	86.3	81.29	87.13	93.80
23	85.9	85.2	84.5	79.25	85.20	91.53
31	85.2	83.1	85.2	79.24	84.50	90.32
39	83.1	84.3	82.7	77.75	83.37	90.11
47	83.1	83.1	81.8	76.48	82.67	88.60
63	82.1	80.2	81.7	75.57	81.33	87.25
79	80.6	80.9	80.3	74.34	80.60	86.24
95	79.2	79.4	79.2	73.45	79.27	85.50
127	78.6	77.8	78.7	72.64	78.37	84.29

Table 5. Measured PSNR(dB) of Y component images

Fingerprinting Code length (bit)	Lena	Korea_ woman	Thai_ woman	Average		
	Image size			Image size		
	256x256			128x128	256x256	512x512
7	93.3	91.5	90.3	84.35	91.70	99.72
11	89.3	90.3	89.3	82.76	89.63	95.39
15	90.3	88.5	88.5	82.12	89.10	95.97
19	87.8	86.8	87.8	81.58	87.47	92.26
23	85.5	86.8	85.9	79.39	86.07	91.41
31	85.9	85.2	84.0	78.78	85.03	91.41
39	84.5	83.1	84.5	78.08	84.03	88.85
47	81.5	84.0	82.9	76.18	82.80	88.24
63	81.5	81.2	81.2	75.39	81.30	87.76
79	80.9	80.2	81.5	74.78	80.87	86.41
95	78.8	79.7	79.7	73.09	79.40	85.52
127	78.0	78.2	78.0	72.28	78.07	84.86

Table 6. Measured PSNR(dB) of gray level images.

And with Eq. (16), the computed result of fingerprinting code length is shown in Fig. 10. In the case of larger 86dB PSNR, the inserted fingerprinting code length in Y component image is shorter than gray level image processing. And in the case of lower 86dB PSNR, the inserted fingerprinting code length of gray level image is shorter than Y component image processing.

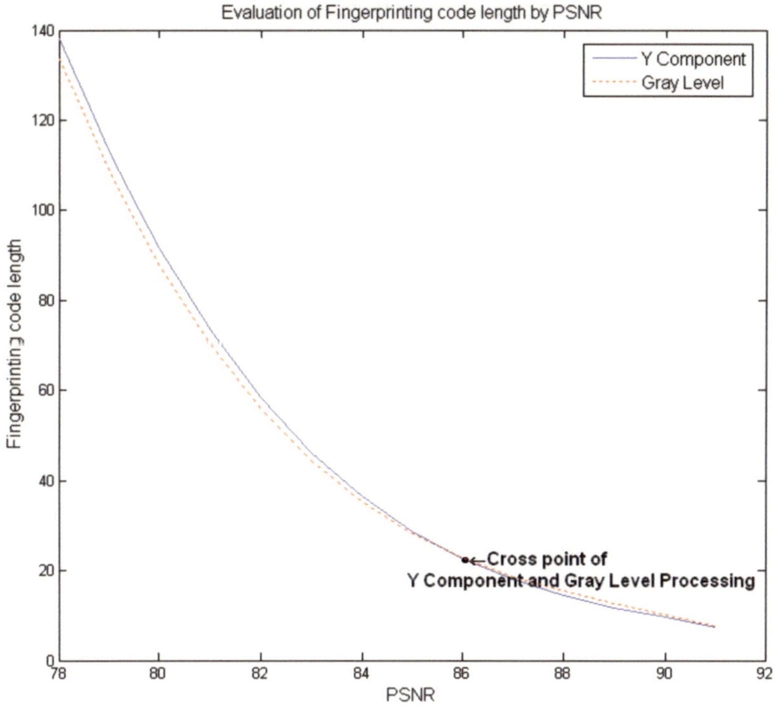

Fig. 10. Evaluation of fingerprinting code length by PSNR value.

Polynomial Coefficient	a_3	a_2	a	C
Y Component	-0.054102	14.677	-1329.2	40,196
Gray level	-0.061901	16.621	-1490	44,609

Table 7. Polynomial coefficients of Eq. (13). (Y component and Gray level)

5. Conclusions

The proposed algorithm in this article, firstly, multimedia fingerprinting code is generated base on BIBD code. Secondly, the usable collusion codes are evaluated for the effect increasing of anti-collusion by the proposed scheme, and the usable collusion codes could be manifesting for an attending colluder would be changing a non-attending user lucratively or a non-attending user would be changing an attending colluder unfortunately. Thirdly, for the increasing image quality, the fit fingerprinting code length is evaluated when user fingerprinting code is inserted into content.

It confirmed that the efficiency of useful collusion codes is 44.13%, the tracing number of the attending colluder is extending to n-1 users with 1-resilient code. Thus, this fingerprinting code would be enough satisfying the criteria of ACC. Furthermore, if it emphasizes a protection or security of content copyright, an inserted fingerprinting code length can't but be long more, and then image content's quality can't but relatively decrease.

The creator or proprietor of content is desiring to keep high PSNR image content, they can choose a fit fingerprinting code length according to the desirable PSNR value. As a experimental results, the reference values of PSNR and fingerprinting code length are evaluated 86dB and 22bits each to the image of Y component and gray level both. When 7~127bits BIBD code was used as fingerprinting code for multimedia content, in the choice of larger 86dB PSNR, the fingerprinting code length will be great to insert into Y component image for shorter than gray level transform. On the other hand, in the choice of lower 86dB PSNR, the fingerprinting code length will be great to insert into gray level image for shorter than Y component transform.

In this article, the implemented algorithm could be widely applied to trace up the illegal distributor of multimedia content on the various colluded attacks, which consisted of Logical operation and Averaging of fingerprinting code base on BIBD code.

6. Acknowledgment

This study was supported in part by Korea Government, Ministry of Education, Science and Technology Fund 2011-0026144.

And this article is rearranged (IDC), 2010 6th International Conference on, Print ISBN: 978-1-4244-7607-7, INSPEC Accession Number: 11526187

7. References

[1] Jie Yang, Pingg Liu and Guo Zhen Tan, "The Digital Fingerprint Coding Based on LDPC," *ICSP'04 Proceedings*, pp.2600-2603, 2004.

[2] K. H. Rhee, "DRM Implementation by Multimedia Fingerprint," *IEEK Computer Society*, Vol.46, No.3, pp.50~56, 2009. 5.

[3] K. H. Rhee, "An Embedded Watermark into Multiple Lower Bit planes of Digital Image," *IEEK Computer Society*, Vol. 43, No. 8, pp.101-109, 2006. 11.

[4] D. Boneh and J. Shaw, "Collusion-secure fingerprinting for digital data," *IEEE Tran. on Information Theory*, vol. 44, pp. 1897–1905, September 1998.

[5] Trappe W., Min Wu, Ray Liu K.J., "Collusion-resistant fingerprinting for multimedia," *IEEE International Conference on Acoustics, Speech, and Signal Processing 2002, Proceedings (ICASSP '02)*, vol.4, pp.IV-3309-IV-3312, 13-17 May 2002.

[6] Lin W. S., Zhao H. V., Ray Liu K. J., "Scalable Multimedia Fingerprinting Forensics with Side Information," *IEEE International Conference on Image Processing, 2006*, pp.2293-2296, 8-11 Oct. 2006

[7] W. G. Kim, S. H. Lee and Y. S. Seo, "Robustness Digital Fingerprinting Technology to Collusion Attack," *KIISE*, ISSN 1015-9908, Vol.23, No. 8, pp. 52~60, Sept. 2005

[8] Jie Yang, Xiaoxia Xu, "A Robust Anti-collusion Coding in Digital Fingerprinting System," *IEEE Asia Pacific Conference on Circuits and Systems, APCCAS 2006*, pp.996 - 999, 4-7 Dec. 2006

[9] Shashanka D., Bora P.K, "Collusion Secure Scalable Video Fingerprinting Scheme," International Conference on Advanced Computing and Communications, *ADCOM 2007*, pp.641-647, 18-21 Dec. 2007

[10] Jie Yang, Xiaoxia Xu, "A Robust Anti-collusion Coding in Digital Fingerprinting System," *The 8th International Conference on Signal Processing*, Volume 4, 2006

[11] Zang Li and Trappe W, "Collusion-resistant fingerprints from WBE sequence sets," *IEEE International Conference on Communications, ICC 2005*, Vol. 2, pp. 1336-1340, 16-20 May 2005.

[12] In Koo Kang, Choong-Hoon Lee, Hae-Yeoun Lee, Jong-Tae Kim, Heung-Kyu Lee, "Averaging attack resilient video fingerprinting," *IEEE International Symposium on Circuits and Systems, ISCAS 2005*, Vol. 6, pp.5529-5532, 23-26 May 2005.

[13] J. S. Noh, K. H. Rhee, "Detection of Colluded Multimedia Fingerprint by Neural Network," *IEEK Computer Society*, Vol.43, No.4, pp.80~87, July 2006.

[14] K. H. Rhee, "Detection of Colluded Multimedia fingerprint using LDPC and BIBD," *IEEK Computer Society*, Vol.43, No.5, pp.68~75, Sept. 2006.

[15] J. Kilian, T. Leighton, L. R. Matheson, T. G. Shammon, R. E. Tarjan and F. Jane, "Resistance of Digital Watermarks to collusive Attacks," *Tech. Rep., TR-585-98, Dept. of Computer Science*, Princeton University, 1998.

[16] Wade Trappe, Min Wu, Jane Wang and K. J. Ray Liu, "Anti-collusion Fingerprinting for Multimedia," *IEEE Tran. on Signal Processing*, VOL.51, NO.4, pp.1069~1087, April 2003.

[17] F. Ergun, J. kilian and R. Kumar, "A note on the limits of collusion-resistant watermarks," *in Eurocrypt '99*, pp.140-149, 1999.

[18] J. K. Su, J. J. Eggers and B. Girod, "Capacity of digital watermarks subjected to an optimal collusion attack," in *European Signal Processing Conference (EUSIPCO 2000)*, 2000.

[19] Willard H. Clatworthy, "Tables of two-associate-class partially balanced design," *National Bureau of Standards*, Washington D.C., U.S., 1973.

[20] D. R. Stinson and R. Wei, "Combinatorial Properties and Construction of Traceability Schemes and Frame proof codes," *J. of Discrete mathematics,* Jan. 1997.

[21] H. Vicky Zhao, MinWu, Z. JaneWang, and K. J. Ray Liu, "Forensic Analysis of Nonlinear Collusion Attacks for Multimedia Fingerprinting," *IEEE Transactions on Image Processing,* Vol. 14, No. 5, pp.646-661, May 2005

[22] Shuhui Hou, Tetsutaro Uehara, Takashi Satoh, Yoshitaka Morimura and Michihiko Minoh, "Integrating Fingerprint with Cryptosystem for Internet-Based Live Pay-TV System," *Security and Communication Networks, Volume 1, Issue 6,* pp.461 - 472, 18 Nov. 2008.

[23] Byung-Ho Cha, and C.-C. Jay Kuo, "Robust MC-CDMA-Based Fingerprinting Against Time-Varying Collusion Attacks," *IEEE Transactions on Information Forensics and Security,* Vol. 4, NO. 3, pp.302-316, September 2009.

[24] Jae-Min Seol and Seong-Whan Kim, "A Scalable Fingerprinting Scheme for Tracing Traitors/Colluders in Large Scale Contents Distribution Environments," *Proceedings of the 2005 5th International Conference on Intelligent Systems Design and Applications (ISDA'05),* 2005.

[25] Dalwon Jang and Chang D. Yoo, "A Novel Embedding Method for an Anti-Collusion Fingerprinting by Embedding Both a Code and an Orthogonal Fingerprint," *ICASSP 2006,* pp.V485-488, 2006.

[26] Yongdong Wu, "Linear Combination Collusion Attack and its Application on an Anti-Collusion Fingerprinting," *ICASSP 2005,* pp.II13-16, 2005.

[27] Wade Trappe, Min Wu, and K. J. Ray Liu, "Anti-Collusion Codes: Multi-User and Multimedia Perspectives," *Image Processing. 2002. Proceedings 2002 International Conference on,* Vol. 2, pp.II149-II152, 2002.

[28] InKoo KANG, Kishore SINHA and Heung-Kyu LEE, "New Digital Fingerprint Code Construction Scheme Using Group-Divisible Design," *IEICE Trans. Fundamentals, Vol.E89–A, NO.12,* pp.3732-3735, December 2006

[29] J. Dittmann, "Combining Digital watermarks and Collusion Secure Fingerprints for Customer Copy Monitoring," *Proc. IEE Seminar Sec. Image & Image Auth.,* pp. 128-132, Mar. 2000.

[30] F. Sebe and Domingo-Ferrer, "Short 3-Secure Fingerprinting Codes for Copyright Protection," *Lecture Notes in Computer Science,* Vol. 2384, pp. 316-327, 2002.

[31]http://news.joins.com/component/htmlphoto_mmdata/200907/htm_20090727152308c000c010-001.JPG, 10. Oct. 2008

[32] Sanjay Kr. Singh1, D. S. Chauhan, Mayank Vatsa, Richa Singh,"A Robust Skin Color Based Face Detection Algorithm," Tamkang Journal of Science and Engineering, Vol. 6, No. 4, pp. 227-234 (2003) 227

[33] http://www.roman10.net/?p=485

Part 4

Bridging the Semantic Gap in Multimedia

8

Enhancing Multimedia Search Using Human Motion

Kevin Adistambha[1], Stephen Davis[1], Christian Ritz[1],
Ian S. Burnett[2] and David Stirling[1]
[1]*University of Wollongong,*
[2]*RMIT University,*
Australia

1. Introduction

Over the last few years, there has been an increase in the number of multimedia-enabled devices (e.g. cameras, smartphones, etc.) and that has led to a vast quantity of multimedia content being shared on the Internet. For example, in 2010 thirteen million hours of video uploaded to YouTube (http://www.youtube.com). To usefully navigate this vast amount of information, users currently rely on search engines, social networks and dedicated multimedia websites (such as YouTube) to find relevant content. Efficient search of large collections of multimedia requires metadata that is human-meaningful, but currently multimedia sites generally utilize metadata derived from user-entered tags and descriptions. These are often vague, ambiguous or left blank, which makes search for video content unreliable or misleading. Furthermore, a large majority of videos contain people, and consequently, human movement, which is often not described in the user entered metadata.

To compensate for the lack of metadata, which is crucial for efficient search, there has been research into automated techniques for the extraction of metadata to create multimedia description formats. The latter can generally be described as *temporal* (e.g. a point in time within a video when something happens), or *non-temporal* (e.g. a video was created by John Doe). Popular metadata formats such as Dublin Core (Weibel et al. 1998) are typically used as a *non-temporal* description format. e.g., using Dublin Core to describe the whole video clip, while other description formats, such as MPEG-7 (Martínez 2004), are capable of describing multimedia in both a *temporal* (i.e., Color Structure Descriptor) and *non-temporal* (i.e., parts of MPEG-7 Multimedia Description Schemes (MDS)) manner. In the context of search, both temporal and non-temporal metadata sets are both important.

One approach to multimedia search for action sequences is description of the action in terms of a *Subject-Verb-Object* construct similar to RDF (W3C 2004). For example, one can search for *"John Doe runs and then jumps into a lake"*, or *"Jane Doe runs in a circle by a tree"*. In this analogy, Dublin Core might be used to provide the *Subject* description, and MPEG-7 the *Object* description: Dublin Core can describe a person in general terms (subject), and MPEG-7 can accurately describe a lake (object). However, using this construct, the crucial description of the *Verb* is missing. The question becomes, how do we describe a person running, jumping, walking, etc.?

Consider a simple scenario where John Doe has just come back from a holiday and uploaded 100 videos taken while away all at once to YouTube. As a result of the single upload, John did not have the time to annotate all of his videos individually. When one of his friends wanted to search for the video that contained the funny moment that everyone was talking about (when he jumped into a lake), it was not possible to search for that exact moment using current description technologies. Instead, John's friends would need to look at each of the 100 videos to find it and it is likely that their enthusiasm would wane. Even if some of the metadata was automatically extracted/generated (Dublin Core: uploaded by John Doe, MPEG-7: spatio-temporal color descriptors), it is not currently possible to perform a human motion search in a temporal manner. With 35 hours of video uploaded every minute to YouTube (http://www.youtube.com), this is becoming a real, immediate problem to be solved. This chapter provides a solution to the missing verb description in the Subject-Verb-Object multimedia search for the case of human motion, by proposing a searchable human motion description that can be used in conjunction with existing metadata technologies

The rest of this chapter is structured as follows: Section 2 provides related work in human motion description area. Section 3 provides the detail of the new human motion description format that is simple and searchable. Section 4 concludes the chapter and provides possible future work in this area.

2. Related work

2.1 Multimedia description schemes

Multimedia description schemes describe content (e.g. video and motion capture) with different detail granularities in terms of their semantic description of the underlying raw data. Existing methods include the Dublin Core metadata that describes the media using high-level descriptors (e.g. title, subject, creator, creation date), and MPEG-7 as an overarching description format. MPEG-7 combines many description schemes that can describe the content of audiovisual data in terms of many aspects including color and sound characteristics. MPEG-7 Part 5 Multimedia Description Scheme (MDS) also provides a high level semantic description similar to Dublin Core (although Dublin Core was designed to describe formats not limited to multimedia). In the case of the *Subject-Verb-Object* analogy described in Section 1, the *Subject* and *Object* portion of multimedia description are adequately represented by both Dublin Core and MPEG-7, while the *Verb* portion is not. Unfortunately, these description schemes do not provide a temporal representation of human motion.

2.2 Motion capture based human motion description

With the advent of motion capture technologies and the relatively low cost of processing power nowadays, people have been recording an increasing amount of motion for games development and movies, and hence the problem of how to catalogue the motion and to search the resulting motion capture databases is becoming increasingly relevant. The state of the art in this area is the work of Mueller et. al. (Mueller et al. 2009) and Guerra-Filho et. al.

(Gutemberg Guerra-Filho & Yiannis Aloimonos 2007). Mueller developed the concept of a "motion template", where a number of example sequence of a given motion are analyzed and their common features recognized. The result of this analysis is the template for that specific motion. Some tolerance was designed into the system, so that minor differences in movements would still be recognized as the same motion (hence the term "template"). In contrast, Guerra-Filho developed the Human Action Language that takes inspiration from written language and defines a motion as a series of small actions connected together to form larger, more complex motions. The key concepts of the Human Action Language are compactness of description (describing an action with the least amount of symbols, called atoms), view-invariance (a 3D motion should be able to be projected into a 2D plane), selectivity (the ability to differentiate between different atoms) and reconstructivity (reconstruction of a described motion back into its motion capture representation). Barbic et al (Barbič et al. 2004) explores the use of Principal Component Analysis (PCA) and Gaussian Mixture Model (GMM) to perform automatic segmentation of motion capture data, due to their observation that a motion capture session tends to get longer as more motion is captured, especially if natural behavior of the actor during the capture session is desired. Barbic et. al. achieved high accuracy using the PCA approach. Similarly, Li et. al. (Li et al. 2007) explored the use of Singular Value Decomposition (SVD) to extract features in a continuous motion capture data to perform automatic motion segmentation into distinct motion classes. Most recently, VideoMocap by Wei et. al. (Wei & Chai 2010) provides a method to extract a motion capture-like 3D representation of the human body from 2D video. This is achieved by manually annotating the joints in keyframes in the video, and by using physics-based interpolation method to reconstruct the 3D skeleton of the human body accordingly. The work by Gu et. al.(Gu et al. 2010) further performed action and gait recognition on a reconstructed 3D model of the human body from video using a Hidden Markov Model (HMM) based approach; the reconstruction of the 3D human body by Gu et.al. combines manual annotation of the body joints with a hierarchical skeleton model similar to motion capture representation of the human body.

Although significant progress has been made in the area of human motion from a numerical point of view using GMM, PCA, SVD, HMM, or physics-based methods, annotating motion data in a structured manner (from either video or motion capture) for search purposes is noticeably absent. Advances in the form of Human Action Language and Motion Templates are bridging the gap between semantic and numeric descriptions of human motion, but both technologies are not designed with general multimedia search that can work together with existing metadata technologies.

2.3 Dance notation based human motion description

Labanotation (Laban & Lange 1975) was developed by Rudolf Laban to record dance movements using a series of symbols written on a special staff where each place in the staff denotes a major limb such as both legs, both arms, the torso, and the head. This popular notation served as the basis for some technologies for human motion descriptions.

The work by Nakamura (Nakamura & Hachimura 2006) provides a crossover between Labanotation and motion capture. The goal of Nakamura is to provide a well-formed Labanotation description of motion capture data in XML, called LabanXML and is defined using Document Type Definition (DTD). The work in LabanXML is further extended to include the full Labanotation as described in (Ann Hutchinson 1970) in the form of

MovementXML by Hatol (Hatol 2006). In contrast to the DTD approach used in LabanXML, MovementXML utilizes the more modern XML Schema approach while also providing a more complete Labanotation description. Both LabanXML and MovementXML provide direct translation from handwritten Labanotation directly into XML. Further, the work by Loke et al (Loke et al. 2005) explores the possibilities of using a Labanotation-based effort metric to serve as an input for a human-computer interface.

In terms of computer-based multimedia search, dance notation based techniques rely on musical concepts of "beats" and "measures" to provide timing information, and encapsulate the motion descriptions in the context of those timing parameters. These metrics do not align with the actual timing information in a recorded motion (e.g. in a video) that is based on the number of frames captured per second. Since arguably music-based timing information also depends on the type of motion being performed (e.g. a slow walk would have a slower "beat" compared to a sprint), objective and consistent timing information is required for a searchable human motion description.

2.4 Summary

Most of the literature describing human motion has focused on translating the raw data into low-level metadata, often at the frame or near-frame level. These techniques do not provide high level metadata that can describe human motion (e.g., running, walking). Ideally, metadata describing human motion for multimedia should also contain these high-level descriptors such that videos containing these motions can easily be searched by entering some simple keywords. It should not be too detailed and include the idiosyncrasies of an individual's movements (such as provided by motion capture data) but detailed enough to identify the moment of interest (e.g. when John in Section 1 jumps into a lake) so as to provide a precise temporal match of a motion. Motion descriptions such as LabanXML and MovementXML provides a direct translation from the underlying dance notation, and hence suffers from a searchability point of view due to their reliance on dance notation's musical concepts which generally does not have a corresponding counterpart in computer-based multimedia file formats. Although one can potentially describe human motion using a combination of MPEG-7 descriptors, the resulting descriptors would be complex and not conducive to a search environment where an efficient, simple, and scalable human motion description is required.

3. The human motion description format

3.1 Requirements

To answer the question of the missing verb in multimedia search as described in Section 1, a searchable Human Motion Description format would have to meet the following requirements:

1. *Compatibility with existing multimedia description formats*: The description would only need to serve as a bridge between highly temporal and non-temporal multimedia description formats for search purposes. Therefore, it needs to work together with other description formats, notably Dublin Core and MPEG-7.
2. *Limb based*: To describe human motion accurately, the movement of individual major limbs such as the arms and the legs has to be described. Further, the traditional human

motion annotation such as Labanotation is limb-based, proving the flexibility and accuracy of a limb-based approach. In terms of search, a search for a hand waving motion would result in a standing and waving motion and walking and waving motion, in effect expanding or restricting the detail level of the search according to the wishes of the user.

3. *Anatomical plane-based:* To describe a motion independent of the direction that the body is facing, the anatomical planes of the human body (Fig. 1) provides a fixed frame of reference relative to the body itself.
4. *Non-reconstruction*: Since the description would only describe general, temporal movements of the body, reconstruction for motion playback purposes (e.g. motion capture formats) is not needed. This requirement would prevent the description scheme to be too complicated and too detailed to search.
5. *Temporal*: It needs to be able to describe human motion temporally to provide a detailed description that can be used to search for a specific moment in time of a motion. E.g. it has to be able to search for a *"running then jumping"* motion, with a clear separation between the running and the jumping portions of the motion.

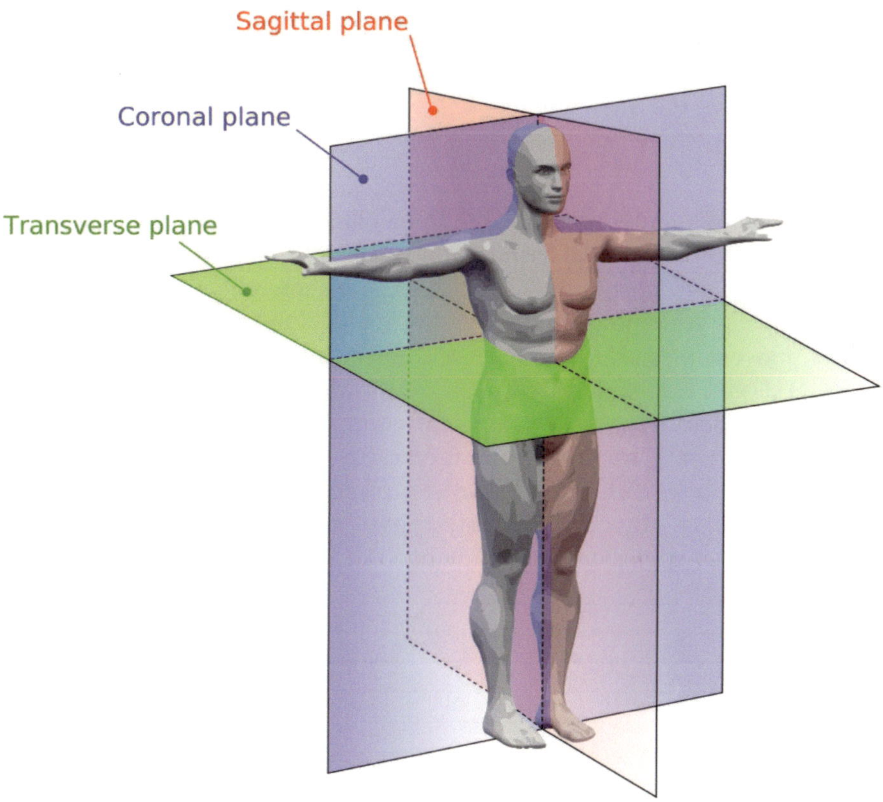

Fig. 1. Graphical representation of the anatomical planes that divides the body (Mrabet 2008) The Sagittal plane divides the left/right sections of the body, the Coronal plane divides the front/back sections of the body, and the transverse plane divides the top/bottom sections of the body. (Licensed under Creative Commons Attribution and ShareAlike license (CC-BY-SA)).

3.2 Design and XML schema visualization

Taking into account all the outlined requirements in Section 3.1, the Human Motion Description (HMD) format has been implemented as an XML Schema (see the visualization of the schema in Fig. 2). XML was chosen as it provides maximum compatibility between existing popular description formats - Dublin Core can be described using XML, and MPEG-7 is entirely XML-based. The core elements of the HMD schema is as follows (see Fig. 2):

- The element <motion> that encapsulates the motion description format, with an optional *fps* attribute that specifies the number of recorded frames per second in the annotated motion.
- The elements <sagittal>, <coronal>, and <transverse> that encapsulate descriptions in their respective axis:
  - The Sagittal plane divides the body between left and right.
  - The Coronal plane divides the body between front and back portions.
  - The Transverse plane divides the body between upper and lower portions.
- The elements<leg>, <arm> and <torso> describe the movements of the limbs, which contains optional attributes:
  - *side*: specifies either the left or the right side for the arms and the legs.
  - *dir*: describes the direction of the movement.
  - *frame*: describes the frame number in the media when the movement started.
  - *occur*: for repetitive motions, describes how many times the exact motion is repeated.

In HMD, the motion of a limb is described in three planes simultaneously (sagittal, coronal, and transverse). The full directional descriptors for each plane are shown in Table 1, and the relationships between elements in the XML Schema are shown in Fig. 2. In Fig. 2, each limb has three directional descriptors, with the restriction that only one direction is to be specified for a movement (since a limb cannot move in two directions in the same plane simultaneously). Using the plane-based description format, this enables HMD to describe 3D motion, even for describing a 2D video. For example in Fig. 2, the arms in the sagittal plane can move in forward, backward, and center directions. In the coronal plane in right, left, and center directions, and in the transverse plane in high, low, and level directions. Exceptions are the "*center*" direction that only applies to the sagittal and coronal plane, and the "*none*" direction that applies to all three planes.

Direction	**Meaning**		
	Sagittal	**Coronal**	**Transverse**
forward	Forward	-	-
backward	Backward	-	-
left	-	Left	-
right	-	Right	-
center	Toward neutral position	Toward neutral position	-
high	-	-	Up
low	-	-	Down
level	-	-	Middle position
none	Not moving/held in place	Not moving/held in place	Not moving/held in place

Table 1. Directions of limb movements according to the body planes.

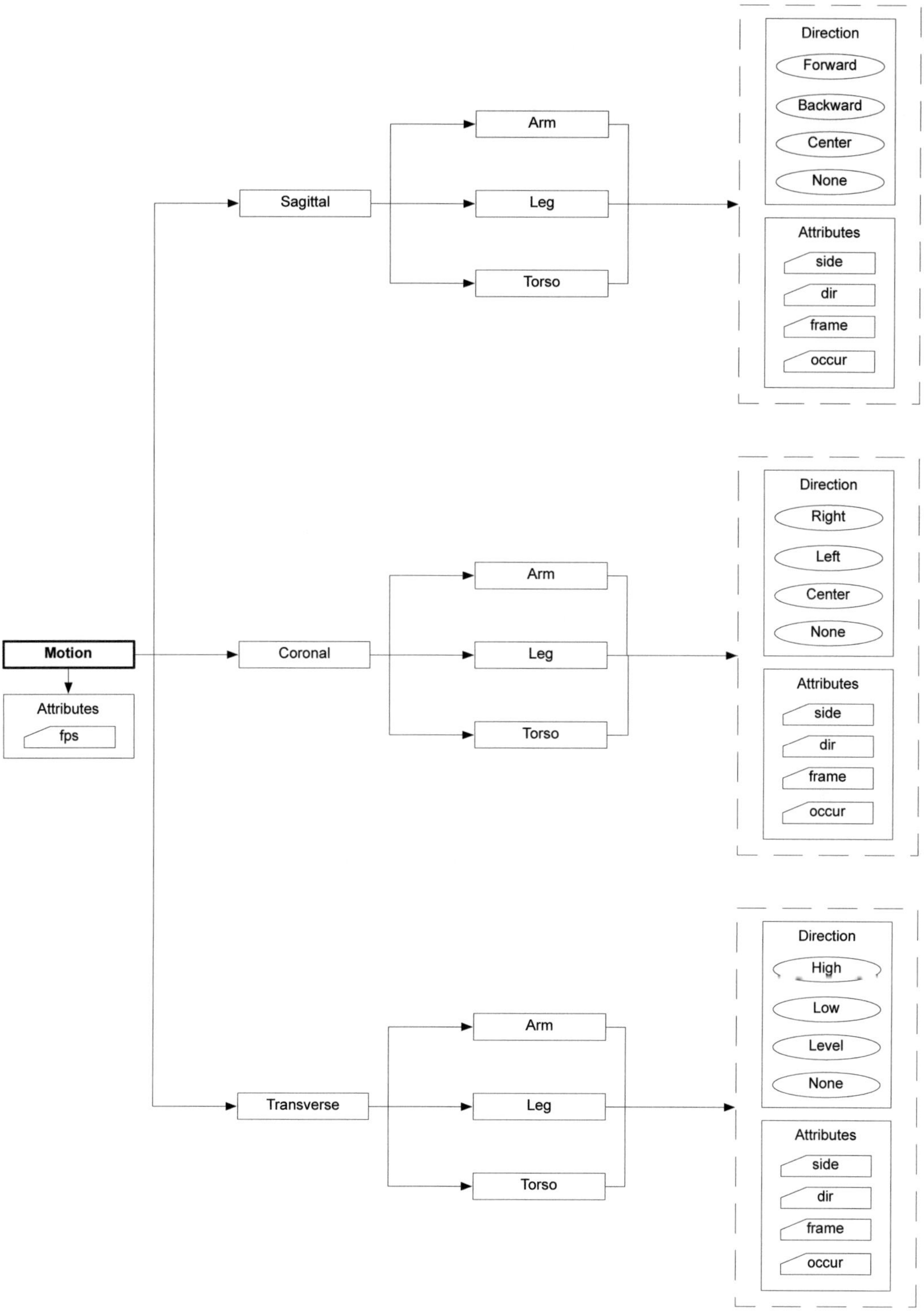

Fig. 2. Visualization of the Human Motion Description (HMD) schema element hierarchy.

3.3 Example: Using HMD to describe a motion

To illustrate the use of the HMD XML Schema as defined in Section 3.2, an example description using a walking motion is presented in Fig. 3 and Fig. 4. Fig. 3 illustrates a conceptual diagram of a HMD description of the leg movements in a walking forward motion. The sagittal, coronal, and transverse plane form individual description tracks, inside of which are the actual description of the limb movements. Specifying the frame number of the moment when the movement was made by the limb provides temporal information. The example in Fig. 3 depicts a four step walking motion starting with the right leg:

- The sagittal plane description track shows that the leg moves forward starting with the right leg.
- The coronal plane description track shows that the first movement of the right leg involves movement to the right, and the left leg movement involves movement to the left. In walking motion, the movement is slight, as the center of the mass of the body is moving according to the leg that is to receive the body weight in walking.
- The transverse plane description track shows that the legs move in a level direction.

In combination, the tracks provide a detailed description of the movements of the legs within the three body planes. The XML instantiation (based on the Schema) is shown in Fig. 4, where the *frame* attribute is present to denote the exact frame where each leg-forward motion is performed.

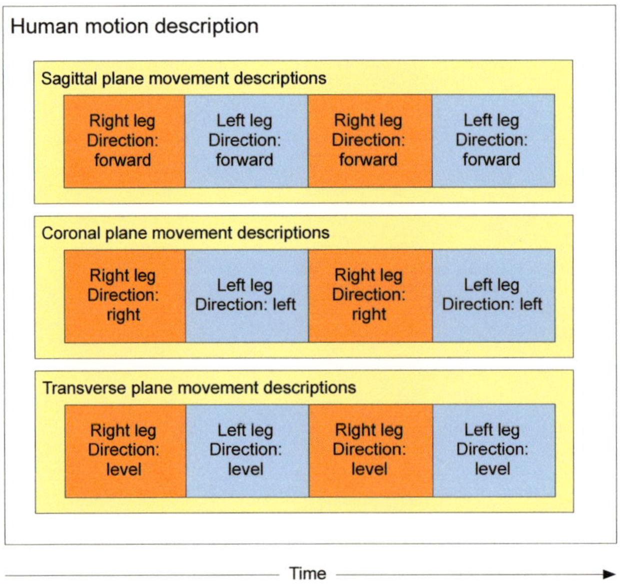

Fig. 3. An example diagram of the human motion description describing leg movement temporally in three separate planes.

Using the John Doe scenario in Section 1, a description of a running and jumping motion is shown in Fig. 5. In the running portion of the description, the leg forward motion appears to have exactly the same description as in the walking motion in Fig. 4. This is expected since both walking and running motion involves the same leg-moving-forward aspect. The difference is the timings involved. Note that in Fig. 4 there are 60 frames separations between the motions, while in Fig. 5 the separation between motions is 40 frames. The shorter timing of the leg forward motion in Fig. 5 provides the differentiating factor between walking and running motions.

```
<hmd:motion fps="120">

  <sagittal>
    <leg side="right" dir="forward" frame="1" />
    <leg side="left" dir="forward" frame="60" />
    <leg side="right" dir="forward" frame="120" />
    <leg side="left" dir="forward" frame="180" />
  </sagittal>

  <transverse>
    <leg side="right" dir="level" frame="1" />
    <leg side="left" dir="level" frame="60" />
    <leg side="right" dir="level" frame="120" />
    <leg side="left" dir="level" frame="180" />
  </transverse>

</hmd:motion>
```

Fig. 4. Example XML instantiation from the HMD schema describing a walking forward motion.

```
<hmd:motion fps="120">

   <sagittal>

      <!-- run... -->
      <leg side="right" dir="forward" frame="1" />
      <leg side="left" dir="forward" frame="40" />
      <leg side="right" dir="forward" frame="80" />

      <!-- ...and jump (both feet off the ground) -->
      <leg side="left" dir="none" frame="120" />
      <leg side="right" dir="none" frame="120" />

   </sagittal>
   <transverse>

      <!-- run... -->
      <leg side="right" dir="level" frame="1" />
      <leg side="left" dir="level" frame="40" />
      <leg side="right" dir="low" frame="80" />

      <!-- ...and jump (both feet off the ground) -->
      <leg side="left" dir="none" frame="120" />
      <leg side="right" dir="none" frame="120" />
   </transverse>

</hmd:motion>
```

Fig. 5. Example XML describing John Doe's running and jumping motion using HMD.

Describing walking and running in a similar fashion provides an advantage: there is no need to provide separate descriptions for different motions that involves the same limb movement if the timings are all that differentiate the motions. In this way, walking, walking slowly, running, jogging, and sprinting can be described consistently and logically.

In the latter portion of John Doe's description in Fig. 5 marked as jumping, the jumping motion is described using the "*none*" attribute for the legs, which means that both feet are off the ground (simultaneously, in Fig. 5, as the motions for both legs occurred at the same frame number).

3.4 Example: Using HMD description fragments for a temporal query

While HMD is primarily a description format, fragments of HMD can be employed to perform temporal queries. An illustration of using a HMD fragment-to-HMD description query is shown in Fig. 6 by constructing parts of a walking motion, such as walking four steps in a forward direction starting with the right leg as viewed from the sagittal plane (from the side). The query portion of the illustration in Fig. 6 (with example XML fragment shown in Fig. 7) forms a subset of the walking motion description shown in Fig. 3 and Fig. 4. To perform a temporal search for a motion, the server would therefore search for a description that is the superset of the incoming query.

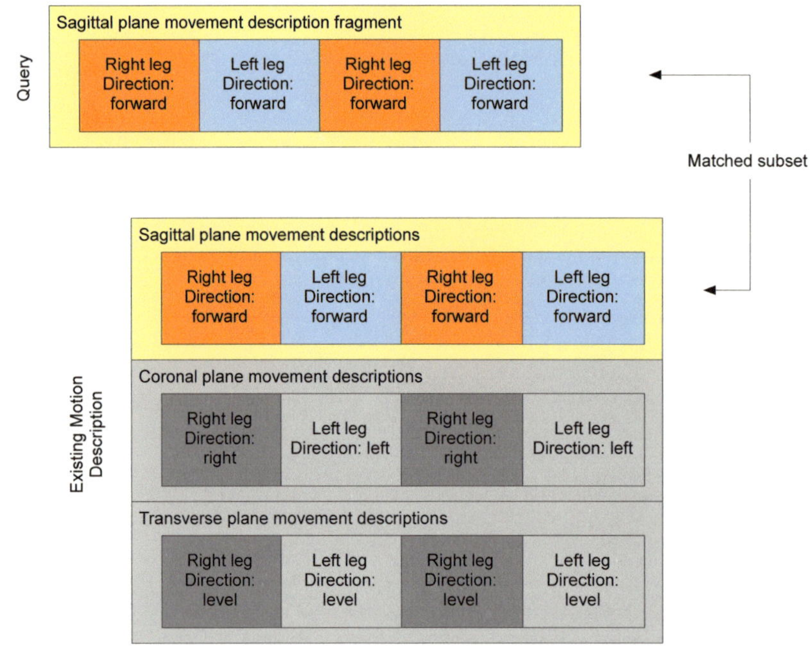

Fig. 6. An illustration of HMD temporal matching example by matching the incoming query to a subset of an existing description.

```
<hmd:motion fps="120">

  <sagittal>
    <leg side="right" dir="forward" frame="1" />
    <leg side="left" dir="forward" frame="60" />
    <leg side="right" dir="forward" frame="120" />
    <leg side="left" dir="forward" frame="180" />
  </sagittal>

</hmd:motion>
```

Fig. 7. Example XML of an HMD fragment forming a temporal query.

By matching a subset of an existing description, it is possible to perform a search using only a specific body plane, since the body planes divides the body in a constant manner no matter the direction that the body is facing. For example, when searching a walking forward motion, the coronal plane movement is irrelevant. Similarly, when searching for a sidestepping motion, the movement of the sagittal plane is, in turn, irrelevant.

Another feature of HMD is the ability to match any number of repetitions of movement as detailed in Section 3.2. For example, to search for a walking forward motion, the query only contains the description of a leg forward movement with the "occur=*unbounded*" attribute. This signifies that the desired match is a leg forward motion that occurred for an undetermined number of repetitions. A block diagram of the "*unbounded*" attribute in use in a matching scenario is shown in Fig. 8. An XML instantiation example based on the HMD Schema is shown in Fig. 9. The query formed in Fig. 9 will match the example XML description shown in Fig. 4.

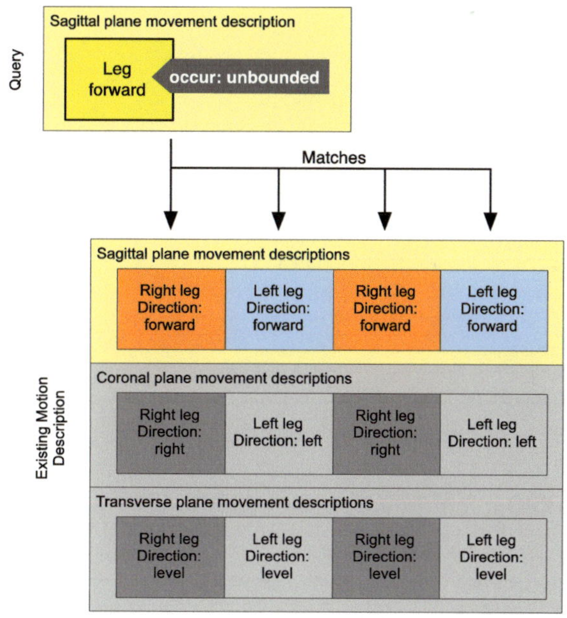

Fig. 8. An illustration of the "*unbounded*" occurrence of leg forward motion as a query term. The query term matches the same walking forward motion previously described.

```
<hmd:motion>

   <sagittal>
      <leg dir="forward" occur="unbounded" />
   </sagittal>

   <transverse>
      <leg dir="level" occur="unbounded" />
   </transverse>

</hmd:motion>
```

Fig. 9. Example XML fragment for using the "*unbounded*" attribute of HMD to form a query for multiple repetitive forward leg motions.

In the case of the John Doe example in Section 1, the running and jumping portion of the query is instantiated as shown in Fig. 10. In Fig. 10, the movements of the legs in the sagittal and transverse planes initially follow the description shown in Fig. 9. However, both legs are described to be using the *"none"* direction, which signifies that the feet are off the ground.

```
<hmd:motion>
   <sagittal>

      <!-- run... -->
      <leg dir="forward" occur="unbounded" />

      <!-- ...and jump (both feet off the ground) -->
      <leg side="left" dir="none" occur="1" />
      <leg side="right" dir="none" occur="1" />

   </sagittal>
   <transverse>

      <!-- run... -->
      <leg occur="unbounded" />

      <!-- ...and jump (both feet off the ground) -->
      <leg side="left" dir="none" occur="1" />
      <leg side="right" dir="none" occur="1" />
   </transverse>
</hmd:motion>
```

Fig. 10. XML instantiation of John Doe's running and jumping query from Section 1.

3.5 Example: Using HMD in conjunction with Dublin Core and MPEG-7 for search result filtering

Going back to the *Subject-Verb-Object* query concept described in Section 1, the search term *"John Doe running and then jumping into a lake"* can be thought of as a series of increasingly strict search filters.

Fig. 11 illustrates the flow of the filtering process involved in a detailed temporal search using human motion. The terms are separated according to their *Subject-Verb-Object* construct, with the subject described using Dublin Core (*John Doe*), the verb using HMD (*…running and jumping into…*), and the object using MPEG-7 (*…a lake*). Working together, the *Subject-Verb-Object* provides an increasingly strict filtering criteria for the media to be searched: Assuming that John Doe is searching for his own video that he uploaded to YouTube (100 of them in this scenario), he is searching for a video of himself running and jumping (there are 10 videos that matches the description), and only one of him actually jumping into a lake.

The example in Fig. 11 illustrates that HMD was intended to work together with existing multimedia description formats, the combination of which can provide a detailed temporal search using human motion.

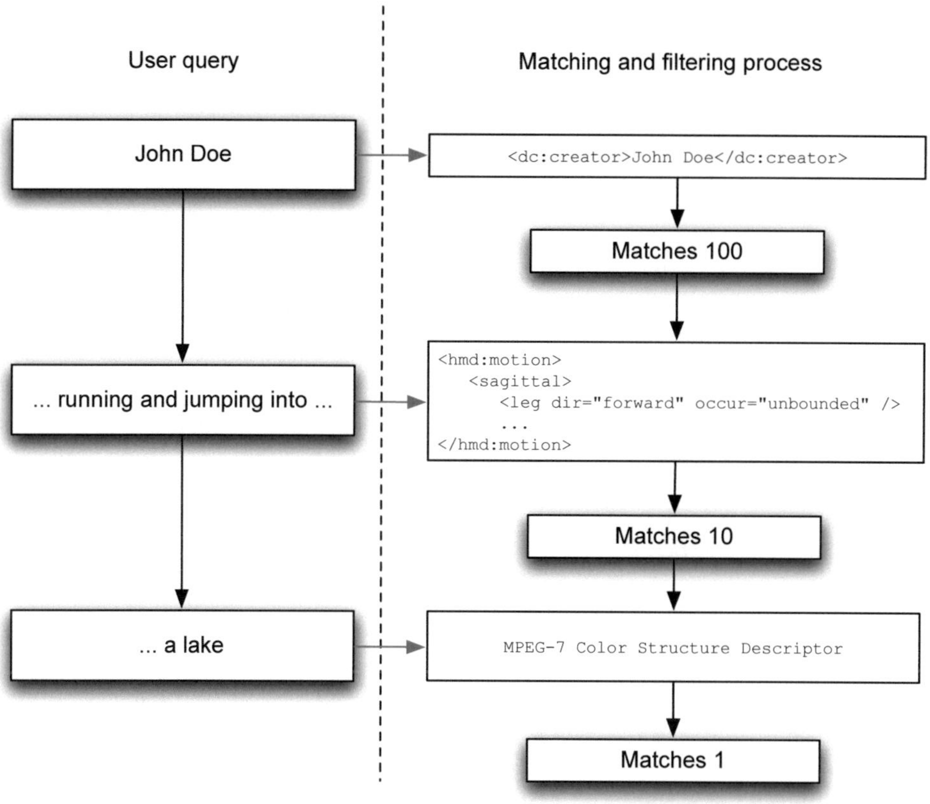

Fig. 11. An illustration of using HMD in conjunction with Dublin Core and MPEG-7 to perform a detailed search of a video using the query terms as an increasingly strict filtering process.

4. Conclusions and future work

This chapter has demonstrated a human motion description format designed for human motion enhanced multimedia search. Multimedia search using existing description formats can be thought of as increasingly strict search filtering based on a *Subject-Verb-Object* construct, where a non-temporal Dublin Core can describe the *Subject*, and temporal MPEG-7 descriptors can describe the *Object* portions of the construct. However, the important *Verb* portion is missing, which HMD intends to fill.

HMD was not designed to replace either Dublin Core or MPEG-7. Instead, it was designed to work in conjunction with both existing standards to provide a richer multimedia query environment, where a detailed query such as "*John Doe running and jumping into a lake*" can be performed with high temporal accuracy. HMD is based on XML Schema, which provide interoperability with any future description format that is based on XML. Key features of HMD include temporal matching for queries, limb-based description of motion using anatomical body planes that provides a constant frame of reference independent of the direction that the body is facing, and the ability to match arbitrarily repeated motions (such as leg movements in walking) using a single query term.

For future work, investigation into possible automatic extraction of HMD descriptions will be performed using a limb-based feature extraction as described in (Adistambha et al. 2011) as a basis. With automatic extraction, a user can upload a video to a video-sharing site such as YouTube, and using HMD, the uploaded video can be immediately indexed for detailed temporal searches involving human motions.

5. References

Adistambha, K. et al., 2011. Limb-based Feature Description of Human Motion. In International conference on signal processing and communication systems (to be presented). Honolulu, Hawaii.

Ann Hutchinson, 1970. *Labanotation; or, Kinetography Laban: the system of analyzing and recording movement*, Oxford University Press.

Barbič, J. et al., 2004. Segmenting motion capture data into distinct behaviors. In *Proceedings of Graphics Interface 2004*. Canadian Human-Computer Communications Society, pp. 185-194.

Gu, J. et al., 2010. Action and gait recognition from recovered 3-D human joints. *Systems, Man, and Cybernetics, Part B: Cybernetics, IEEE Transactions on*, 40(4), pp.1021-1033.

Gutemberg Guerra-Filho & Yiannis Aloimonos, 2007. A Language for Human Action. *IEEE Computer Magazine*, 40(5), pp.60-69.

Hatol, J., 2006. *MovementXML: A representation of semantics of human movement based on Labanotation*. Simon Fraser University.

Laban, R. & Lange, R., 1975. *Laban's principles of dance and movement notation*, in 1956 and 1970 under title: Principles of dance and movement notation Includes indexes.

Li, C., Zheng, S.Q. & Prabhakaran, B., 2007. Segmentation and recognition of motion streams by similarity search. *ACM Transactions on Multimedia Computing, Communications, and Applications (TOMCCAP)*, 3(3), p.16-es.

Loke, L., Larssen, A.T. & Robertson, T., 2005. Labanotation for design of movement-based interaction. In *Proceedings of the second Australasian conference on Interactive entertainment*. Sydney, Australia: Creativity \& Cognition Studios Press, pp. 113-120. Available at: http://portal.acm.org.ezproxy.uow.edu.au/citation.cfm?id=1109180.1109197 [Accessed December 10, 2009].

Martínez, J.M., 2004. MPEG-7 Overview. Available at: http://mpeg.chiariglione.org/standards/mpeg-7/mpeg-7.htm [Accessed October 9, 2011].

Mrabet, Y., 2008. *Planes of human anatomy*, Available at: http://commons.wikimedia.org/wiki/File:Human_anatomy_planes.svg.

Mueller, M., Baak, A. & Seidel, H.-P., 2009. Efficient and Robust Annotation of Motion Capture Data. In ACM SIGGRAPH/Eurographics Symposium on Computer Animation.

Nakamura, M. & Hachimura, K., 2006. An XML representation of labanotation, LabanXML, and its implementation on the notation editor LabanEditor2. *Pregled Nacionalnog centra za digitalizaciju*, pp.47-51.

W3C, 2004. RDF Primer. Available at: http://www.w3.org/TR/rdf-primer/ [Accessed October 11, 2011].

Wei, X. & Chai, J., 2010. Videomocap: modeling physically realistic human motion from monocular video sequences. *ACM Transactions on Graphics (TOG)*, 29(4), pp.1-10.

Weibel, S. et al., 1998. Dublin core metadata for resource discovery.

9

Ensemble Learning with LDA Topic Models for Visual Concept Detection

Sheng Tang[1], Yan-Tao Zheng[2], Gang Cao[3], Yong-Dong Zhang[1] and Jin-Tao Li[1]

[1]*Advanced Computing Research Laboratory, Beijing Key Laboratory of Mobile Computing and Pervasive Device, Institute of Computing Technology, Chinese Academy of Sciences, Beijing,*

[2]*Google Inc, Mountain View, CA*

[3]*Beijing Software Testing & QA Center, Beijing,*

[1,3]*China*

[2]*USA*

1. Introduction

With the rapid growth of multimedia application technologies and network technologies, especially the proliferation of Web 2.0 and digital cameras, there has been an explosion of images and videos in the Internet. For example, the volume of videos uploaded to the YouTube every minute is amounting to 48 hours by May 2011, having doubled in the last two years. Such huge video collections hold useful yet implicit and nontrivial knowledge about various domains. To manage and utilize these resources effectively, video concept detection becomes a very important subject of intensive research by a large research community (Over et al., 2008). It is an integral part of visual data mining that is automatically extracting such knowledge from the huge unstructured visual data. It aims to automatically annotate video shots or keyframes with respect to a semantic concept (Tang et al., 2012). Ranging from objects like *airplane* and *car* to scenes like *urban street* and *sky*, semantic concepts serve as good intermediate semantic features for video content indexing and understanding, and thus, spurring much research attention (Jiang et al., 2010; Naphade & Smith, 2004; Snoek et al., 2006; Zheng et al., 2008). Essentially, concept detection is a classification task, in which a binary classifier is usually learned to predict the presence of a certain concept in a video shot or keyframe (image). Traditional concept detection methods are mainly global classification: use supervised machine learning techniques, such as single Support Vector Machine (SVM), etc., over whole training dataset.

Study on pedestrian classification (Munder & Gavrila, 2006) showed that the benefit of selecting the best combination of features and pattern classifiers was less pronounced than the gain obtained by increasing the training set, even though the base training set already involved many thousands of samples (Enzweiler & Gavrila, 2009). In other words, the data matters most (Enzweiler & Gavrila, 2009). For visual concept detection, this was also pointed out in (Huiskes et al., 2010), and made the authors simply use more data rather than design more intelligent classification algorithms and image representations since

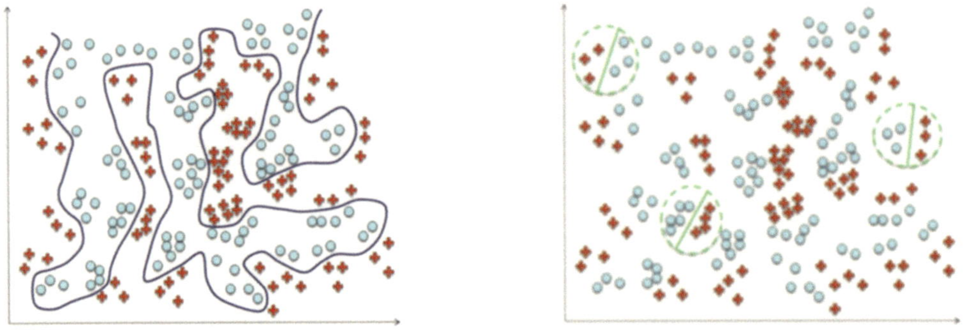

(a) Single SVM (b) The proposed method

Fig. 1. Illustration of the differences of optimal separating hyperplanes between (a) and (b). For single SVM, each test instance will use the same holistic complex hyperplane (the blue curve), while for the proposed method, a test instance will trigger very fewer number of local classifiers, e.g. 3 green dashed circles in (b), with much simpler hyperplanes (green lines) to fire.

large-scale data can also directly benefit visual concept detection. Inspired by these studies, for multimedia data of high dimension and diversified patterns, it is necessary to construct large scale training dataset to reflect all sorts of patterns as much as possible. However, there exist some challenges for global classification methods trained on large scale dataset: huge intra-class variations, low training efficiency, and low testing efficiency resulting from complex classification hyperplane as shown in Figure 1(a). To address these difficulties, the focus of this work is to develop an ensemble learning method based on Latent Dirichlet Allocation (LDA) topic models for large scale concept detection.

Ensemble learning refers to the process of combining multiple classifiers to provide a single and unified classification decision. Recent research have demonstrated, both theoretically (Krogh & Vedelsby, 1995) and empirically (Opitz & Shavlik, 1996a;b), that a good ensemble of localized classifiers can outperform a single (best) classifier learned over the entire dataset. Furthermore, learning a set of "smaller" localized classifiers usually possesses more efficient algorithmic complexity than a global classifier. Additionally, the former localized classifiers are generally more effective since their optimal separating hyper-planes may be much simpler to discriminate the data as illustrated in Figure 1(b), hence have better generalization performance than the latter due to the aforementioned problem of the huge intra-class variation. This motivates us to adopt an ensemble learning approach for concept detection.

There are, in general, two essential ingredients in a good ensemble classifier, which are: (1) the diversity of classifiers in the ensemble (Kuncheva & Whitaker, 2005), and (2) the fusion of classifiers (Opitz & Maclin, 1999; Zhang & Zhou, 2011). Diversity means that classifiers in the ensemble should possess different decision knowledge and make uncorrelated errors. In this way, the error of individual classifiers will not be the same and propagated to the ensemble, ensuring that individual classifiers have different "inductive biases", and thus, complement each other. The fusion of the classifier in the ensemble, on the other hand, is regarding how to coordinate individual classifiers for the final classification decision in a unified and theoretically principled fusion.

The most common way to achieve diversity is to train individual classifiers by using different training data. For example, the well known Bagging and Boosting (Freund & Schapire, 1997) adopt this approach by randomly selecting (via re-sampling) different sets of training data for each individual classifier. Despite of simplicity, this approach ignores the intrinsic structure of data exemplars. To achieve classifier diversity, intuitively, similar data exemplars should be grouped together to train a localized classifier, as the simple subspace complexity usually leads to more effective localized classifier. The challenge here is how to group the data effectively. In this chapter, we investigate an instance grouping method via topic modeling.

Topic modeling is a newly emerging approach to analyze large volumes of unlabeled text (Griffiths & Steyvers, 2004). It specifies a statistical sampling technique to describe how words in documents are generated based on (a small set of) hidden topics. Particularly, we investigate the semantic grouping method through estimating the topical structure of large visual data under the framework of latent Dirichlet allocation (LDA)(Blei et al., 2003).

(a) Car

(c) Dog

(b) Car

(d) Cat

Fig. 2. Illustration of the insight from psychophysical studies that humans can perform coarse categorization between left column cars (a, b) and right column animals (c, d) quite easily and quickly, followed by successive finer but slower discrimination between different types of cars (a) and (b), or between different kinds of animals (c) dog and (d) cat.

As shown in Figure 2, our proposed solution is motivated by the insight from psychophysical studies that humans can perform coarse categorization of visual objects quite easily and quickly, followed by successive finer but slower discrimination (Kuncheva, 2004; S. Thorpe & Marlot., 1996). Specifically, since all the pictures of the same category often have some local parts in common, such as all the cars have common wheels and animals have common eyes and legs as shown in the Figure 2, we propose an ensemble learning with LDA topic models due to their great advantages in exploiting the co-occurrences of local features or visual words to discover intrinsic common or similar structures of data. The proposed ensemble learning can scale up to large data sets through combination of unsupervised semantic grouping and supervised learning. First, we use generative LDA model (Blei et al., 2003) to mine the hidden topical structure of large visual data, and then perform coarse categorization by grouping the large-scale training data set with huge variations into many diversified small topic localities. Second, we perform the successive finer discrimination by training each topic locality to generate multiple small effective classifiers. Thereby, the data exemplars within one topic are deemed to be similar in part with respect to the hidden topic structure. The corresponding individual classifier then holds the decision knowledge mostly with respect to the topic. This ensures that the individual classifiers have reasonable diversity in varying regions of expertise. More importantly, for the fusion of classifiers, we propose to utilize the topic mixture coefficients in a generative probabilistic manner. For a given test sample, we adaptively select the most probable classifiers with large topic mixture coefficients for detection, which ensures that a sample is projected to only a few topic with top ranked non-zero coefficients. The resulting ensemble model is, therefore, sparse, in the way that only a small number of classifiers in the ensemble will fire on a testing sample as illustrated in Figure 1(b). Consequently, the efficiencies of both training and testing resulting can be greatly improved.

In summary, the main contribution of this chapter is that we propose a novel ensemble learning method for video concept detection by LDA topic modeling. Our preliminary results on the TREC Video Retrieval Evaluation (TRECVid) benchmark can be found in (Tang et al., 2008), and preliminary results on pornography detection for online videos can be found in (Tang et al., 2009). This chapter is an extension of both conference papers, and more detailed results of extensive tests on the TRECVid 08 benchmark and pornography detection will be provided to show that the proposed approach achieves promising results and outperforms existing approaches.

In the rest of the chapter, we first review the related work on concept detection, ensemble learning and LDA topic models in Section 2. Then, we elaborate on the details of the proposed ensemble learning algorithm in Section 3, which includes ensemble construction with LDA topic models and coordination of individual classifiers. Two systems based on the proposed ensemble learning algorithm, TRECVid concept detection system and online pornography filtering system are introduced in Section 4, and experimental results of the two systems are also given in Section 4. Finally, we present the conclusive remarks along with discussion for future work in Section 5.

2. Related work

2.1 Concept detection

Concept detection is a challenging yet useful task that has attracted attentions of many researchers. Early work on concept detection focuses on concept-specific handcrafted rules for tailor-made solution (A. Vailaya & Zhang, 1998; Smith & Chang, 1997; Szummer & Picard, 1998; Zhang et al., 1995). Distilling these rules automatically, machine learning approaches have then become the research focus, wherein a variety of classification techniques are explored. Majority of existing machine learning approaches are generally composed of five major steps (Jiang, 2009) as shown in Fig.3:

- **Preprocessing**: A video consists of a sequence of shots separated by shot boundaries including cuts and gradual transitions. Since video shots are often the basic unit for concept detection, videos are segmented into shots based on various shot boundary detection methods which uses different key frame features such as color histogram in (Yuan et al., 2007), SIFT in (Chang, Lee, Hong & Archibald, 2008), and similarity measurements. We refer readers to (Smeaton et al., 2010; Yuan et al., 2007) for a recent review on the subject. After shot boundary detection, either the middle I-frame or a set of

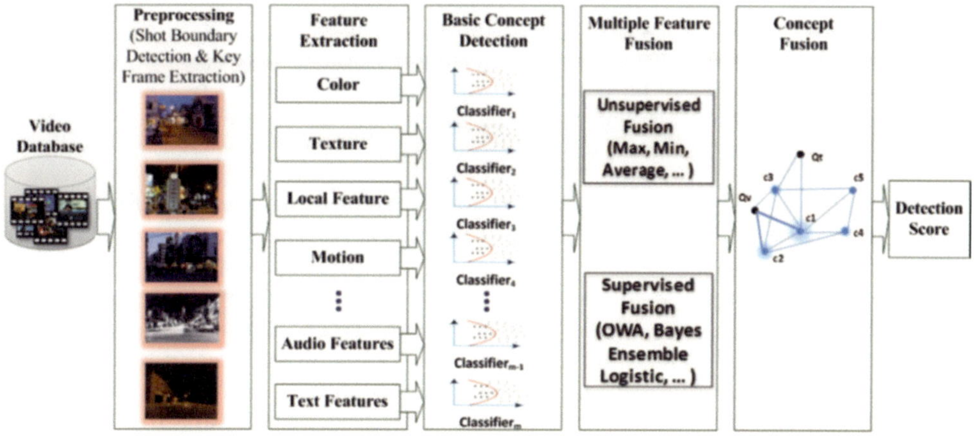

Fig. 3. General procedure of concept detection

key frames may be selected from each shot to represent the content for further detection (Borth et al., 2008).

- **Low-level feature extraction**: The purpose of feature extraction is to convert the shots or keyframes into a low dimensional feature vectors. Generally, two types of visual keyframe features are often used: global and local. Global features include (Chang, He, Jiang, Khoury, Ngo, Yanagawa & Zavesky, 2008; Ngo et al., 2009): color or edge histograms, correlograms, grid-based color moment and wavelet texture, histogram of oriented gradients (HOG) (Dalal & Triggs, 2005), local binary patterns (LBP) (Ojala et al., 1996), GIST (Siagian & Itti, 2007) and Gabor feature (Zhu et al., 2008), etc. Bag of Visual Words (BoVW) is the most widely adopted local feature which is based on a vocabulary of visual words clustered by a set of SIFT features (Lowe, 2004), and weighted by various schemes such as the traditional TF, TF-IDF, and the soft-weighting scheme which has been demonstrated to be more effective than the traditional ones (Jiang et al., 2010). Audio features such as in (Tang et al., 2007) are less frequently used while spatial temporal features including motion features, such as Space-Time Interest Points (STIP) (Laptev, 2005), are coming into use such as in (Jiang & *et al.*, 2010) despite their expensive extraction.
- **Basic concept detection**: namely, uni-modality learning with a variety of classification techniques such as SVM (Cao et al., 2006), Gaussian Mixture Model (Amir et al., 2003), Hidden Markov Model (Pytlik et al., 2005), graph-based semi-supervised learning (Tang et al., 2010; 2011; Wang, Hua, Hong, Tang, Qi & Song, 2009), etc. The choice of different kernel functions for classification of BoW features was studied in (Jiang et al., 2010), and a novel neighborhood similarity measure beyond traditional distance measurement was proposed to explore the local sample and label distributions for concept detection in (Wang, Hua, Tang & Hong, 2009) recently.
- **Multiple feature fusion**: including both early fusion (i.e., vector concatenation) of multiple features, and late fusion of multiple classifiers (Snoek et al., 2005). Late fusion is widely used for efficiency and accuracy, and there are two common approaches to calculate the weight for each classifier: unsupervised, such as min, max, and average in (Amir et al., 2003), kernel fusion in (S. Ayache & Gensel, 2007), fusion with membership vector such as LDA topic mixture coefficients in (Tang et al., 2008), etc., and supervised, such as ordered weight averaging in (Tang et al., 2007).

- **Concept fusion**: Besides the above multi-modality fusion methods based on multiple features, contextual fusion techniques (Hauptmann et al., 2007; Jiang, 2009; Qi et al., 2007; Weng & Chuang, 2008) are emerging by exploiting inter-concept relationships, such as taking into account the detection scores of nearby objects in the scene, to improve the accuracy of detection.

The major challenge of concept detection lies primarily in the existence of the well-known semantic gap (Smeulders et al., 2000) between the low level visual features and the users's semantic interpretation of visual data, and the fact that different video shots w.r.t a certain concept often possess huge variations among different visual appearances, camera shooting and video editing styles, etc. This diversity renders video shots of the same semantic concept to have varying visual patterns. Therefore, the resultant huge intra-class variation hinders the performance of most machine learning approaches. Domain change caused by the mismatch between different domains (genres or sources (Borth et al., 2010)) may worsen this problem, which raises domain adaptation in concept detection, known as cross-domain learning techniques (Jiang et al., 2008; Ngo et al., 2009; Snoek et al., 2010), including our recent concept detection work on pseudo relevance feedback based domain transfer learning (Xu, Tang, Zhang & Li, 2011) and multi-modality transfer based on multi-graph optimization (Xu, Tang, Zhang, Li & Zheng, 2011), for transferring detectors trained in source domain to the target domain. For a comprehensive review on concept detection, refer to (Jiang, 2009; Snoek & Worring, 2009), and the high level feature extraction (or semantic indexing since the year 2010) task of TRECVid (Smeaton et al., 2006; 2009) as well as its workshop papers (NIST, 2001-2010) since TRECVid provides a large video data collection, uniform evaluation criteria, a workshop for active participants to discuss their approaches, and hence can be widely regarded as the actual standard for performance evaluation of concept based video retrieval systems (Snoek & Worring, 2009).

This chapter is an extension of our previous work (Tang et al., 2008), which attempts the concept detection in the framework of ensemble learning. In the proposed scheme, the individual classifiers and their fusion weights are learned in a unified framework without any additional classifier selection module.

2.2 Ensemble learning

Ensemble learning (Kuncheva, 2004; Rokach, 2010) coordinates the outputs of multiple classifiers using diversified data to improve the performance. Empirically, ensemble methods tend to yield better results when there is a significant diversity among the constituent classifiers (Kuncheva & Whitaker, 2005). The diversity of classifier outputs plays a critical role on the success of ensemble learning. Existing methods of constructing ensembles include Bayesian voting, manipulation on the training examples and input features, etc (Dietterich, 2000). Correspondingly, for concept detection in particular, Snoek and Worring (Snoek & Worring, 2009) identified three common approaches to achieve some form of independence (diversity) for coordination, which are using (1) separate features, (2) separate classifiers, and (3) separate set of labeled examples.

This work focuses on the manipulation on the training examples for classifier diversity, which can be generally classified into two schemes: (1) separate sampling of labeled instances, and (2) instance space partitioning. As for separate sampling of labeled examples, two most widely used strategies are Bagging and Boosting:

- **Bootstrap aggregating (Bagging):** Bagging (Breiman, 1996) aims at developing independent classifiers, and the diversity necessary to make the ensemble work is created by taking bootstrap replicates as the training sets. The samples are pseudo-independent because they are sampled with replacement from the same development set.
- **Boosting and AdaBoost**: Boosting (Freund & Schapire, 1997) is a general method for improving the performance of a weak classifier. Similar to bagging, Boosting develops the classifiers by resampling the training set, while contrary to bagging, the resampling mechanism in boosting focus on most useful sample in each consecutive iteration (Rokach, 2010). AdaBoost (Adaptive Boosting) (Y. & E., 1996) is a popular ensemble algorithm that improves the simple boosting algorithm via an iterative process. The main idea is to give more focus to patterns that are harder to classify (Rokach, 2010).

Parallel to the above sampling-based partitioning approaches, many space-based partition approaches have been developed for partitioning the training set into subsets according to their belonging to some part of the input space (Rokach, 2010). Particularly, inspired by the idea that similar instances should be assigned to the same subspace, researchers attempt to use some clustering method as a possible tool for partitioning the instance space recently. Lior Rokach proposed the naive decomposition method based on K-Means algorithm (Rokach, 2010). SVM-KNN was proposed in (Zhang et al., 2006) to train an SVM improvisedly by using the K nearest neighbors of the test sample, but for large-scale dataset such as TRECVid, it is too time-consuming to search for the K nearest neighbors and train an SVM for each test sample. Furthermore, it is evident that if a test image is only partially similar with the expected training images, the latter may not fall within the range of the K nearest neighbors if K is small, which turns in vain the subsequent training and testing. Recently, we proposed a localized multiple kernel learning method for realistic human action recognition based on multiple features (Song et al., 2011), and sparse ensemble learning for visual concept detection (Tang et al., 2012) by exploiting a sparse non-negative matrix factorization process to for ensemble construction and fusion.

In this chapter, we propose a novel space-based partitioning scheme by exploiting Latent Dirichlet Allocation (LDA) (Blei et al., 2003) to partition the instance space into small topic subspaces (Tang et al., 2008).

2.3 LDA topic models

2.3.1 Vector space modeling

The first major progress in text processing was due to the vector space modeling (VSM) (Salton & McGill, 1986), in which "bag of words (BoW)" has been adopted to represent a document as a vector of frequency histogram where each dimension is associated with one term of the vocabulary and each entry is weighted by the term frequency (TF) or term frequency-inverse document frequency (TF-IDF) to reduce the importance of indiscriminant words that appear in many documents. Thereby, the whole corpus is represented as term-document matrix whose rows are indexed by the terms of the vocabulary and whose columns are indexed by the documents.

2.3.2 Latent Semantic Analysis

To address the inherent drawbacks of the VSM, such as the difficulty of capturing inter- and intra document statistical structure and the incompact description of the corpus (Alsumait et al., 2010), Latent Semantic Analysis (LSA) (Deerwester et al., 1990) has been introduced to reduce the term-document matrix through singular value decomposition (SVD). However, the computation of the SVD is expensive, and the reduced feature space is very difficult to interpret (Alsumait et al., 2010).

2.3.3 Probabilistic Latent Semantic Analysis

To better understand LSA statistically, probabilistic Latent Semantic Analysis (pLSA) was proposed (Hofmann, 1999) as an alternative to LSA by applying Bayesian methods to document modeling. The pLSA model is a generative model which uses a probabilistic sampling process to generate words in documents based on the latent topics. It associates the documents d with a mixture of latent topics z weighted by the posterior $p(z|d)$, and represents each topic by a distribution over words w that appear in it $p(w|z)$. The graphical model of pLSA is shown in Fig.4(a). As shown by the figure, the joint probability of a document d and a word w_{di} can be given as:

$$p(d, w_{di}) = p(d)p(w_{di}|d) \tag{1}$$

Given that the observation pairs (d, w_{di}) are assumed to be generated independently, the conditional probability $p(w_{di}|d)$ can be computed by marginalizing over topics z_k. Therefore, the joint probability $p(d, w_{di})$ can be computed as:

$$p(d, w_{di}) = p(d) \sum_{k=1}^{K} p(z_k|d)p(w_{di}|z_k) \tag{2}$$

where K is the total number of latent topics, $p(z_k|d)$ is the probability of topic z_k occurring in document d, and $p(w_{di}|z_k)$ is the probability of word w_{di} occurring in a particular topic $p(z_k)$.

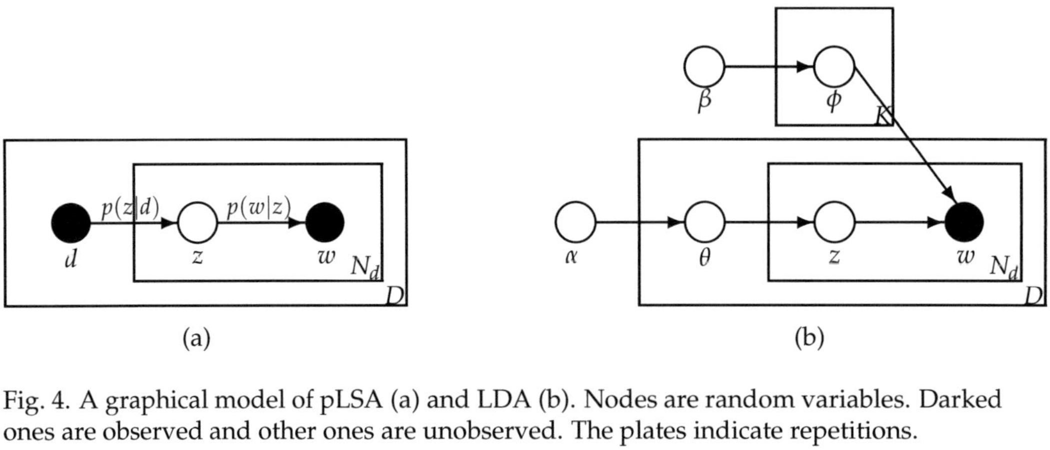

Fig. 4. A graphical model of pLSA (a) and LDA (b). Nodes are random variables. Darked ones are observed and other ones are unobserved. The plates indicate repetitions.

Actually, the pLSA is non-parametric pseudo-generative model since the document d is a dummy random variable indexed by the by the documents in a training set (Alsumait et al., 2010; Blei et al., 2003), and there is no natural way to use it to assign probability to a new testing observation (Li & Perona, 2005). Additionally, the model parameters grows linearly with the number of training examples (Li & Perona, 2005). Consequently, pLSA has the limitation of overfitting, hence poor generability for unseen documents (Blei et al., 2003). Despite its limitation, pLSA has invoked a huge amount of work in statistical machine learning and text mining, which resulting in a class of probabilistic topic models aiming at discovering these hidden variables based on hierarchical Bayesian analysis (Alsumait et al., 2010).

2.3.4 LDA

LDA (Blei et al., 2003) is a three-level hierarchical Bayesian network, a truely generative probabilistic model for a corpus of documents. The basic idea of LDA is that documents are represented by a mixture of topics where each topic is a latent multinomial variable characterized by a multinomial distribution over a fixed vocabulary of words (Alsumait et al., 2010). A graphical model of LDA is shown in Fig.4(b). As shown by the figure, through introducing Dirichlet priors α on the document distributions over topics and β on the topic distributions over words, the generative model of LDA is complete and is capable of generalizing the topic distributions for generating unseen documents (Alsumait et al., 2010).

The generative process of the LDA is described as follows (Blei et al., 2003):

1. Generate K topic multinomials ϕ_k over a fixed vocabulary of words from a Dirichlet prior $Dir(\phi_k|\beta)$ given by β; $(p(\phi_k|\beta))$.
2. Generate D document multinomials θ_d over K topics from a Dirichlet prior $Dir(\theta_d|\alpha)$ given by α; $(p(\theta_d|\alpha))$.
3. For each document d in the corpus, and for each word w_{di} in the document d:
   (a) Sample a topic z_{di} from the document multinomial θ_d; $(p(z_{di}|\theta_d))$.
   (b) Sample a word w_{di} from the topic multinomial ϕ_z; $(p(w_{di}|\phi_{z_{di}}))$.

The joint distributions of the LDA model is:

$$p(\{w_{di}\},\{z_{di}\},\{\phi_k\},\{\theta_d\}|\alpha,\beta) = \prod_{k=1}^{K} p(\phi_k|\beta) \prod_{d=1}^{D} p(\theta_d|\alpha) \prod_{i=1}^{N_d} p(z_{di}|\theta_d)p(w_{di}|\phi_{z_{di}}) \tag{3}$$

where α and β are hyperparameters of Dirichlet priors, and ϕ_k , θ_d and z_{di} are hidden variables to be inferred.

2.3.5 LDA topic models in computer vision

Recently, inspired by its great success in finding useful structures in many kinds of documents in the field of text processing (Griffiths & Steyvers, 2004), LDA topic model, has been widely applied to computer vision problems such as object segmentation (Wang & Grimson, 2007), scene categorization (Li & Perona, 2005), action recognition (Niebles et al., 2008; Wang, 2011; Wang & Mori, 2009) and event detection(Pan & Mitra, 2011).

Under topic models, analogous to BoW in text processing, "Bag of visual words (BoVW)" (Jiang et al., 2007; Jurie & Triggs, 2005; Sivic & Zisserman, 2003; Zhang et al., 2007) is usually used to represent visual contents (such as key frames) as visual words. BoVW has first been introduced by Sivic in the case of video retrieval (Sivic & Zisserman, 2003) and became very popular in the fields of image retrieval and categorization due to its efficiency and effectiveness. After extraction of visual features, such as local features SIFT (Lowe, 2004) or SURF (Bay et al., 2006), BoVW consists of two main steps: visual vocabulary construction and feature quantization. Generally, various clustering methods are used to build the visual vocabulary by clustering features in to visual words (centroids) which are analogous to stems in text processing. Then, visual features are quantized into visual words and visual contents are represented as the frequencies of visual words. Topic models will compute latent concepts by exploring the co-occurrence of visual words to learn the models of different patterns without manual annotation of training samples (Wang, 2011). Compared with other approaches, one of the major advantages of topic models is their unsupervised nature which is very important for discovering different patterns from large volumes of video data (Wang, 2011).

3. Algorithm

3.1 Preliminaries and problem formulation

In the task of concept detection, a video shot keyframe is processed to detect the presence of a set of predefined concepts. Let x denote the visual feature for the keyframe.

For each concept, we have a training set $X = \{x_i, i = 1, 2, ..., N\}$ with label $Y = \{y_i \in \pm 1, i = 1, 2, N\}$. The concept detection is thus naturally formulated as a classification task. Here, we adopt the binary classification in the framework of SVM (Vapnik, 1995) and aim to learn an ensemble discriminant function $F(x_t)$ for a test sample x_t

$$F(x_t) = \sum_{k=1}^{K} \Psi_k(x_t) \cdot (\langle \omega_k, \Phi(x_t) \rangle + b_k). \tag{4}$$

The discriminant function $F(x_t)$ is an ensemble of K localized classifiers that are built on instance localities π_k respectively, where $\Psi_k(x_t)$ are the gating functions that governs how localized classifiers $f_k(x_t)$ are coordinated for the final classification of test sample x_t.

Solving the primal SVM problem, we obtain $\omega = \sum_i \beta_i y_i \Phi(x_i)$. As plugging ω into Eq.(5), the ensemble discriminant function $F(x_t)$ becomes:

$$F(x_t) = \sum_{k=1}^{K} \Psi_k(x_t) \cdot \left(\sum_{i \in \pi_k} \beta_i y_i \langle \Phi(x_t), \Phi(x_i) \rangle + b_k \right). \tag{5}$$

Learning the ensemble discriminant function $F(x_t)$ can be decomposed into two steps: (1) computing the instance locality model and (2) estimating the localized kernel classifier parameters. The first step learns the instance localities π_k and gating function $\Psi_k(x_t)$.

In the next subsections, we describe the proposed data instance partitioning approach based on LDA topic model , and the coordination of individual classifiers based on LDA coefficients. Fig.5 shows the overall framework of the proposed ensemble learning method.

3.2 Ensemble construction with LDA topic models

We employ LDA to model the relationship between images to discover the hidden structures and perform coarse categorization for ensemble construction and fusion.

3.2.1 LDA topic modeling

To construct the ensemble, the first step is learn the instance locality π. Suppose we have a set of $D(d = 1, \ldots, D)$ keyframes (or shots) containing words from a vocabulary of size V. Each instance (a shot or keyframe) d is represented as a sequence of N_d visual words $w = (w_1, \ldots, w_{N_d})$. We set the number of latent topics K to the number of the above instance localities, i.e., the number of localized classifiers in the ensemble. Then, the LDA process that generates each instance d in the corpus is:

1. Choose the number of visual words N_d from $Poisson(\xi)$.

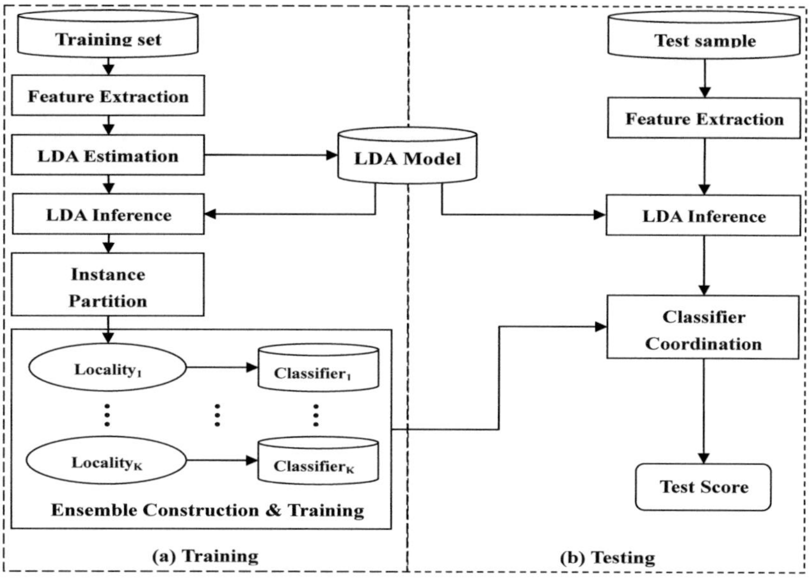

Fig. 5. The overall framework. The proposed ensemble first exploits LDA to represent data instances as a mixture of hidden topics and partition the data space into topic localities, and then coordinates the individual classifiers in each topic locality for final classification based on the topic mixture of LDA topics which is naturally achieved during LDA inference without additional classifier selection.

2. Choose the mixing proportions θ of the current instance d over K topics from $Dir(\alpha)$.
3. For each of the N_d visual words w_i:
   (a) Choose a topic z_i from $Multinomial(\theta)$.
   (b) Choose a visual word w_i from the multinomial distribution $p(w_i|z_i, \beta)$.

Here, the topic mixture θ is a multinomial distribution which is generated by K-dimensional Dirichlet distribution parameterized by the Dirichlet priors α. Additionally, the matrix β of size $K \times V$ is the parameter of the distribution of visual words conditioned on each topic locality, and each element of β corresponds to the probability $p(w_i|z_k)$.

The joint distributions of the LDA model is:

$$p(\theta, z, w|\alpha, \beta) = p(\theta|\alpha) \prod_{i=1}^{N_d} p(z_i|\theta) p(w_i|z_i, \beta) \tag{6}$$

where w is the set of words observed in the current instance, and z is their corresponding topic.

As mentioned in the previous section, under LDA topic models, BoVW feature (Sivic & Zisserman, 2003) (including other frequency-based features such as color histogram and edge histogram etc.) is usually used to represent keyframe. Therefore, the vocabulary size V is equal to the size M of the feature for LDA estimation. In some practice, $V = M + 1$ since a dummy word irrelevant to all other words should be included in the vocabulary. Additionally, in our proposed ensemble learning method, LDA is used only for partition ensemble construction and individual classifier coordination. The features used for LDA can be different from the features for SVM.

In the proposed ensemble construction, we need to know how an instance is mixed over K hidden topic localities. So we must infer the posterior distribution of the hidden variables for a set of words w observed in the instance (shot or keyframe):

$$p(\theta, z|w, \alpha, \beta) = \frac{p(\theta, z, w|\alpha, \beta)}{p(w|\alpha, \beta)} \tag{7}$$

where θ is specific to each instance and represents its latent topics distribution.

Generally, it is computationally intractable to perform above inference and parameter estimation for the LDA model. Up to now, two main approximation algorithms have been proposed to solve the problem: (1) variational inference Expectation-Maximization (EM) adopted in (Blei et al., 2003); and (2) gibbs sampling adopted in (Griffiths & Steyvers, 2004) which is easier to compute than the former method.

Once the topic mixture θ is inferred, we can know how topic localities are mixed in the current instance. There for we can exploit it to determine which localities the instance should be partitioned into as shown in the next subsection.

3.2.2 Adaptive instance-locality assignment

After LDA inference of the topic mixture θ, we can allocate the instance x_i to a few L localities, according to the top L large elements of $\theta = \{\theta_1, \ldots, \theta_K\}$. The greater the element θ_i is, the

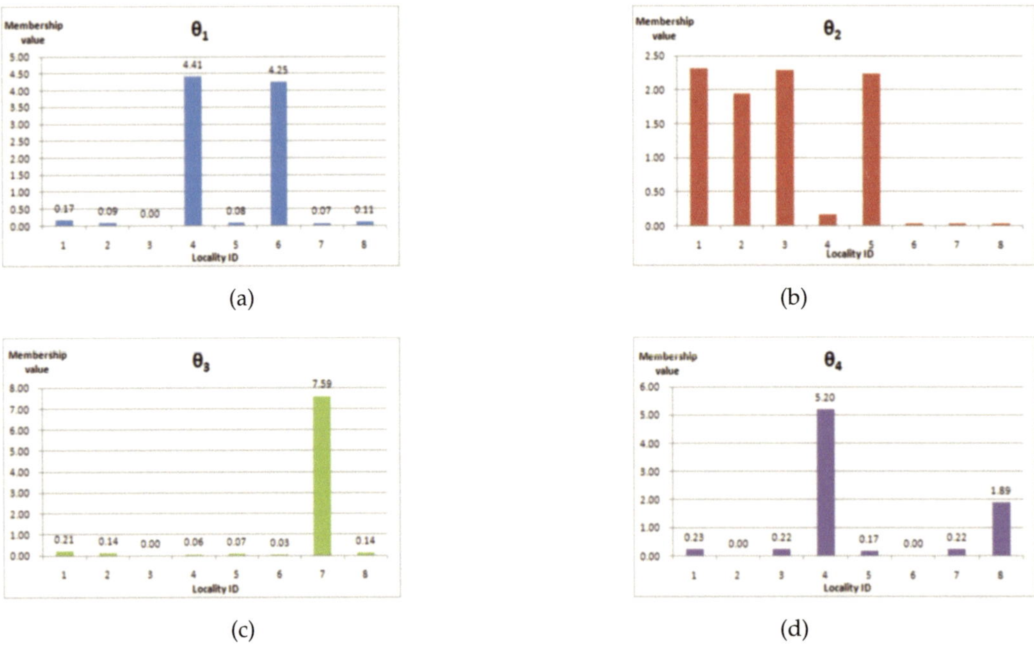

Fig. 6. Illustration of various distributions of topic mixture vector θ. Each bar denotes the value of one data instance in a topic locality. Intuitively, the data instance should be ideally assigned to a small number of localities with relatively large values only.

Algorithm: Adaptive Instance Assignment

Input: Topic mixture $\theta = \theta_1, \ldots, \theta_K \in R^K$;
Thresholds: $Th_{adj}, Th_{sum} \in [0, \ldots, 1]$;
Replication parameter: L.

Output: Locality index set: U; Normalized topic mixture: θ.

l_1-Normalize θ: $\theta_i \leftarrow \theta_i / \parallel \theta \parallel_1, i = 1, \ldots, K$;
Sort: $[\theta, Index]$ = sort(θ,'descend');
$S \leftarrow 0, Len \leftarrow min(K, L), U \leftarrow \emptyset$;
$U \leftarrow U \cup \{Index_1\}$;
for ($i = 1$; $i < Len$; i++)
  if ($\theta_{i+1}/\theta_i < Th_{adj}$)
    break;
  $S \leftarrow S + \theta_{i+1}$;
  if ($S > Th_{sum}$)
    break;
  $U \leftarrow U \cup \{Index_{i+1}\}$;
end for;
if ($i + 1 < K$)
  reset: $\theta_j \leftarrow 0, j = i + 2, \ldots, K$;
l_1-Normalize θ: $\theta_j \leftarrow \theta_j / \parallel \theta \parallel_1, j = 1, \ldots, i + 1$;
Return U, θ.

Fig. 7. Adaptive instance assignment algorithm

more probably the instance is related to the corresponding i^{th} topic locality. Here, L is a replication parameter to control the maximum number of localities that a data instance can be assigned. This effectively controls the replication degree of instance.

One challenge here is that the topic mixture value of θ_i in θ may vary greatly, and it is not reasonable to assign the data instance to localities with very small values. For example in Fig.6, the data instance should be ideally assigned to a small number of localities with relatively large mixture values only. To do so, we leverage an ordered operator to select valid localities in an adaptive manner.

The main idea is to detect the abrupt decrease in two adjacent elements in the normalized and sorted (in descending order) topic mixture θ. If the ratio of the mixture value θ_{i+1} to the former θ_i is greater than the a given adjacent threshold (Th_{adj}) and the accumulated sum of the vector values is below a given accumulation threshold (Th_{sum}), then assign the data instance to the corresponding locality. Finally, we reset all the elements θ_j after the abrupt decrease in θ the to zero, and re-normalize the topic mixture vector θ. The adaptive instance-locality assignment algorithm is shown in Fig.7.

After grouping all the instances in the training set to localities, we finish coarse categorization by partitioning large-scale training data set into K small topic localities according to topic mixture θ of instances. Then, we train a linear discriminative classifier for each locality to learn the instance localities π_k. Once all the local classifiers are trained, we finish the ensemble construction and training process.

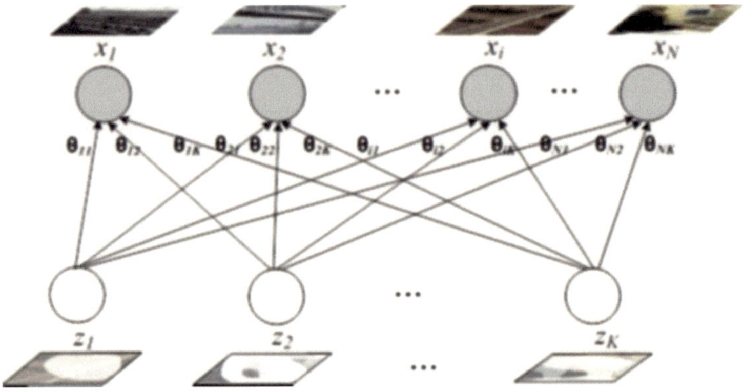

Fig. 8. In the probabilistic generative process of LDA, the observed data instances (documents) are represented as a mixture of hidden topics, and the topic mixture vector θ determines how an instance x is mixed over K hidden topic localities. Note that after reseting of θ in the above adaptive instance assignment, most connections between x and z will be of zero coefficients.

3.3 Coordination of individual classifiers

As shown in Fig.5, after LDA inference of test instances during testing process, we need to coordinate the learned local classifiers for the final classification.

The coordination of classifiers in the ensemble concerns learning the gating function $\Psi_k(x_t)$ in the Equation 5 for a test sample x_t. As shown in Fig.8, in the probabilistic generative process of LDA, the observed data instances (documents) are represented as a mixture of hidden topics, and the topic mixture vector θ determines how an instance x is mixed over K hidden topic localities. Therefore, in the LDA generative model, the influence of a topic locality z_k on x_t is represented by the connection strength θ_{tk}. We, therefore, utilize this influence to coordinate individual classifiers by setting $\Psi_k(x_t) = \theta_{tk}$. Note that after resetting of θ in the above adaptive instance assignment, most weak connections between x and z will be of zero coefficients. In other words, for a testing sample x_t, as only a few number ($T \leq L$ is the resultant size of the locality index set U returned by the algorithm) of large topic mixture coefficients are non-zero which trigger the corresponding number T of local classifiers to fire.

3.4 Analysis and discussion

3.4.1 The number of localities

The optimal tuning of the number of localities K is not necessary, since the instance space partitioning is a coarse process to group data. K can be roughly determined by the ratio of total number of training samples N to the desired average size of topic set which should be generally no more than ten thousands for the consideration of classifier training efficiency.

3.4.2 Computational complexity

The separate training of individual classifiers on each locality gives rise to the parallelism of SVM training. Assume that each locality possesses $O(N \cdot T/K)$ data instances. Since the theoretical computational complexity of SVM training (without considering space problem) is between $O(n^2)$ and $O(n^3)$ (n denotes the number of training samples) depending on the value of the hyper-parameter C (Bordes et al., 2005). Then the complexity of learning its classifier is between the lower bound $O((N \cdot T/K)^2)$ and upper bound $O((N \cdot T/K)^3)$. The total complexity of the ensemble is between $K \cdot O((N \cdot T/K)^2) = \frac{T^2}{K} \cdot O(N^2)$, and $K \cdot O((N \cdot T/K)^3) = \frac{T^3}{K^2} \cdot O(N^3)$, which is much more efficient than the complexity of the single SVM that is learned over the entire dataset since $T \leq L \ll K$. Furthermore, if we take the space problem into consideration, as the number of training instances N grows, the large kernel matrix cannot be stored in memory and the cost of computing each kernel value is relatively high because Kernel values must be computed on the fly or retrieved from a cache of often accessed values (Bordes et al., 2005), which makes single SVM impractical. On the other hand, it means that the ensemble can scale up to large scale training dataset.

Similarly, the testing speed can be considerably improved since a testing instance belongs to only a few T localities and invokes the corresponding local classifiers only. The test complexity of the ensemble is $O(N_{sv})$, where N_{sv} is the number of support vectors (SV) which is proportional to number of training samples. Assume the testing data instance are assigned to only T localities as illustrated in Figure 1(b), then the number of training samples in all firing classifiers can be estimated to be $N \cdot T^2/K$ in average. Therefore, the testing efficiency can be considerably improved. This makes it practical for online detection in spite of large training data set.

3.4.3 Cross validation for classifier parameter optimization

Cross validation is widely used for parameter optimization of classifiers, such as the cost parameter C in soft-margin SVMs and the width parameter g of the Gaussian kernel for SVM classifiers. It has great influence on video classification performance (van Gemert et al., 2006). However, it is very time consuming for large scale training set. For the individual SVM classifier training on each locality, we do not adopt SVM cross validation due to the two facts: (1) the diversity of the ensemble makes uncorrelated decisions for each classifier thus complement each other, which makes cross validation less important compared with the case of single SVM training; (2) for the unbalanced data sets such as TRECVid, traditional accuracy-based SVM cross validation may not be good for model selection. Perhaps AP or InfAP based cross validation is more preferable.

4. System and evaluation

Based on the proposed LDA ensemble learning method, we developed two systems to test its effectiveness: (1)TRECVid concept detection system; (2) Online pornography filtering system. We will introduce them briefly as follows.

4.1 TRECVid concept detection system

To evaluate the performance of our proposed method, we developed a video concept detection system based on the TRECVid 08 video benchmark collection (Over et al., 2008). The preliminary results have been reported in our recent papers (Tang et al., 2008).

4.1.1 Datasets and experimental setup

In TRECVid 08, 20 concepts are used for evaluation as listed in Table 1. Its development set consists of 109-hour documentary videos of 43,616 keyframes(shots), and testing set of 109-hour videos of 35,766 keyframes(shots).

There are two kinds of the annotation efforts for the development set (Snoek & Worring, 2009): one is our manual annotation (Tang et al., 2008) and the other is collaboration annotation

ID	Concept	#Pos	#Hit	ID	Concept	#Pos	#Hit
1001	Classroom	241	64	1011	Harbor	217	35
1002	Bridge	186	30	1012	Telephone	203	106
1003	Emergency-Vehicle	103	22	1013	Street	1799	458
1004	Dog	136	94	1014	Demonstration-Or-Protest	159	87
1005	Kitchen	289	124	1015	Hand	1879	630
1006	Airplane-flying	80	64	1016	Mountain	265	140
1007	Two-people	4140	1090	1017	Nighttime	490	316
1008	Bus	106	47	1018	Boat-Ship	506	210
1009	Driver	302	364	1019	Flower	620	319
1010	Cityscape	331	337	1020	Singing	441	133

Note: The column "#Pos" denotes the number of positive training samples in the development set, and the column "#Hit" denotes the number of hits in the groundtruth of the test set provided by TRECVid.

Table 1. The list of 20 concepts in TV08.

Proposed (L=1)	Proposed (L=6)	Single-SVM	Bagging
0.116	0.138	0.130	0.132

Table 2. MAP Comparison of the proposed method, Single-SVM and Bagging on TV 08.

launched by Laboratory of Informatics of Grenoble (LIG) (Ayache & Quénot, 2008). In our experiments, we used the combination of both ours and LIG's annotation. The number of positive training samples and number of hits in the groundtruth are also shown in Table 1. The evaluation criteria used here is the inferred average precision (InfAP) (Yilmaz & Aslam, 2006) or inferred mean average precision (Inf MAP). InfAP is a very good estimate for average precision (AP). AP is the average of precisions computed at the point of each of the relevant documents for considering the order in the ranked sequence of documents, and it is one of the most commonly used system-oriented measures of retrieval effectiveness (Smeaton et al., 2009). InfAP was adopted to replace AP in TRECVid since 2005 to save large amount of judging effort as verified by Yilmaz and Aslam (Yilmaz & Aslam, 2006).

4.1.2 Features and ensemble parameters

We use the released VIREO-374 features (Jiang et al., 2010) to train and test our system. The primary visual feature we adopt is the local BoVW) features, due to its widely reported effectiveness. The BoVW representation is a histogram based on a visual vocabulary of 500 visual words clustered by a set of about 500,000 SIFT features (Lowe, 2004), and weighted by a soft-weighting scheme for taking into account the significance of each visual word in the keyframe, which has been demonstrated to be more effective than the traditional TF/TF-IDF weighting schemes (Jiang et al., 2010).

There are three principal types of parameters in the LDA ensemble construction and SVM training phase of the proposed ensemble:

(1) The number of localities K: we set $K = 100$ empirically;

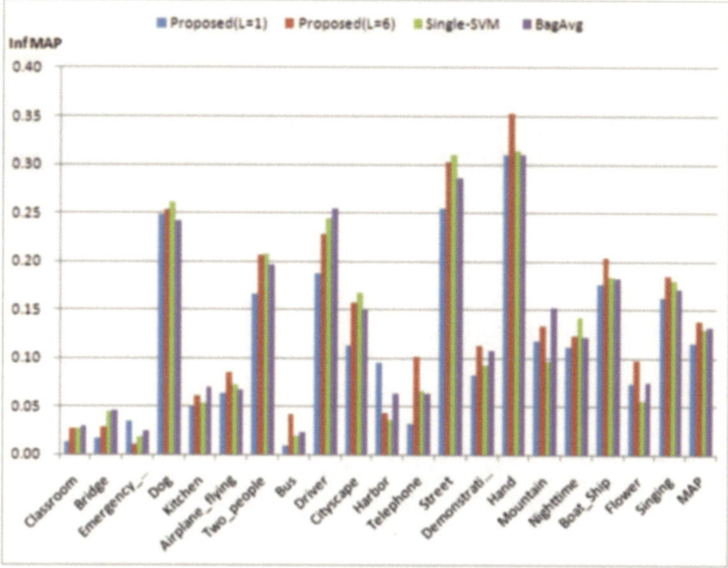

Fig. 9. Comparison of AP for each concept on TV 08 by different runs. As shown, the proposed method outperforms single SVM and Bagging.

(2) Parameters for the adaptive instance-locality assignment, and our recommendation is: the replication parameter $L = 6$, and the two thresholds: $Th_{adj} = 0.2$, $Th_{sum} = 0.95$. Th_{adj} and Th_{adj} is not so important since they can be determined empirically;

(3) For the individual SVM classifier of each locality, we utilize the default RBF kernel, and we do not adopt SVM cross validation according to the aforementioned reasons.

4.1.3 Experimental results

To investigate the effectiveness of the proposed ensemble, we compare its performances with the widely used single SVM method over the entire data set, and the well known ensemble learning approach - Bagging by imitating the random generation of $K = 100$ training subsets through sampling with replacement from the development set (Efron & Tibshirani, 1993).

The proposed ensemble learning ($L = 6$) gives rise to an MAP of 0.138, which is 6.2% relatively higher than the single SVM of MAP 0.130, and 4.5% higher than Bagging of MAP 0.132 as shown in Table 2. Fig.9 also shows the comparison of AP for each concept. As shown, the proposed method outperforms single SVM on evidently on 11 out of 20 concepts, which are object-oriented concepts like "Airplane-flying", "Bus", "Telephone", "Hand", "Boat-Ship", "Flower". Most of the rest concepts in which single SVM performs better are scene-oriented concepts like "Cityscape", "Street" and "Nighttime". As compared with Bagging, we can also see that the proposed method are better for object-oriented concepts.

Our conjecture is that the object-oriented concepts have intrinsic structures consisting of different subcategories (such as different kind of canoes and steamers associated with the concept "Boat-Ship") of common objects (such as "wheels" for the concept "Car"), which have similar local features, and hence makes LDA exhibit obvious advantages in capturing visual contents by exploiting the co-occurrences of visual words for instance space partitioning during ensemble construction. On the other hand, scene-oriented concepts are too diversified to have common parts such as "Street" and "Nighttime".

Additionally, for the proposed method with the case of $L = 1$, its performances are greatly reduced as shown in Fig.9, even worse than the single SVM method. We attribute this to the insufficient positive training samples in most of topic localities due to the over-partition without replication of samples.

Besides the better accuracy, the proposed ensemble also enables much more efficient training than the single SVM. According to the previous computational complexity analysis, the lower bound complexity of the proposed ensemble ($L = 6$) is $\frac{L^2}{K} \cdot O(N^2)$, which is 0.36 of the single SVM. This is verified from the actual ratio (0.077) of the proposed training time (6.0 hours) to that of single SVM (78.3 hours), while the actual total number of training samples of the proposed amounts to about 250,000, approximately $L = 6$ times as that of single SVM.

4.2 Online pornography filtering system

Due to the explosion of images and videos in the Internet, the chances of individuals encountering adult-oriented contents such as pornographic images and videos increase dramatically, which has become a serious global socio-cultural problem. Therefore, it is of great importance to detect and filter these harmful contents to provide a cleaner internet environment for the sake of young adolescents' healthy growth.

Most existing methods for pornography filtering attempt to exploit text contents to classify web pages (Rowley et al., 2006). However, the textual approaches suffer from significant limitations such as dependence of languages, and unavailability of texts. Previous work on pornographic image detection can be divided into two broad categories (Hu et al., 2007; Rowley et al., 2006): skin-based methods (Zeng et al., 2004; Zheng, 2004) that are based primarily on skin color or texture, and model-based methods(Forsyth & Fleck, 1999) which analyze the shapes of skin colored regions to determine their similarity to human figures. Both categories rely heavily on skin detection which lacks sufficient robustness against significant variations in races, lighting conditions, textures, sex-positions, and other factors.

Due to the importance of data (Enzweiler & Gavrila, 2009), we first established a large-scale training image dataset to include all the kinds of possible variations aforementioned as much as possible. Then, in order to handle large-scale dataset both efficiently and effectively, we used the proposed LDA ensemble learning framework to develop an online pornography filtering system for detecting and monitoring images and video keyframes in the Internet, and the system is being used by governments and companies in real application. The details of the system are introduced as follows. The preliminary results have been published in our recent paper (Tang et al., 2009).

4.2.1 Construction of large-scale training dataset

We established a large-scale training image (including key-frames extracted from videos) dataset for pornography detection. Thanks to the proliferation of digital images and videos, it was no longer a difficult task to establish a large database with totally 420,615 training image samples collecting from a wide variety of diverse origins. We collected 1,108 pornographic videos from off-line VCD sources. We also captured about 20,000 short pornographic video clips from online media streams by the skin-based detection method (Zheng, 2004) from Dec 2007 to Dec 2008. We downloaded about 65,000 non-pornographic videos from YouTube, Tudou, YouKu and other websites. The non-pornographic images were mainly from Corel database while the pornographic images were downloaded from Pinkworld. After collection,

Samples	Images	Video Keyframes	Total
Positive	21,699	44,128	65,827
Negative	51,680	303,108	354,788

Table 3. Sample distribution of training dataset

we annotated all the images and keyframes after data collection and keyframe extraction. During annotation, in order to distinguish true pornographic images from non-pornographic bodies, we regarded only the images with exposed woman breast, anus, genital organs, or sexual intercourse scenes as positive samples, while others as negative samples regardless of exposed skin area. Details of the sample distribution are listed in Table 3. Up to now, few pornographic image detection systems are based on such a large-scale database with more than 10^5 images. To our best knowledge, the reported number of pornographic positive training samples is usually less than 10^4 images.

4.2.2 Features and ensemble parameters

We extracted the following three kinds of keyframe features in the system:

1. Color Histogram (CH) (Amir et al., 2005): This is a 166-dimensional histogram, a global representation of keyframe which is based on the distribution of pixels in an uniformly partitioned HSV color space.

2. Color Moments (CM) (Stricker & Orengo, 1995): To further incorporate spatial relationship into the color content, a keyframe is partitioned into a 5×5 grid and each patch is represented using the first three moments of the color distribution in LAB color space, i.e. the mean, standard deviation and the third root of the skewness of each color channel. The color moments for each patch are then concatenated to form a 255-dimensional feature vector. In our implementation (Chua et al., 2009), we pre-compute the transformation coefficients for color moment feature extraction which can provide up to five times speed up over the traditional extraction method.

3. Edge Histogram (EH) (Amir et al., 2005): It is localized edge histograms from a 5-region layout consisting of four corner regions and a center overlapping region, represented as a 320-dimensional vector with 8 edge direction bins and 8 edge magnitude bins based on a Sobel filter (64-dimensional) for each grid.

Through our hierarchical combination of unsupervised clustering and supervised learning, we used CH for LDA categorization at the top layer; and the prior fusion (concatenation) of the CM and EH for finer discrimination at the bottom layer (CM+EH, 545-dimensional). We used CH for coarse categorization due to its relatively lower dimension and faster extraction, while the concatenation of the two sets of features for finer discrimination for further removal of false detection caused by many existing skin-based methods. To meet the online detection speed requirements, we did not use the effective bag-of-visual-word features based on local features such as SIFT. Although there is no special emphasis on detecting skin, skin detection is actually included in the latent semantic analysis of the color histogram and training of SVM models with color moment.

We set the number of localities $K = 40$, the replication parameter $L = 1$, and the two thresholds: $Th_{adj} = 0.2$, $Th_{sum} = 0.95$. For the individual SVM classifier of each locality, we utilize the default RBF kernel, and we do not adopt SVM cross validation.

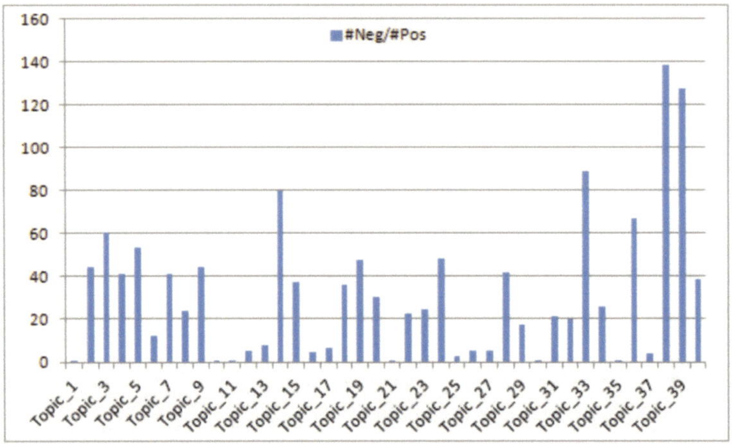

Fig. 10. Distributions of Negative/Positive samples over the $K = 40$ topics

4.2.3 Experimental results

After training all the $K = 40$ individual SVM classifiers, we collected the test image/keyframe samples from some companies independently. The total 7110 test samples include 1695 pornographic samples and 5415 non-pornographic samples.

Figure 10 show the distributions of the Negative/Positive samples over the $K = 40$ topics. We can see that the Negative/Positive ratio varies greatly from 0.29 in the topic 11 to 138.42 in the largest topic 38, which means there are more pornographic samples than non-pornographic ones in the topics (1, 10, 11, 21, 30 and 35) where the ratio is less than 1, while there are relatively much fewer pornographic samples in the topics (such as 38 and 39) where the ratio is very large. Compared with the nearly uniform distribution of Negative/Positive samples generated by random sampling, this imbalanced distribution of positive samples over topics indicates that LDA can mine the hidden structures of images effectively.

For comparison, we implemented the skin-based method in (Zheng, 2004) and used it for collecting our training database as mention above. We also implemented single SVM method with the same feature CM+EH over randomly selected 120, 000 samples from our training data set. We did not use the whole training dataset for single SVM due to the impractical amount of training computation.

The ROC curves for our proposed ensemble learning (LDA-SVM), SVM, and the skin-based method are shown in Figure 11, which indicates that the LDA-SVM is much more effective than other two methods. Particularly, when we set the detection score threshold to 0.95, the false positive rate can reach as low as 0.11% (only 6 out of 5415 non-pornographic samples are recognized pornographic ones) while keeping the recall rate still around 50% (840 out of 1695 pornographic samples are correctly recognized). On the other hand, when we set the detection score threshold to 0.5, the precision and recall rates can reach as high as 95.12% (corresponding to false positive rate of 4.88%) and 90.09% respectively.

To test the effectiveness of our coordination method with topic mixture θ, we use the average fusion method for comparison, and its ROC curve is shown in Figure 11 (the cyan one marked as LDA-SVM(AVG)). Since all the 40 SVM models is used for average fusion, its test time is 667ms about 13.6 times slower than that (49 ms) of our coordination method. So we can conclude that using the topic mixture coefficients for adaptive fusion is effective and efficient.

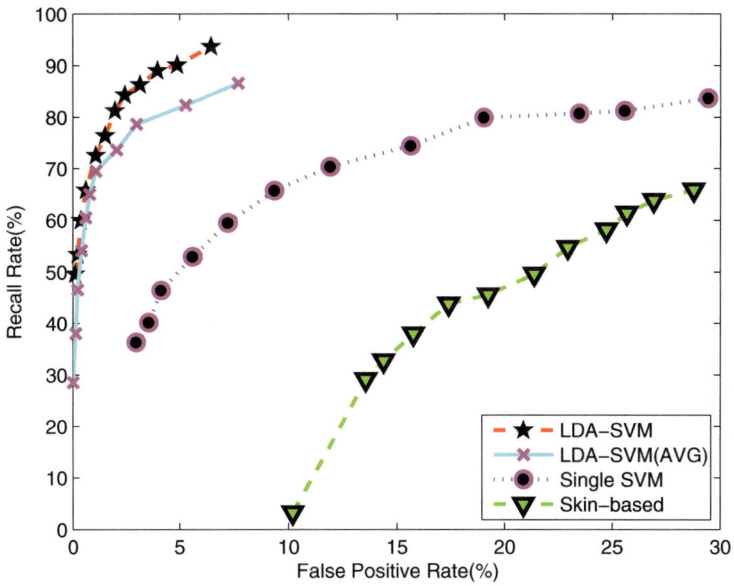

Fig. 11. ROC Curves for Pornography Detection

Methods	SVM	LDA-SVM
Training samples	120,000	420,615
Number of SVs	24,112	1,842 per topic
Training time	72 hours	6 hours
Testing time(320×240)	667 ms	49 ms

Table 4. Training & testing time of SVM methods

The training time, testing time and the numbers of samples and SVs of the single SVM method and LDA-SVM are shown in Table 4, which indicates the high training and testing efficiency of the proposed method.

5. Conclusion and future work

In this chapter, motivated by the insight from psychophysical studies, we propose a novel ensemble learning framework in LDA topic models for large scale concept detection through combination of unsupervised semantic grouping and supervised learning. Classifier diversity is achieved by digging the intrinsic topic structure of large visual data under the framework of LDA topic modeling. For the ensemble fusion, the individual classifiers are then coordinated based on the large LDA topic mixture coefficients in a generative probabilistic manner, which is naturally achieved without any additional classifier selection module. As the individual classifiers are often more compact due to their training on the smaller topic localities, and only a small number of classifiers in the ensemble will fire on a testing sample, the testing efficiency can be considerably improved. This makes it practical for online concept detection despite of large training data set. Extensive tests on the TRECVid 08 benchmark and pornography detection show that the proposed ensemble learning achieves promising results and outperforms existing approaches.

Several issues are worthy of further investigation. First, optimal feature, kernel selection and removal of redundant samples along with high-dimensional indexing should be taken into consideration to further improve the performance. Then, the individual classifiers trained in each locality can be further explored for cross-domain concept detection. Finally, it is of great importance to use tags of web images to avoid laborious annotation of training samples.

6. Acknowledgments

This work was supported by National Nature Science Foundation of China (60873165).

7. References

A. Vailaya, A. K. J. & Zhang, H.-J. (1998). On image classification: City images vs. landscapes, *Pattern Recognition* 31: 1921–1936.

Alsumait, L., Wang, P., Domeniconi, C. & Barbarĺć, D. (2010). *Embedding Semantics in LDA Topic Models*, John Wiley & Sons, Ltd.

Amir, A., Argillander, J., Campbell, M. & *et al.* (2005). IBM Research TRECVID-2005 Video Retrieval System, *NIST TRECVID Workshop*.

Amir, A., Berg, M., Chang, S.-F. & *et al.* (2003). Ibm research trecvid-2003 video retrieval system, *NIST TRECVID Workshop*.

Ayache, S. & Quénot, G. (2008). Video corpus annotation using active learning, *Proceedings of the IR research, 30th European conference on Advances in information retrieval*, ECIR'08, pp. 187–198.

Bay, H., Tuytelaars, T., Gool, V. & L. (2006). Surf: Speeded up robust features, *9th European Conference on Computer Vision*.

Blei, D. M., Ng, A. Y. & Jordan, M. I. (2003). Latent dirichlet allocation, *Journal of Machine Learning Research* .

Bordes, A., Ertekin, S., Weston, J. & Bottou, L. (2005). Fast kernel classifiers with online and active learning, *J. Mach. Learn. Res.* 6: 1579–1619.

Borth, D., Ulges, A. & Breuel, T. (2010). *Adapting Web-based Video Concept Detectors for Different Target Domains*, Bentham Science Publishers, chapter 6.

Borth, D., Ulges, A., Schulze, C. & Breuel, T. (2008). Keyframe extraction for video tagging & summarization., *Informatiktage*, Vol. S-6 of *LNI*, GI, pp. 45–48.

Breiman, L. (1996). Bagging predictors, *Mach. Learn.* 24: 123–140.

Cao, J., Lan, Y., Li, J. & *et al.* (2006). Intelligent multimedia group of Tsinghua University at trecvid 2006, *NIST TRECVID Workshop*.

Chang, S.-F., He, J., Jiang, Y.-G., Khoury, E. E., Ngo, C.-W., Yanagawa, A. & Zavesky, E. (2008). Columbia university/vireo-cityu/irit trecvid2008 high-level feature extraction and interactive video search, *NIST TRECVID Workshop*.

Chang, Y., Lee, D. J., Hong, Y. & Archibald, J. (2008). Unsupervised video shot detection using clustering ensemble with a color global scale-invariant feature transform descriptor, *J. Image Video Process.* 2008: 9:1–9:10.

Chua, T.-S., Tang, S., Trichet, R., Tan, H. K. & Song, Y. (2009). Moviebase: A movie database for event detection and behavioral analysis, *Proceedings of ACM Multimedia 2009 Workshop on Web-Scale Multimedia Corpus*.

Dalal, N. & Triggs, B. (2005). Histograms of oriented gradients for human detection, *Proceedings of the 2005 IEEE Computer Society Conference on Computer Vision and Pattern Recognition (CVPR'05) - Volume 1 - Volume 01*, CVPR '05, IEEE Computer Society, Washington, DC, USA, pp. 886–893.

Deerwester, S., Dumais, S., Furnas, G., Landauer, T. & Harshman, R. (1990). Indexing by latent semantic analysis, *Journal of the American Society for Information Science* 41: 391–407.

Dietterich, T. G. (2000). Ensemble methods in machine learning, *Multiple classifers systems* 1857: 1–15.

Efron, B. & Tibshirani, R. (1993). *An Introduction to the Bootstrap*, Chapman & Hall.

Enzweiler, M. & Gavrila, D. M. (2009). Monocular pedestrian detection: Survey and experiments, *IEEE Transactions on Pattern Analysis and Machine Intelligence* 31: 2179–2195.

Forsyth, D. A. & Fleck, M. M. (1999). Automatic detection of human nudes, *Int. J. Comput. Vision* 32: 63–77.

Freund, Y. & Schapire, R. E. (1997). A decision-theoretic generalization of on-line learning and an application to boosting, *Journal of Computer and System Sciences* 55(1): 119–139.

Griffiths, T. L. & Steyvers, M. (2004). Finding scientific topics., *Proceedings of the National Academy of Sciences* pp. 5228–5235.

Hauptmann, A., Yan, R. & Lin, W.-H. (2007). How many high-level concepts will fill the semantic gap in news video retrieval?, *Proceedings of the 6th ACM International Conference on Image and video retrieval*, ACM, pp. 627–634.

Hofmann, T. (1999). Probabilistic latent semantic analysis, *Proceedings of Uncertainty in Artificial Intelligence, UAI*.

Hu, W., Wu, O., Chen, Z., Fu, Z. & Maybank, S. (2007). Recognition of pornographic web pages by classifying texts and images, *IEEE Transactions on Pattern Analysis and Machine Intelligence* 29: 1019–1034.

Huiskes, M. J., Thomee, B. & Lew, M. S. (2010). New trends and ideas in visual concept detection: the mir flickr retrieval evaluation initiative, *Proceedings of the international conference on Multimedia information retrieval*, MIR '10, ACM, New York, NY, USA, pp. 527–536.

Jiang, W., Zavesky, E., Chang, S.-F. & Loui, A. (2008). Cross-domain learning methods for high-level visual concept classification, *International Conference on Image Processing*.

Jiang, Y.-G. (2009). *Large Scale Semantic Concept Detection, Fusion, and Selection for Domain Adaptive Video Search*, PhD thesis, City University of Hong Kong.

Jiang, Y.-G. & *et al.* (2010). Columbia-UCF TRECVID 2010 Multimedia Event Detection: Combining Multiple Modalities, Contextual Concepts, and Temporal Matching, *NIST TRECVID Workshop*.

Jiang, Y. G., Ngo, C. W. & Yang, J. (2007). Towards optimal bag-of-features for object categorization and semantic video retrieval, *Proceedings of ACM Conference on Image and video retrieval*, pp. 494–501.

Jiang, Y.-G., Yang, J., Ngo, C.-W. & Hauptmann, A. G. (2010). Representations of keypoint-based semantic concept detection: A comprehensive study, *IEEE Transactions on Multimedia* 12: 42–53.

Jurie, F. & Triggs, B. (2005). Creating efficient codebooks for visual recognition, *Proceedings of International Conference on Computer Vision*.

Krogh, A. & Vedelsby, J. (1995). Neural network ensembles, cross validation, and active learning, *Proceedings of Advances in Neural Information Processing Systems*, pp. 231–238.

Kuncheva, L. I. (2004). *Combining Pattern Classifiers: Methods and Algorithms*, John Wiley & Sons, Inc.

Kuncheva, L. I. & Whitaker, C. J. (2005). Controlling the diversity in classifier ensembles through a measure of agreement, *Pattern Recognition* 38(11): 2195 – 2199.

Laptev, I. (2005). On space-time interest points, *Int. J. Comput. Vision* 64: 107–123.

Li, F.-F. & Perona, P. (2005). A bayesian hierarchical model for learning natural scene categories, *Proceedings of the 2005 IEEE Computer Society Conference on Computer Vision and Pattern Recognition (CVPR'05) - Volume 2 - Volume 02*, CVPR '05, pp. 524–531.

Lowe, D. G. (2004). Distinctive image features from scale-invariant keypoints, *International Journal of Computer Vision* 60(2): 91–110.

Munder, S. & Gavrila, D. (2006). An experimental study on pedestrian classification, *IEEE Transactions on Pattern Analysis and Machine Intelligence* 28: 1863–1868.

Naphade, M. R. & Smith, J. R. (2004). On the detection of semantic concepts at trecvid, *Proceedings of ACM International Conference on Multimedia*, pp. 660–667.

Ngo, C.-W., Jiang, Y.-G., Wei, X.-Y., Zhao, W., Liu, Y., Wang, J., Zhu, S. & Chang, S.-F. (2009). Vireo/dvmm at trecvid 2009: High-level feature extraction, automatic video search, and content-based copy detection, *NIST TRECVID Workshop*.

Niebles, J., Wang, H. & Fei-Fei, L. (2008). Unsupervised learning of human action categories using spatial-temporal words, *International Journal of Computer Vision* 79: 299–318.

NIST (2001-2010). TRECVID workshop papers, Website. http://www-nlpir.nist.gov/projects/tvpubs/tv.pubs.org.html.

Ojala, T., Pietikäinen, M. & Harwood, D. (1996). A comparative study of texture measures with classification based on featured distributions, *Pattern Recognition* 29(1): 51–59.

Opitz, D. & Maclin, R. (1999). Popular ensemble methods: An empirical study, *Journal of Artificial Intelligence Research* 11: 169–198.

Opitz, D. W. & Shavlik, J. W. (1996a). Actively searching for an effective neural network ensemble, *Connect. Sci.* 8(3): 337–354.

Opitz, D. W. & Shavlik, J. W. (1996b). Generating accurate and diverse members of a neural-network ensemble, *Proceedings of Advances in Neural Information Processing Systems*, pp. 535–541.

Over, P., Awad, G., Rose, R. T., Fiscus, J. G., Kraaij, W. & Smeaton, A. F. (2008). Trecvid 2008 - goals, tasks, data, evaluation mechanisms and metrics, *NIST TRECVID Workshop*.

Pan, C.-C. & Mitra, P. (2011). Event detection with spatial latent dirichlet allocation, *Proceeding of the 11th annual international ACM/IEEE joint conference on Digital libraries*, JCDL '11, pp. 349–358.

Pytlik, B., Ghoshal, A., Karakos, D. & Khudanpur, S. (2005). TRECVID 2005 Experiment at Johns Hopkins University: Using Hidden Markov Models for Video Retrieval, *NIST TRECVID Workshop*.

Qi, G. J., Hua, X. S., Y. Rui, J. T., Mei, T. & Zhang, H. J. (2007). Correl-ative multi-label video annotation, *ACM International Conference on Multimedia*.

Rokach, L. (2010). *Pattern Classification Using Ensemble Methods*, World Scientific Publishing Company.

Rowley, H., Jing, Y. & Baluja, S. (2006). Large scale image-based adult content filtering, *International Conference on Computer Vision Theory and Applications*.

S. Ayache, G. Q. & Gensel, J. (2007). Classifier fusion for svm-based multimedia semantic indexing, *European Conference on Information Retrieval*.

S. Thorpe, D. F. & Marlot., C. (1996). Speed of processing in the human visual system, *Nature* 381: 520–522.

Salton, G. & McGill, M. J. (1986). *Introduction to Modern Information Retrieval*, McGraw-Hill, Inc., New York, NY, USA.

Siagian, C. & Itti, L. (2007). Rapid biologically-inspired scene classification using features shared with visual attention, *IEEE Trans. Pattern Anal. Mach. Intell.* 29: 300–312.

Sivic, J. & Zisserman, A. (2003). Video google: A text retrieval approach to object matching in videos, *Proceedings of ICCV*, p. 1470.

Smeaton, A. F., Over, P. & Doherty, A. R. (2010). Video shot boundary detection: Seven years of trecvid activity, *Comput. Vis. Image Underst.* 114: 411–418.

Smeaton, A. F., Over, P. & Kraaij, W. (2006). Evaluation campaigns and trecvid, *Proceedings of the 8th ACM International Workshop on Multimedia Information Retrieval*, ACM Press, pp. 321–330.

Smeaton, A. F., Over, P. & Kraaij, W. (2009). High-Level Feature Detection from Video in TRECVid: a 5-Year Retrospective of Achievements, *in* A. Divakaran (ed.), *Multimedia Content Analysis, Theory and Applications*, Springer Verlag, Berlin, pp. 151–174.

Smeulders, A. W. M., M.Worring, Santini, S., Gupta, A. & Jain, R. (2000). Content-based image retrieval at the end of the early years, *IEEE Transactions on Pattern Analysis and Machine Intelligence* 22(12): 1349–1380.

Smith, J. R. & Chang, S.-F. (1997). Visually searching the web for content, *IEEE MultiMedia* 4: 12–20.

Snoek, C. G. M. & Worring, M. (2009). Concept-based video retrieval, *Found. Trends Inf. Retr.* 2(4): 215–322.

Snoek, C. G. M., Worring, M., van Gemert, J. C., Geusebroek, J.-M. & Smeulders, A. W. (2006). The challenge problem for automated detection of 101 semantic concepts in multimedia, *Proceedings of ACM Conference on Multimedia*, pp. 421–430.

Snoek, C. G., van de Sande, K. E., de Rooij, O. & *et al.* (2010). The mediamill trecvid 2010 semantic video search engine, *NIST TRECVID Workshop*.

Snoek, C., Worring, M. & Smeulders, A. (2005). Early versus late fusion in semantic video analysis, *Proceedings of the ACM International Conference on Multimedia*, Singapore, pp. 399–402.

Song, Y., Zheng, Y.-T., Tang, S. & *et al.* (2011). Localized multiple kernel learning for realistic human action recognition in videos, *IEEE Transactions on Circuits and Systems for Video Technology* 21(9).

Stricker, M. A. & Orengo, M. (1995). Similarity of color images, *Storage and Retrieval for Image and Video Databases (SPIE)*, pp. 381–392.

Szummer, M. & Picard, R. W. (1998). Indoor-outdoor image classification, *IEEE International Workshop on Content-based Access of Image and Video Databases, in Conjunction with ICCVąŕ98*.

Tang, J., Hong, R., Yan, S., Chua, T.-S., Qi, G.-J. & Jain, R. (2010). Image annotation by graph-based inference with integrated multiple/single instance representations, *IEEE Transactions on Multimedia* pp. 131–141.

Tang, J., Hong, R., Yan, S., Chua, T.-S., Qi, G.-J. & Jain, R. (2011). Image annotation by knn-sparse graph-based label propagation over noisily tagged web images, *ACM Trans. Intell. Syst. Technol.* **2**: 14:1–14:15.

Tang, S., Li, J.-T., Li, M. & *et al.* (2007). Trecvid 2007 high-level feature extraction by MCG-ICT-CAS, *NIST TRECVID Workshop*.

Tang, S., Li, J.-T., Li, M., Xie, C., Liu, Y., Tao, K. & Xu, S.-X. (2008). Trecvid 2008 high-level feature extraction by MCG-ICT-CAS, *NIST TRECVID Workshop*.

Tang, S., Li, J., Zhang, Y., Xie, C., Li, M., Liu, Y., Hua, X., Zheng, Y.-T., Tang, J. & Chua, T.-S. (2009). Pornprobe: an lda-svm based pornography detection system, *Proceedings of the 17th ACM international conference on Multimedia*, MM '09, pp. 1003–1004.

Tang, S., Zheng, Y.-T., Wang, Y. & Chua, T.-S. (2012). Sparse ensemble learning for concept detection, *IEEE Transactions on Multimedia* 14(1).

van Gemert, J. C., Snoek, C. G. M., Veenman, C. J. & Smeulders, A. W. M. (2006). The influence of cross-validation on video classification performance, *Proceedings of the 14th annual ACM international conference on Multimedia*, MULTIMEDIA '06, ACM, New York, NY, USA, pp. 695–698.

Vapnik, V. N. (1995). *The nature of statistical learning theory*, Springer-Verlag.

Wang, M., Hua, X.-S., Hong, R., Tang, J., Qi, G.-J. & Song, Y. (2009). Unified video annotation via multi-graph learning, *IEEE Transactions on Circuits and Systems for Video Technology* 19(5).

Wang, M., Hua, X.-S., Tang, J. & Hong, R. (2009). Beyond distance measurement: Constructing neighborhood similarity for video annotation, *IEEE Transactions on Multimedia* 11(3).

Wang, X. (2011). Action recognition using topic models, *in* T. B. Moeslund, A. Hilton, V. Krĺźger & L. Sigal (eds), *Visual Analysis of Humans*, Springer London, pp. 311–332.

Wang, X. & Grimson, E. (2007). Spatial latent dirichlet allocation, *Proceeding of Neural Information Processing Systems Conference (NIPS)*.

Wang, Y. & Mori, G. (2009). Human action recognition by semilatent topic models, *IEEE Trans. Pattern Anal. Mach. Intell.* 31: 1762–1774.

Weng, M.-F. & Chuang, Y.-Y. (2008). Multi-cue fusion for semantic video indexing, *ACM International Conference on Multimedia*.

Xu, S., Tang, S., Zhang, Y. & Li, J. (2011). A pseudo relevance feedback based cross domain video concept detection, *Proceedings of the Third International Conference on Internet Multimedia Computing and Service*, ICIMCS '11.

Xu, S., Tang, S., Zhang, Y., Li, J. & Zheng, Y.-T. (2011). Multi-modality transfer based on multi-graph optimization for domain adaptive video concept annotation, *Neurocomputing* 74.

Y., F. & E., S. R. (1996). Experiments with a new boosting algorithm, *Machine Learning: Proceedings of the Thirteenth International Conference*, pp. 325–332.

Yilmaz, E. & Aslam, J. A. (2006). Estimating average precision with incomplete and imperfect judgments, *Proceedings of the 15th ACM international conference on Information and knowledge management*, CIKM '06, pp. 102–111.

Yuan, J., Wang, H., Xiao, L., Zheng, W., Li, J., Lin, F. & Zhang, B. (2007). A Formal Study of Shot Boundary Detection, *IEEE Transactions on Circuits and Systems for Video Technology* 17.

Zeng, W., Gao, W., Zhang, T. & Liu, Y. (2004). Image guarder: An intelligent detector for adult images, *Asian Conference on Computer Vision*, ACCV '04, Jeju Island, Korea, pp. 1080–1084.

Zhang, H., Berg, A. C., Maire, M. & Malik, J. (2006). Svm-knn: Discriminative nearest neighbor classification for visual category recognition, *Proceedings of Conference on Computer Vision and Pattern Recognition (CVPR)*, pp. 2126–2136.

Zhang, H.-J., Tan, S. Y., Smoliar, S. W. & Gong, Y. (1995). Automatic parsing and indexing of news video, *Multimedia Systems* 2: 256–266.

Zhang, J., Marsza, M., Lazebnik, S. & Schmid, C. (2007). Local features and kernels for cassification of texture and object categories: a comprehensive study, *International Journal of Computer Vision*, 73(2): 213–238.

Zhang, L. & Zhou, W.-D. (2011). Sparse ensembles using weighted combination methods based on linear programming, *Pattern Recogn.* 44: 97–106.

Zheng, H. (2004). *Maximum entropy modeling for skin detection: with an application to Internet filtering*, PhD thesis, Univeristľę des Sciences et Technologies de Lille, France.

Zheng, Y.-T., Neo, S.-Y., Chua, T.-S. & Tian, Q. (2008). Probabilistic optimized ranking for multimedia semantic concept detection via RVM, *Proceedings of ACM Conference on Image and Video Retrieal (CIVR)*, pp. 161–168.

Zhu, J., Hoi, S. C., Lyu, M. R. & Yan, S. (2008). Near-duplicate keyframe retrieval by nonrigid image matching, *Proceeding of the 16th ACM international conference on Multimedia*, MM '08, ACM, New York, NY, USA, pp. 41–50.

Part 5

Managing Multimedia Content and Metadata

10

Mconf: An Open Source Multiconference System for Web and Mobile Devices

Valter Roesler[1], Felipe Cecagno[1],
Leonardo Crauss Daronco[1] and Fred Dixon[2]
[1]Federal University of Rio Grande do Sul,
[2]BigBlueButton Inc.,
[1]Brazil
[2]Canada

1. Introduction

Deployment of videoconference systems have been growing rapidly for the last years, and deployments nowadays are fairly common, avoiding thousands of trips daily. Video conferencing systems can be organized into four groups: Room, Telepresence, Desktop and Web.

1.1 Groups of videoconference systems

Room videoconference systems are normally hardware based and located in meeting rooms or classrooms, as seen in Fig. 1, which shows examples of a Polycom[1] equipment. Participants are expected to manually activate and call a remote number in order to begin interacting. Other solutions of room videoconference systems are Tandberg[2] (which is now part of Cisco), Lifesize[3] and Radvision (Scopia line)[4].

Telepresence videoconference systems are a variation of room systems in that the room environment and the equipments are set in order to produce the sensation that all participants are in the same room, as shown in Fig. 2, which shows the Cisco Telepresence System[5]. To accomplish the "presence sensation", the main approaches are: a) adjust the camera to show the remote participant in real size; b) use speakers and microphones in a way that the remote sound comes from the participant position; c) use high definition video in order to show details of the participants; d) use a complementary environment, as the same types of chairs, same color in the rooms, and same type of table on the other sides. The same vendors of room videoconference systems provide also telepresence solutions.

---

[1] http://www.polycom.com/
[2] http://www.tandberg.com/
[3] http://www.lifesize.com/
[4] http://www.radvision.com/
[5] http://www.cisco.com/

Desktop videoconference systems are a variation of room systems in that instead of dedicated hardware equipment to perform the videoconference, they use software and off-the-shelf webcams, as showed in Fig. 3, illustrating Vidyo[6] and Vsee[7].

Fig. 1. Polycom room videoconference systems

Fig. 2. Cisco telepresence videoconference system

With desktop systems, a user installs and launches the software on their computer. With the rapid advancement of personal computer hardware and high-definition webcams, the gap in quality between room video conferencing and desktop video conferencing is narrowing. Some other examples of desktop videoconference solutions are EVO[8], Skype[9], ooVoo[10], Megameeting[11], Ekiga[12] and Sightspeed[13]. Previously hardware-only vendors are also

---

[6] http://www.vidyo.com/
[7] http://vsee.com/
[8] http://evo.caltech.edu/evoGate/
[9] http://www.skype.com/
[10] http://www.oovoo.com/
[11] http://www.megameeting.com/
[12] http://ekiga.org/

providing desktop systems as well, like Radvision (Scopia Desktop line) and Polycom (Polycom PVX). Desktop systems can be used as a means of performing personal videoconferences, or, when used with a LCD projector, they serve as low-end room videoconferences or even low-end telepresence videoconferences.

Fig. 3. Vidyo and Vsee Desktop videoconference systems

One example of a desktop system is IVA (Interactive Video and Audio), whose architecture is depicted in Fig. 4, showing one local "Telecentre", where the teacher and local students stand, and many "Remote Points", where the remote students stays. Telecentre and Remote Points communicate through superior quality (roughly 2 Mbps each point) to provide high-quality audio and video, allowing to the teacher perform his/hers classes synchronously keeping the class pedagogical quality [Roesler, 2009] [Roesler, 2010]. The teacher sees each remote point through a 46" television, and each remote point sees the teacher through a 46" television and also the teacher´s presentation, as his/hers computer screen is also transmitted.

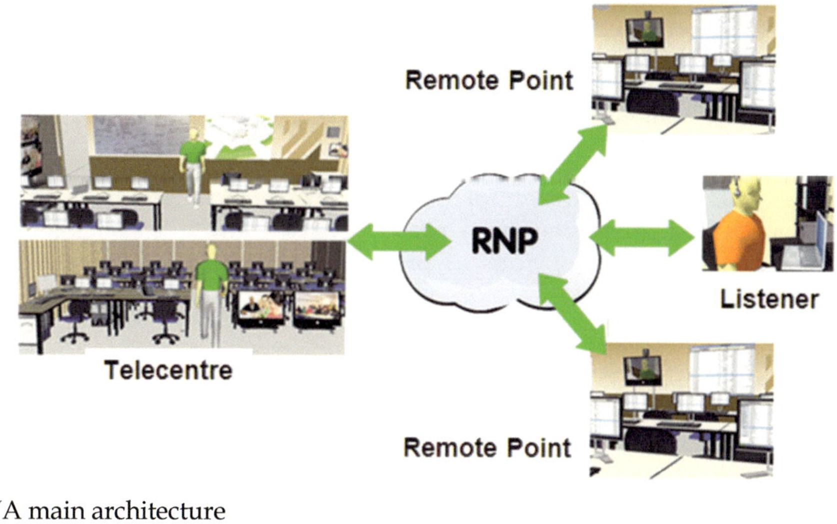

Fig. 4. IVA main architecture

[13] http://www.sightspeed.com/

Web-based videoconference systems, or web conference systems, run within a web browser, as seen in Fig. 5, which shows Adobe Connect[14] and BigBlueButton[15]. The advantage for users of web conferencing systems is the simplicity of deployment: users need only open a hypertext link within their browser to launch the system. Another advantage is interoperability among different operational systems: users may be running Chrome in Linux, Internet Explorer in Windows, Safari in MacOS, and so on, but everyone still has the same experience.

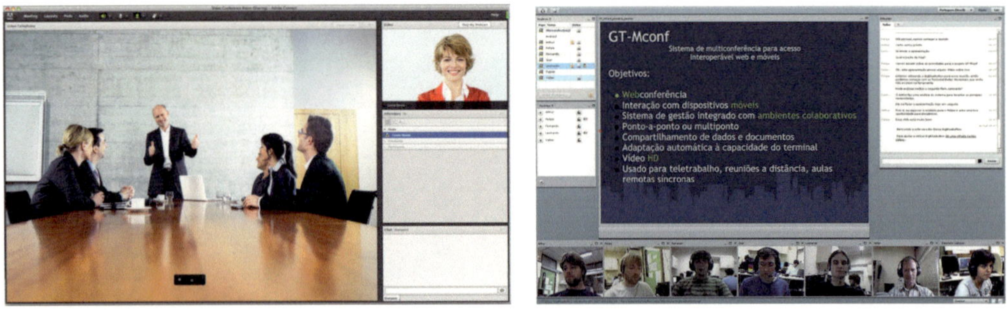

Fig. 5. Adobe connect and BigBlueButton web videoconference systems

While some web conferencing systems are open source, such as BigBlueButton, or free to use, such as Google plus hangout[16], most require purchase of licenses or subscription from a hosting vendor. Examples of hosted systems are, Webex[17], GotoMeeting[18], Vyew[19], Anymeeting[20], Mikogo[21], and Buddymeeting[22].

1.2 Other issues related to videoconference systems

One issue with using any of the conferencing systems is lack of interoperability. In order to accomplish interoperability among different vendors, common standards must be followed. The two most prominent standards are H.323 [ITU-T H.323, 2009] and SIP (Session Initiation Protocol) [Rosenberg, 2002], and both are used worldwide to allow interoperability among different systems. The basic idea of these protocols is to have some common messages to initiate the session and exchange capabilities. Using the information exchanged, the different parties in the conference can agree in the same group of audio and video codecs, as well as the data protocol, allowing the interoperability.

Sometimes the MCU (Multipoint Control Unit) is responsible for adapting different user bandwidths and codecs, composing many user videos in a single transmission, however, this adaptation have its costs in terms of processing power and delay inserted in the videoconference.

[14] http://www.adobe.com/products/adobeconnect.html
[15] http://www.bigbluebutton.org/
[16] https://plus.google.com/
[17] http://www.webex.com/
[18] http://www.gotomeeting.com/
[19] http://vyew.com
[20] http://www.anymeeting.com/
[21] http://www.mikogo.com/
[22] http://www.buddymeeting.com/

Some videoconference systems, like Vidyo and Google plus hangout, follow a scalable video encoding. Scalable video encoders are designed to include more flexibility to multimedia systems. Basically, a scalable encoder generates a multi-layer output, e.g. an output composed by multiples streams. A special stream, called as *base layer*, allows the video reconstruction with minimum detail level, while the others streams, called *enhancement layers*, can increase the video quality in a complementary way (each layer enhances the video generated by the previous one) [Huang, 2007].

The scalable approach is well suitable to multi-rate users, as represented in Fig. 6 for three layers. A user in a low bandwidth environment (a congested 3G connection, for example), receives only one layer, getting the worst quality. Other user in a better connection can receive 2 layers, improving the quality, and a third user in a good network receives the three layers, presenting a superior quality.

The advantage of Scalable Video Coding is that the MCU (or other central element) does not need to transcode video anymore, as the video encoding is performed by the end users, so, it need only to redirect network packets, minimizing its processing demands and the network delay.

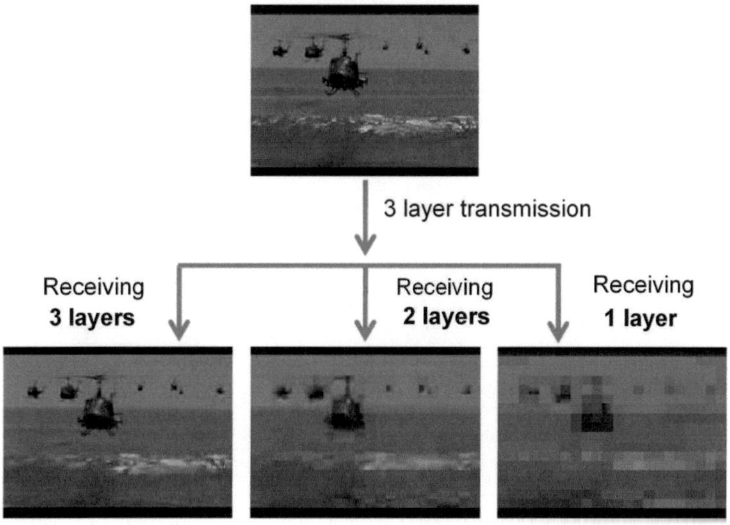

Fig. 6. Scalable video playback

1.3 Requirements of videoconference systems

Related to the features expected in a videoconference system, the following items list some metrics to compare different systems according to the user objective.

- Meeting recording for asynchronous access through video on demand (VOD)
- Whiteboard
- Application and Desktop sharing, as well as documents presentation
- Public and Private chat
- SIP or H.323 standards support for interoperability
- LMS support / integration to facilitate exchange of files and definition of agenda

- Conference scheduling and participants invitation
- Notes for registering the meeting agenda, for example
- Polls in order to vote for some issue in debate
- Moderation, authorization, access rights
- Federated networks support allowing the user to use the same password in different applications, including videoconference
- Exchange of files
- Administrative users with knowledge and power to change remote settings, to help someone who do not know how to set its microphone, for example
- Feedback about the network conditions in order to take some measure if the bandwidth is too low;
- Scalability to hundreds or thousands of simultaneous users in different virtual rooms
- Cryptography
- Mobile support

The focus of this chapter is in a web conference system called Mconf (Multiconference system for interoperable access between web and mobile devices), composed of three main parts: web portal; web conference server; web conference client in the browser / mobile devices.

This chapter aims to describe in a simple way some technical issues and user possibilities regarding the Mconf project. As the project is open source, it is expected to bring some information and motivation to its use.

The following sections will present these three parts in more detail. Section 2 presents the Mconf system in a general way. Section 3 focuses on BigBlueButton, the web conference system integrated with Mconf. Section 4 presents the web portal. Section 5 presents the Mconf mobile application, while Section 6 brings some conclusions and future directions.

2. Mconf overview

This session presents an overview of the Mconf project and its main building blocks, seen in Fig. 7.

The conferencing component of Mconf is BigBlueButton (BBB), an open source web conferencing system developed for distance education, providing the real-time sharing of voice, video, slides, desktop, and chat, besides recording. While focused on distance education, it has the same features at the core than other commercial web conferencing systems. Since BigBlueButton is open source, the Mconf team has the option to improve the code and contribute those improvements back to the BBB team.

The second block of the Mconf architecture is the web portal (Mconf-Web), a Ruby on Rails application that provides creation of virtual rooms, discussion forums, and event scheduling.

The third block is the Android client, which is compatible to both BBB and Mconf-Web. The Android client allows web conference managing and fully participation through mobile devices.

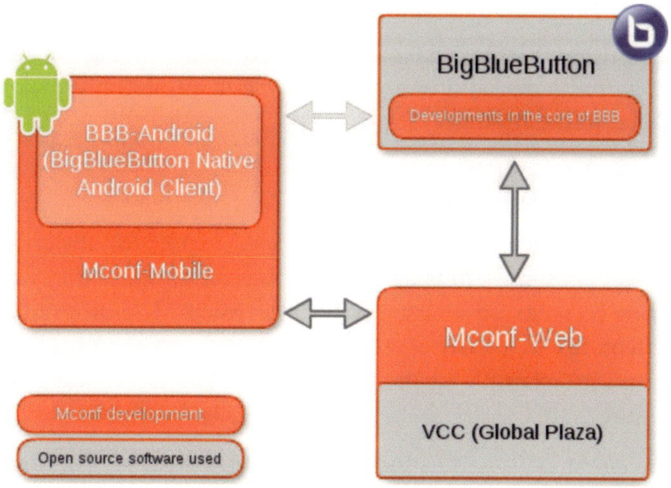

Fig. 7. General view of the Mconf project

Besides that, it is worth mentioning the possibility of federated service and scalability. These issues are described in the following paragraphs.

Mconf-Web has recently been integrated with a Shibboleth[23] module, providing federated login in the website. Shibboleth is a middleware architecture that allows users of different security domains to employ their security information to access a federated service.

Mconf-Web is able to obtain user identity from any identity provider that follows the Shibboleth architecture with few configurations, providing access to any user that is registered in this federation. Currently, Mconf-Web is one of the services provided for the Brazilian federation named CAFe (Federated Academic Community)[24].

Related to scalability, one BigBlueButton server is designed to support about 25 simultaneous users with video and audio, so, a scalability strategy must take place to increase the service capacity. Of course, a powerful hardware could be used to increase the number of users, but it will not scale to 1000 users, for example.

For the audio communication, BigBlueButton uses FreeSWITCH[25], an open source telephony platform that is used as a VoIP server. FreeSWITCH is already scalable, allowing the VoIP service to be spread across multiple FreeSWITCH servers, which would increase a lot the capacity of the web conferencing service since the voice processing is very CPU intensive. However, there isn't yet a way to scale the other components of BigBlueButton through multiple servers.

The solution being developed by Mconf includes a monitor module on BigBlueButton that generates statistics like CPU, memory and network, that are collected by the web portal. When there is a new room to be created, the web portal decides which server is more suitable to the target users, based on statistics plus geographic location and delay.

[23] http://shibboleth.net/
[24] http://www.rnp.br/servicos/cafe.html
[25] http://www.freeswitch.org/

Besides that, it is possible to use this solution through a commercial or private cloud computing infrastructure. Virtual machines of web conferencing servers are enabled or disabled depending on the demand in a given moment, all of them managed automatically by the web portal scalability module.

3. BigBlueButton web conferencing

BigBlueButton is an open source web conferencing system for distance education. The BigBlueButton project started in 2007 at Carleton University (Ontario, Canada) as an effort to replace an existing commercial web conferencing system. The project has since evolved to provide the core features of synchronized presentation, chat, video, audio, and desktop sharing. Fig. 8 shows an example of its interface presenting its main windows, which are described in the figure.

The BigBlueButton client runs within the Adobe Flash Player[26]. The BigBlueButton server manages the individual sessions, keeps all users in sync, and records the sessions for later playback.

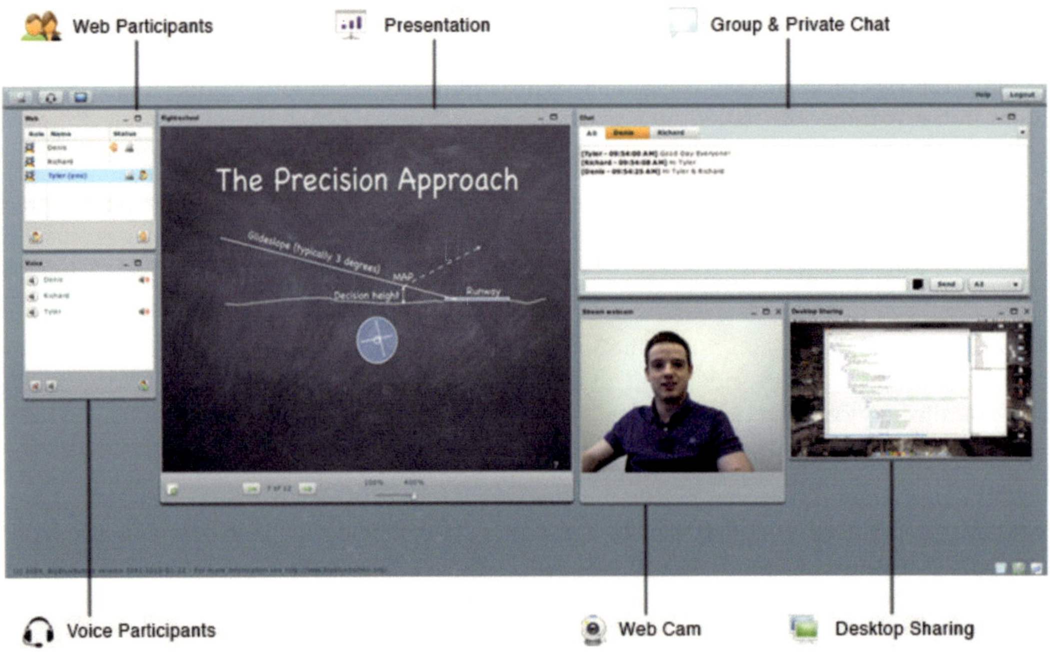

Fig. 8. Example of a BBB web conference

Users enter a BigBlueButton session in one of two roles: viewer or moderator. A viewer has the capabilities to a) interact with others through chat, b) share their webcam, c) join the audio conference, and d) raise their hand. A moderator has all the capabilities of a user, and in addition can a) mute/unmute users, b) eject a user from the conference, and c) make any user the current presenter.

[26] http://www.adobe.com/products/flashplayer/

The presenter has the ability to a) upload slides to the presentation area, b) control the slide view for all users, c) annotate the slide with the whiteboard, and d) share their desktop.

Compared with commercial web conferencing systems, BigBlueButton lacks some features, such as remote control of desktops; however, the project has stated its goal to focus on simplicity and ease when implementing the core features for web conferencing.

3.1 BBB architecture

BigBlueButton has a client and a server component. The client is written in Action Script. The server components are mostly written in Java. The three main components of the BigBlueButton server are the real-time server, application server, and voice conferencing server. Fig. 9 presents its main building blocks and communications.

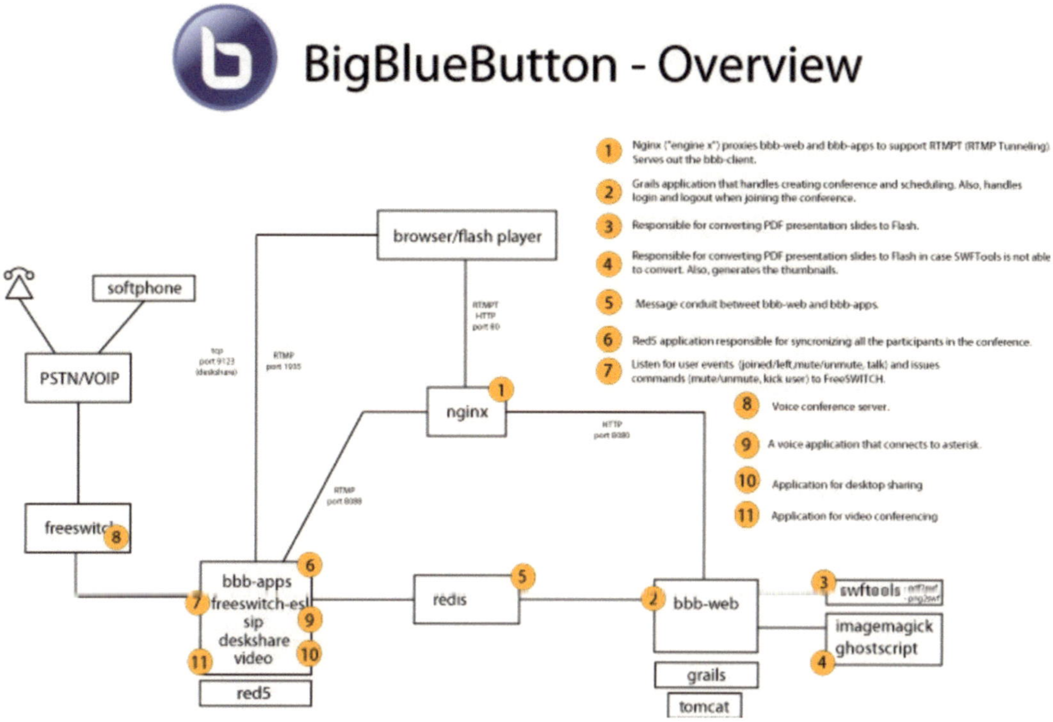

Fig. 9. BBB overview

The real-time server of BigBlueButton is based on red5[27], an open source implementation of Adobe's Flash Media Server[28]. BigBlueButton implements a number of server-side applications, called bbb-apps (see in figure), that keeps the video, audio, and chat in sync between the remote BigBlueButton clients and the application server.

[27] http://red5.org/

[28] http://www.adobe.com/products/flashmediaserver/

The application server, called bbb-web (see in figure), is a Java-based application running within an Apache Tomcat[29]. The bbb-web application handles all API calls and requests by the client to upload slides.

The voice conferencing server is built on FreeSWITCH[30], a scalable open source cross-platform telephony platform. Incoming audio packets from the BigBlueButton client are routed to FreeSWITCH through red5phone, an open source voice over IP (VoIP) phone that uses the Session Initiation Protocol (SIP) to communicate with FreeSWITCH.

3.2 Integration of BigBlueButton with other software

The BigBlueButton project does not bundle any built-in web-based applications, such as a system for scheduling sessions; rather, it provides an API that others can use to integrate with 3rd party applications.

BigBlueButton provides an HTTP-based API that includes commands to create, join, and end a meeting. Since the API is HTTP-based, a 3rd party application can control the BigBlueButton server with simple URL requests. Integration with a 3rd party application requires the writing of a plug-in for the 3rd party application (such as Moodle). Many of the most popular open source applications have a plug-in architecture specifically for integration with external systems such as BigBlueButton.

For example, Fig. 10 shows the BigBlueButton plug-in for Moodle, which enables a teacher setup and schedule BigBlueButton sessions from within the Moodle interface[31].

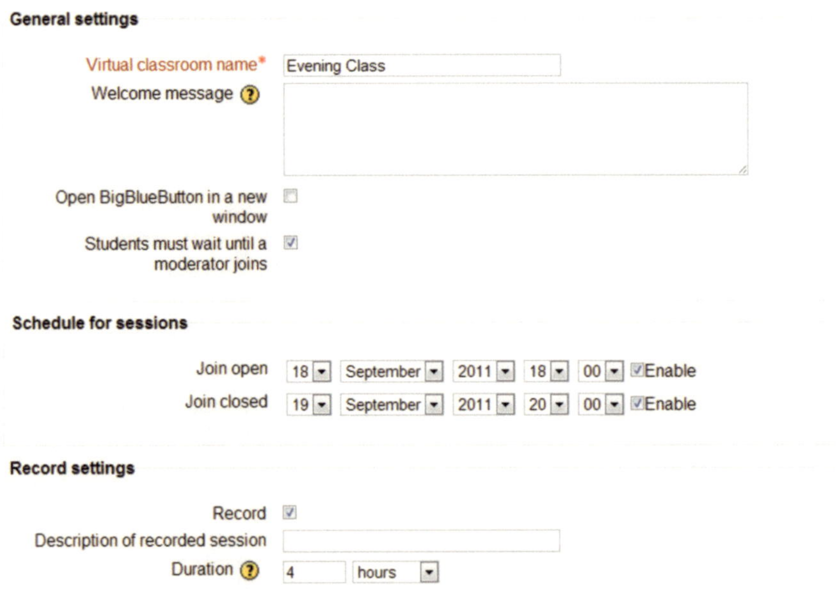

Fig. 10. Integration BBB and Moodle

29 http://tomcat.apache.org/
30 http://www.freeswitch.org/
31 http://moodle.org/

Using the BigBlueButton plug-in a teacher can configure properties for the BigBlueButton session. Examples of properties are the name of the link in Moodle, restricting student's access to an on-line session until a moderator (teacher) has joined, or restricting access to specific times within the Moodle calendar.

When the record property is set to true, the BigBlueButton server will record the audio, slides, and chat from a meeting for later playback within an HTML5 compatible browser (such as FireFox and Chrome), as seen in Fig. 11.

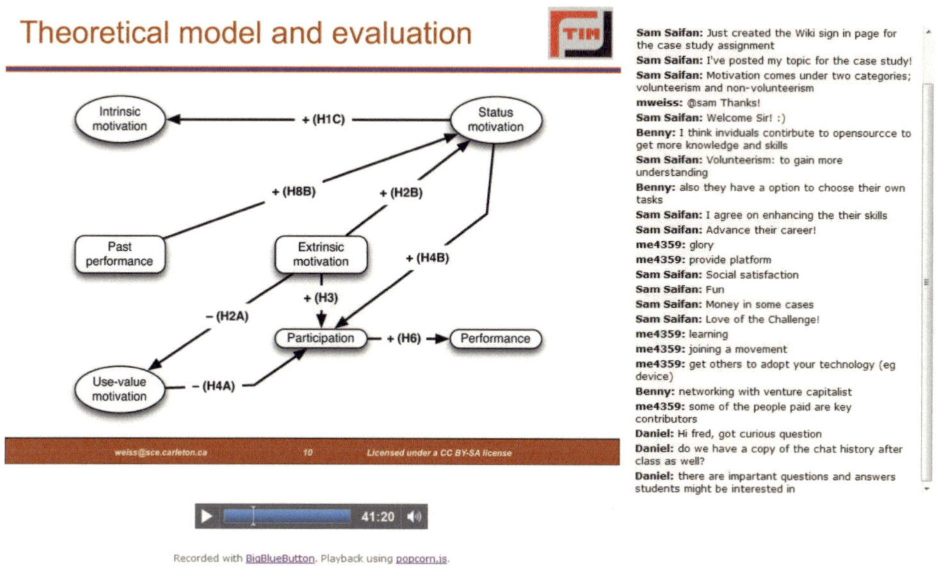

Fig. 11. Playback of a recorded lecture within BigBlueButton

4. Mconf web portal

The objective of the Mconf web portal is to provide user authentication, permission control, scheduling, among others. These kinds of tasks are left in BBB to third-party applications, such as the integrations with Moodle and Joomla, for instance. Furthermore, the web portal aims to provide facilities to manage multiple servers and provide load balance, for example.

The most important roles of Mconf-Web are listed below:

- User authentication
- Permission control
- Ability to manage multiple meetings (and meeting rooms)
- CRUD operations (create, read, update, delete) on rooms
- Ability to manage multiple servers
- CRUD operations on servers
- Monitoring interface
- Load balancing
- Conference scheduling
- Usage statistics

- Asynchronous access to the recordings (audio, video, presentations)
- Pre-upload of documents

Mconf-Web can be compared to other integrations already existent for BigBlueButton, except that it has a different focus and interaction model. BigBlueButton has a strong focus on distance education, but Mconf focuses mainly on virtual meetings, not necessarily for education. Different focuses will result in different application requirements, especially for the user interface, in this case the web application Mconf-Web.

Mconf-Web uses a web application called Global Plaza as the basis for Mconf-Web. Global Plaza is an open source web application that aims to enable virtual meetings through an event based social network. Its model fits very well the requirements imposed in Mconf. In the following of this section we will explore each of the points commented above, starting with a description of Global Plaza and then Mconf-Web.

4.1 About global plaza

Global Plaza is a web application developed in Ruby on Rails[32], providing events as social media in the Internet [Quemada, 2010]. Global Plaza was developed in the European Global Project[33] as an open source application and is also available for use in the Internet[34]. The GLOBAL project has ended on October 31, 2010, but as an open source application Global Plaza is still available for use.

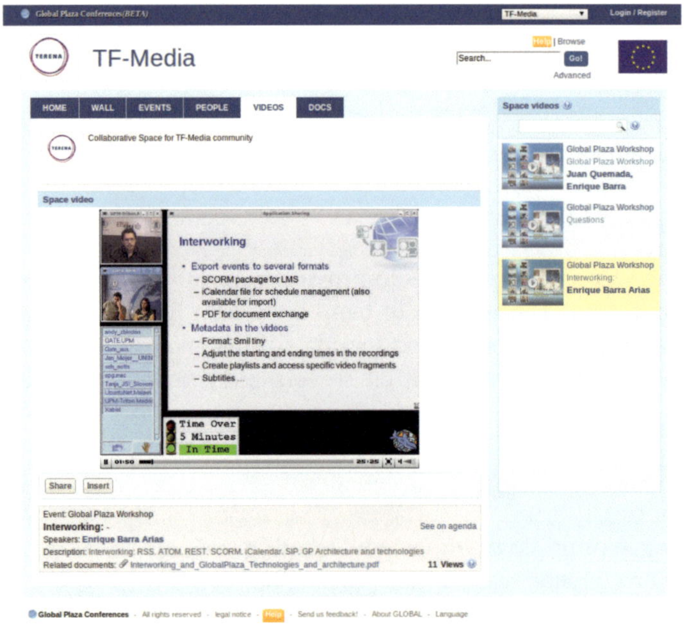

Fig. 12. Video inside the TF-Media's space in Global Plaza

[32] http://rubyonrails.org/
[33] http://www.global-project.eu/
[34] http://globalplaza.org

In Global Plaza, the registered users can create three types of events: (a) in person, where you just have a date and agenda in the website; (b) virtual meetings, possibly with streaming and recording; and (c) virtual congress, large virtual meetings, usually needing an on-site operator. These events happen inside spaces (or communities), that are a places where people with similar interests can interact. Fig. 12 shows one space inside Global Plaza where a recorded video is being played through the web interface.

The Global Plaza application is just the web interface in a stack of applications used to provide the full set of features. For web conferencing it uses the Isabel system [Quemada, 2005], that also requires several components.

From the feature set needed by Mconf, Global Plaza provides user authentication, permission control, management of meetings (inside events), scheduling, and access to the recording. Some other features, such as usage statistics, can be easily leveraged from the framework used by Global Plaza. It is important to observe that most of these features are tightly coupled with Isabel and had to be adapted for its use with BigBlueButton.

4.2 Mconf web portal details

This section will detail the main features of Mconf web portal. Some features are inherited from Global Plaza, and the differences between Mconf-Web and Global Plaza will be discussed later.

Mconf-Web is a social network of users, spaces and events. Users can create and join spaces (communities) and can create and participate in events. All the events are held inside a community from a defined start date to an end date.

Fig. 13 shows the user home page in Mconf-Web. This page has links to the most used features in the website. The label "Web conference room" shows the access point to the user´s web conference room (to start a meeting and invite people to his meeting, for example). The label "Communities" allows access to the user communities (or spaces). The label "Recent activity" shows messages, events, news and attachments related to the user. The label "Agenda" depicts the section where the user can see the upcoming events, and the label "Inbox" shows the latest internal messages which arrived. These features will be further explained in the following of this section.

A community in Mconf-Web can be public or private. A public community can be viewed by anyone, even by visitors that do not have an account in Mconf yet. But, even though everyone can view it, only authorized people can alter it (create events and post messages, for example). Private communities, however, can only be viewed by authorized people. A private community can be created by a user and the access can be given only to people from the same workplace, for instance. Nobody else is able to see the activity inside this community (even though everybody is able to know that the community exists).

4.2.1 Web conferences

In Mconf-Web there are two types of web conference rooms: users' rooms and communities' rooms. When a user registers in Mconf web portal, he/she automatically receives a permanent web conference room (a user room). This room can be shared with anyone the user wants to, even with people that do not have a Mconf account. The user rooms are public by default, so anyone with its link will be able to access it. But it can be made private so that only people with the defined password can join the web conference.

Every community created in Mconf also has a permanent web conference room associated (a community room). If the community is public, the room is public, otherwise the room is private and there will be a password associated to it.

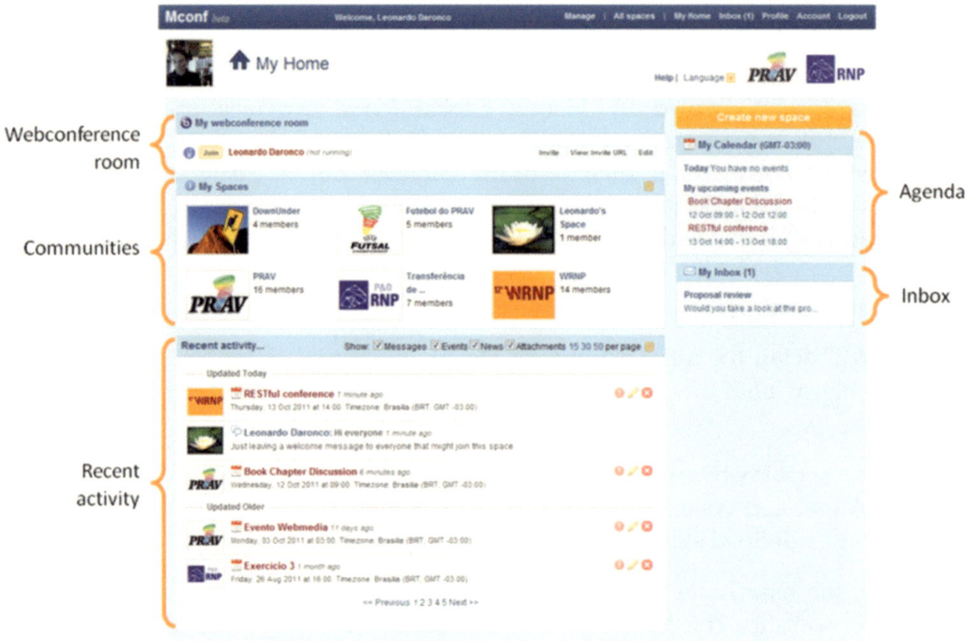

Fig. 13. Main page of the Mconf web portal

The permissions inside a web conference will depend on several factors, but mostly on these:

- Who is the user?
- Is it a user room or a community room?
- Is the room public or private?

The permissions available are the ones already discussed in the BigBlueButton section (section 3): moderator, viewer and presenter. The presenter role is the only one that can be defined during the meeting using the application interface. The other roles are defined before the user joins the conference, and it's Mconf-Web that should decide if the user is a moderator or a viewer.

In a user room, the owner will always be a moderator and the only one that can start the meeting in the room. If the owner is not in the meeting, no one else will be able to join. Everybody else will have the viewer role.

An exception to this rule happens when the room is made private. When the user marks the room as private, he/she will be asked for two passwords: the viewer password and the moderator password. Any person invited must use one of these passwords to join the conference, and the password will define the role of this person. Fig. 14 exhibits the web page shown when an anonymous user tries to join a private web conference.

In a community room all members who belong to the community are moderators, so any of them can start a meeting in this room. In a public community, everybody else will be able to join and will receive a viewer role (including anonymous users). In a private community, a password will be asked when a non member tries to join the meeting and this password will define the user's role in the conference.

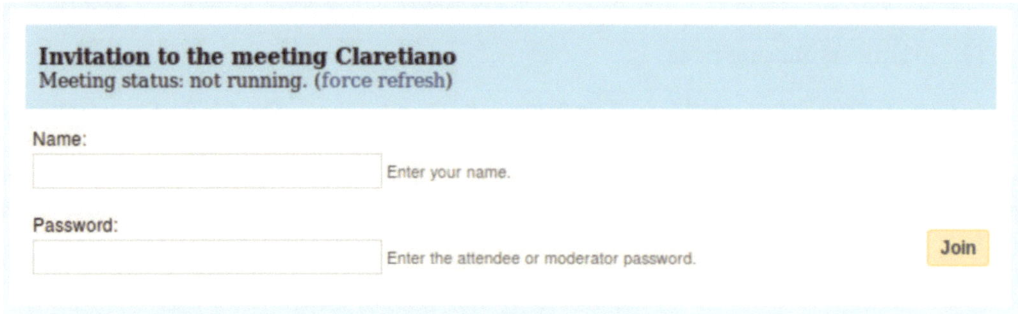

Fig. 14. Anonymous user invited to a private web conference

In Mconf-Web any user can start a web conference with just a few clicks, as shown in Fig. 15. After logging in the website, the user can simply click in the "join" button and the web conference will start. The same is valid for a community: after creating a community, any member can simply click in the "join" button and start the web conference.

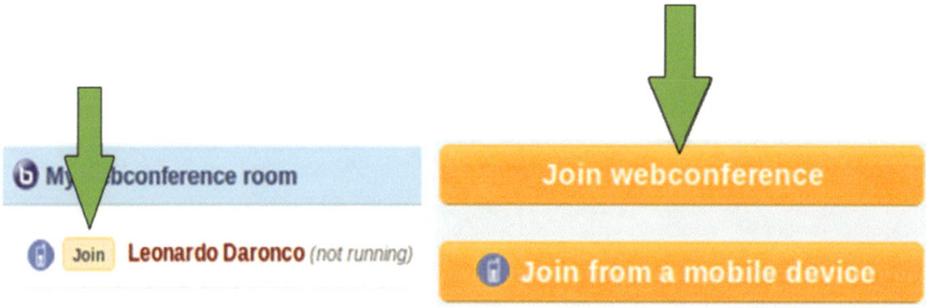

Fig. 15. Joining a web conference

4.2.2 Other features

Mconf-Web has still some other features not specifically related to web conferencing but that add value to the application and can improve the user experience.

One of these features is the document sharing, where users can share any kind of documents inside a community. These documents can be accessed by any member of the community and, if the community is public, they can be accessed by anyone. Documents can also be tagged and versioned, so that it is easier to search for them later on. Fig. 16 shows the documents sharing page.

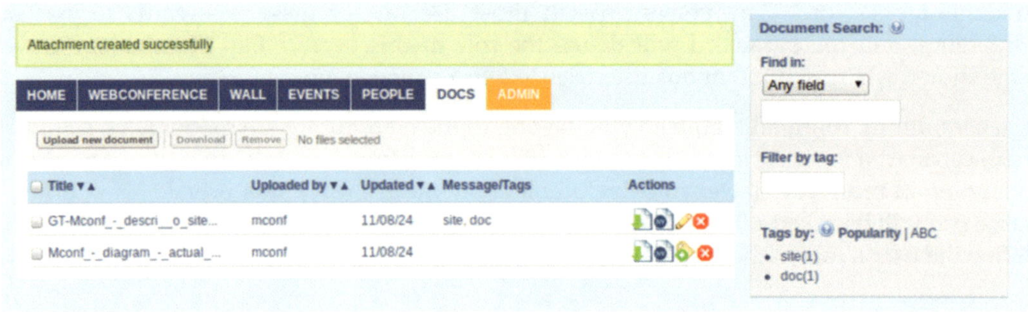

Fig. 16. Documents sharing page

Communities have also a wall board and a notice board, where any kind of text messages can be posted and all members will be notified. In the user's homepage, there's a digest of the recent activity that includes the latest documents shared, messages and news posted, and events created. The user also has a calendar that shows the next events, as illustrated in Fig. 17.

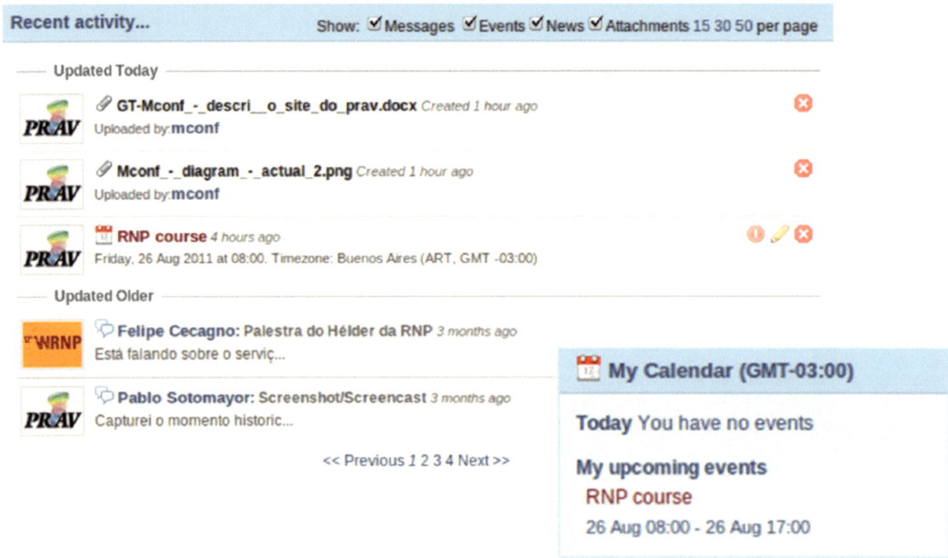

Fig. 17. User's recent activity and calendar

The website has also an internal messaging system, that works similarly to an email system and that users can use to communicate with each other.

Mconf-Web is fully available in English and Portuguese (BR) and partially translated to Spanish, French and German.

4.3 Main differences between Mconf-Web and global plaza

The most important difference between Mconf-Web and Global Plaza is the use of BigBlueButton as a replacement for Isabel. BigBlueButton is very different from Isabel and follows a different approach to reach the same goal: provide a web conference environment. Mconf uses BigBlueButton due to all its features already detailed in the section 3 and due to its open source nature and great community support and activity.

BigBlueButton has many advantages over Isabel, so this can be considered not only as a different approach but as an evolution in the web application specially for the open source community.

One downside of this replacement is that some features in Global Plaza had to be disabled before they were adapted to be used with BigBlueButton. This is the case of the streaming and recording features. BigBlueButton has only recently included recording in its core and this still needs to be integrated in the web application in the near future.

As already mentioned, the project supporting Global Plaza has ended in the end of 2010, so it's development has been greatly reduced since then. It is originally developed using the version 2.3.4 of Ruby on Rails, an old version that was since 2010 replaced by the version 3. So other of the most important differences included by Mconf-web was the migration to Ruby version 3.

The migration for Ruby on Rails 3 was especially important for the libraries developed to integrate the web application with BigBlueButton. These libraries will be detailed in the following sections, but it is important to consider that they were developed in the latest version of the framework so that they can be used with any other web application that uses the same framework.

The way a user can create and participate in web conferences has also been vastly modified. Global Plaza is a very event-centered application, and users need to create an event to be able to hold a web conference. Everything revolves around events.

In Mconf-Web, web conferences are easier to be held. The user can create a web conference from his homepage or from a community very easily, while events are only a mean to schedule a web conference inside a community.

Besides that, several things were also changed in the application's interface in order to make it simpler and easier to be used.

4.4 Implementation details

The most important thing that should be added regarding the implementation is that all the integration between the framework Rails and BigBlueButton was developed in two libraries (called "gems" in Ruby). With these libraries, the front end application (in this case Global Plaza) can be replaced by any other Rails application and all the integration with BigBlueButton would still be functional. In other words, it is now easy to start a new front end application and integrate it with BigBlueButton.

Fig. 18 shows how the application, the gems and BigBlueButton interact with each other. The gems were built in two levels: (1) a basic library for Ruby that simply performs HTTP calls to contact BigBlueButton's API; and (2) a library for Rails that is targeted for web applications and contains common data models and controlling logic to interact with BigBlueButton.

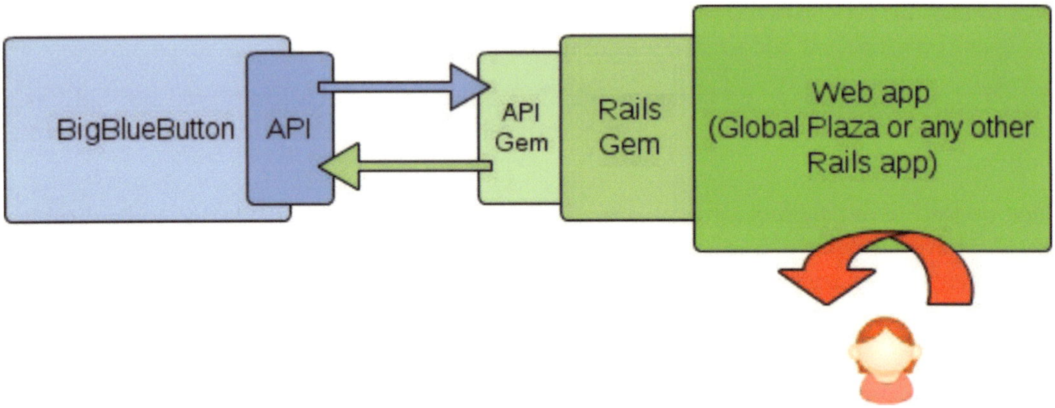

Fig. 18. A front end Rails application and the gems to interact with BigBlueButton

The basic gem (1) is called "bigbluebutton-api-ruby"[35] and can be used by any Ruby application (it is not necessary to be a Rails application). It contains methods to perform every API call possible in BigBlueButton and utility functions to adapt the response (XML files) to be friendlier to a Ruby application.

The other gem is called "bigbluebutton_rails"[36] and is specific for Rails. It implements several features that a web application needs to use BigBlueButton. The most important features are:

- Provides data models to manipulate BigBlueButton servers and conference rooms;
- Allows multiple servers and multiple conference rooms;
- Full API access using bigbluebutton-api-ruby;
- Easy way to join conferences: simply create a room and call a defined URL;
- Possibility to create private rooms, that require a password to join;
- Deals with visitors (users that are not logged), allowing (or forbidding) them to join rooms;
- Server activity monitor;
- Includes default views (web pages) used in the interaction with BigBlueButton (create rooms and servers, join a room, invite people to join, and others).

5. Mobile devices integration in Mconf

This session will discuss the development details of the Mconf Android client. There are two possibilities of interaction using Android devices, shown in Fig. 19 and Fig. 20: the first one is through a web browser, and the system works like in a regular PC, using Adobe Flash Player (shown in Fig. 19a); the other way is through the Android native application (shown in Fig. 19b and Fig. 20). There are two Android native applications, named Mconf-mobile and BBB-Android, which are described in section 5.2.

[35] https://github.com/mconf/bigbluebutton-api-ruby
[36] https://github.com/mconf/bigbluebutton_rails

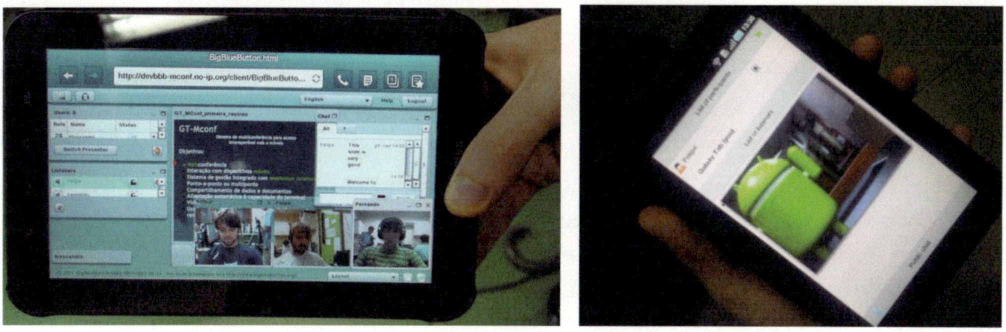

Fig. 19. Examples of web conference in a tablet using: a) flash or b) the Android application

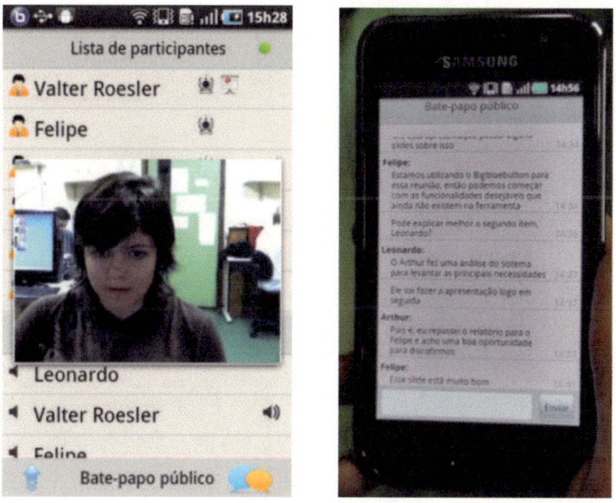

Fig. 20. Examples of web conference in a smartphone using the Android application

The Android operational system was chosen because of its big growth and popularity, in addition to a non-bureaucratic development and easy distribution for the applications.

The BigBlueButton web application used on PCs also runs on Android 2.2 and above, since these Android versions support the Adobe Flash Platform. However, there are several usability limitations when adapting the user interface to a (often small) touch screen display. It would be an option to develop a new flash based client adapting the user interface to mobile devices, but since audio and video capture is still not supported by Adobe Flash Player on Android, it would be impossible to develop a client with all the desired features, so, the group in Mconf two Android native applications were developed (see section 5.2).

Most features are the same in the web-based application and the Android application, however, a few are still in development on the native application, such as the presentation, the whiteboard and the possibility to display several participant videos in the same screen. These capabilities will be gradually added in order to cover all the features existent on the web application, with the advantage of having audio and video capture since the beginning.

Another advantage of the adopted approach is that the native application can be distributed in the official Android marketplace, what is not possible with a web application. The native Android application developed is compatible with Android 2.0 and above, and the details will be presented hereafter.

5.1 Architecture

The Mconf for Android is built upon many open source applications and libraries. Also, the support for mobile devices doesn't require any modification on the server side. The solution architecture is presented in Fig. 21. The figure depicts the software layers of both mobile applications developed (BBB-Android and Mconf-Mobile - see section 5.2), and each block is detailed hereafter.

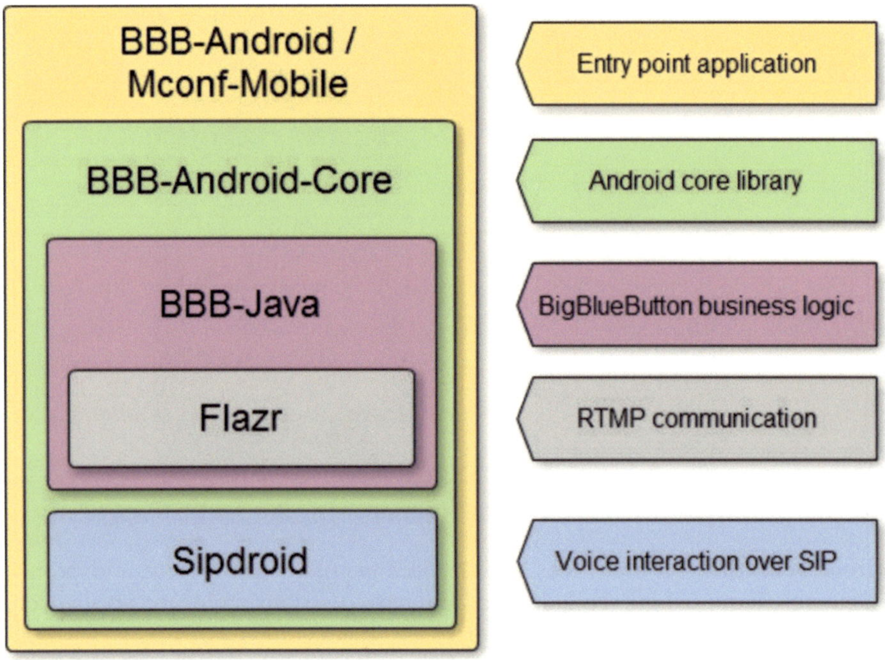

Fig. 21. Mconf mobile architecture

5.1.1 Sipdroid[37]

Considering that the BigBlueButton system uses a VoIP server to handle the audio streams, the strategy of integrating an existing VoIP open source solution to the application was adopted. The Sipdroid is one of the most popular SIP phones on Android Market, and the access to the source code has enabled the Sipdroid to be transformed in a library, which could be consumed by another Android application or library.

[37] http://sipdroid.org

Speex[38], the default audio codec of BigBlueButton, is among the audio codecs supported by Sipdroid. It is implemented in C and compiled through the Android NDK.

This integration of Sipdroid with Mconf has enabled the addition of the audio interaction feature with a very low development cost.

5.1.2 Flazr[39]

All the RTMP (Real Time Messaging Protocol) [Adobe, 2009] communication between the application and the Red5[40] server is done through the Flazr library, a Java open source implementation of protocols used for multimedia streaming. This library implements important parts of the RTMP protocol, such as the initial handshake and handlers for messages of control, audio, video, and also Remote Procedure Calls.

However, the library does not support Remote Shared Objects (RSO), an indispensable requirement for the complete communication with the server. For example, information such as join and leave of participants, video transmitting or the "raise hand" features are actions broadcasted through the *participantsSO* object. Public chat message exchanges are broadcasted through the *chatSO* object.

Then, an extension of the library was developed to add support for RSO. The implementation of the shared objects management and multiplexing/demultiplexing of messages were based on the Red5 source code and the RTMP protocol specification.

5.1.3 BBB-Java

The BBB-Java is a library developed in the Mconf project to be used by the Android client. This library implements the communication logic between a generic Java application and a BigBlueButton server. The library is loosely coupled with the Android application, in order to enable and encourage the development of new third party applications integrated to the web conference system. Also, the library can be used to create robot applications, which would help to perform stress and behavior tests.

5.1.4 BBB-Android-Core

BBB-Android-Core is another developed library which implements the session handle after the user joins a meeting, and it uses BBB-Java to interact with the BigBlueButton server. This library is written mainly in Java, using the Android Software Development Kit (SDK), and a small fraction of CPU intensive code was developed in C/C++ over the Native Development Kit (NDK).

An optimized compilation of the FFmpeg[41] library was used to handle video encoding and decoding, and it was compiled only with the H.263 codec enabled (the default video codec of BigBlueButton). FFmpeg is a library written in C which implements many audio and video codecs.

---

38 http://www.speex.org
39 http://flazr.com/
40 http://red5.org/
41 http://ffmpeg.org

5.2 Mobile applications

In Mconf two web conference client applications for mobile devices were developed. One is called *Mconf-Mobile*, and the other is *BBB-Android*. Both are depicted in Fig. 22.

Mconf-Mobile is an application integrated with the Mconf web portal. It implements the login screen of the session, and using it the user authenticates and looks for the meetings he has permission to join. After joining a meeting, the session is handled by the *BBB-Android-Core* library.

BBB-Android is an application for direct use with BigBlueButton. Through it, the user can join, as participant or moderator, any running meetings, and also create new meetings.

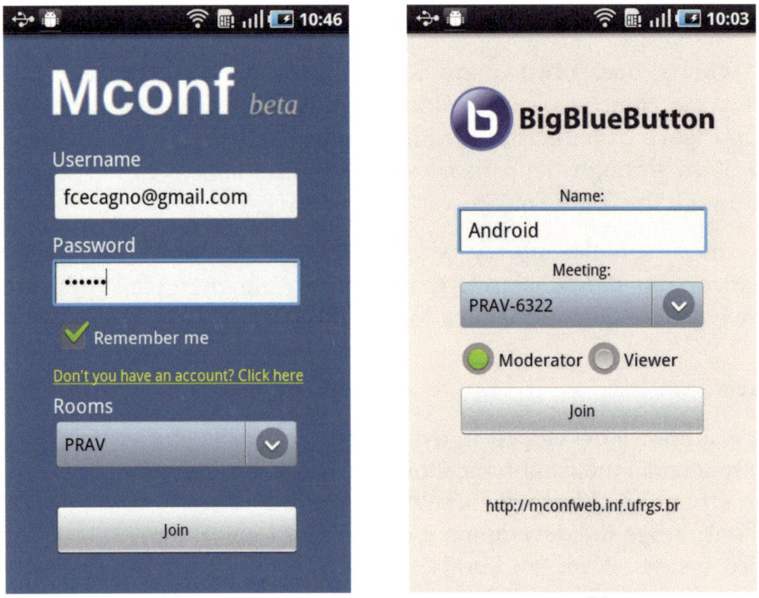

(a) (b)

Fig. 22. Mobile applications: (a) Mconf-Mobile; (b) BBB-Android

The main difference between *BBB-Android* and *Mconf-Mobile* is that *BBB-Android* connects directly to a BigBlueButton instance, without any interaction with the web portal. Because of that, it is necessary to know previously the server address, differently from *Mconf-Mobile*, where the user has to know simply the web portal URL.

5.3 Main functionalities

This section presents the main functionalities of the Android application.

5.3.1 Chat

Just like the BigBlueButton web client, the Android application provides chat interaction through public and private message exchange. The public chat is implemented as a sliding bar on the main screen, and the private chat is accessed pressing on the participant name with whom the user wants to start a conversation.

5.3.2 Audio

When the user joins the voice conference, two buttons are presented on the main screen in order to enable the user to interact: the buttons *Lock speak* and *Push to talk*, as seen in Fig. 23. *Lock speak* means that the microphone is always open, and *push to talk* means that the microphone is only open when the user is pressing this button. They are essential for a good quality interaction, because the high microphone sensitivity on mobile devices can result in noise and acoustic echo problems.

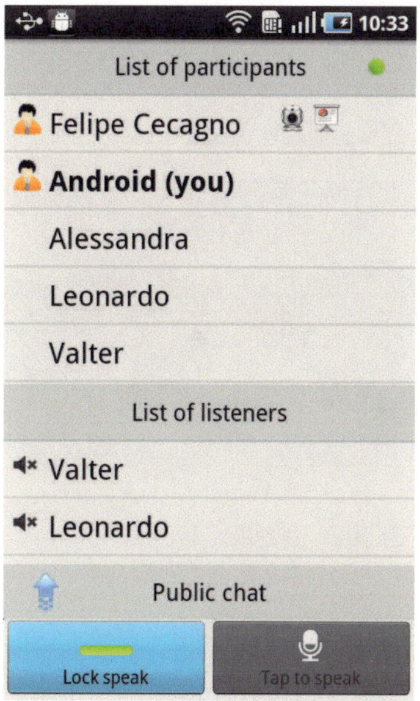

Fig. 23. Voice interaction

5.3.3 Video

When a participant is publishing his video to the session, a webcam icon appears in the main screen, as seen for "Felipe Cecagno" in Fig. 24. The Android application enables the user to playback any participant's video being published, as well as capturing and publishing its own video camera. If the user puts the mobile in horizontal mode, it shows the video in full screen.

If a user joins a session with the moderator permission, he/she will be able to perform some management actions, such as turning any participant into presenter, muting or unmuting a noisy participant, lowering hand of a participant that wants to talk or even kicking out a participant from the session.

These kind of features suggest a new use case for the application: a professor using the white board to explain the lesson for a group of students connected remotely doesn't need to stay in front of his computer during the lecture, but can use the mobile device as a remote control to manage the conference.

6. Conclusion and future directions

This article presented two main contributions: a) one survey of videoconference systems and trends in the area; b) technical and implementation details about the Mconf project, which involves a complete web conference solution, contemplating the triptych web portal / web conference environment / mobile devices.

Initially, the survey presented different deployments of videoconference systems and some trends, as scalable video, high definition and usability.

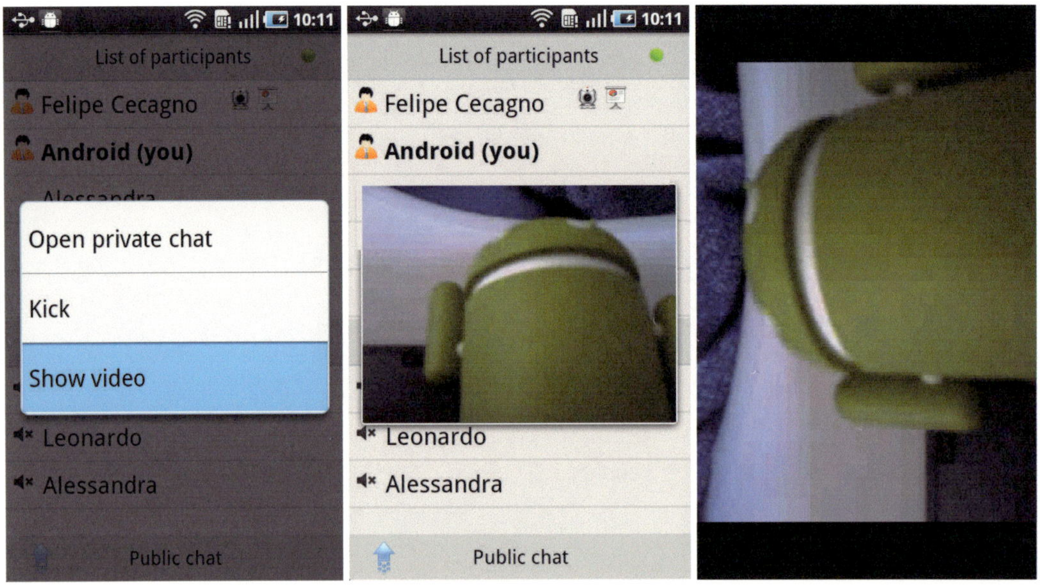

Fig. 24. Video interaction allows playback and also sending the mobile video

After that, the chapter focused on the Mconf system, which provides an open source web conference solution based on BigBlueButton, Global Plaza and some own developments, like the mobile solution.

Mconf provides a tool with good quality, scalability, simplicity, mobile access and recording. Scalability is provided by balancing the various web conference rooms among different servers, monitoring constantly the servers' activity to better choose the best one to start the new room. This is the principle of cloud computing, and it is very suitable to this application. One issue is the cloud delay, and the server must be chosen taking also the delay into consideration. Security is provided through the use of Federated login and data encryption. Federated login is a reality nowadays, simplifying greatly the permission handling.

There is a long road ahead, however, and the main future developments are:

- To create an HTML5 client, in order to have web conference in other mobile platforms such as iOS and Windows Phone;
- To simplify the web portal, allowing the user to know who is available in each community and create easily a web conference with them;

- To allow interaction with room systems like Polycom, using H.323 or SIP.

All the source code of the Mconf project is available under open source licenses in https://github.com/mconf. The main links are:

- Mconf version of BigBlueButton: https://github.com/mconf/bigbluebutton
- Mconf-Mobile (and BBB-Android): https://github.com/mconf/mconf-mobile
- Mconf-Web: https://github.com/mconf/mconf-web

The project information and updates are available in the Google Code wiki at http://code.google.com/p/mconf/wiki/Home. The main subjects are related to the Mconf installation, Mconf-mobile, Mconf-Web and the customized BigBlueButton. Also there is a virtual machine with the entire environment already installed.

Furthermore, there is a demo server available at http://mconf.org. This demo server has about 100 communities and 250 users worldwide.

7. Acknowledgment

We would like to express our sincere gratitude to RNP (Research National Network) for sponsoring the Mconf project.

Also we would like to thank BBB Foundation for bringing such a helpful tool for the world, and for being very active and effective regarding BBB development.

8. References

Adobe Systems Incorporated. Real Time Messaging Protocol Chunk Stream. At: http://wwwimages.adobe.com/www.adobe.com/content/dam/Adobe/en/devnet/rtmp/pdf/rtmp_specification_1.0.pdf. June, 2009. Accessed in Sept, 2011.

Huang H-S, Peng W-H and Chiang T. Advances in the Scalable Amendment of H.264/AVC. Proc. of. Advances Visual Cont. Analysis and Adaptation for Multimedia Communication, jan. 2007. pp 68-76.

ITU-T H.323 v7 H Series: Audiovisual and Multimedia Systems: Infrastructure of audiovisual services - Systems and terminal equipment for audiovisual services. Dec, 2009.

Quemada, Juan. Presentation at the 2nd TF-Media Task Force meeting, May 30, 2010. At. http://www.terena.org/activities/media/meeting2/slides/20100530-tnc-juan.pdf

Quemada, Juan; et al. Isabel: an application for real time collaboration with a flexible floor control. International Conference on Collaborative Computing: Networking, Applications and Worksharing, IEEE Computer Society (2005).

Roesler, Valter, Coelho, Luiz. Distributed Classes: Convergence of distance learning and presence learning through a videoconference system. In TNC 2010: Terena Networking Conference 2010. Vilnius, Lithuania. May, 2010.

Roesler, Valter; Husemann, Ronaldo; Costa, Carlos H. A new multimedia synchronous distance learning system: The IVA study case. In Proceedings of the 24th Annual ACM Symposium on Applied Computing, SAC2009. Honolulu, Hawaii. March, 2009.

Rosenberg, J., Schulzrinne, H., Camarillo, G., Johnston, A., Peterson, J., Sparks, R., Handley, M., and Schooler, E. SIP: Session Initiation Protocol. IETF: Internet Engineering Task Force. RFC 3261, Jun, 2002.

High-Dimensional Indexing for Video Retrieval

Catalin Calistru[2,3], Cristina Ribeiro[1,3] and Gabriel David[1,3]
[1]*FEUP, Faculdade de Engenharia da Universidade do Porto*
[2]*ISPGAYA, Instituto Superior Politécnico Gaya*
[3]*INESC, Porto*
Portugal

1. Introduction

The video retrieval task raises many fundamental questions in computer vision and information retrieval, such as how to represent video items, what information can be directly extracted from them, and how to explore such information in order to satisfy the user's information need. Video items are intrinsically complex, and the analysis of their content requires heavy computing processes. Excepting the case of text, multimedia content analysis does not result in the high-level concepts required by the generality of the search tasks. This brings about the so-called "semantic gap", clearly identified as the main issue in multimedia retrieval Gudivada & Raghavan (1995); Smith (2007). Text communication is based on concepts, expressed in the user's language and close to the way humans think. Searching text items may require a number of processing techniques like pattern matching, stemming, finding synonyms, translating, natural language analysis. Supposing that the user expresses his information need through words, the set of retrieved documents includes those containing precise or imprecise word matches and can be continuously enlarged to more and more semantically related documents. In the case of a video repository, however, there is not such a clear semantic channel between the object's content and the user information need. The automatic video analysis may produce many descriptors related to the contents, the so-called low-level descriptors Bober (Jun 2001); Manjunath et al. (2001); Mufit Ferman et al. (2000), but hardly produces accurate descriptions close enough to human concepts Snoek & Smeulders (2010); Tesic & Smith (2006). This is a problem for a wide range of video-based applications, other than search and retrieval, such as human-computer interface, security and surveillance, copyright protection, and personal entertainment.

While significant progress has been achieved towards narrowing the 'semantic gap' in image and audio retrieval, Celma & Serra (2008); Smeulders et al. (2000); Yan & Hauptmann (2007), there are no satisfactory systems for video retrieval Smith (2007); Snoek & Worring (2005); Snoek, Worring, van Gemert, Geusebroek & Smeulders (2006). In fact, the video retrieval techniques overlap significantly with the image-based ones. In practice, video repositories Westerveld (2005) are treated as statical sets of representative images, the keyframes. True video search systems, capable of analyzing the whole spatio-temporal information available in video are nor yet available Ekin et al. (2004); Snoek et al. (2003).

The 'semantic gap' is not the single problem to be solved in video retrieval. For example, a retrieval system should rank all the video items in a dataset by their degree of similarity to a given query, where the similarity is typically assessed by means of some similarity distance between the video items and the query. However, it is not yet fully understood how to convey the human similarity judgments in terms of distance computations. It is not even clear whether the similarity computation should be of metric nature or not Eidenberger (9-11 Dec. 2002); Santini & Jain (1997). Although metric-based similarity computations are frequently preferred, the choice is not based on a clear criteria for the selection of similarity measures. Recent studies on distance metrics Yu et al. (2006) provide some insight on this issue. However, except in the case of specific application domains, where the ranking criteria are established a priori, the video retrieval systems must account for flexibility in the choice of similarity measures.

While the issues mentioned earlier, namely the 'semantic gap' and the variability of metrics, are concerned with retrieval effectivity, there is more to retrieval that must be considered. For example, the emerging retrieval systems are expected to be seamlessly integrated into existing databases, which raises questions related to database organization, such as the data/metadata dichotomy Bulterman (2004); Kosch et al. (2005), or how to integrate the video search engines with the existing search facilities Chaudhuri et al. (2005). But the most important issue, from the point of view of integration with existing database systems, is the search efficiency in the context of continuously growing datasets. It is widely accepted that the growth rate of multimedia content production increases the length of time it takes to process a dataset, from its production until it is available for search; we will refer to this as the time to search issue.

Analyzing current multimedia search approaches IBM (2008); Wactlar et al. (1999) from the time to search point of view, we observe that, if machine learning techniques are used to extract high-level concepts, large training times are required. The manual annotation alternative Shneiderman et al. (2006), although essential in many cases, cannot keep the pace with the growth rate of video productions. On the other hand, if search relies on low-level similarity, in a query-by-example fashion, a short time to search can be achieved Calistru et al. (2006); Tesic (2004). Two main directions can be followed: effectivity-oriented, where finding relevant objects is the priority, and efficiency-oriented, where the quality of results is traded for speed. The goal here is to tackle the video search and retrieval tasks from both the efficiency and the effectiveness points of view. The idea is to build an indexing system that can search—with the shortest possible time to search—in large datasets of low-level descriptors, and incrementally integrate, as they become available, high-level information from the manual and automatic annotators.

The chapter is organized as follows. Sections, 2, 3, and 4 offer insights into three essential retrieval aspects, namely features and descriptors, similarity models, and multidimensional indexing. As retrieval systems do not operate with the video items themselves, but with representations thereof, Section 2 reviews the feature types that can be extracted, how they are being represented, and what is their impact in retrieval. In Section 3, we discuss a second important issue in retrieval, namely how to discriminate between items. In order to be comparable, all the video items must share a common representation type, and, depending on the representation, a range of similarity measures can be applied. Considering the large volume of high-dimensional feature data and the variety of similarity measures, efficient and versatile indexing methods are needed. This brings about the efficiency aspect, which we strengthen in Section 4. This section comprises a review of the current state of the art in multidimensional indexing, and continues to identify a set of requirements that indexes for video data should comply. In sections 5 and 6 we illustrate a video retrieval case study where, using a custom-designed high-dimensional index, the BitMatrix, we efficiently index a large set of high-dimensional descriptors. Section 5 presents the BitMatrix, showing that it relies on bitwise operations, can be conveniently arranged for efficient sequential access, and can be easily broken into segments for distributed or parallel processing. Moreover, it adapts gracefully to continuously growing datasets, such as the video contents produced by cameras. In the sequel, a set of BitMatrix-based experiments, carried on in both synthetic and real datasets, such as TRECVID 2007 are presented in Section 6. We show that our search strategy can cope with the trade-off between flexible video ranking, required for capturing the multitude of similarity facets, and query execution speed. The last section includes a chapter summary and some current research trends.

2. Features and descriptors

Feature extraction is the process of obtaining descriptors from multimedia items. When the items are digitized versions of some real world objects, it is important to note that the items properties are not necessarily the properties of the objects in the world. The digitizations are obtained by sensory means and sensor limitations introduce a so-called "sensory gap". For example, due to lighting conditions, a red car can appear as white in a video shot. It is easy to imagine that a color-based search for shots that contain red cars would not find that video shot. Although this is a trivial example, in many critical domains such as medicine, the 'sensory gap' must be seriously taken into consideration. However, throughout this section we are not concerned with this issue; the relationship between real world objects and multimedia items is not explored.

In a first, and most common categorization, the features can be either low or high-level. The low-level features are the ones directly obtained from the multimedia items, such as color, texture, shape, motion and audio features Deselaers et al. (2004). They are used in several application domains, namely object recognition, surveillance, diagnostics and content-based retrieval.

The high level features consist of keywords or more complex natural language formulations that capture human concepts. For the text-based multimedia items, high-level descriptors can be directly extracted from the content itself, but for the other modalities a direct semantic connection to human concepts does not exist. High-level descriptors can be obtained by means of either automatic Jiang et al. (2005); Zhang & Chen (2003) or manual annotations. Whatever the annotation type, there are arguments for and against their use. For instance, the manual annotations are considered subjective and expensive to obtain, but if domain experts validate the annotations, they can be accurate Shneiderman et al. (2006); Yee et al. (2003). An argument in favor of automatic annotations is that they are cheaper to obtain when trained concept detectors already exist. However, such detectors are available only for a small number of concepts and often provide low accuracy rates. If concepts such as 'water', 'sky', 'cars', 'faces' or 'outdoors' are relatively well-detected, concepts such as 'entertainment' or aspects such as preferences Bartolini et al. (2005) or moods Hanjalic (2006) are far from being correctly identified. To cope with the automatic concept detection challenges, the multimedia communities are currently establishing concept lexicons Naphade et al. (2006); Snoek, Worring, van Gemert, Geusebroek & Smeulders (2006), focusing on the concepts that are feasible for automatic detection Hauptmann et al. (2007); Snoek, Worring, Geusebroek, Koelma, Seinstra & Smeulders (2006); Yang & Hauptmann (2006).

Beside the low/high-level categorization, the features can also be local/global and variant/invariant. If the feature extraction targets specific item regions, the features are called local and if the whole item is analyzed, the features are called global. A feature is considered either variant or invariant depending on how the feature values are sensitive to item transformations. For example, if the shape feature values of an image are insensitive to rotation, such a feature is called rotation-invariant. The variance/invariance can be judged with respect to other transformations, such as scaling, location change, illumination variation, viewpoint transformations, or occlusions.

Feature representations are typically incorporated as descriptors. According to the feature types presented above, the descriptors can be considered low/high-level, local/global and variant/invariant. Between features and descriptors there is a one to many relation, as a feature can be represented in multiple ways. For example, DominantColor, ColorStructure and ScalableColor descriptors Manjunath et al. (2001) are all color descriptors. Low-level descriptors consist predominantly of vectorial data. The DominantColor descriptor, for example, consists of an RGB-tuple (red, green, blue). The color histogram descriptors are even larger vectors of 128 or 256 values. The entire set of descriptors can be viewed as a vectorial space, also called the feature space, which generally has hundreds or thousands of dimensions.

A possible question to address here is: what descriptors should be extracted that would help finding relevant multimedia items Deselaers et al. (2004); Jiang et al. (2007)? As an answer to such a question, one may expect a set of descriptors that guarantees up to some degree of confidence that an effective retrieval system can be built on top of it. Such an answer is difficult to obtain, because the retrieval quality is a problem that surpasses the choice of descriptors. However, we can say that retrieval based on low-level features is already mature Flickner et al. (1995); Rehatschek et al. (2004); Smith & Chang (1996); Wactlar et al. (1996), but inferring high-level features is still a challenging task Gevers & Smeulders (2004); Hanjalic (2006); Huijbregts et al. (2007); Smeulders et al. (2000); Xiong et al. (2006). As the high-level feature extraction depends, up to some extent, on the low-level features, we expect that the use of low-level features will still grow Burghouts & Geusebroek (2009).

Recent years have been marked by a shift from global and variant descriptors, such as color histograms and global shape descriptors, to local invariant ones, such as keypoints Burghouts & Geusebroek (2009), region-based, and local shape characterizations. This shift is explained by the complexity of the multimedia items. The semantics covered by a whole item is too deep for global descriptors to cope with. It has been observed that local descriptors correspond better to item parts such as objects or persons. Invariance also became increasingly important because it helps identifying objects under various circumstances.

3. Similarity models

The similarity models are the means by which the multimedia items can be compared. Although the choice of a specific similarity model is generally dependent on the features that are involved, in this section we ignore this type of dependency. The main question has a general nature: how can one discriminate among video items? We start with a preliminary discussion on what similarity is, and then continue with a review of several similarity models.

3.1 About similarity

The similarity between two multimedia items can be seen generically as a relationship between them. There are domains, such as geometry, in which the similarity is precisely defined: two geometrical objects are called similar if one is congruent to the result of a uniform scaling (enlarging or shrinking) of the other. With this definition we can easily assess the similarity between geometric objects. For example, two circles are always similar to each other, two squares are always similar to each other, and two triangles are similar if and only if they have the same values for the three angles. But unlike geometric similarity, which is precise, similarity in retrieval is imprecise and depends on numerous facets of the items, on the user and on the interaction context.

There is a difference between similarity and matching Kherfi et al. (2004), which may lead to different approaches. Matching requires a comparison between two items—a binary operator— to check whether the items are identical or not; it is used for copy identification, for example. But similarity, although it sometimes uses matching techniques, is a more complex process, requiring knowledge from very diverse domains. In modeling similarity, the similarity judgments are often based on subjective features grouping which yield user-dependent degrees of similarity Gentner (1988); Santini & Jain (1997).

In retrieval, similarity is evaluated by some comparison between a given query and the items' feature values (descriptors). The features that can be checked for relevance range from low-level ones such as color or shape, to high-level and subjective ones such as a feelings or moods Dimitrova (2004); Hanjalic (2006). In the sequel, the most common similarity models are presented.

3.2 The Vector Space Model

In the Vector Space Model, (VSM) both the queries and the objects are represented as points in high-dimensional vector spaces. Although created as a text retrieval model, Faloutsos & Oard (1995); Salton (1971); Van Rijsbergen (1979) VSM is not restricted to the text modality. Generic multimedia items can be captured, given that their feature types, such as color, texture, shape, or motion have vectorial representations.

Assuming a vector space with N dimensions, an item D_k is represented by a vector $D_k = [d_{k0}, d_{k1}, .., d_{kN}]$ and a query Q by a vector $Q = [q_0, q_1, .., q_N]$, where N depends on the feature type, d_{ki} and q_i are the D_k and Q feature values for dimension i. The similarity between Q and D_k is then computed as a distance $d(Q, D_k)$, where d can take a large variety of forms, Datta et al. (2008) such as cosine similarity, Faloutsos & Oard (1995); Salton (1971); Van Rijsbergen (1979) quadratic distance, Böhm, Kriegel & Seidl (2001); Ishikawa et al. (1998) L_p distance, Aggarwal et al. (2001); Howarth & Rüger (2005b); Yan & Hauptmann (2007) Chebyshev distance, Li et al. (2006) Earth Mover's Distance, Carson et al. (1999); Rubner et al. (2000); Wu & Bretschneider (2004) and localized metrics Aggarwal & Yu (2000); Cha (2003); Howarth & Rüger (2005a).

3.3 Feature Contrast Model

The Feature Contrast Model (FCM), also known as Tversky's model Tversky (1977), is a similarity model that does not assume a metric nature for the human perception, which is the default assumption in the VSM model. The triangle inequality and the symmetry axioms were considered too restrictive.

Unlike the vector space model, which represents the items as points in a vector space, Tversky treats them as sets of binary predicates. Let X and Y be two feature sets corresponding to items x and y. The contrast model obtains the similarity of the two items by combining the common features ($X \cap Y$) and the distinctive features ($X \setminus Y$ and $Y \setminus X$):

$$Sim(x,y) = f(X \cap Y) - \alpha f(X \setminus Y) - \beta f(Y \setminus X). \quad (1)$$

The formula in Equation 1 is not a metric, because the symmetry axiom does not hold. Tversky's view on similarity assessment was extended to geometric Santini & Jain (1997) and fuzzy feature contrast Santini & Jain (1999) models. Comparisons with the Euclidean distance Eidenberger & Breiteneder (2003), and with various other metrics for MPEG-7 descriptors Eidenberger (2003) have shown that in many cases the FCM performs better. However, the FCM has been criticized for not capturing relationships between features Rada et al. (1989) .

3.4 Probabilistic Model

The idea behind the Probabilistic Model (PM) is to predict the probability that a given multimedia item will be relevant to a given query. It relies on the assumption that the distribution of some concepts throughout the collection, or within some subset of it, may be informative of the likely relevance of the items. With this assumption, accurate estimates of the probabilities can be obtained and the documents can be ranked according to this probability of relevance Benitez & Chang (2002); Bohm et al. (2007); H.R.Turtle (1991); Larson et al. (1996); Macdonald & Ounis (2006); Robertson (1997).

3.4.0.1 Language-based models

A special category of probabilistic models, the Language-based Models (LM) Kraaij (2005); Ponte & Croft (1998); Zhai & Lafferty (2001) propose to statistically model the use of language in a multimedia collection in order to estimate the probability that a query is generated from a particular document. The main idea is that, if the query could have come from the document, then that document is likely to be relevant.

3.5 Generative Model

In this model, every object is considered as the outcome of a process that generated it. The idea is to include in the similarity assessment knowledge about the likelihood of existence of the objects to be compared. It has been argued that the generative processes are important since they help the selection of critical features for similarity comparison Kemp et al. (2005).

As an example, Kemp et al. ask which is more similar to a given nutritious mushroom: a mushroom identical except for its size, or a mushroom identical except for its color? They suggest that knowing how mushrooms are formed, i.e. their generative process, we can be sure that mushrooms grow from small to large and their final size depends on the amount of sunlight and soil fertility. Therefore, it is more likely that the differently-sized mushroom is more similar than the differently-colored.

When applied to multimedia retrieval, the generative models follow probabilistic approaches. Under the assumption that each item was obtained from some specific generative process, the similarity is assessed through the probability that the query is an outcome of the item's process Westerveld (2004).

3.6 Rank Aggregation Model

In this model the assumption is that several independent rankings with respect to a query object already exist and these have to be merged into a single results list. Thus, the model is not directly applicable on the original feature values, but on intermediate rank lists. As an example, we can have a situation, where several descriptors are involved in the similarity computation and metrics adapted to each descriptor are required. In such a case, descriptor-wise rank lists are obtained, and a further aggregation strategy is required.

The common approach for the aggregation of several rank lists is to use scoring functions, such as *min* or *average* in order to compute overall scores. Depending on the aggregation function and the termination condition, several aggregation algorithms such as *Fagin's Algorithm, Threshold Algorithm, medrank* Fagin et al. (2003) and *Quick-Combine* Güntzer et al. (2000), have been proposed.

3.7 Preference Relations Model

The scoring functions used in aggregation models are quantitative and assign scores to multimedia items based on their feature values. When multiple rankings exist, user preferences for one result set or another are modeled with weights. However, the scores and weights have a limited expressive power, since not all the user preferences can be translated into quantitative expressions. The preference-based similarity model appeared as an alternative.

Figure 1(a) illustrates a first example. A small database composed of five objects is assumed, where object o_1 is preferred to object o_2 and o_3 is preferred to o_4. There is no preference between o_1, o_3 and o_5. If we try to capture these preferences with a scoring function, the object scores can be assigned in the following manner:

$$S(o_1) = S(o_3) = S(o_5) > S(o_2) = S(o_4). \tag{2}$$

Let's assume now that object o_1 is deleted from our database, as in Figure 1(b). Looking at the preferences we see that in the absence of o_1, o_2 should not be second to other objects, but looking at the scores we have $S(o_3) = S(o_5) > S(o_2) = S(o_4)$, which do not place o_2 among the top objects. That happens because the scoring function evaluates the similarity only by quantitative means, not accounting for the relations with the other objects in the database.

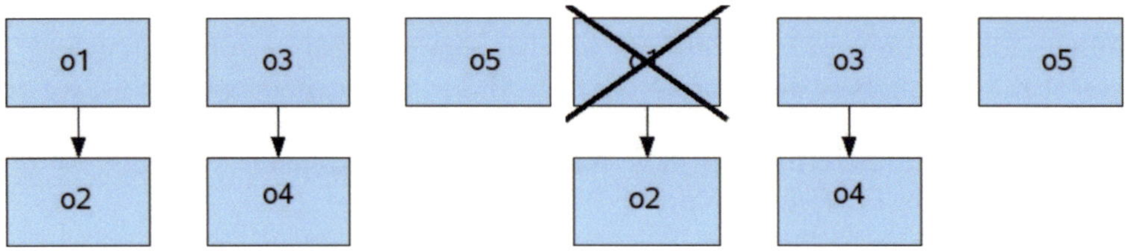

(a) Before o_1 removal (b) After removing o_1

Fig. 1. Preference Diagram

As an alternative to scoring functions, Chomicki Chomicki (2002; 2003) proposes a similarity approach based on qualitative preference relations. This technique requires that, given two objects o_i and o_j, there must exist a binary relation —the preference relation— that states whether o_i is preferred to o_j ($o_i \succ o_j$) or not ($o_i \not\succ o_j$). If $o_i \succ o_j$ we also say that o_i *dominates* o_j. If neither $o_i \not\succ o_j$ nor $o_j \not\succ o_i$, then we have that $o_i \sim o_j$, which represents the *indifference relation*. Assuming that queries are expressed by means of preference relations, it is possible to define an operator, called *skyline-operator* Börzsönyi et al. (2001) or *winnow* Chomicki (2002), that computes the set of preferred objects, i.e. all the objects that are not dominated by the others. The skyline operator is defined as:

$$skyline(DB) = \{o \in DB | \nexists p \in DB, p \succ o\}. \tag{3}$$

In the previous example, after the deletion of o_1, o_2 becomes a skyline object, i.e. is not dominated by any other object. In preference-based retrieval applications such as Bartolini et al. (2005); Leubner & Kießling (2002), sequent skyline iterations are reported and the partial object sets are ranked: the set of skyline objects, followed by the skyline of the remaining objects, and so on. Although it is a ranking without scores, also called a qualitative ranking, the interest in having retrieval systems that take into account the user preferences led to an increasing adoption of skyline-based similarity models Balke & Güntzer (2004); Bartolini & Ciaccia (2005); Godfrey et al. (2005); Papadias et al. (2005); Pei et al. (2005); Yuan et al. (2005)

3.8 Network Model

The idea behind this model is to represent the items as nodes in a network, with *part-of* or *is-a* relations between items. The most representative class for network models are the semantic networks, where the nodes of the network are concepts, eventually coming from predefined ontologies. Such a representation mode is often referred to as a conceptual graph Nguyen & Corbett (2006). The measure of similarity between two nodes(concepts), is the length of the shortest path between them. Usually the semantic neighborhood of radius r of a concept C is defined as the set of all the concepts that have the distance to C smaller than r.

Ekin et al. Ekin et al. (2004) propose a semantic model dedicated to video retrieval with entities and relations between them. Instantiations of this model are graphs, allowing for graph-based queries, while the similarity is obtained by graph-based matching.

3.9 Hybrid approaches

In current multimedia retrieval prototypes, similarity is assessed with hybrid approaches, i.e. by combining various similarity models. Schwering, for example Schwering (2005), introduces a hybrid model for semantic similarity that combines the network model, in the form of semantic network, with the geometric model. The resulting model becomes a network of vector spaces, where each node of the net represents a concept, and each concept is further mapped to a vector space. The similarity is obtained in two phases: first the query concepts are aligned with the concepts available in the model using semantic networks techniques and then a metric is applied on the corresponding vector spaces. Raubal proposes a similar approach Raubal (2004).

4. Multidimensional indexing methods

We have seen in the previous section that the similarity between multimedia items can be evaluated with a wide range of models. Among them, the VSM-based retrieval models are by far the most used. Therefore, there is an increasing interest in speeding similarity-based retrieval on top of such models. We remind that in VSM the multimedia items are modeled as points in a high-dimensional vector space and the similarity between them is assessed with metric-based distance computations. Given a query object q from a universe of objects $\mathcal{O}$ and a metric function d, finding similar objects means identifying particular sets of objects:

- the *Nearest Neighbor Set* $NN(q)$, defined as $\{o \in \mathcal{O} | \forall v \in \mathcal{O}, d(q,o) \leq d(q,v)\}$;
- the *k- Nearest Neighbors Set* $NN_k(q)$, defined as the set of k elements closest to q in $\mathcal{O}$, i.e. a set objects $A \subseteq \mathcal{O}$, such that $| A | = k$ and $\forall o \in A, v \in \mathcal{O} - A, d(q,o) < d(q,v)$;
- the *approximate Nearest Neighbor Set* $(NN_A(q))$, which is the set of objects $\{o \in \mathcal{O} | d(q,o) \leq (1+\epsilon) * d(q, NN(q)), \epsilon > 0\}$.

The computation of these neighbor sets becomes challenging when dimensionality increases, a problem often referred to as the "curse of dimensionality" Beyer et al. (1999); Indyk & Motwani (1998). In practice, the naive and inefficient approach of simply comparing the query vector to all feature vectors has proved comparable, sometimes even more efficient than especially designed indexing methods such as the "R-tree" Beckmann et al. (1990). Due to the increasing importance of search in high-dimensional spaces, a great diversity of indexing methods have been proposed in recent years. In spite of their diversity, they all avoid looking at every object by creating groups of objects with common properties. Under the assumption that the grouped objects are requested or pruned together, checking the groups instead of individual objects saves time. For example, the objects in a distance range can be pruned or not just by checking the range's minimum and maximum values. In the following we review the most used multidimensional indexing methods.

4.1 Spatial Access Methods

Spatial Access Methods (SAM), also called feature-based methods, partition the space based on the values of the vectors along each independent dimension.

SAM are based on tree data structures with two types of nodes: data nodes (the leaves) and directory nodes. The information stored in directory nodes describe space regions obtained

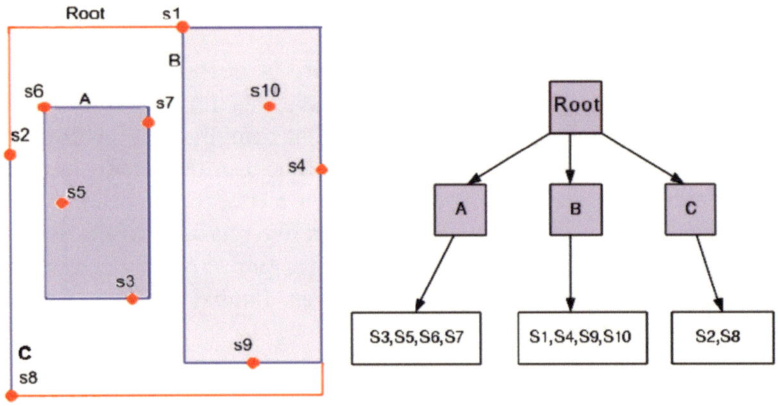

Fig. 2. An R-Tree example

with various partitioning strategies. There can be strategies such as data partitioning (DP) which uses minimum bounding regions (MBR) such as *R-tree*, *R^*-tree* Beckmann et al. (1990), *X-tree* Berchtold et al. (1996), bounding spheres such as $SS - tree$ White & Jain (1996), MBR and bounding spheres such as $SR - Tree$, generic minimum bounding regions (hyper rectangle, cube, sphere) such as the $TV - tree$, the $BBD - tree$ Arya et al. (1998) and space partitioning methods (SP) such as the $kDB - tree$, $Hybrid - tree$, $SH - tree$ Böhm, Berchtold & Keim (2001).

The most representative SAM approach, the *R-tree*, is illustrated in Figure 2. The left-hand side of the figure shows the MBR around 10 data points s_1, to s_{10}. The tree structure on the right-hand side of Figure 2 follows the containment hierarchy obtained from the data partitioning.

The nodes of the SAM trees contain information about the MBR that they cover, such as their coordinates. This kind of information grows exponentially with the number of dimensions, leading to the growth of each tree node and of the index itself. The larger the nodes are, the fewer can fit in a disk page; accessing such an index becomes more difficult. Another important issue is the high-overlapping between the MBR stored at the same level in the tree. Although they cannot be observed in our example because we have few data points and few dimensions, the overlappings lead to an increased number of branches to be searched. The costs of maintaining SAM structures cover aspects such as space, index re-creation, updates, insertions and MBR split managements.

4.2 Metric Access Methods

Like SAM, the Metric Access Methods (MAM) Chávez et al. (2001); Hjaltason & Samet (2003) are also based on tree-structures, but they work with relative distances between the objects rather than their absolute positions in space. MAM have gained an important role due to the fact that conventional SAM approaches stop being efficient in high-dimensional data. They are also required for search in distance-only data sets, i.e. those that cannot be mapped to vector spaces. An example thereof is a set of text documents that use the edit metric Yujian & Bo (2007) to measure the distance between documents.

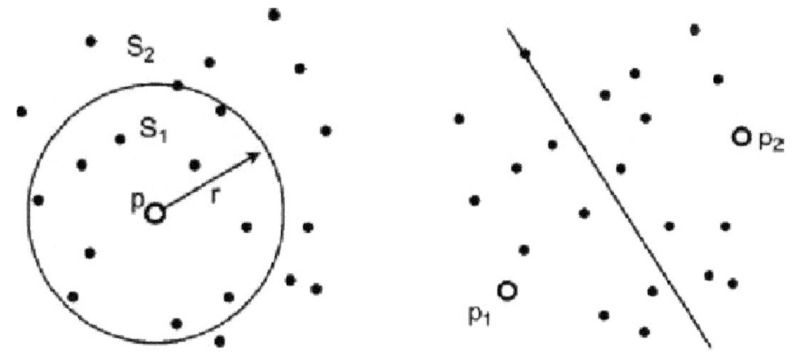

Fig. 3. Ball and Hyperplane partitioning; figure taken from Hjaltason & Samet (2003)

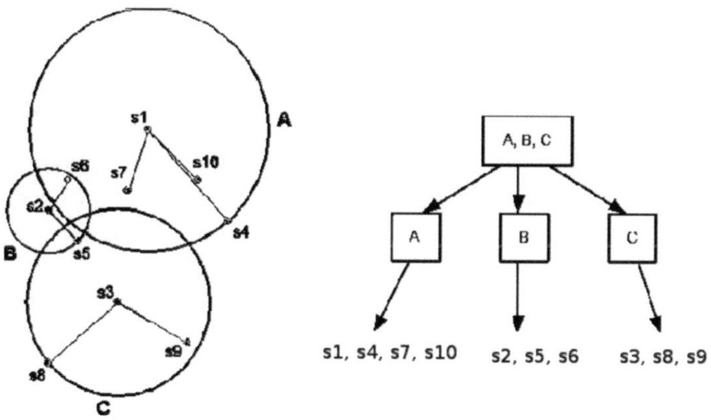

Fig. 4. An M-Tree example

MAM build their tree-structures by recursively partitioning the data set into subsets at each node level Chávez et al. (2001). Two main partitioning schemes have been identified by Hjaltson and Samet Hjaltason & Samet (2003): *ball partitioning* and *generalized hyperplane partitioning*, illustrated in Figure 3. With the *ball partitioning* approach, the data set is partitioned based on the distance from one specified object, called *vantage point* or *pivot*: two subsets are generated: the first subset inside the circle around the pivot, and the second subset outside the ball. Among ball partitioning trees the most referenced are *Vantage-Point Tree (VP-tree), Multi-Vantage Point Tree (MVPT)* Bozkaya & Ozsoyoglu (1999), *Vantage-Point Forest (VPF), Burkhard-Keller Tree (BKT)* and *Fixed Queries Tree (FQT)* Hjaltason & Samet (2003). With the *hyperplane partitioning* approach, at each step two points p_1 and p_2 are selected. Elements closer to p_1 than to p_2 go into the left sub tree and those closer to p_2 go into the right sub tree. Among hyperplane partitioning structures we enumerate *Bisector Tree (BST), Generalize Hyperplane Tree (GHT), Geometric Near-neighbor Access Tree (GNAT).* and the *M-tree*Ciaccia et al. (1997).

An M-tree example for a small set of 10 objects is shown in Figure 4. The objects are stored in the leaf nodes, while the internal nodes, also called *routing objects*, store pointers to child nodes and the covering radius for the children they enclose.

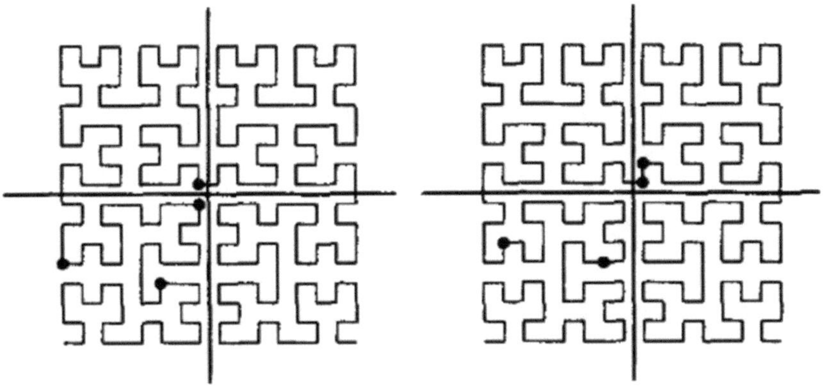

Fig. 5. Space filling curve; figure taken from Liao et al. (2001)

The applicability of the MAM methods ranges from "native" distance-only datasets to high-dimensional datasets for which conventional SAM are no longer efficient Digout & Nascimento (2005). Their advantage is that the relative distances between objects can be pre-computed at index creation time, avoiding heavy distance computations at search time. However, this advantage is also a constraint because the distance measure used at creation time must be used at search time. Given that the distance measure must be established in advance, searching with user-defined metrics that capture personalized criteria becomes difficult. It has been shown, however, that metrics from certain classes of parameterizable distance functions could be used Ciaccia & Patella (2002).

4.3 Single-dimension mapping

Single-dimension mapping approaches map the points in the high-dimensional space to single-dimensional values for which efficient techniques such as the B-tree Bayer & McCreight (1972) exist.

Querying high-dimensional data in single-dimensional space considers the smallest and largest values among all the dimensions of each data point Yu et al. (2004) and Ooi et al. (2000). Another single-dimensional mapping method sorts the data points according to their positions on a space-filling curve Liao et al. (2001). The list obtained in this way is stored in a B-tree structure. In practice, several shifted copies of the data points (maximum $N + 1$, where N is the space dimensionality) are used. Each copy of the data points produces a separate, differently ordered list, which is stored in a separate B-tree. The left part of Figure 5 illustrates a space filling curve that touches the original data points. On the right part, the same curve touches the shifted data with one unit up and one to the right.

With the "iDistance" approach, Jagadish et al. (2005) a data partitioning (see Section 4.1) technique is initially applied, followed by a single-dimensional mapping within each region. The mapping process consists of sorting the objects in each region on the distance to a specific reference point, such as the region's center. The reference points are then indexed in a $B^+ - tree$ structure. The "iDistance" has been applied on local subspaces Shen et al. (2007), previously obtained with principal components analysis Jolliffe (1986).

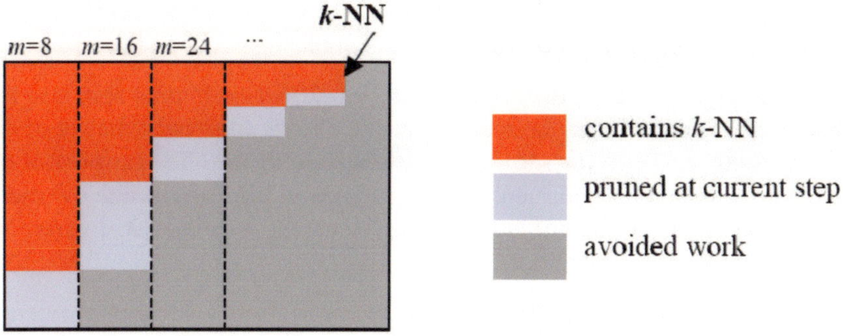

Fig. 6. Example of BOND technique; figure taken from Arjen et al. (2002)

4.4 Data decomposition

Data decomposition methods treat each dimension as a separate list, and their goal is to obtain the answer of the query by accessing a minimum number of lists and as few objects as possible in each of the visited lists.

Branch and Bound on Vertically Decomposed Data (BOND) Arjen et al. (2002), adopts vertical decomposition as storage organization. That means it decomposes the data into multiple tables, one for each dimension. Therefore, the information for a specific object is distributed into multiple tables. The algorithm accumulates the distances between the query object and all data vectors, by scanning the dimensional projections one-by-one. After processing a few dimensions, *partial* distances of k-nearest neighbors are exploited to discard safely from further consideration those vectors that cannot possibly participate in the result. This process is graphically illustrated in Figure 6. It can be observed that groups of 8 dimensions are successively scanned; *m* represents the total number of visited dimensions. After reading each group, based on partial distances, a set of objects is pruned. The iterative application of this process quickly reduces the candidate set (the upper part of the figure) to just a small database sample.

4.5 Data approximation structures

The methods described here are based on a result obtained by Weber et al. Weber et al. (1998), which indicate that MAM and SAM are outperformed by a simple sequential scan whenever the dimensionality is above 10. Considering this result, a sequential scan is inevitable when searching high-dimensional datasets. Under this assumption, the VA-file method Tesic & Manjunath (2003); Weber et al. (1998) constructs a vector of approximations, significantly smaller than the original data and sequentially scans it. The vector of approximations is the result of a space division in a number of cells; all the objects contained in a cell are represented by a common approximation. When searching for nearest neighbor for example, the entire vector of approximations is scanned. Based on their minimum/maximum distance to the query the majority of approximations are filtered. For the remaining ones the corresponding exact data points have to be accessed. The critical factor of VA-file' performance is the filtering step. If too many approximations remain, a lot of objects have to be accessed and the advantage of an approximation file is lost. Discussions and improvements of the VA-file pruning strategy have been reported Wang & You (2006).

Also using a grid of cells, the IGrid Aggarwal & Yu (2000) maintains separate lists for the objects in each cell. The similarity between any two objects uses only the set of dimensions for which the two objects lie in the same range (the *proximity set*). The number of objects that are accessed is kept small as the dimensionality increases, but the storage overhead is 100% because all the objects are copied into the indexing structure. Bitmap IGrid variants have also been proposed Cha (2003); Goldstein et al. (2004).

The process of partitioning a high-dimensional space is itself a specific problem requiring dimension-wise discretization strategies Fayyad & Irani (1992). One possibility is to create dimension-wise histograms of the distance values from the points to the data center Jagadish, H.V. and Beng Chin Ooi and Heng Tao Shen and Kian-Lee Tan (2006) . The number of bins in each dimension's histogram gives the number of intervals. Another data approximation technique uses a partitioning strategy based on a graph model Aggarwal et al. (1999).

4.6 Which indexing method to use?

The SAM and MAM high-dimensional indexing methods divide the search space in a set of minimum bounding regions hierarchically organized in tree structures. At search time, the MBR that don't overlap the query region are filtered. As dimensionality increases, the distances from a query object to the nearest and the farthest objects are almost in the same range. Practically, the nearest neighbor becomes indistinctive from other neighbors Katayama & Satoh (2001), loosing its meaningfulness Aggarwal (2002); Beyer et al. (1999). In such conditions, the smallest query region that contains the nearest neighbor will overlap most of the MBR, making them non-prunable. The consequence is that the search methods end up accessing all the nodes of their structures in a pseudo-random fashion, which is more time consuming than a simple sequential scan —a problem often referred to as the "curse of dimensionality" Beyer et al. (1999); Indyk & Motwani (1998).

To overcome this problem, Katayama et al. have proposed a distinctive-sensitive approach for tree-based structures Katayama & Satoh (2001), testing the distinctiveness of the nearest neighbor in the course of search operation. When the nearest neighbor is considered indistinctive, search returns a partial result. Other indexing methods, such as the ones presented in Section 4.3, resort to single-dimension mapping. Another approach, presented in Section 4.4, uses specific aggregations with the goal of visiting only a fraction of the dataset. Finally, the data approximation methods sequentially access a compressed version of the data.

Choosing the proper index for a given situation should be the result of especially designed tests that consider various approaches. A given indexing approach could behave well in some situations and worse in others. For example, in Wang & You (2006) an important improvement over the original method in Weber et al. (1998) has been reported just by using a different metric. To our knowledge, test frameworks for the whole range of high-dimensional indexing methods are not yet publicly available. The currently available frameworks, such as GIST Hellerstein et al. (1995), SP-GIST Aref & Ilyas (2001) and XXL den Bercken et al. (2001) provide only a subset of the existing indexing methods. GIST provides a tree-based template indexing structure. XXL, while also offering tree-based indexing templates, focuses on implementations of advanced database queries (cursors, iterators) independent from the underlying data types and data structures. MMDI Gonçalves et al. (2007) is built with the goal of supporting virtually any high-dimensional index. However, at the moment, only approaches that cannot be tested in GIST or XXL have been implemented.

4.7 Video retrieval requirements

Considering the variety of indexing approaches, it is important to have a set of requirements specific to the video indexing domain, against which any given index can be checked for compliance. The following set of requirements strengthen the need for flexibility of the high-dimensional indexes.

- Data preprocessing;
- Frequency of updates;
- Varying dimensionality;
- Any dimensional subspace;
- Support for different metrics;
- Support for weighted queries;
- Multiple query objects.

Data preprocessing can be a dominant effort when dealing with diverse descriptors and high-dimensional spaces. Tasks such as the normalization of the feature vectors and dimensional reduction may be required for index construction.

Many multimedia databases are statical in nature; this is the case with archives, where append is the common operation. But there are cases where updates are quite often. When new objects are added to the database, they have to be processed and included in the indexes. On the other and, if a new feature is extracted, or the quality of some feature extraction tool improves, existing objects will be processed and the new descriptors incorporated as an update.

The dimensionality of the search space is directly related to the number of descriptors, as each descriptor contributes new dimensions. Adding a histogram descriptor, for instance, increases the dimensionality by the number of bins the histogram has been quantized (8, 16, 32, 256).

If the user is familiar with the descriptors that are being used, the interface may offer the choice of a subset of features at query time. The user may then use only color descriptors in one search and texture descriptors in another one, for instance.

Searching by different components of the feature space often implies using different metrics for each component. Aggregation is required in this case and it may be done in different ways, such as using arithmetic aggregation functions.

The user may want to stress the relevance of some features, and in this case weights can be used.

The query may be specified as a composition of various objects. This happens, for example, when relevance feedback is used and the user selects multiple objects as positive/negative examples after some exploratory search.

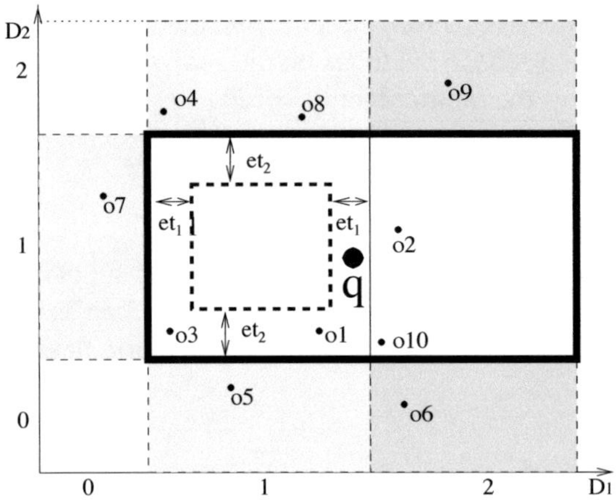

	D1			D2			Cardinalities	
	0	1	2	0	1	2	Naive	Exp
o1		1			1		2	2
o2			1		1		1	2
o3		1			1		2	2
o4		1				1	1	1
o5		1		1			1	1
o6			1	1			0	1
o7	1				1		1	1
o8		1				1	1	1
o9			1			1	0	1
o10			1		1		1	2
q_{Naive}		1			1			
q_{Exp}		1	1		1			

Fig. 7. BitMatrix

5. BitMatrix-based multidimensional indexing

In this section the focus is also maintained on high-dimensional indexing by presenting an indexing approach, BitMatrix, Calistru et al. (2006) that satisfies most of the requirements previously identified, and has been successfully applied in video retrieval.

The main idea behind the BitMatrix is to construct a collection of bitmap signatures that can be sequentially analyzed and processed with bitwise operations in order to prune the search space. Following a data approximation approach, in the spirit of VA-File Weber et al. (1998) and IGrid Aggarwal & Yu (2000), each of the N dimensions are partitioned in k ranges. A partition of a dimension D is a set of ranges

$$\pi_D = \{r_i = [l_i, u_i], i = 1 \ldots k_D\},$$

where l_i, u_i are the lower and upper bounds of range i. The partitioning scheme $(k_1, k_2, \ldots, k_N)$ is used to obtain bitmap signatures for all the objects in a dataset $\mathcal{O}$ arranged as lines in a matrix. For each dimension the signatures contain 1 for the range where the object belongs and 0 for the other ranges. The search algorithm selects objects based on the cardinality (number of bits set to 1) of the bitwise AND between object and query signatures. Only the objects that obtain scores above an established cardinality threshold are then exhaustively analyzed to compute their exact distance. Figure 7 illustrates a two-dimensional space having each dimension partitioned in three ranges. The 10 objects in Figure 7 have their signatures arranged in a BitMatrix; for simplicity, we ignore the zeros. For a given query object q, with signature q_{Naive}, the cardinality column *Naive* contains the results of the bitwise AND between each of the 10 object signatures and q_{Naive}. In this example, if the cardinality threshold is set to 2, the search algorithm prunes object o_2, which happens to be the nearest neighbor. This happens because, for all the dimensions, only the objects in the same range as q are considered. However, this effect can be controlled by using modified query regions (expansions) and various cardinality thresholds. Expanding the query region along dimension D_1 corresponds to a change in the query signature from q_{Naive} to q_{Exp}. The cardinality column *Exp* contains the results of the bitwise AND between the 10 object signatures and q_{Exp}. With the same cardinality threshold, i.e. 2, o_2 becomes part of the selected objects. In general, the variations in query signature and cardinality threshold control the trade-off between precision and speed.

5.1 The BitMatrix and the retrieval requirements

The BitMatrix index and the associated similarity search methods are proposed to solve the common requirements in multimedia retrieval.

5.1.0.2 Multiple query objects

The proposed method easily supports multiple query objects. This is a common requirement in multimedia retrieval in general, and in particular for supporting relevance feedback search iterations. The independent object signatures are merged into a common query signature which is used in the sequel to search the BitMatrix.

5.1.0.3 Subspace selection

The importance of each individual dimension of the search space has already been examined in works like BOND Arjen et al. (2002) and LDC Koudas et al. (2004). Similarly, the BitMatrix search algorithm can be applied on selected subspaces. The subspace selection feature is useful for speeding up the search in at least two situations. First, when the dimensions of the original search space are not of equal importance. They may be ordered by decreasing importance and only a first subset of them used in the search. The second situation arises when enough objects have been pruned after analyzing only some of the subspaces. The analysis of the remaining subspaces can thus be avoided and the search can stop earlier.

5.1.0.4 Index management: insert, update, delete

The insertion of a new object in the BitMatrix, accounts for computing its signature and adding it as a new line in the matrix. The size of the BitMatrix grows linearly with the number of objects and with the dimensionality. The precise size of the BitMatrix is $(\Sigma_{D=1}^{N} k_D) * |\mathcal{O}|$ bits. To update an existing object its signature has to be modified through bitwise operations. To delete an object, the corresponding line is removed from the matrix.

The BitMatrix index retains most of sequential scan's flexibility with good quality of the approximations and a much better time performance. It can be conveniently arranged for efficient sequential access and optimized bitwise operations. It can also be broken into segments for distributed or parallel processing.

5.2 Evaluation of the BitMatrix method

The BitMatrix evaluation has been performed on two datasets: a set of 9908 real image histograms having 256 dimensions, named the i9000 dataset, and a synthetic dataset, i10000, of 10000 objects independent and identically-distributed in all of its 80 dimensions. The dimensions partitioning strategy for both datasets was 7 ranges per dimension, where the range computation is based on k-means clustering ($k = 7$).

5.2.1 Recall performance

The experiments were geared towards observing the BitMatrix performance for nearest neighbor search ($NN(q)$) and k-nearest neighbors search ($NN_k(q)$). To illustrate the $NN_k(q)$

	i9000 256 dimensions, 7 ranges/dimension							
	$NN(q)$				$NN_{10}(q)$			
ct	Naive(et=0)		**et=0,01**		Naive(et=0)		**et=0,01**	
	Recall	accessed	Recall	accessed	Recall	accessed	Recall	accessed
0.73	0.6	0.2%	0.7	0.4%	0.39	0.2%	0.48	0.4%
0.67	0.78	0.8%	0.87	1.0%	0.61	0.8%	0.68	1.0%
0.55	0.93	2.9%	0.95	3.8%	0.86	2.9%	0.9	3.8%
0.47	**0.97**	**6.0%**	**0.99**	**7.4%**	**0.91**	**6.0%**	**0.94**	**7.4%**
0.40	**1.0**	**10.9%**	**1.0**	**13.5%**	**0.93**	**10.9%**	**0.96**	**13.5%**
	i10000 80 dimensions, 7 ranges/dimension							
	$NN(q)$				$NN_{10}(q)$			
	Naive (et=0)		**et=0,01**		Naive (et=0)		**et=0,01**	
0.60	0.24	0.19%	0.25	0.21%	0.08	0.19%	0.09	0.21%
0.50	0.55	1.99%	0.57	2.31%	0.33	1.99%	0.35	2.31%
0.40	0.78	8.16%	0.84	9.32%	0.57	8.16%	0.62	9.32%
0.35	0.90	17.0%	0.93	19.2%	0.77	17.0%	0.80	19.2%
0.30	0.90	32.2%	0.94	34.21%	0.85	32.2%	0.87	34.21%

Table 1. Testing the BitMatrix on two datasets

search performance, we compare the approximate BitMatrix results with the exact *k-nearest neighbors*. We use the recall rate for this purpose. Assuming R as the $NN_k(q)$ set and A as the set of approximate neighbors obtained with the BitMatrix, the recall rate is

$$\frac{|A \cap R|}{|R|}.$$

Beside the recall rate scores, we also record the percentage of objects that are effectively accessed, i.e that remain after the pruning phase. This is expressed as the ratio of $|A|$ to the size of the dataset: $\frac{|A|}{sizeofdataset}$.

Table 1 shows average values for the two measures (recall rate, and % of objects accessed) with respect to $NN(q)$ and $NN_{10}(q)$ across random sets of 100 queries. The cardinality thresholds are in the first column. With a cardinality threshold of 0.55 for instance, less than 3% of i9000 is accessed, the average recall rate is 0.93 (relative to NN) and 0.86 (relative to NN_{10}). The experiments have shown that the trade-off between quality of retrieval and speed can be tuned with the available expansion mechanism. For example, with the cardinality threshold 0.47, about 6% of i9000 is accessed, and the recall rate relative to NN_{10} is 0.91. If range expansion is performed the NN_{10} recall becomes 0.94 at 7.4% accessed objects, while for a smaller cardinality threshold (ct = 0.4) the NN_{10} recall is 0.93 at 10.9% accessed objects. With an increase in recall (0.94 vs 0.93) and less 3.5% (7.4% vs 10.9%) objects accessed, expansion should be preferred in this case.

The results for the second dataset, i10000, are presented in the second half of Table 1. The numbers indicate lower performance than on i9000. Much larger amounts of the i10000 have to be analyzed in order to obtain acceptable recall rates. Note however that i10000 is a synthetic dataset independent and identically-distributed (uniform distribution) across all the dimensions, thus not a realistic one. The expansion mechanism clearly improves the recall rate in this case as well.

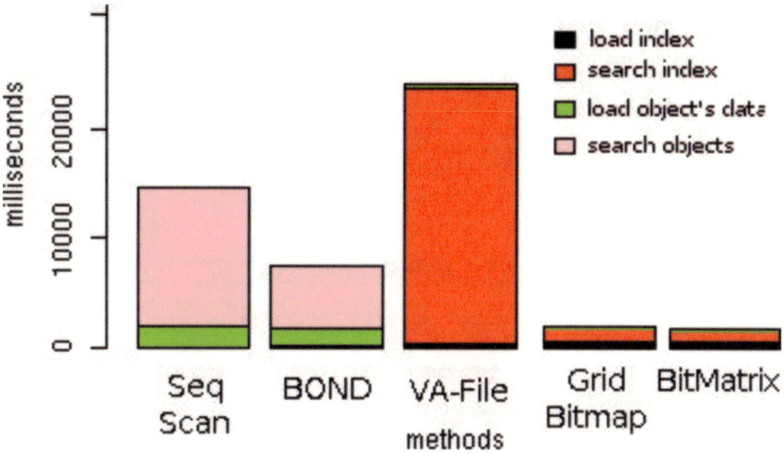

Fig. 8. Comparing methods that use the euclidean metric

5.2.2 Time performance

Another set of experiments have been designed to observe the time performance of the BitMatrix as a memory-based indexing method. A specific framework for high-dimensional indexing evaluation has been used Gonçalves et al. (2007), and the experiments were run on i9000 dataset. The MMDI allowed us to test a set of 5 methods: Sequential Scan, Bond, VA-File, GridBitmap, and BitMatrix. The time columns in Figure 8 have four components: the time to load the index in memory (if such an index exists), the time to search it, the time to load objects data, and the time to search them. The total time for the BitMatrix is clearly smaller than the values for Sequential Scan and Bond and is in the same range as the GridBitmap. The VA-file's time is not favorable to the method as it is tested using the same partitioning scheme as GridBitmap and BitMatrix; with 7 ranges in each of the 256 dimensions, there are 7^{256} approximation cells, with the non-empty ones having at most one object. Thus, VA-file has to access much more cells than real objects.

BitMatrix has been also evaluated in an independent multimedia retrieval test Acar et al. (2008), where it has been shown to outperform a slim-tree index.

6. BitMatrix-based video retrieval—A case study

In this section we report on the implementation of a BitMatrix-based video retrieval system. The experiments have been performed on the TRECVID 2007 dataset, which consists of 100 hours of videos from the BBC and the Danish national television.

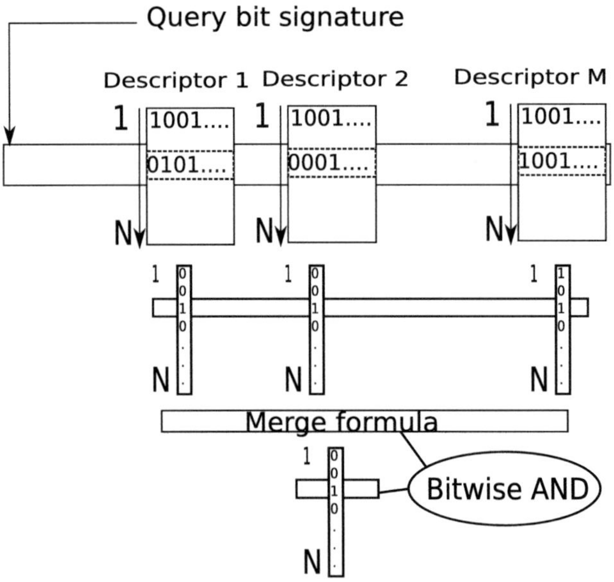

Fig. 9. Answer computation

6.1 Features and descriptors

This case study integrates the whole range of available descriptors, from low- to high-level ones. The list of low-level descriptors includes ColorLayout, ColorStructure, ScalableColor and ColorMoments for color, EdgeHistogram, Homogeneous Texture, Wavelet texture and Haralick for texture, RegionShape for shape, Scale Invariant Feature Transform Lowe (2003) (for interest points, Spectral Centroid, Spectral Rollof Point, Spectral Flux, Compactness, Spectral Variability, Root Mean Square, Fraction of Low Energy Windows, Zero Crossings, Strongest Beat, Beat Sum, Strength of Strongest Beat, Mel Frequency Cepstral Coefficient, Linear Predictive Coding and Area Method of Moments for audio.

The high-level features, such as the concepts automatically obtained with special detectors Jiang et al. (2007) have been used to create a high-level descriptor, named the "Concepts" descriptor. The "Concepts" descriptor construction is based on a 39-dimensional concept space —a vector space where each concept is a dimension. The concept space $C^n = \{c_1, c_2, .., c_n\}$, where c_i is a dimension corresponding to the ith concept and n is the total number of concepts. Each of the annotated objects can be represented as a vector: $(v_1, v_2, .., v_n)$, where each v_i represents the value for the ith conceptual dimension.

With this representation, the "Concepts" descriptor can be indexed with multidimensional techniques. This allows the use the BitMatrix for the entire range of low and high-level descriptors.

6.2 Indexing and search

The indexing strategy has been to build descriptor-wise BitMatrix indexes off-line. This allows an independent analysis of several similarity facets and an experimental evaluation of the contribution of each descriptor to the retrieval tasks. The answer of a query-by-example

Fig. 10. Color-based results

with respect to the color feature, for example, can be obtained with several color descriptors, each one showing a different facet of color similarity. Their usefulness for the search topics is evaluated empirically.

The overall search process fits into the query-by-example paradigm, where the answer computation is performed with respect to a combination of descriptors. Note however, that when the "Concepts" descriptor is included in the combination , the search paradigm becomes a combination of a typical query-by-example and a query-by-semantic-example Rasiwasia et al. (2006). For example, the search can start with an image or video shot of a natural scene and expect similar video items with respect to the ColorLayout, ColorStructure (color), EdgeHistogram (texture), and "Concepts" descriptors.

Starting with a set of example objects, the first step is to translate their feature vectors into a bit signature and then pass it to the BitMatrix-based answer computation step, as illustrated in Figure 9. In the sequel, several binary lists, one for each selected descriptor, are obtained by searching the corresponding BitMatrix indexes. We refer to these lists as binary lists because, as shown in Section 5, the objects that obtain scores above an established cardinality threshold are marked with 1, while the others are marked with 0.

Finally, the binary lists are aggregated with merge formulas. For example, a merge formula may count the number of binary lists in which each object appears; weights can also be assigned to each list. Figure 9 illustrates a merge formula that performs a bitwise AND between corresponding positions of each binary list. As all have their third positions set to 1,

Fig. 11. "Concepts" and audio-based results

the bitwise AND yields a 1 in the final result set, meaning that the third object will be among the retrieved objects.

Note that instead of constructing binary lists, the object cardinalities, or even their exact distances to the query objects can be recorded. In such a case, the lists aggregation can be achieved by implementing rank-aggregation approaches, such as Fagin et al. (2003) and Güntzer et al. (2000). The preference for binary lists is motivated by the lack of distinctiveness between the scores of the nearest neighbors in high-dimensional spaces Katayama & Satoh (2001). Moreover such binary lists can be aggregated with bitwise operations, which improves the overall efficiency.

6.3 Parametrization

The cardinality thresholds used to obtain the binary lists were empirically determined by performing several query-by-example iterations per descriptor. If high thresholds are used, few objects are returned, while the use of small thresholds allows too many objects to appear in the answer set. Cardinality thresholds were considered acceptable when allowing a number of objects in the 500-700 range—an appropriate number of objects to be visually inspected in a user interface.

The merge formula for the binary list aggregation has been the bitwise AND, which can be efficiently computed with bitwise operations and sequential access.

Fig. 12. Texture-based results

6.4 Search results

Search experiments were performed on top of the TRECVID 2007 dataset, containing educational, cultural and youth-oriented programs, news magazines and historical footage videos. Beside the great variety of subject matter, the video material has been primarily in Dutch, without repetitive parts such as commercials, or repeated news footage.

While the TRECVID community is mainly focused on benchmarking the effectiveness of video retrieval, the goal here was to tackle the retrieval problem from both effectiveness and efficiency aspects.

Figures 10, 11 and 12 show several result sets consisting of video shots from the TRECVID 2007 dataset. Figure 10 shows the results of a color-based query-by-example; all the color descriptors enumerated in Section 6.1 are involved. Figure 11 shows the results for the "Find shots of a people walking or riding a bicycle" query; the search started with video samples of people walking or riding bicycles and involved the "Concepts" and all the audio descriptors. Figure 12 shows the results of a texture-based query-by-example search; the query image is the one in the upper left corner of Figure 12 and the answer was obtained using all the texture descriptors mentioned earlier: Edge Histogram, Haralick texture, Homogeneous Texture, Region Shape, and Wavelet Texture.

The quality of the retrieval is evaluated by calculating average precision results. Four components are typically required: a fixed number of multimedia objects to be searched on, a fixed number of topics from which the queries will be chosen, an evaluation criteria such as

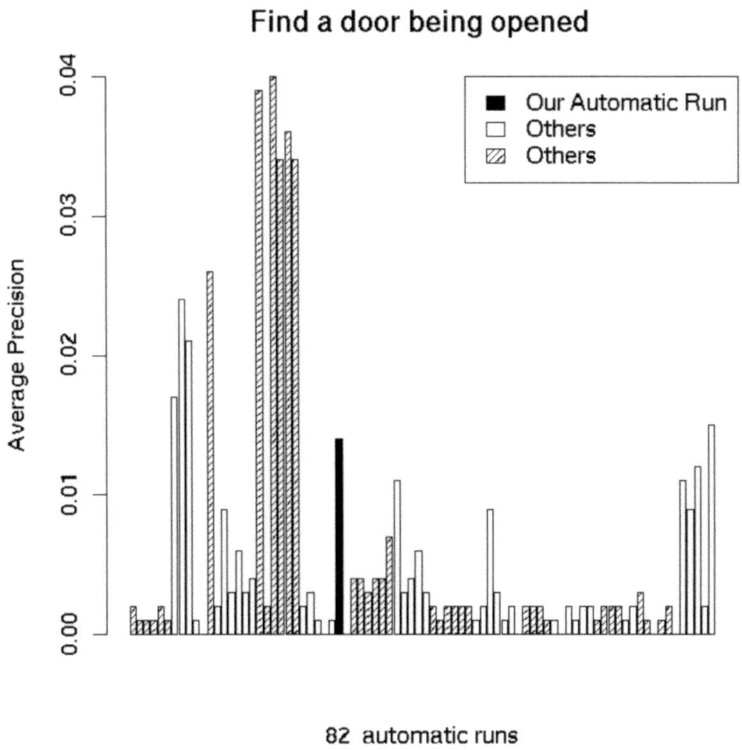

Fig. 13. Average precision results

the precision/recall measure, and the relevance judgments or ground truth; TRECVID offered them all. The average precision was measured per-topic, based on the positions of the relevant documents. The precision is measured at every rank at which a relevant document is obtained and then averaged over all relevant documents to obtain the average precision:

$$AP = \frac{\sum_{r=1}^{N} P(r) \times relevant(r)}{size\,of\,ground\,truth}.$$

r is the rank, N is the number of retrieved documents, $relevant()$ is a binary function on the relevance at a given rank, and $P()$ is the precision at that rank. Figures 13 and 14 illustrate the average precision results obtained for two topics, namely "Find shots of a door being opened" and "Find shots of a waterfront with water and buildings".

Overall, the precision results indicate that our retrieval system's effectivity was comparable to the others. However, by indexing the whole spectrum of descriptors with the same index type—the BitMatrix—we have been able to speed up the query computation, making a step further towards a database-ready retrieval system.

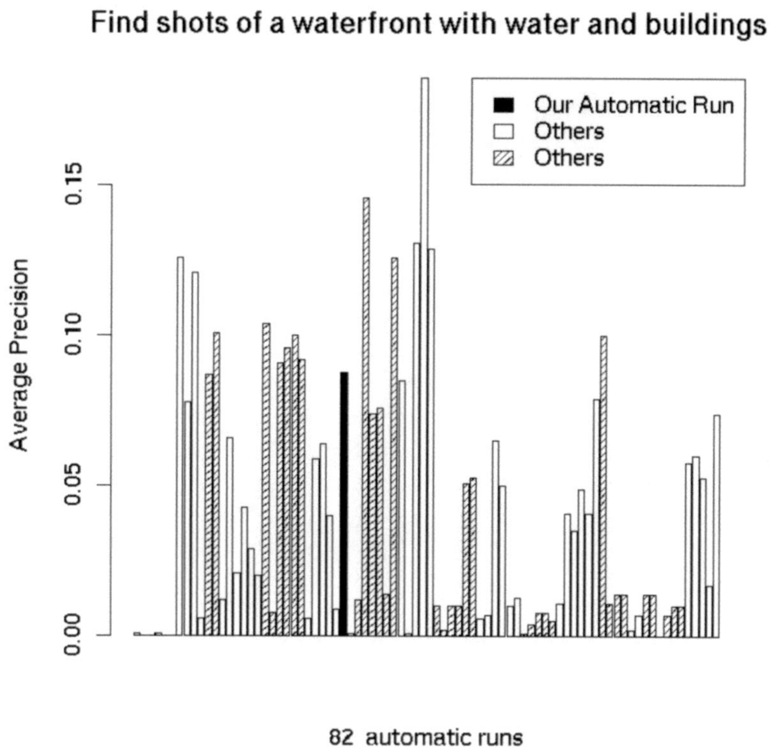

Fig. 14. Average precision results

7. Summary

Representing, managing and retrieving video data is required in a wide range of application domains. Current tools for video analysis are time consuming and can be very time consuming on large datasets. With the growth of multimedia mass production we must shift from simple collection paradigms to well-organized multimedia repositories.

Existing multidimensional indexing methods are not yet prepared for the variety of features and similarity models in multimedia objects. In order to work with as many feature representations and similarity models as possible, the high-dimensional indexing techniques should at least be able to access individual dimensions, should easily incorporate new objects as well as new sets of dimensions. Flexible ranking mechanisms that capture user preferences are also an important requirement.

The indexing structure that we have presented, the BitMatrix, is a highly parameterizable index structure offering a large space for experimentation: similarity threshold, number of dimensions processed in each step, and dimension processing order for the case of weighted dimensions. It also supports multiple query objects at a time, which is especially useful for relevance feedback. The BitMatrix index retains most of sequential scan's flexibility with good quality of the approximations and a much better time performance. It can be conveniently arranged for efficient sequential access and optimized bitwise operations. It can also be broken into segments for distributed or parallel processing.

However, when application requirements are not that tough, other type of indexing methods may be appropriate. For example, if a specific metric is established, or when the significance of individual dimensions can be lost, metric-based access methods, such as LSH Datar et al. (2004) or iDistance Jagadish et al. (2005) can be used. As we have stated in Section 4.6, a given indexing approach could behave better in some situations than others.

The proposed BitMatrix index is expected to adapt well to the distributed and parallel paradigms, allowing its use in software frameworks for parallel computations over large data sets, such as "MapReduce" Dean & Ghemawat (2008). MapReduce allows to split an application among a set of machines by dividing the job into Map and Reduce parts. The BitMatrix search algorithm can have a Map phase, taking the initial bit matrix, splitting it into smaller bit matrices, and sending the parts to different machines—so all would be searched at the same time. The Reduce phase will then combine the partial results to get a single answer set. This approach will allow larger amounts of high-dimensional data to be efficiently searched, in a scalable manner.

8. References

Acar, E., Arslan, S., Yazici, A. & Koyuncu, M. (2008). Slim-tree and BitMatrix index structures in image retrieval system using MPEG-7 Descriptors, *Content-Based Multimedia Indexing, 2008. CBMI 2008. International Workshop on* pp. 402–409.

Aggarwal, C. C. (2002). Towards meaningful high-dimensional nearest neighbor search by human-computer interaction, *Data Engineering, 2002. Proceedings. 18th International Conference on*, pp. 593–604.

Aggarwal, C. C., Hinneburg, A. & Keim, D. A. (2001). On the surprising behavior of distance metrics in high dimensional space, *Lecture Notes in Computer Science* 1973: 420–434. URL: *citeseer.ist.psu.edu/aggarwal01surprising.html*

Aggarwal, C. C., Wolf, J. L. & Yu, P. S. (1999). A new method for similarity indexing of market basket data, *SIGMOD '99: Proceedings of the 1999 ACM SIGMOD international conference on Management of data*, ACM Press, New York, NY, USA, pp. 407–418.

Aggarwal, C. C. & Yu, P. S. (2000). The IGrid index: reversing the dimensionality curse for similarity indexing in high dimensional space, *KDD '00: Proceedings of the sixth ACM SIGKDD international conference on Knowledge discovery and data mining*, ACM Press, New York, NY, USA, pp. 119–129.

Aref, W. G. & Ilyas, I. F. (2001). SP-GiST: An Extensible Database Index for Supporting Space Partitioning Trees, *J. Intell. Inf. Syst.* 17(2-3): 215–240.

Arjen, P. d. V., Mamoulis, N., Nes, N. & Kersten, M. (2002). Efficient k-NN search on vertically decomposed data, *SIGMOD '02: Proceedings of the 2002 ACM SIGMOD international conference on Management of data*, ACM Press, pp. 322–333.

Arya, S., Mount, D. M., Netanyahu, N. S., Silverman, R. & Wu, A. Y. (1998). An optimal algorithm for approximate nearest neighbor searching fixed dimensions, *J. ACM* 45(6): 891–923.

Balke, W.-T. & Güntzer, U. (2004). Multi-objective query processing for database systems., *VLDB*, pp. 936–947.

Bartolini, I. & Ciaccia, P. (2005). Optimal incremental evaluation of preference queries based on ranked sub-queries., *SEBD*, pp. 308–315.

Bartolini, I., Ciaccia, P., Oria, V. & Özsu, M. T. (2005). Integrating the results of multimedia sub-queries using qualitative preferences, *SEBD*, pp. 308–315.

Bayer, R. & McCreight, E. M. (1972). Organization and maintenance of large ordered indices, *Acta Informatica.* 1: 173–189.

Beckmann, N., Kriegel, H.-P., Schneider, R. & Seeger, B. (1990). The r*-tree: an efficient and robust access method for points and rectangles, *SIGMOD Rec.* 19(2): 322–331.

Benitez, A. B. & Chang, S.-F. (2002). Multimedia knowledge integration, summarization and evaluation., *MDM/KDD*, pp. 39–50.

Berchtold, S., Keim, D. A. & Kriegel, H.-P. (1996). The X-tree: An index structure for high-dimensional data, *in* T. M. Vijayaraman, A. P. Buchmann, C. Mohan & N. L. Sarda (eds), *Proceedings of the 22nd International Conference on Very Large Databases*, Morgan Kaufmann Publishers, San Francisco, U.S.A., pp. 28–39.
URL: *citeseer.ist.psu.edu/berchtold96xtree.html*

Beyer, K., Goldstein, J., Ramakrishnan, R. & Shaft, U. (1999). When Is "Nearest Neighbor" Meaningful?, *Lecture Notes in Computer Science* 1540: 217–235.
URL: *citeseer.ist.psu.edu/article/beyer99when.html*

Bober, M. (Jun 2001). Mpeg-7 visual shape descriptors, *Circuits and Systems for Video Technology, IEEE Transactions on* 11(6): 716–719.

Böhm, C., Berchtold, S. & Keim, D. A. (2001). Searching in high-dimensional spaces: Index structures for improving the performance of multimedia databases, *ACM Comput. Surv.* 33(3): 322–373.

Bohm, C., Gruber, M., Kunath, P., Pryakhin, A. & Schubert, M. (2007). Prover: Probabilistic video retrieval using the gauss-tree, *Data Engineering, International Conference on* 0: 1521–1522.

Böhm, C., Kriegel, H.-P. & Seidl, T. (2001). Adaptable similarity search using vector quantization, *DaWaK '01: Proceedings of the Third International Conference on Data Warehousing and Knowledge Discovery*, Springer-Verlag, London, UK, pp. 317–327.

Börzsönyi, S., Kossmann, D. & Stocker, K. (2001). The skyline operator, *Proceedings of the 17th International Conference on Data Engineering*, IEEE Computer Society, Washington, DC, USA, pp. 421–430.

Bozkaya, T. & Ozsoyoglu, M. (1999). Indexing large metric spaces for similarity search queries, *ACM Trans. Database Syst.* 24(3): 361–404.

Bulterman, D. C. A. (2004). Is It Time for a Moratorium on Metadata?, *IEEE Multimedia* 11(4): 10–17.

Burghouts, G. J. & Geusebroek, J.-M. (2009). Performance evaluation of local colour invariants, *Comput. Vis. Image Underst.* 113(1): 48–62.

Calistru, C., Ribeiro, C. & David, G. (2006). Multidimensional Descriptor Indexing: Exploring the BitMatrix., *in* Sundaram et al. (2006), pp. 401–410.

Carson, C., Thomas, M., Belongie, S., Hellerstein, J. M. & Malik, J. (1999). Blobworld: A system for region-based image indexing and retrieval, *Third International Conference on Visual Information Systems*, Springer.
URL: *citeseer.ist.psu.edu/carson99blobworld.html*

Celma, Ò. & Serra, X. (2008). Foafing the music: Bridging the semantic gap in music recommendation, *J. Web Sem.* 6(4): 250–256.

Cha, G.-H. (2003). Bitmap indexing method for complex similarity queries with relevance feedback, *MMDB '03: Proceedings of the 1st ACM international workshop on Multimedia databases*, ACM Press, New York, NY, USA, pp. 55–62.

Chaudhuri, S., Ramakrishnan, R. & Weikum, G. (2005). Integrating db and ir technologies: What is the sound of one hand clapping?, *CIDR*, pp. 1–12.

Chávez, E., Navarro, G., Baeza-Yates, R. & Marroquín, J. L. (2001). Searching in metric spaces, *ACM Comput. Surv.* 33(3): 273–321.

Chomicki, J. (2002). Querying with Intrinsic Preferences, *EDBT '02: Proceedings of the 8th International Conference on Extending Database Technology*, Springer-Verlag, London, UK, pp. 34–51.

Chomicki, J. (2003). Preference formulas in relational queries, *ACM Trans. Database Syst.* 28(4): 427–466.

Ciaccia, P. & Patella, M. (2002). Searching in metric spaces with user-defined and approximate distances, *ACM Trans. Database Syst.* 27(4): 398–437.

Ciaccia, P., Patella, M. & Zezula, P. (1997). M-tree: An efficient access method for similarity search in metric spaces, *VLDB '97: Proceedings of the 23rd International Conference on Very Large Data Bases*, Morgan Kaufmann Publishers Inc., pp. 426–435.

Datar, M., Immorlica, N., Indyk, P. & Mirrokni, V. S. (2004). Locality-sensitive hashing scheme based on p-stable distributions, *SCG '04: Proceedings of the twentieth annual symposium on Computational geometry*, ACM Press, New York, NY, USA, pp. 253–262.

Datta, R., Joshi, D., Li, J. & Wang, J. Z. (2008). Image retrieval: Ideas, influences, and trends of the new age, *ACM Computing Surveys* to appear: to appear.
URL: *http://infolab.stanford.edu/ wangz/project/imsearch/review/JOUR/datta.pdf*

Dean, J. & Ghemawat, S. (2008). Mapreduce: simplified data processing on large clusters, *Commun. ACM* 51(1): 107–113.

den Bercken, J. V., Blohsfeld, B., Dittrich, J.-P., Krämer, J., Schäfer, T., Schneider, M. & Seeger, B. (2001). XXL - A Library Approach to Supporting Efficient Implementations of Advanced Database Queries, *VLDB '01: Proceedings of the 27th International Conference on Very Large Data Bases*, Morgan Kaufmann Publishers Inc., San Francisco, CA, USA, pp. 39–48.

Deselaers, T., Keysers, D. & Ney, H. (2004). Features for image retrieval – a quantitative comparison, *DAGM 2004, Pattern Recognition, 26th DAGM Symposium*, LNCS, Tbingen, Germany.
URL: *citeseer.ist.psu.edu/deselaers04features.html*

Digout, C. & Nascimento, M. A. (2005). High-dimensional similarity searches using a metric pseudo-grid., *ICDE Workshops 1174*.

Dimitrova, N. (2004). Context and memory in multimedia content analysis, *IEEE MultiMedia* 11(3): 7–11.

Eidenberger, H. (2003). Distance measures for MPEG-7-based retrieval, *MIR '03: Proceedings of the 5th ACM SIGMM international workshop on Multimedia information retrieval*, ACM Press, New York, NY, USA, pp. 130–137.

Eidenberger, H. & Breiteneder, C. (2003). Visual similarity measurement with the feature contrast model, *in* M. M. Yeung, R. W. Lienhart & C.-S. Li (eds), *Proceedings SPIE Storage and Retrieval for Media Databases Conference*, Vol. 5021, SPIE, pp. 64–76.

Eidenberger, H.; Breiteneder, C. (9-11 Dec. 2002). An experimental study on the performance of visual information retrieval similarity models, *Multimedia Signal Processing, 2002 IEEE Workshop on* pp. 233–236.

Ekin, A., Tekalp, A. M. & Mehrotra, R. (2004). Integrated Semantic-Syntactic Video Modeling for Search and Browsing, *IEEE Transactions on Multimedia* 6(6): 839–851.

Fagin, R., Kumar, R. & Sivakumar, D. (2003). Efficient similarity search and classification via rank aggregation, *SIGMOD '03: Proceedings of the 2003 ACM SIGMOD international conference on Management of data*, ACM Press, New York, NY, USA, pp. 301–312.

Faloutsos, C. & Oard, D. W. (1995). A survey of information retrieval and filtering methods, *Technical report*, Univ. of Maryland Institute for Advanced Computer Studies Report, College Park, MD, USA.

Fayyad, U. M. & Irani, K. B. (1992). On the handling of continuous-valued attributes in decision tree generation, *Mach. Learn.* 8(1): 87–102.

Flickner, M., Sawhney, H., Niblack, W., Ashley, J., Huang, Q., Dom, B., Gorkani, M., Hafner, J., Lee, D., Petkovic, D., Steele, D. & Yanker, P. (1995). Query by Image and Video Content: The QBIC System, *IEEE Computer* 28(9): 23–32.

Gentner, D. (1988). Structure-mapping: A theoretical framework for analogy, *in* A. Collins & E. E. Smith (eds), *Readings in Cognitive Science: A Perspective from Psychology and Artificial Intelligence*, Kaufmann, San Mateo, CA, pp. 303–310.

Gevers, T. & Smeulders, A. W. M. (2004). *Content-Based Image Retrieval: An Overview*, IMSC Press Multimedia Series, 1st edn, Prentice Hall.

Godfrey, P., Shipley, R. & Gryz, J. (2005). Maximal vector computation in large data sets, *VLDB '05: Proceedings of the 31st international conference on Very large data bases*, VLDB Endowment, pp. 229–240.

Goldstein, J., Platt, J. C. & Burges, C. J. C. (2004). Redundant Bit Vectors for Quickly Searching High-Dimensional Regions., *Deterministic and Statistical Methods in Machine Learning*, pp. 137–158.

Gonçalves, B., Calistru, C., Ribeiro, C. & David, G. (2007). An Evaluation Framework for Multidimensional Multimedia Descriptor Indexing, *Workshop on Multimedia Databases and Data Management*.

Gudivada, V. N. & Raghavan, V. V. (1995). Content-based image retrieval systems, *Computer* 28(9): 18–22.

Güntzer, U., Balke, W.-T. & Kießling, W. (2000). Optimizing multi-feature queries for image databases, *in* A. E. Abbadi, M. L. Brodie, S. Chakravarthy, U. Dayal, N. Kamel, G. Schlageter & K.-Y. Whang (eds), *VLDB 2000, Proceedings of 26th International Conference on Very Large Data Bases, September 10-14, 2000, Cairo, Egypt*, Morgan Kaufmann, pp. 419–428.

Hanjalic, A. (2006). Extracting moods from pictures and sounds: towards truly personalized tv, *Signal Processing Magazine, IEEE* 23(2): 90–100.
URL: *http://ieeexplore.ieee.org/xpls/abs_all.jsp?arnumber=1621452*

Hauptmann, A., Yan, R. & Lin, W.-H. (2007). How many high-level concepts will fill the semantic gap in news video retrieval?, *CIVR '07: Proceedings of the 6th ACM international conference on Image and video retrieval*, ACM, New York, NY, USA, pp. 627–634.

Hellerstein, J. M., Naughton, J. F. & Pfeffer, A. (1995). Generalized search trees for database systems., *VLDB*, pp. 562–573.

Hjaltason, G. R. & Samet, H. (2003). Index-driven similarity search in metric spaces, *ACM Trans. Database Syst.* 28(4): 517–580.

Howarth, P. & Rüger, S. (2005a). *Image and Video Retrieval*, Vol. http://www.springerlink.com/content/eq86j0456l73ax78, Springer Berlin / Heidelberg, chapter Trading Precision for Speed: Localised Similarity Functions, pp. 415–424.

Howarth, P. & Rüger, S. M. (2005b). Fractional distance measures for content-based image retrieval, *ECIR*, pp. 447–456.

H.R.Turtle (1991). *Inference Networks for Document Retrieval*, PhD thesis, University of Massachusetts.
URL: *citeseer.ist.psu.edu/turtle91inference.html*

Huijbregts, M., Ordelman, R. & de Jong, F. (2007). Annotation of heterogeneous multimedia content using automatic speech recognition, *Proceedings of the second international conference on Semantics And digital Media Technologies (SAMT)*, Lecture Notes in Computer Science, Springer Verlag, Berlin.

IBM (2008). Marvel: Multimedia Analysis and Retrieval, http://mp7.watson.ibm.com/marvel/.

Indyk, P. & Motwani, R. (1998). Approximate nearest neighbors: towards removing the curse of dimensionality, *Proc. of 30th STOC*, pp. 604–613.
URL: *citeseer.ist.psu.edu/article/indyk98approximate.html*

Ishikawa, Y., Subramanya, R. & Faloutsos, C. (1998). Mindreader: Querying databases through multiple examples, *VLDB '98: Proceedings of the 24rd International Conference on Very Large Data Bases*, Morgan Kaufmann Publishers Inc., San Francisco, CA, USA, pp. 218–227.

Jagadish, H. V., Ooi, B. C., Tan, K.-L., Yu, C. & Zhang, R. (2005). iDistance: An adaptive B+-tree based indexing method for nearest neighbor search, *ACM Trans. Database Syst.* 30(2): 364–397.

Jagadish, H.V. and Beng Chin Ooi and Heng Tao Shen and Kian-Lee Tan (2006). Toward Efficient Multifeature Query Processing, *Knowledge and Data Engineering, IEEE Transactions on* 18(03): 350–362.

Jiang, W., Chan, K. L., Li, M. & Zhang, H. (2005). Mapping low-level features to high-level semantic concepts in region-based image retrieval, *CVPR '05: Proceedings of the 2005 IEEE Computer Society Conference on Computer Vision and Pattern Recognition (CVPR'05) - Volume 2*, IEEE Computer Society, Washington, DC, USA, pp. 244–249.

Jiang, Y.-G., Ngo, C.-W. & Yang, J. (2007). Towards optimal bag-of-features for object categorization and semantic video retrieval., *in* N. Sebe & M. Worring (eds), *CIVR*, ACM, pp. 494–501.
URL: *http://dblp.uni-trier.de/db/conf/civr/civr2007.html#JiangNY07*

Jolliffe, I. T. (1986). *Principal component analysis*, Springer-Verlag.

Katayama, N. & Satoh, S. (2001). Distinctiveness-Sensitive Nearest Neighbor Search for Efficient Similarity Retrieval of Multimedia Information, *Proceedings of the 17th International Conference on Data Engineering*, IEEE Computer Society, Washington, DC, USA, pp. 493–502.

Kemp, C., Bernstein, A. & Tenenbaum, J. B. (2005). A generative theory of similarity, *The Twenty-Seventh Annual Conference of the Cognitive Science Society*.

Kherfi, M. L., Ziou, D. & Bernardi, A. (2004). Image retrieval from the world wide web: Issues, techniques, and systems, *ACM Comput. Surv.* 36(1): 35–67.

Kosch, H., Boszormenyi, L., Doller, M., Libsie, M., Schojer, P. & Kofler, A. (2005). The Life Cycle of Multimedia Metadata, *IEEE Multimedia* 12(1): 80–86.

Koudas, N., Ooi, B. C., Shen, H. T. & Tung, A. K. H. (2004). Ldc: Enabling search by partial distance in a hyper-dimensional space, *ICDE '04: Proceedings of the 20th International Conference on Data Engineering*, IEEE Computer Society, Washington, DC, USA, p. 6.

Kraaij, W. (2005). Variations on language modeling for information retrieval, *SIGIR Forum* 39(1): 61.

Larson, R. R., McDonough, J., O'Leary, P., Kuntz, L. & Moon, R. (1996). Cheshire II: designing a next-generation online catalog, *J. Am. Soc. Inf. Sci.* 47(7): 555–567.

Leubner, A. & Kießling, W. (2002). Personalized keyword search with partial-order preferences., *SBBD*, pp. 181–193.

Li, H., Shi, R., Chen, W. & Shen, I. (2006). Image tangent space for image retrieval, *ICPR06*, pp. II: 1126–1130.

Liao, S., Lopez, M. A. & Leutenegger, S. T. (2001). High dimensional similarity search with space filling curves, *Proceedings of the 17th International Conference on Data Engineering*, IEEE Computer Society, Washington, DC, USA, pp. 615–622.

Lowe, D. (2003). Distinctive image features from scale-invariant keypoints, *International Journal of Computer Vision*, Vol. 20, pp. 91–110.
URL: *citeseer.ist.psu.edu/lowe04distinctive.html*

Macdonald, C. & Ounis, I. (2006). Searching for expertise using the terrier platform, *SIGIR '06: Proceedings of the 29th annual international ACM SIGIR conference on Research and development in information retrieval*, ACM, New York, NY, USA, pp. 732–732.

Manjunath, B., Ohm, J.-R., Vasudevan, V. & Yamada, A. (2001). Color and texture descriptors, *Circuits and Systems for Video Technology, IEEE Transactions on* 11(6): 703–715.

Mufit Ferman, A., Krishnamachari, S., Murat Tekalp, A., Abdel-Mottaleb, M. & Mehrotra, R. (2000). Group-of-frames/pictures color histogram descriptors for multimedia applications, *Image Processing, 2000. Proceedings. 2000 International Conference on* 1: 65–68 vol.1.

Naphade, M., Smith, J. R., Tesic, J., Chang, S.-F., Hsu, W., Kennedy, L., Hauptmann, A. & Curtis, J. (2006). Large-Scale Concept Ontology for Multimedia, *IEEE MultiMedia* 13(3): 86–91.

Nguyen, P. H. P. & Corbett, D. (2006). A basic mathematical framework for conceptual graphs, *IEEE Transactions on Knowledge and Data Engineering* 18(2): 261–271.

Ooi, B. C., Tan, K.-L., Yu, C. & Bressan, S. (2000). Indexing the edges - a simple and yet efficient approach to high-dimensional indexing, *Proceedings of the Nineteenth ACM SIGMOD-SIGACT-SIGART Symposium on Principles of Database Systems, May 15-17, 2000, Dallas, Texas, USA*, ACM, pp. 166–174.

Papadias, D., Tao, Y., Fu, G. & Seeger, B. (2005). Progressive skyline computation in database systems., *ACM Trans. Database Syst.* 30(1): 41–82.

Pei, J., Jin, W., Ester, M. & Tao, Y. (2005). Catching the best views of skyline: a semantic approach based on decisive subspaces, *VLDB '05: Proceedings of the 31st international conference on Very large data bases*, VLDB Endowment, pp. 253–264.

Ponte, J. M. & Croft, W. B. (1998). A language modeling approach to information retrieval, *SIGIR '98: Proceedings of the 21st annual international ACM SIGIR conference on Research and development in information retrieval*, ACM, New York, NY, USA, pp. 275–281.

Rada, R., Mili, H., Bicknell, E. & Blettner, M. (1989). Development and application of a metric on semantic nets, *Systems, Man and Cybernetics, IEEE Transactions on* 19(1): 17–30.

Rasiwasia, N., Vasconcelos, N. & Moreno, P. J. (2006). Query by semantic example, *in* Sundaram et al. (2006), pp. 51–60.

Raubal, M. (2004). Formalizing conceptual spaces, *FOIS 2004: Proceedings of the Third International Conference*, IOS Press, A. Varzi and L. Vieu. Amsterdam, NL, pp. 153–164.

Rehatschek, H., Schallauer, P., Bailer, W., Haas, W. & Wertner, A. (2004). An innovative system for formulating complex, combined content-based and keyword based queries, *in* S. Santini & R. Schettini (eds), *Proceedings of the SPIE conference on Internet Imaging*, pp. 160 – 169.

Robertson, S. E. (1997). *The probability ranking principle in IR*, Morgan Kaufmann Publishers Inc., San Francisco, CA, USA.

Rubner, Y., Tomasi, C. & Guibas, L. J. (2000). The earth mover's distance as a metric for image retrieval, *Int. J. Comput. Vision* 40(2): 99–121.

Salton, G. (1971). *The SMART Retrieval System—Experiments in Automatic Document Processing*, Prentice-Hall, Inc., Upper Saddle River, NJ, USA.

Santini, S. & Jain, R. (1997). Similarity is a Geometer, *Multimedia Tools Appl.* 5(3): 277–306.

Santini, S. & Jain, R. (1999). Similarity measures, *IEEE Trans. Pattern Anal. Mach. Intell.* 21(9): 871–883.

Schwering, A. (2005). Hybrid model for semantic similarity measurement, *in* R. Meersman, Z. Tari, M.-S. Hacid, J. Mylopoulos, B. Pernici, Ö. Babaoglu, H.-A. Jacobsen, J. P. Loyall, M. Kifer & S. Spaccapietra (eds), *OTM Conferences (2)*, Vol. 3761 of *Lecture Notes in Computer Science*, Springer, pp. 1449–1465.

Shen, H. T., Zhou, X. & Zhou, A. (2007). An adaptive and dynamic dimensionality reduction method for high-dimensional indexing, *The VLDB Journal* 16(2): 219–234.

Shneiderman, B., Bederson, B. B. & Drucker, S. M. (2006). Find that photo!: interface strategies to annotate, browse, and share, *Commun. ACM* 49(4): 69–71.

Smeulders, A. W. M., Worring, M., Santini, S., Gupta, A. & Jain, R. (2000). Content-Based Image Retrieval at the End of the Early Years, *IEEE Trans. Pattern Anal. Mach. Intell.* 22(12): 1349–1380.

Smith, J. (2007). The real problem of bridging the 'semantic gap', *MCAM07*, pp. 16–17.

Smith, J. R. & Chang, S.-F. (1996). VisualSEEk: A Fully Automated Content-Based Image Query System, *ACM Multimedia*, pp. 87–98.
URL: *citeseer.ist.psu.edu/smith96visualseek.html*

Snoek, C. G. M., Member, S. & Worring, M. (2003). Multimedia event based video indexing using time intervals, *IEEE Trans. on Multimedia* 7: 2004.

Snoek, C. G. M. & Smeulders, A. W. M. (2010). Visual-concept search solved?, *IEEE Computer* 43(6): 76–78.

Snoek, C. G. M. & Worring, M. (2005). Multimodal video indexing: A review of the state-of-the-art, *Multimedia Tools Appl.* 25(1): 5–35.

Snoek, C. G. M., Worring, M., Geusebroek, J., Koelma, D., Seinstra, F. & Smeulders, A. (2006). The Semantic Pathfinder: Using an Authoring Metaphor for Generic Multimedia Indexing, *IEEE Trans. Pattern Anal. Machine Intell.* 28(10): 1678–1689.

Snoek, C. G. M., Worring, M., van Gemert, J. C., Geusebroek, J.-M. & Smeulders, A. W. M. (2006). The challenge problem for automated detection of 101 semantic concepts in multimedia, *MULTIMEDIA '06: Proceedings of the 14th annual ACM international conference on Multimedia*, ACM, New York, NY, USA, pp. 421–430.

Sundaram, H., Naphade, M. R., Smith, J. R. & Rui, Y. (eds) (2006). *Image and Video Retrieval, 5th International Conference, CIVR 2006, Tempe, AZ, USA, July 13-15, 2006, Proceedings*, Vol. 4071 of *Lecture Notes in Computer Science*, Springer.

Tesic, J. (2004). *Managing Large-scale Multimedia Repositories*, PhD thesis, University of California, Santa Barbara.
URL: *http://vision.ece.ucsb.edu/publications/04ThesisTesic.pdf*

Tesic, J. & Manjunath, B. (2003). Nearest neighbor search for relevance feedback, *cvpr* 02: 643.

Tesic, J. & Smith, J. R. (2006). Semantic labeling of multimedia content clusters., *ICME*, IEEE, pp. 1493–1496.
URL: *http://dblp.uni-trier.de/db/conf/icmcs/icme2006.html#TesicS06*

Tversky, A. (1977). Features of similarity, *Psychological Review* 84: 327–352.

Van Rijsbergen, C. J. (1979). *Information Retrieval, 2nd edition*, Dept. of Computer Science, University of Glasgow.
URL: *citeseer.ist.psu.edu/vanrijsbergen79information.html*

Wactlar, H. D., Christel, M. G., Gong, Y. & Hauptmann, A. G. (1999). Lessons learned from building a terabyte digital video library, *Computer* 32(2): 66–73.

Wactlar, H. D., Kanade, T., Smith, M. A. & Stevens, S. M. (1996). Intelligent access to digital video: Informedia project, *Computer* 29(5): 46–52.

Wang, Q. & You, S. (2006). Fast similarity search for high-dimensional dataset, *ISM '06: Proceedings of the Eighth IEEE International Symposium on Multimedia*, IEEE Computer Society, Washington, DC, USA, pp. 799–804.

Weber, R., Schek, H.-J. & Blott, S. (1998). A Quantitative Analysis and Performance Study for Similarity-Search Methods in High-Dimensional Spaces, *Proc. 24th Int. Conf. Very Large Data Bases, VLDB*, pp. 194–205.
URL: *citeseer.ist.psu.edu/weber98quantitative.html*

Westerveld, T. (2004). *Using generative probabilistic models for multimedia retrieval*, Ph.d. thesis, University of Twente, Enschede, The Netherlands.

Westerveld, T. (2005). TRECVID as a Re-Usable Test-Collection for Video Retrieval, *Proceedings of the Multimedia Information Retrieval Workshop 2005*.

White, D. A. & Jain, R. (1996). Similarity indexing with the ss-tree, *ICDE '96: Proceedings of the Twelfth International Conference on Data Engineering*, IEEE Computer Society, Washington, DC, USA, pp. 516–523.

Wu, L. & Bretschneider, T. (2004). Vp-emd tree: An efficient indexing strategy for image retrieval, *in* H. R. Arabnia (ed.), *CISST*, CSREA Press, pp. 421–426.

Xiong, Z., Zhou, X. S., Tian, Q. & TS, Y. R. H. (2006). Semantic retrieval of video - review of research on video retrieval in meetings, movies and broadcast news, and sports, *Signal Processing Magazine, IEEE* 23(2): 18–27.

Yan, R. & Hauptmann, A. G. (2007). A review of text and image retrieval approaches for broadcast news video, *Inf. Retr.* 10(4-5): 445–484.

Yang, J. & Hauptmann, A. G. (2006). Annotating News Video with Locations., *CIVR*, pp. 153–162.

Yee, K.-P., Swearingen, K., Li, K. & Hearst, M. (2003). Faceted metadata for image search and browsing, *CHI '03: Proceedings of the SIGCHI conference on Human factors in computing systems*, ACM, New York, NY, USA, pp. 401–408.

Yu, C., Bressan, S., Ooi, B. C. & Tan, K.-L. (2004). Querying high-dimensional data in single-dimensional space, *The VLDB Journal* 13(2): 105–119.

Yu, J., Amores, J., Sebe, N. & Tian, Q. (2006). A new study on distance metrics as similarity measurement, *Multimedia and Expo, IEEE International Conference on* 0: 533–536.

Yuan, Y., Lin, X., Liu, Q., Wang, W., Yu, J. X. & Zhang, Q. (2005). Efficient computation of the skyline cube, *VLDB '05: Proceedings of the 31st international conference on Very large data bases*, VLDB Endowment, pp. 241–252.

Yujian, L. & Bo, L. (2007). A normalized levenshtein distance metric, *IEEE Trans. Pattern Anal. Mach. Intell.* 29(6): 1091–1095.

Zhai, C. & Lafferty, J. (2001). A study of smoothing methods for language models applied to ad hoc information retrieval, *SIGIR '01: Proceedings of the 24th annual international ACM SIGIR conference on Research and development in information retrieval*, ACM, New York, NY, USA, pp. 334–342.

Zhang, C. & Chen, T. (2003). *From Low Level Features to High Level Semantics*, CRC Press, chapter 27.
URL: *citeseer.ist.psu.edu/619954.html*

12

Challenges and the Solutions for Multimedia Metadata Sharing in Networks

Hochul Shin
Samsung Electronics Co., LTD,
South Korea

1. Introduction

Nowadays, multimedia devices such as PCs, smart phones, and televisions have large storage capacities to store a lot of multimedia files and high-speed network ability to connect with each other and the Internet. The demand for multimedia content sharing in networks is scaled up supported by the availability of storage capability and network speed. Thus, innovative infrastructures and technologies have been introduced to efficiently share multimedia contents in distributed systems.

One of the fundamental features of this sharing is metadata acquisition from the multimedia devices, because users in clients need to obtain information about multimedia contents from servers before they decide to manipulate or share the contents. However, obtaining multimedia metadata across multiple servers in networks usually results in high round-trip latency from a request to the response. Since this isn't responsive enough, a user may feel the user interface sluggish, delayed or frozen for significant periods.

Additionally, users expect that the Search function with certain conditions and Sort function by the titles, the artists, the dates, etc. of contents are supported regardless of the location of the contents or the number of servers. However, adding additional protocols to support various kinds of metadata-based service is very difficult to implement and deploy due to the interoperability problem.

Caching responses, historical and statistical information based prefetching, aggressive link based prefetching, full prefetching, and metadata database object acquisition, and the metadata aggregator-based centralized solution have been introduced to resolve these poor responsiveness and limitation of service extensibility from a user's perspective. Some solutions have several usability problems such as long warm-up time or have a lack of service extensibility, while others hurt the interoperability of the multimedia metadata sharing system.

In this chapter we introduce the solutions and guide you in order to figure out their limitations, pros and cons. This chapter is structured as follows: Section 2 covers the multimedia metadata sharing solutions and the examples; Section 3 explains the critical problems of metadata acquisition in multimedia sharing systems; Section 4 introduces the solutions to the problems; Conclusion section briefly restates challenges and the solutions for multimedia metadata sharing in networks.

2. Multimedia metadata sharing solutions

As demand for multimedia content sharing in networks has grown rapidly, innovative infrastructures and technologies have been introduced to efficiently browse multimedia content lists, control playbacks, and deliver multimedia contents in distributed systems.

Fig. 1. A typical multimedia sharing scenario of DLNA

Thus, Universal Plug and Play Audio and Video (UPnP AV) architecture[1] has been introduced as a candidate for multimedia distribution middleware for local networks, becoming widespread in many multimedia devices and software solutions in PCs. This architecture has been supervised by Digital Living Network Alliance (DLNA) [2] , a forum supported by many companies in the consumer electronics, multimedia, entertainment, and mobile industries.

The key of the UPnP AV architecture and DLNA is multimedia metadata sharing. Therefore, their specifications and guidelines have protocols and constraints for multimedia metadata sharing.

---

[1]DLNA. http://www.dlna.org. A non-profit collaborative trade organization has more than 250 member companies to make their products compatible with each other. The DLNA published its first set of Interoperability Guidelines in June 2004 and the first set of DLNA Certified products began appearing in market thereafter. To become certified, products pass through the DLNA Certification Program.

[2]UPnP AV Architecture. UPnP AV is an audio and video extension of UPnP. It defines three device classes, actions and events among the classes.

2.1 UPnP AV

UPnP was defined by the UPnP Forum [3] as what brings easy-to-use, flexible, standards-based connectivity to peer-to-peer networks. It is an open architecture that uses established standards such as IPv4 [4], HTTP [5], XML [6], and SOAP [7]. The UPnP AV architecture defines AV device classes the general interaction between its Control Points and devices.

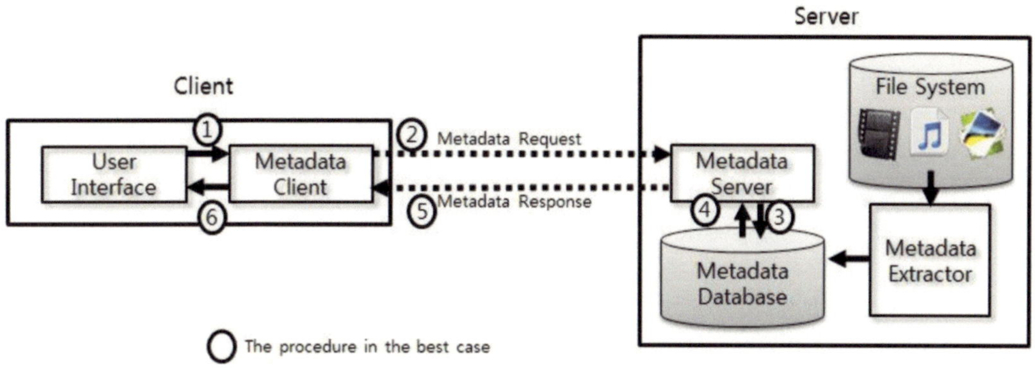

Fig. 2. A typical metadata sharing system and the acquisition procedure

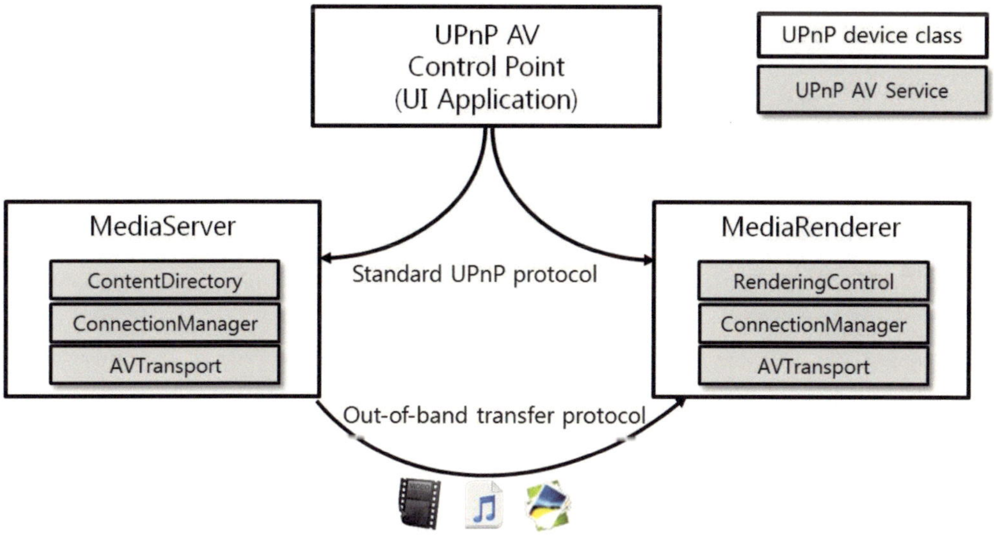

Fig. 3. A content playback scenario involves three distinct UPnP AV components: a Media Server, a Media Renderer, and an UPnP AV Control Point

---

[3] UPnP Forum. http://www. upnp.org. Formed in October 1999, UPnP Forum is an industry initiative of more than 954 leading companies in computing, printing and networking; consumer electronics; home appliances, automation, control and security; and mobile products.
[4] Internal Protocol version 4.
[5] Hypertext Transfer Protocol.
[6] Extensible Markup Language. http:// www.w3.org/XML/.
[7] Simple Object Access Protocol. http://www.w3.org/TR/soap/.

2.1.1 UPnP AV device classes

An UPnP AV Control Point is a device class responsible for coordinating and synchronizing distributed devices and a Media Server [8] is a device class defined as the source device of the media content responsible for exposing and streaming multimedia. In order to correspond with user inputs for the playback of multimedia contents, the Control Point coordinates, synchronizes, and interacts with its devices acting as a source called the Media Server and a sink called the Media Renderer [9].

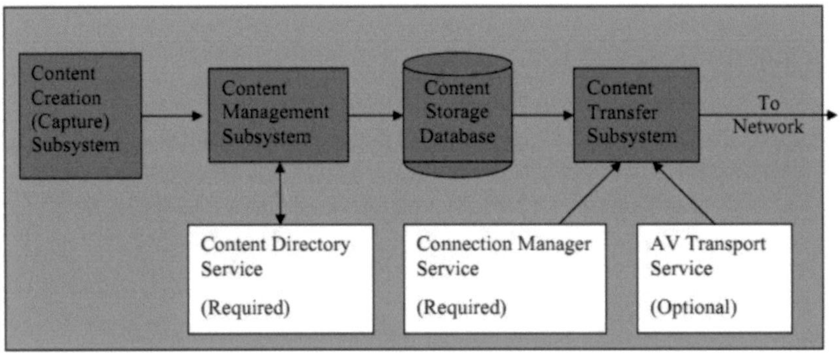

Fig. 4. The conceptual structure of UPnP MediaServer

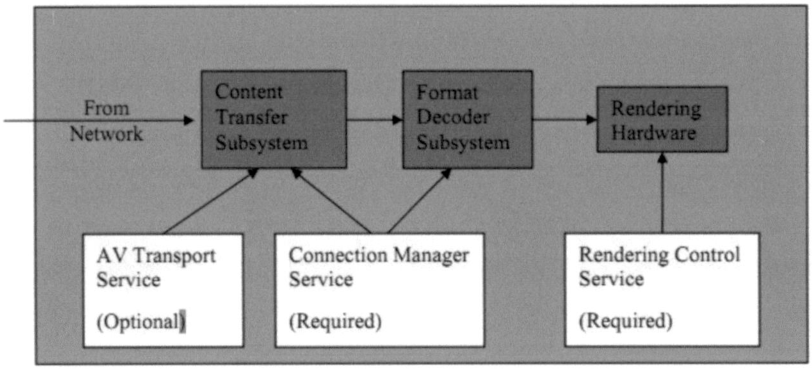

Fig. 5. The conceptual structure of UPnP MediaRenderer

2.1.2 Metadata exchange in UPnP AV devices

The Media Server exposes its contents via the Content Directory service (CDS) which establishes and maintains the hierarchical structure of UPnP container objects. Each object has multimedia content information and metadata such as the type, creator, date, and locator to access it and each CDS may have a unique structure and various objects. UPnP defines two requests to inspect a CDS such as Browse to browse the CDS structure and Search to obtain items conforming to specified search terms. A Browse request is mandatory in all CDSs, but a Search request is optional in UPnP AV specification. UPnP also defines

[8]UPnP MediaServer. http://www.upnp.org/specs/av/UPnP-av-MediaServer-v1-Device.pdf.
[9]UPnP MediaRenderer. http://www.upnp.org/specs/av/UPnP-av-MediaRenderer-v1-Device.pdf.

two events such as SystemUpdateID [10] and ContainerUpdateIDs [11] to indicate the change in the CDS. UPnP AV architecture defines the control messages expressed in XML using SOAP. SOAP is similar to RPC where the client sends a request to the server and the server sends a response to the client. This architecture also standardizes the transport layer for SOAP in the architecture using HTTP. SOAP in HTTP is used for high interoperability when exchanging information in networks.

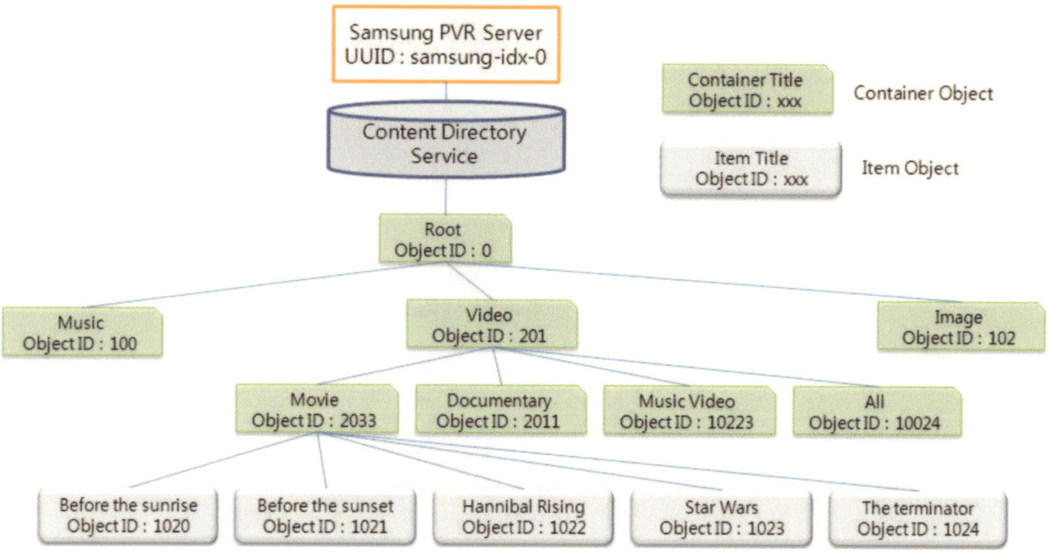

Fig. 6. An example of the hierarchical CDS structure

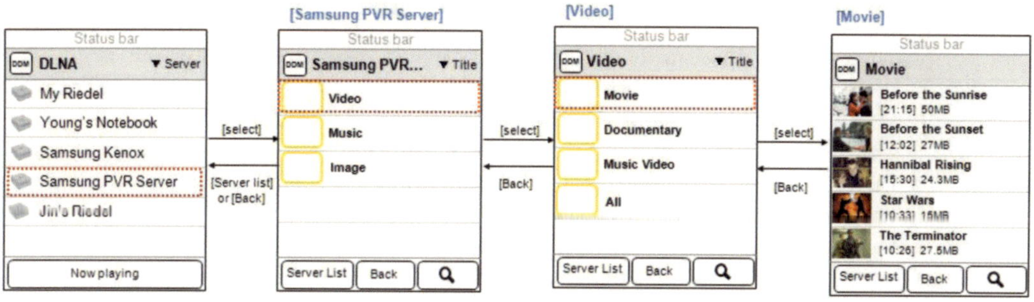

Fig. 7. An example of browsing the content list in the UPnP AV Control Point. The hierarchical structure of the CDS in figure 3 was navigated by Browse requests in this Example

---

[10]SystemUpdateID. When any content in the CDS is added, removed, or changed, the SystemUpdateID event must be delivered to all the subscribed UPnP AV Control Points. A mandatory event of UPnP AV specification.

[11]ContainerUpdateIDs. When any content in specific containers in the CDS is added, removed, or changed, the ContainerUpdateIDs event with the information on the containers should be delivered to all the subscribed UPnP AV Control Points. A optional event of UPnP AV specification.

2.2 DLNA

The aim of the DLNA is to enable end-to-end interoperability among the digital multimedia devices storing, playing and sharing digital content and help put an end to the fragmentation of multimedia sharing standards for multimedia devices. As a collaboration of the world's leading consumer electronics, PC and mobile companies, the DLNA has created design guidelines for DLNA Certified products that can work together — no matter what the brand is. The DLNA has been based on the UPnP AV architecture, and put some constraints on the metadata exchange protocols of the architecture to ensure interoperability among devices in local networks.

Fig. 8. DLNA certified products (http://www.dlna.org/products)

3. Challenges of multimedia metadata sharing solutions

Poor performance due to the round-trip latencies between the servers and clients is a typical problem of network-based solutions. Since some additional protocols to express the metadata hurt the responsiveness of multimedia applications, multimedia sharing systems suffer from serious usability problems due to poor responsiveness. Additionally, because multimedia metadata are distributed across several multimedia devices and the sharing protocols meet some constraints to improve interoperability, the extensibility of the metadata based services is usually poor. For instance, even if you want to sort multimedia contents according to geographic information, the UPnP AV architecture and DLNA don't support that. Thus, you should introduce your own propriety protocol hurting interoperability.

3.1 Performance

A common serious usability problem in multimedia sharing systems in networks is poor responsiveness of metadata acquisition. Generally, 100 to 200ms is the threshold beyond which users will perceive a lag in an application [12]. However, metadata acquisition in the

[12]Beigbeder, T., et al., (2003). The effects of loss and latency on user performance in Unreal Tournament, Proc. NetGames, (2004), pp. 144-151.

systems causes long round-trip latencies, due mainly to the protocol exchange mechanism. For this reason, interactive multimedia sharing applications have suffered and caused inconvenience to users. To avoid this problem, some solutions have tried to aggregate all the metadata in a controller device which has a user interface. In that case, a user usually suffers from long warm-up time to gather metadata instead of the responsiveness problem which was discussed above.

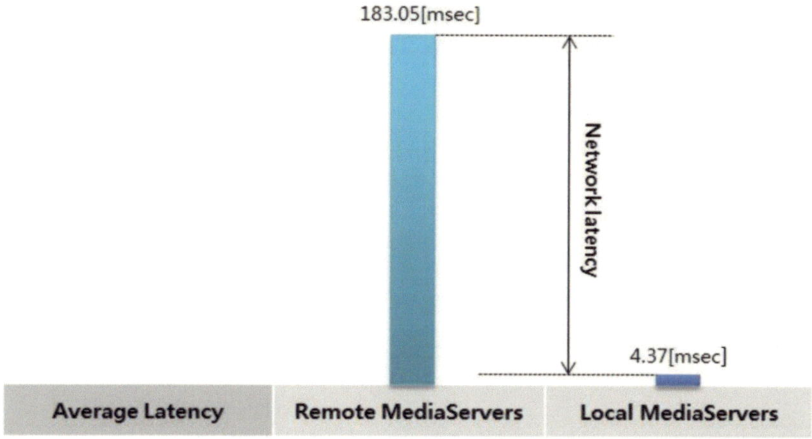

Fig. 9. The comparison of average latencies of UPNP AV's Browse requests to obtain metadata [13]. The round-trip latencies of Browse requests with local MediaServers were definitely short

3.2 Service extensibility problem

Another critical problem is a lack of additional metadata-based functions such as search and sort with a title, date, or type of contents that provide convenient ways for the user to find expected multimedia content. However, if multimedia metadata spreads over several servers, it is difficult to implement these functions. Moreover, the functions also cause high round-trip latencies.

4. Solutions

To address challenges such as poor responsiveness and limitation of service extensibility from a user's perspective as we described above, several solutions such as caching responses, historical and statistical information based prefetching, aggressive link based prefetching, full prefetching, metadata database object acquisition, and the metadata aggregator-based centralized solution have been introduced.

4.1 Caching

Caching the metadata in the client is one classical solution. The response to a user's metadata request is stored in a cache. In this case, since the round-trip latency of a metadata

[13]Hochul, S., (2008). Achieving Low Latency of Multimedia Content Browsing in UPnP AV Architectures

request with a cache hit is definitely short, a user may be satisfied with a very fast response. Additionally, with a larger number of cache entries, the cache hit rate tends to be higher.

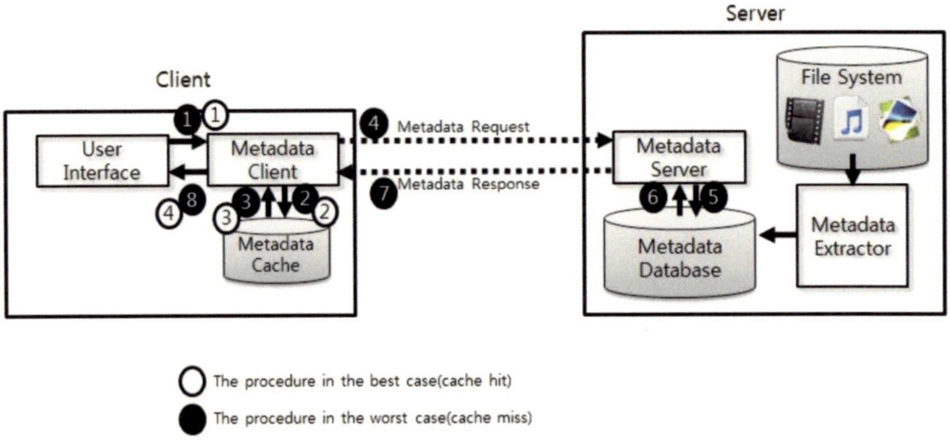

Fig. 10. An example of metadata sharing systems with caching and the acquisition procedure

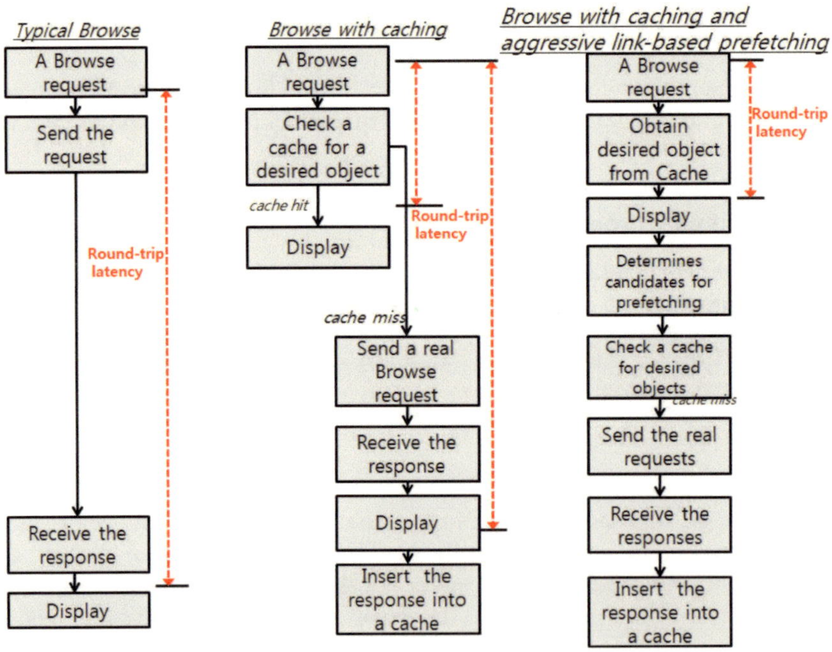

Fig. 11. The comparison of round-trip latency of a user's Browse requests in UPnP AV architecture with the typical, caching, and prefetching

However, cache misses which are known as cold start or compulsory misses during cache warm-up are unavoidable and a cache does not guarantee 100% cache hit rate even after cache warm-up is completed. Moreover, it is difficult for caching to meet users' needs of using a variety of metadata-based functions because the cache can only store part of the whole metadata.

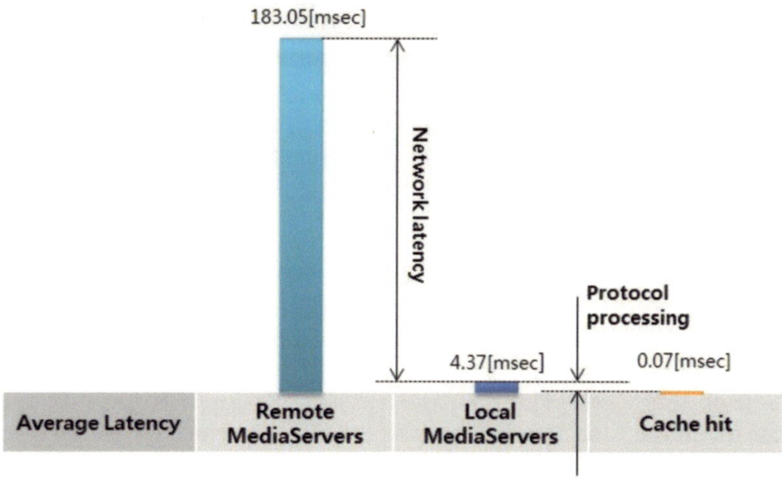

Fig. 12. The comparison of evaluated average latencies of Browse requests. Cache hits reduced the latencies dramatically[14]

4.2 Prefetching

Another solution is prefetching metadata responses to the expected requests. This means that a client sends requests based on users' prior requests and stores the responses in the cache before the user requests them. The prefetching seems necessary to prevent cache misses and this could dramatically improve the round-trip latencies from the user's perspective if the response to the request is already stored in the cache. There are several kinds of prefetching algorithms such as prefetching based on historical and statistical information, aggressive link based prefetching, and full prefetching before a user's first input.

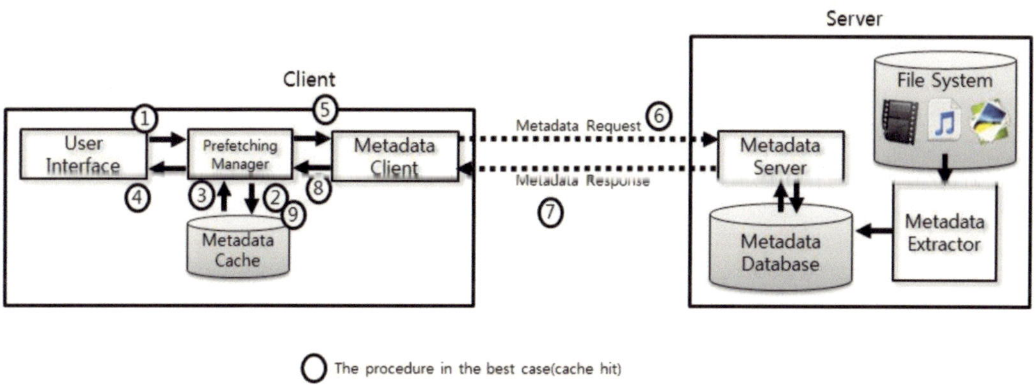

Fig. 13. An example of metadata sharing systems with prefetching. The steps from 5 to 9 are to obtain metadata for users' future requests according to historical and statistical information or the hierarchical structure of the contents before the next request

[14]Hochul, S., (2008). Achieving Low Latency of Multimedia Content Browsing in UPnP AV Architectures

4.2.1 Historical and statistical information based prefetching

To increase cache hit rate, we can predict users' expected requests based on historical and statistical data, for example, a prediction based on what kinds of multimedia contents have been chosen or what search keywords have been used by the user. However, cache miss is inevitable because a user's preference can always be changed.

4.2.2 Aggressive link based prefetching

Aggressive link based prefetching means that all possible links that a user may select must be prefetched. Multimedia metadata is usually stored and expressed as a hierarchical structure. So, while a user navigates the structure, all metadata in links the user can move will be obtained in advance before the user moves to one of the links. It ensures a cache hit rate of 100% at all times except in the case that a user's input is faster than the response acquisition for the links. Also, it is not suitable for cases in which a link has a lot of items or that there are a lot of links that the user can move.

4.2.3 Full prefetching

The third solution is more aggressive to improve the usability. The solution is that the entire metadata stored in the servers is copied into the client using metadata acquisition protocols, even if the initial setup time is very long. It establishes the illusion of the original metadata storage at the client. After this has been established, users can access the storage with very low latencies and a variety of metadata-based functions can be supported as if the metadata storage is real. However, the whole metadata acquisition at the initial setup time may cause the huge protocol processing, data access time and the heavy traffic in networks due to very complicated low level protocol exchange, XML processing and retrieval of metadata from the database in the server and to the client.

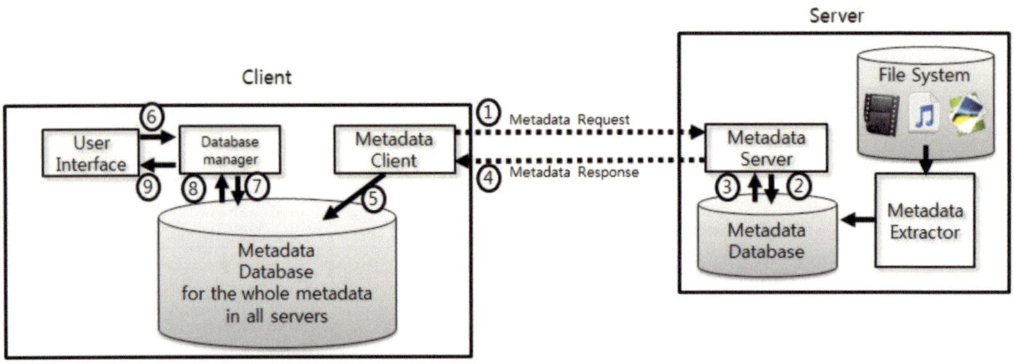

Fig. 14. An example of metadata sharing systems with full prefetching. The steps from 1 to 5 are to obtain the whole metadata in all the servers via metadata exchange protocols and establish the illusion of metadata storage. Then, a user's request refers to the illusion instead of the real servers

4.3 Metadata database object acquisition

The establishment of the illusion of metadata storage at the client is very effective for usability except for a very long initial setup time. Therefore, we propose a more aggressive solution that copies the metadata database object itself from the servers to the client instead of copying metadata. If a client uses the same schema for metadata database as the servers, we can directly copy the database object from the servers to the client, and the client then can access the database object without a very complicated and redundant metadata acquisition method in the network. Database object acquisition protocol is relatively much simpler than metadata acquisition protocol. For example, a typical multimedia metadata acquisition method uses HTTP and SOAP for extensibility, interoperability, and flexibility of services.

On the other hand, these protocols are very complicated and cause very long round-trip latencies to exchange metadata. However, to obtain the database object, we can use the FTP which is a very simple and fast protocol. Additionally, since multiple database objects can be referred to in order to respond to user's requests, various metadata-based functions can be very easily implemented.

However, this solution requires the unified interface to the metadata database across several servers and clients. Thus, unlike the other solutions, changing both the servers and clients is required to apply this solution to your application.

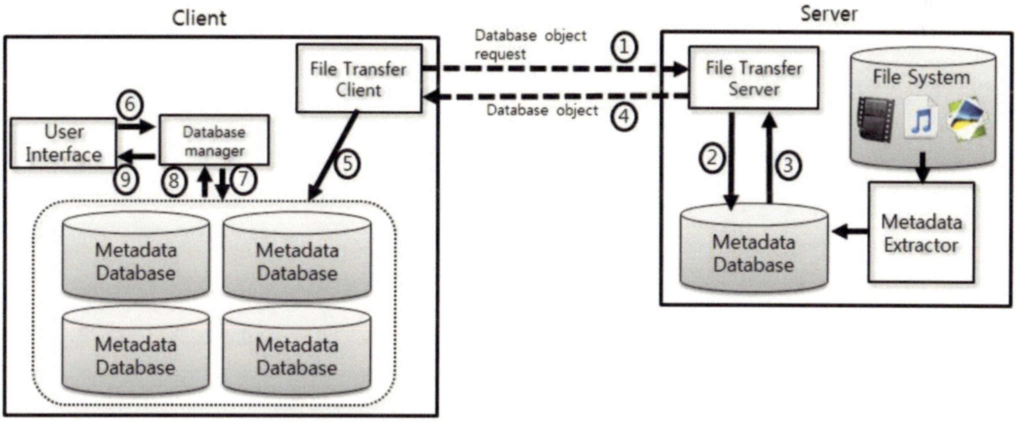

Fig. 15. An example of metadata sharing systems with Metadata database object acquisition. The steps from 1 to 5 are to obtain the whole metadata in all servers via file transfer protocols and establish the illusion of metadata storage. Then, a user's request refers to the illusion instead of the real servers

4.4 Metadata aggregator-based centralized solution

To obtain metadata in distributed systems, a client must access all the servers which causes the service extension problem. For example, if a user wants to get items ordered by dates, the client must send messages to all the servers to obtain metadata, wait for the replies and then sort them. If the whole metadata is aggregated in one server, a client can only access this server instead of all the servers. Also, the caching mechanism or prefetching mechanism can be used for the clients. The aggregator is suitable to run on non-mobile devices working with many metadata servers. If there are a few servers, it is not beneficial to apply this solution to that environment.

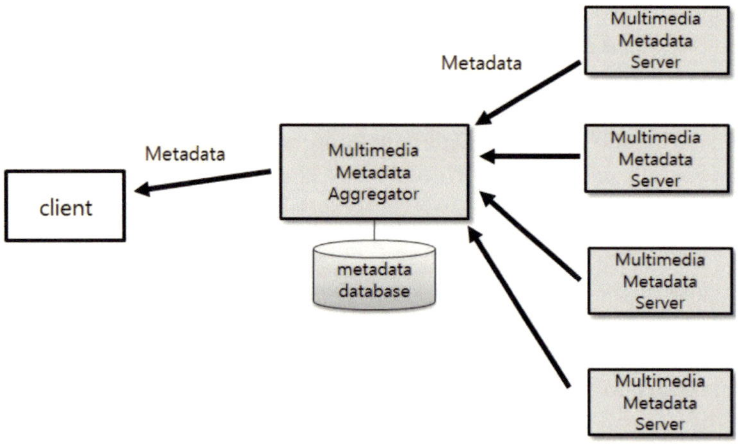

Fig. 16. The conceptual diagram of metadata sharing systems with a metadata aggregator

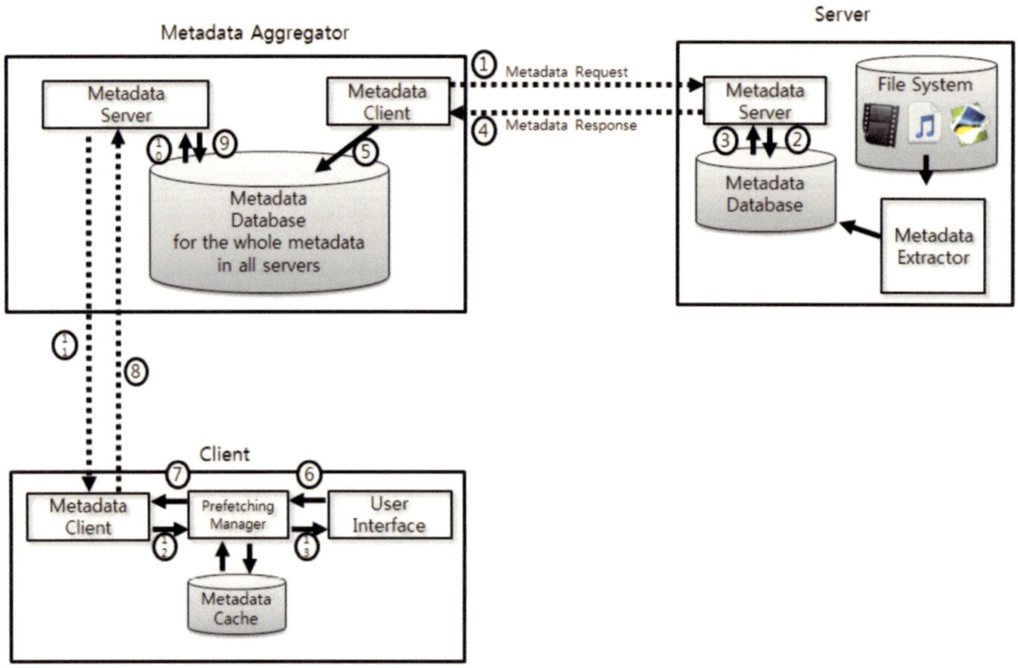

Fig. 17. An example of metadata sharing systems with a metadata aggregator. The steps from 1 to 5 are to obtain the whole metadata from all the servers and fill the metadata aggregator with the metadata from the servers. Then, a client accesses the aggregator instead of all the servers in the network

4.5 Comparison of the solutions

Any solution described above does not resolve both the performance and service extensibility problem of metadata sharing solutions for multimedia sharing systems as follows.

Metadata sharing solutions	Required time for the first service	The best case round trip latency	The worst case round trip latency	Possibility of the worst case	The extensib-ility of metadata based services	The scope of implem-entation
Typical	No	Long	-	-	Low	-
Historical and statistical information based prefetching	No	Short	Long [15]	High [16]	Low	Client
Aggressive link based prefetching	No	Short	Long	Low [17]	Low	Client
Full prefetching	Very long	Short	-	-	High	Client
Metadata database object acquisition	Long	Short	-	-	High	Server and Client [18]
Metadata aggregator (client)	No [19]	-	-	-	High	Aggregator and Client

Table 1. Comparison of the metadata sharing solutions

5. Conclusion

In this chapter, we have presented the typical problems of metadata sharing. The latency problem and service extensibility problem are typical and crucial in industrial solutions but very difficult to resolve. To address those problems, caching responses, historical and statistical information based prefetching, aggressive link based prefetching, full prefetching, metadata database object acquisition, and the metadata aggregator-based centralized solution have been introduced and these have their own limitations, pros, and cons. Thus, you should understand that each solution has its own pros, cons, and limitations and figure out what solutions can be applied to your application. Most of all, the most important factor you should consider when you choose the solutions is how to satisfy users of your application.

[15]It depends on the cache algorithm, the number of cache entries, and cache replacement algorithm.

[16]When cache-miss happens, long round-trip time is required.

[17]It depends on the number of links, the duration between a user's two inputs, and the speed of servers' response.

[18]The metadata database object acquistion protocol must be implemented on the servers and clients. Also, the clients must be able to figure out that the servers support that protocol.

[19]It takes long time to the aggregator gathers the whole metadata from the servers in the network. Then the clients can use the metadata immediately.

6. References

Andresen, D., et al., (2004). *LYE: a high-performance caching SOAP implementation*, Parallel Processing, ICPP 2004. International Conference, pp. 143 - 150 vol.1.

Beigbeder, T., et al., (2003). *The effects of loss and latency on user performance in Unreal Tournament*, Proc. NetGames, (2004), pp. 144-151.

Berners-Lee, T., et al., (1996). *Hypertext Transfer Protocol – HTTP/1.0*, RFC 1945

Cao, P., Felten, et al., (1995). *A study of integrated prefetching and caching strategies*, Proceedings of the 1995 ACM SIGMETRICS joint international conference on Measurement and modeling of computer systems, (May 1995), pp. 188-197, Ottawa, Ontario, Canada.

Cohen, E., & Kaplan, H., (2000). *Prefetching the means for document transfer: A new approach for reducing Web latency*. In Proceedings of IEEE INFOCOM, Tel Aviv, Israel, (March 2000)

Davis, D., Parashar, P. (2002). *Latency Performance of SOAP Implementations Cluster Computing and the Grid*, 2002. 2nd IEEE/ACM International Symposium (May 2002) pp. 407–407.

Davison, B., (2002). *Predicting web actions from HTML content*, Proceedings of the thirteenth ACM conference on Hypertext and hypermedia, (June 2002), College Park, Maryland, USA.

Devaram, K & Andresen, D., (2003). *Soap optimization via parameterized client-side caching.* Fifteenth IASTED International Conference on Parallel and Distributed Computing and Systems, Marina del Ray, CA, USA, (Nov. 2003), pp. 785-790.

Duchamp, D., (1999). *Prefetching hyperlinks*, Proceedings of the 2nd conference on USENIX Symposium on Internet Technologies and Systems, (October 1999), pp. 12-12, Boulder, Colorado.

Duncan, B, & Heron, R., (2005). *Query caching in a system with a content directory service*, Publication Number:WO/2005/031607.

Hochul, S., (2008). *Achieving Low Latency of Multimedia Content Browsing in UPnP AV Architectures*, The Second International Conference on Mobile Ubiquitous Computing Systems Services and Technologies, pp. 56-63.

Kroeger, M., et al., (1997). *Exploring the Bounds of Web Latency Reduction from Caching and Prefetching*, Proceedings of the USENIX Symposium on Internet Technologies and Systems, (December 1997)

Padmanabhan, N., & Mogul, C., (1996). *Using predictive prefetching to improve World Wide Web latency*, Computer Communication Review, (July 1996), pp. 22-36, Proceedings of SIGCOMM '96.

Ritchie, T. & Kuehnel, T., (2002). *UPnP AV Architecture: 1*, UPnP Forum, Available from http://www.upnp.org/specs/av/UPnP-av-AVArchitecture-v1-20020625.pdf

Ritchie, T. et al., (2003). *UPnP Device Architecture 1.1*, UPnP Forum, Available from http://www.upnp.org/specs/arch/UPnP-arch-DeviceArchitecture-v1.1.pdf

Sarukkai , R., (2000). *Link prediction and path analysis using Markov chains*, Proceedings of the 9th international World Wide Web conference on Computer networks : the international journal of computer and telecommunications networking, (June 2000), pp.377-386, Amsterdam, The Netherlands.